PRAISE FOR *Jerusalem, Jerusalem*

"James Carroll's *Jerusalem, Jerusalem* should be required reading for all: it is a lucid, calm, deeply compelling history of the literal and symbolic significance of that city, at the heart and origins of Judaism, Christianity and Islam. From Abraham's sacrifice of Isaac through Charlemagne and Spinoza to Adolf Eichmann and Billy Graham, Carroll marshals an extraordinary range of sources to illuminate the interwoven violence and redemption that define Jerusalem in the world entire, up to this day." — **Claire Messud, author of** *The Emperor's Children*

"James Carroll writes with Jesuitical passion about a city that is defined by its arguments. The pace of the book is breathless, its candor exhilarating." — *New Jersey Star-Ledger*

"The compelling follow-up to [Carroll's] best-selling *Constantine's Sword*. . . his use of Jerusalem as a prism to examine the development of monotheism, and his prescription for what he believes might be a more positive future path, provide a powerful and provocative intellectual journey." — *BookPage*

"A gripping account of how Jerusalem has fired the spiritual imagination of the West from Biblical times to the present — and a deeply personal meditation on the religious impulse itself, and its dark double, sacred violence. More than a rebuke to jihadists and religious extremists, this book challenges secularists who believe that, for modern Western societies, wars of religion are a thing of the past."
— **Michael Sandel, author of** *Justice: What's the Right Thing To Do?*

"What a remarkable book! I was blown away by the breadth and depth of it. This is going to be another hugely important book for James Carroll, right there with *Constantine's Sword*."
— **Reza Aslan, author of** *No god but God*

"One of the broadest and most balanced accounts of the city of King David in recent years. . . Conceptually profound, richly detailed, and wonderfully realized, this book brings to life the dynamic story of the Divided City." — *Publishers Weekly,* **starred review**

Books by James Carroll

Fiction

MADONNA RED

MORTAL FRIENDS

FAULT LINES

FAMILY TRADE

PRINCE OF PEACE

SUPPLY OF HEROES

FIREBIRD

MEMORIAL BRIDGE

THE CITY BELOW

SECRET FATHER

Nonfiction

AN AMERICAN REQUIEM

CONSTANTINE'S SWORD

TOWARD A NEW CATHOLIC CHURCH

CRUSADE

HOUSE OF WAR

PRACTICING CATHOLIC

JERUSALEM, JERUSALEM

Jerusalem, Jerusalem

How the Ancient City
Ignited Our Modern World

James Carroll

MARINER BOOKS
HOUGHTON MIFFLIN HARCOURT
BOSTON · NEW YORK

First Mariner Books edition 2012
Copyright © 2011 by James Carroll

For information about permission to reproduce selections
from this book, write to Permissions, Houghton Mifflin
Harcourt Publishing Company, 215 Park Avenue South,
New York, New York 10003.

www.hmhbooks.com

Library of Congress Cataloging-in-Publication Data
Carroll, James, date.
  Jerusalem, Jerusalem: how the ancient city ignited our
modern world / James Carroll.
    p. cm.
  Includes bibliographical references (p.) and index.
  ISBN 978-0-547-19561-2   ISBN 978-0-547-74762-0 (pbk.)
  1. Jerusalem — History. 2. Jerusalem — Description and travel.
3. Jerusalem — Religion. 4. Jerusalem — Ethnic relations. I. Title.
  DS109.9.C367 2011
  956.94'42 — dc22   2010043034

Printed in the United States of America
DOC 10 9 8 7 6 5 4 3 2 1

The author gratefully acknowledges the use of material in the
following books:
Judaism: Practice and Belief, 63 BCE–66 CE by E. P. Sanders.
Copyright © 1992 by E. P. Sanders. Reprinted with permission
of the publisher, Continuum International Publishing Group.
Violence and the Sacred by René Girard, translated by Patrick
Gregory (pp. 46, 221). Copyright © 1977 The Johns Hopkins
University Press. Reprinted with permission of The Johns
Hopkins University Press. *The Iron Cage* by Rashid Khalidi.
Copyright © 2006 by Rashid Khalidi. Reprinted by permission
of Beacon Press, Boston.

For Dean James Parks Morton
and Rabbi David Hartman
and in memory of
Bishop Krister Stendahl

Oh, what a beautiful city,
Twelve gates to the city, hallelujah.

— African-American spiritual

Contents

Jerusalem, Jerusalem

Introduction: Two Jerusalems

1. Heat

THIS BOOK IS ABOUT the lethal feedback loop between the actual city of Jerusalem and the apocalyptic fantasy it inspires. It is a book, therefore, about two Jerusalems: the earthly and the heavenly, the mundane and the imagined. That doubleness shows up in the tension between Christian Jerusalem and Jewish Jerusalem, between European Jerusalem and Islamic Jerusalem, between Israeli Jerusalem and Palestinian Jerusalem, and between the City on a Hill and the Messiah nation that, beginning with John Winthrop, understands itself in its terms. But all recognizably contemporary conflicts have their buried foundations in the deep past, and this book will excavate them. Always, the story will curve back to the real place: the story of how humans living on the ridge about a third of the way between the Dead Sea and the Mediterranean have constantly been undermined by the overheated dreams of pilgrims who, age in and age out, arrive at the legendary gates with love in their hearts, the end of the world in their minds, and weapons in their hands.

It is as if the two Jerusalems rub against each other like stone against flint, generating the spark that ignites fire. There is the literal fire of wars among peoples and nations, taken to be holy because ignited in the holy city, and that will be our subject. There is the fire of the God who first appeared as a burning bush,[1] and then as flames hovering over the heads of chosen ones.[2] That God will be our subject. But Jerusalem also ignites heat in the human breast, a viral fever of zealotry and true belief that lodged in the DNA of Western civilization. That fever lives—an infection but also, as happens with the mind on fire, an inspiration. And like all good metaphors, fever carries implications of its own opposite, for preoccupation with Jerusalem has been a religious and cultural boon, too. "Salvation is from Jerusalem,"[3] the Psalms say, but the first meaning of the word "salvation" is health. That the image of fever suggests ecstasy, transcendence, and intoxication is also true to our meditation. "Look," the Lord tells the prophet Zechariah, "I am going to make Jerusalem an intoxicating cup to all the surrounding peoples."[4]

Jerusalem fever consists in the conviction that the fulfillment of history depends on the fateful transformation of the earthly Jerusalem into a screen onto which overpowering millennial fantasies can be projected. This end of history is conceived variously as the arrival of the Messiah, or his return; as the climactic final battle at Armageddon, with the forces of angels vanquishing those of Satan (usually represented by Christians as Jews, Muslims, or other "infidels"). Later, the end of history sheds its religiosity, but Jerusalem remains at least implicitly the backdrop onto which millennial images are thrown by social utopias, whether founded by pilgrims in the New World, by communards in Europe, or by Communists. Ultimately, a continuous twentieth- and twenty-first-century war against evil turns out, surprisingly, to be centered on Jerusalem, a pivot point of both the Cold War and the War on Terror. Having begun as the ancient city of Apocalypse, it became the magnetic pole of Western history, doing more to create the modern world than any other city. Only Jerusalem—not Athens, Rome, or Paris; not Moscow or London; not Istanbul, Damascus, or Cairo; not El Dorado or the New York of immigrants' dreams—only Jerusalem occupies such a transcendent place in the imagination. It is the earthly reflection of heaven—but heaven, it turns out, casts a shadow.

Thus, across the centuries, the fancied city creates the actual city, and vice versa. "The more exalted the metaphoric status of Jerusalem," as the Jerusalem scholar Sidra DeKoven Ezrahi writes, "the more dwarfed its geopolitical dimensions; the more expansive the boundaries of the Holy City, the less negotiable its municipal borders."[5] Therefore, war. Over the past two millennia, the ruling establishment of Jerusalem has been overturned eleven times, almost always with brute violence, and always in the name of religion.[6] This book will tell the story of those wars—how sacred geography creates battlefields. Even when wars had nothing literally to do with Jerusalem, the city inspired them with the promise of "the glory of the coming of the Lord . . . with his terrible swift sword," as put by one battle hymn from far away. Metaphoric boundaries obliterate municipal borders, with disputes about the latter spawning expansions of the former, even to distant reaches of the earth.

Jerusalem fever infects religious groups, certainly the three monotheisms that claim the city. Although mainly a Christian epic, its verses rhyme with what Judeans once did, what Muslims took to, what a secular culture unknowingly pursues, and what parties to the city's contemporary conflict embody. Yet if Jerusalem is the fever's chosen niche, Jerusalem is also its antidote. Religion, likewise, is both a source of trouble and a way of vanquishing it. Religion, one sees in Jerusalem as nowhere else, is both the knife that cuts the vein and the force that keeps the knife from cutting. Each tradition enlivens the paradox uniquely, and that, too, is the story.

For Jews, Jerusalem, after the destruction of the Temple by the Babylonians and then the Romans, means that absence is the mode of God's presence. First, the Holy of Holies in the rebuilt Temple of biblical times was deliberately kept vacant—vacancy itself mythologized. Then, after the destruction by Rome, when the Temple was not rebuilt, the holy place was imagined in acts of Torah study and observance of the Law, with a return to Jerusalem constantly felt as coming "next year." Throughout centuries of diaspora, the Jewish fantasy of Jerusalem kept communal cohesion intact, enabled survival of exile and oppression, and ultimately spawned Zionism.

For Christians, the most compelling fact of the faith is that Jesus is gone, present only through the projections of sacramentalism. But in the ecstasies of evangelical fervor, Jesus can still be felt as kneeling in the garden of Gethsemane, sweating blood for "you." So Jerusalem lives as the locus of piety, for "you" can kneel there, too. The ultimate Christian vision of the future—the Book of Revelation—is centered in the city of the Lord's suffering, but now that anguish redeems the very cosmos. Even in the act of salvation, the return of Jesus to Jerusalem is catastrophic.

Muslims came to Jerusalem as occupiers in 637, only five years after the death of Muhammad. That rapidity makes the point. The Prophet's armies, sweeping up out of Arabia in an early manifestation of the cohesion generated by an Islamic feel for the Oneness of God, were also in hot pursuit of Jerusalem. Desert heat this time. The Muslims' visceral grasp of the city's transcendent significance defined their first longing — and their first true military campaign. Islam recognizes God's nearness only in recitation, with chanted sounds of the Qur'an exquisite in their elusiveness and allusiveness both. Yet the Prophet left a footprint in Jerusalem's stone that can be touched to this day — an approximate and singular sacrament. To Muslims, Jerusalem is simply Al Quds, "the Holy."

The three monotheisms of Jerusalem are thus nested in a perennial present, a temporal zone in which the past is never quite the past and the future is always threatening to break in. The linear order of time keeps getting lost in Jerusalem, just as the spatial realm, by being spiritualized, keeps evaporating — except for those who actually live there. For the broader culture, interrupted time means that both psychological wounds and theological insights are transmitted here less by tradition than by a kind of repetition compulsion. These transcendent manifestations of hurt and suspicion and hostility — and ultimately fanaticism — can be overcome only by understanding their very human sources. But a procession of historical vignettes, beginning here and falling into place like pieces of a puzzle, can also make clear that Jerusalem is home to a spacious religious cosmopolitanism that no amount of overheated warping can ruin. Jerusalem, in its worldly history and its symbolic hovering, forces a large-spirited reckoning with religion and politics both — how they work, how they go wrong, how they can be cooled and calmed.

The cults of Jerusalem make plain that each tradition of the Book depends on a revelation of *indirection,* a knowing what is unknowable, which is why each tradition can miss the truth as well as hit it, sponsoring intolerance as much as neighborliness, discord as much as peace. This book is a pilgrimage through the ways of sacred violence, most of which lead, in the West, either from or to this same city. On medieval maps it marks the intersection of Europe, Asia, and Africa. Armies have swarmed out of all three continents to meet here — and now, in the twenty-first century, they arrive from a fourth continent, too. But Jerusalem's geopolitical implications, however much ignited by religion, have been equally transformative of secular forces, for better and worse. Wars can be holy without invoking the name of God. That also gives us our theme. The point here is that for Europe, and for its legacy culture in America, the fever's virus found a succession of hosts in ancient Roman assaults, medieval Crusades, Reformation wars, European colonialism, New World adventures, and the total wars of modernity — all fixed, if variously, upon Jerusalem. The place and the idea of the place mix like combustible chemicals to become a much too holy land, an explosive combination of madness and sanctity, violence and peace, the will of God and the will to power, fueling conflict up to the present day.

Fuel indeed. The Holy Land has come to overlap the most contested geology on the planet: the oil fields of the Middle East. Oil now trumps every great power strategic concern. Its concentration there — the liquid crescent stretching from Iran and Iraq to the Arabian Peninsula — means the broad obsession with dead-centered Jerusalem is not merely mystical. Nor is the threat merely mystical. For the first time in human history, the apocalyptic fantasy of Armageddon could become actual, sparked in the very place where Armageddon began.[7]

2. Jerusalem Today

The gates are still there, punctuating the medieval wall, which is made, like everything, of Jerusalem stone that gleams in the sun. Desert sun. Ancient custom and modern law require that all buildings be uniformly constructed with the off-white limestone, carrying pink highlights, that has been quarried in the highlands of Judea since the time of Solomon. "Jerusalem all of gold," goes a modern psalm, "Jerusalem, bronze and light. Within my heart, I shall treasure your song and sight."[8] The very light of the air surrounding Jerusalem has been described by mystics as "the outer garment of God."[9]

When you approach from almost any direction, the walled city looms dramatically on its pedestal hilltop, above twin valleys that gouge away to the south like the angled shears of a plow, digging deep. One hillside of those valleys, immediately outside the medieval wall and spilling down from it, is terraced with homes of Arab families — Silwan, from which Arabs are now routinely evicted by Jerusalem's municipal authorities.[10] A far hillside, scaling the Mount of Olives, is strewn with Jewish gravestones that, though now reordered, were desecrated, two thousand years apart, by Romans and Jordanian Arabs. Sacred city, eviction city, desecration city, such is the story "the stony hills recall."

If Jerusalem is the text, the state of Israel is the context. It is a country about the size of Massachusetts, with a population of about seven million. It has its New York, which is the urbane, bustling seaside city of Tel Aviv. Jerusalem stands to Tel Aviv as Delphi does to Athens, or Kyoto to Tokyo—or Dresden to Berlin. Yes, destruction is central to the story, and so is a wild diversity. A million Israelis speak Arabic as their first language, and another million speak Russian. But the capital of the Hebrew Republic[11] is Jerusalem. Half a mile above the level of the Mediterranean Sea, which lies almost forty miles to the west, and higher above the planetary low point of the below-sea-level Dead Sea, which lies about twenty miles to the east, Jerusalem's elevation is said to have kept it dry during the Great Flood of Noah—as if the city existed then, as if the Flood were real. Even in the twenty-first century, atop geological and civilizational strata of the ages, layer upon layer of shale, ash, and the crushed rubble of fifty centuries, the trek to Jerusalem is an ascent, an *aliyah* in Hebrew. "The mountain of the House of the Lord shall be established as the highest of the mountains, and shall be raised above the hills."[12] The "going up" to Jerusalem made it the original and quintessential City on a Hill, which would be the mythic point of reference for America—Jerusalem as an idea as much as a place. But from ancient times the going-up made *aliyah* the word for every Jew's approach to the actual Jerusalem, whether for the first time or upon return. Jewish hearts were first to lift, and they still do.

Today the city is well known for its contentions, with its goldenness defined first by the gold of the Dome of the Rock, the Muslim shrine that superseded the Holy of Holies of the Jewish Temple that the Romans destroyed within decades of the death of Jesus. The seventh-century Islamic monument has the magnificence of the sixteenth-century St. Peter's Basilica in Rome, the architecture of which it is said to have inspired. The Dome stands atop the Haram al-Sharif, or Noble Sanctuary, a thirty-five-acre tree-lined esplanade of gardens, porticoes, fountains, and shrines, an area about one-third the size, say, of Vatican City. The golden Dome of the Rock was established with geometrical precision as the organizing center of the area by eight freestanding archways that surround it, a masterly articulation of sacred space. It is balanced at the southern edge of the platform by the massive Al Aqsa Mosque, which is an architectural chronicler of its own history, from Herodian foundations, to Gothic arches erected by Crusaders, to rotund interior pillars that Mussolini donated, to "a kitsch ceiling commissioned by one of the great kitsch kings of our time, Farouk I of

Egypt."[13] But the entire esplanade is regarded as an open-air mosque, and admission of non-Muslims is strictly regulated.

The Noble Sanctuary, anchoring Jerusalem's Muslim Quarter (a phrase Muslims themselves never use, since to them the whole city is Muslim), looms above the Western Wall, the huge retaining embankment, made of massive hewn stones, that alone remains of Herod's Temple. Indeed, Jews refer to the Haram as the Temple Mount, though they rarely ascend it. Instead, with many in earlocks and beards, they daven in the shadow of the Western Wall, or *Kotel*, which is both the border and the heart of the Jewish Quarter. As the surviving remnant of the otherwise obliterated Temple, the wall is believed by the Orthodox never to have been abandoned by the Shekhinah, the presence of God, which was first recognized as dwelling in this place by David, or perhaps by Abraham, three thousand years ago. At all hours, devout Jews, some in fur hats and some in jeans and T-shirts, can be seen at the *Kotel* offering prayers. Together, the Dome of the Rock and the Western Wall overshadow the dull gray but still striking dome of the thousand-year-old Church of the Holy Sepulcher, a few hundred meters to the west, approached through the winding alleys of the Via Dolorosa, where the fourteen traumas of Christ's torture are enumerated and memorialized. Under the dome of the Holy Sepulcher itself are the sites of Christ's prison, the pillar where he was whipped, the hill of Calvary, the stone slab on which his corpse was anointed, the tomb in which he was buried, and the place where, once risen, he encountered Mary of Magdala. Also inside the Holy Sepulcher are the center of the earth and the tomb of Adam.

Other holy places punctuate the crowded enclave of the Old City: the Ethiopian Monastery, the Greek Orthodox Patriarchate, and the Latin Patriarchate in the Christian Quarter; the Cathedral of St. James, the Cenacle (remembered as the place where Jesus celebrated the Last Supper), and King David's Tomb in the Armenian Quarter. That there are such rigidly defined districts tells the story — Jerusalem as the seat of conflict not only between religious groups, but within them. The city is home to thirty religious denominations and fifteen language groups which use seven different alphabets. In the past one hundred years, more than sixty political solutions to the city's conflicts have been proposed by various national and international entities, yet conflict remains.[14] Still, Jerusalem lives. The balance is delicate, which is why, despite its astonishing survival, the city seems forever vulnerable. "Jerusalem is a golden basin," a tenth-century Islamic geographer wrote, then added that it is "filled with scorpions."[15]

Today's Jerusalem has other markers as well. The Old City with its wall and quarters is a tiny island surrounded by a first ring of less congested but still crowded neighborhoods of the nineteenth and early twentieth centuries. Mea Shearim, for example, dating to the 1870s and only the second settlement to be established outside the Old City walls, is home to the Haredim, the most theologically conservative branch of Orthodox Judaism. The district, which contains fifty synagogues, with another hundred not far away, takes its flavor from the long-skirted, covered women and black-suited men, many of whom wear the satin robes, leggings, and fur hats of the eighteenth-century Polish aristocracy that stamped the movement's origins. The odd dress of the ultra-Orthodox was defiantly embraced by Jerusalem Jews in reaction to its being forcibly imposed on them by the Ottoman rulers who required religious minorities to wear readily identifiable costumes. That spirit of sartorial aggression continues. The first Zionists were mainly socialist and secular, farmers not given to the cities of Israel, including Jerusalem, but that changed. Secular Jews might once have openly disdained the premodern pieties of Mea Shearim, but as the Israeli novelist Amos Oz put it in 1982, "Because of Hitler, you have no right to quarrel with this sort of Judaism."[16] Ultra-Orthodox Judaism is a citywide phenomenon now, and the rabbis have lately dominated the government of the municipality. Because most ultra-Orthodox males spend their time studying Torah, they do not hold jobs. From their piety comes poverty.

Two miles to the southwest, yet a world away, is the German Colony, where the Jewish intellectual elite still gather at cafés on Emek Refaim Street as if on the Boul' Mich' — or, better, on the Kudamm. The area was first settled by nineteenth-century German Protestants, who came to convert the Jews of Jerusalem as a way of preparing for the return of the Messiah. By 1941, the Germans resident there were openly sympathetic with Hitler, and were therefore deported en masse by the British, who controlled the city. The district retains its European air. The Israeli café-sitters are the mostly secular, or only loosely religious, children and grandchildren of the socialist founders of the state. At the café entrances stand dark-skinned Ethiopian or Yemeni security guards, who became ubiquitous during the intifadas, or Palestinian uprisings, of the 1990s and early 2000s, and whose main function was never so much to search handbags for terrorist bombs as it was to take the brunt of the blast when the bombs exploded. (During the second uprising, sacrilegiously named the Al Aqsa Intifada, for the mosque, more than 830 Israelis were killed by suicide terrorists, with over 4,600 maimed.[17] In those days, traffic always left a gap of a hundred yards or more ahead of and behind the municipal buses, because so many of them were being blown up.) Such open fear of violence passed, but less pious Jews have felt increasingly ill at ease in Jerusalem, as the municipality, in its governance and its culture, has become more vigorously associated with ultra-Orthodox parties.[18]

Speaking generally, contemporary Israelis are divided between only two parties: one focused, in a formulation of the writer Bernard Avishai, on "Tel Aviv's cool" (high-tech entrepreneurs, software engineers, European-oriented intellectuals), and the other focused on "Jerusalem's fire" (settlements in disputed territory, God-given claims to Greater Israel, antimodern religiosity).[19] This divide has been evident in the past decade in the quiet migration of many Jews, especially younger ones, away from Jerusalem and toward the more cosmopolitan coastal cities. The cafés of the German Colony do not throb the way they once did. Thus, despite the high ultra-Orthodox birthrate, Jews have been declining as a percentage of Jerusalem's population by about six thousand a year.

This is primarily the result of an argument among Jews over what it is to be a Jew. Such Jewish disputes over the meaning of Judaism were a mark of the time of Jesus, with historic consequences. *Jerusalem is defined by its arguments.* Each of its subcultures has its core value, and its capacity for carrying that value to a destructive extreme.[20] Outsiders perceive this intra-Jewish disputation dimly, since one of the surviving characteristics of anti-Semitic thinking is the tendency to define "the Jews" univocally, as if this group were only one thing. Thus contemporary criticisms of Israel, for example, are routinely mounted from outside Israel with little attention to the expressly Jewish voices *within* Israel that steadfastly raise issues of, say, Palestinian dispossession. The inability of many of Israel's critics, especially Europeans, to refrain from sweeping condemnation of "the Jews" repeats the originating Christian mistake — perceiving "the Jews" with such all-encompassing negativity that Jesus was no longer recognized as belonging to this people. Many Israelis, on the other hand, can, after the traumas of the intifadas, think in exactly the same univocal way about "the Palestinians," as if they were all terrorists. To generalize is human.

Arguments and emigration notwithstanding, visitors to today's Jerusalem see a thriving core. Downtown neighborhoods adjacent to Jaffa
Gate, at the northwest corner of the medieval wall, were restored in the
first decade of the new millennium by the Canadian architect Moshe
Safdie, whose trademark urban design arranges markets and apart-
ments in a kind of terraced amphitheater before which the Old City
seems to be taking a theatrical bow. The true stage set, though, is the
temple-like King David Hotel, on the opposite hill from Jaffa Gate, a
1931 structure built of pink limestone to resemble a Semitic palace. The
King David was made famous when, because British Mandate forces
used it as a headquarters, a Jewish underground organization blew it
up in 1946, killing ninety-one. Directly across King David Street is the
equally monumental YMCA, which also dates from the thirties. It was
built with Rockefeller money, and shows it. Flanked by colonnades and
gardens, the Y has a familiar feel because its tiered, art deco tower carries an echo of another spire, and thereby hints at the identity of its
architect — an American named Harmon, whose firm designed the
Empire State Building in New York, where the same tower, mounted
a thousand feet above Fifth Avenue, was designed to double as a sky-
mooring for dirigibles.

The Y is the perfect twenty-first-century Jerusalem institution — a
Christian organization headed by a Jewish chairperson and a Muslim
CEO.[21] At its elegantly terraced entrance is a plaque defining "a place
where political and religious jealousies can be forgotten and international unity be fostered and developed," but the sentiment is taken from
the dedication remarks of Lord Allenby, who, as Jerusalem's World War
I conqueror and 1917 founder of the British Mandate, perhaps did more
to sow the seeds of local conflict than any other person.

Not far away, the Ben Yehuda pedestrian mall in the heart of West
Jerusalem bustles with young Israelis, especially on Saturday night after
Shabbat has ended. T-shirted and wearing blue jeans, sporting the thin
white cables of their iPod ear buds like jewelry, they spill out onto the
pavement from pizzerias and cafés, a joyous throng, citizens of Youth
Nation. On Saturday nights kids might show up from Tel Aviv for a
taste of Jerusalem's heat.

From Ben Yehuda, a second ring of neighborhoods, or half of one,
stretches through modern apartment complexes — all constructed of
the ubiquitous white stone — to the farther hills of West Jerusalem. The
Knesset, or parliament, the Israel Museum, including the Shrine of the

Book where the Dead Sea Scrolls are kept, and, in the more distant hills of Mount Herzl, Yad Vashem, the memorial to the Six Million, partially designed by Safdie, occupy what have become mostly residential areas. About half a million Jews live in Jerusalem, from the well-to-do Ashkenazim who live in Baka, south of the German Colony, to the relatively recent Russian immigrants who occupy ring neighborhoods like Gilo and Har Homa, which are on disputed land across the green line that formerly divided Israel from Jordan.

In East Jerusalem, the matching inner ring is made up of Israeli Arabs (or, as they might prefer, Palestinians with Israeli passports), living in crowded, poorer, but still proud neighborhoods. In Sheikh Jarrah, for example, extremist Jewish settlers — what one former Speaker of the Knesset calls "the 'Jerusalem syndrome' loonies"[22] — have attempted to force Palestinian families out of homes they have lived in for decades. The neighborhood had once been a manorial center of patrician Arab life, home to notable Jerusalem families like that of Sari Nusseibeh, whose father was a governor of Jerusalem in the Jordanian era and who is himself the president of Al-Quds University.[23] Sheikh Jarrah is now contested, but the Arabs have resisted the Jewish settlers' pressures, and other Israelis have rallied to the Arabs, protesting some evictions and preventing many others.[24] About a quarter of a million Arabs live in the city. But fully half of the city's population is made up of the ultra-Orthodox and the Palestinians, both groups being extremely poor and having many children. Poverty and fundamentalist alienation are defining notes of Jerusalem's future.[25] Palestinian alienation may be, if anything, more intense in Jerusalem than in the West Bank or Gaza, because the relative privilege of even poorer Jews is impossible to miss. At present a "reciprocal antipathy"[26] divides the city between groups of extremists on either side of the dispute.

For all of Jerusalem's deep history, two relatively new, mainly concrete structures have stamped it with fresh drama, markers for Arabs and Jews alike, for better and for ill. Like San Francisco with its Golden Gate, the sprawling cityscape at last has a modern icon to compete with all the ancient ones: a soaring entrance gate in the form of a Santiago Calatrava–designed bridge at the most frequently used approach to the city, at Jaffa Road, where all travelers from the coastal plain arrive. Although brand new (constructed as part of a twenty-first-century light-rail system), and although stretching across traffic instead of water, the suspension bridge achieves the character of a triumphal arch, with its dozens of white steel cables strung to a four-hundred-foot angled mast. The superstructure has a mystical resemblance to a heavenly lyre ("Praise him with the lyre and harp!"[27]). The broken lines of the bridge mast also evoke a lightning strike, the cables as flashing electrical pulses, theophany.

But equally defining of the city's topography, not far from Jaffa Road, is the thirty-foot-high concrete wall that snakes between Jewish and Arab areas, part of a four-hundred-mile-long West Bank "security barrier" that began to be built in 2006 to stop attacks from Palestinian suicide bombers. In fact, the suicide bombers stopped coming, and so the wall may be counted as a success. But the wall transforms the city into an ethnic labyrinth. It cuts off most Palestinian sections of East Jerusalem, like Abu Dis, home to Al-Quds University, with its more than six thousand Palestinian students for whom access to Jerusalem proper is effectively closed down. Whatever its security justifications, the wall annexes whole swaths of land for Israel by veering into occupied territories that were captured during the 1967 Six-Day War. The wall preempts negotiations.

If Jerusalem is an Arab text, *its* context are the refugees—the five million survivors and progeny of the 750,000 Arabs who were displaced by the 1948 war, and of the 500,000 who were displaced by the 1967 war. Spread throughout the West Bank and Gaza, and exiled in Jordan, Syria, and Lebanon, they look to Jerusalem, as their ancestors have since the seventh century, but what they see is disheartening. Of greater Jerusalem's quarter of a million Arabs, fully 60,000 are cut off by the security wall and its checkpoints. Not citizens of the Palestinian Authority, which has putative sovereignty over the West Bank, they are, for practical purposes, stateless—and cityless. The Muslim Quarter of the Old City has housing for fewer than 20,000 people, but twice that number have crowded in because Jerusalem Arabs are afraid of being permanently exiled if they cross to the other side of the security barrier.[28] Until recently, it was assumed that East Jerusalem would one day be the capital of the Palestinian state, but the grim divider winds through that prospect less like a question mark than a slash.

But there, too, old habits of the Western mind intrude on this city. Palestinians are reduced to the mere victimhood that is regarded as proper to "Orientals," as if their agency counts for nothing—both in allowing violent nihilists to speak for them and in creating conditions that prevent reconciliation among themselves, much less with Israelis.

Meanwhile, Western critics of Israel, misreading the meaning of Jerusalem, often hold the state to an ideal of human rights to which Palestinians are not held — or Americans, for that matter.[29]

This occurs by means of what might be called the celebration of "the ideal Jew," which accomplishes a denigration with an exaltation. Jews as they exist are measured against Jews as they *should* exist, and are always found wanting. This old mental habit can involve a New Testament assumption that God's chosen people should have recognized Jesus as the Messiah; a medieval Christian rage against the Talmud as a denial of the sufficiency for Jews of the Old Testament; an Enlightenment-era resentment against Jewish "clannishness" that complicates Jewish citizenship; or the contemporary contrast between the socialist idealism of the kibbutzim and the compromised realpolitik of the post-1948 state of Israel. In every case, the imagined Jew is used to justify contempt for the real Jew — much as the imagined Jerusalem ("heavenly Jerusalem") is used to find fault with Jerusalem as it exists. Imagined versus real: that dynamic defines this book.

3. *Hic*

In nearby Bethlehem, the cave of the Nativity, embedded in the crypt of the Byzantine basilica, is marked with a brass seal on the floor inscribed with the Latin words *Hic Incarnatus Est. Hic* means here. The Word became flesh *here:* so Christians say. Muhammad ascended to heaven from *here:* so Muslims say, thinking of the rock on the Haram, where the Prophet's footprint is found. God dwells in the city *here:* so Jews say, bowing before the Shekhinah, who refused to leave the Western Wall even as the Temple was destroyed. For once, the abstractions of belief, the limitations of the human capacity to assign language to the unspeakable, or to apply categories of knowledge to the unknowable — all of this is transformed by the collective experience, shared in different ways by Jews, Christians, and Muslims, that the Holy One has touched the earth *here.*

The ram's horn, the tolling bells, and the muezzin's high-pitched call to prayer — such are the sounds of what otherwise remains silent. Alas, they form a cacophony. Division and dispute, rivalry and tribalism, turf fight and hurled anathemas: ultra-Orthodox Jews against the secular children of Ben-Gurion; European Ashkenazic Jews against Sephardic

Jews of the Middle East; Russian-immigrant Israelis against native-born sabras; Latin Catholics against Greek Orthodox; Turks against Armenians; dark-skinned Ethiopians against racial elites of various traditions; Franciscans, preaching love, against Dominicans, emphasizing mind; modernity against tradition; doctrine against mysticism; and looming over all, Palestinians against Israelis;[30] Jews against Arabs; gun-toting religious Zionists against Jewish atheists; and, within the Arab world, Muslims against Christians, Hamas jihadists against Fatah bureaucrats — all boiling down to a contest of life against death. In every case, the argument is over *hic*.

In the Church of the Holy Sepulcher, the Eastern Orthodox monks and Latin friars have been known to come to physical blows over the schedule of worship, the arrangement of candles, the right to sing praises to the Lord on the very site of his death and resurrection. Nineteenth-century Protestants were so scandalized by the frenzied spirit of argument in the decrepit Holy Sepulcher — because the Catholics and the Orthodox could not agree even on responsibilities for its upkeep, the sanctuary was filthy, the integrity of the structure threatened — they "discovered" a new and better place in which to honor the memory of the resurrection of Jesus. An event of such sublimity could simply not have occurred in a place of such degraded discord. This new holy place was the Garden Tomb, a few hundred yards outside the Old City wall, a set of gentle small hills and chalky limestone caves that, archeologists could attest, had indeed served as an ancient burial ground. That a grove of cedar trees through which tidy pathways wound made the space lovely, and that the reservation was at a blissful remove from the bustle of the conflicted city, only confirmed the sense that this had to have been the site of Jesus' resurrection. The aesthetic truth of the Garden Tomb trumped all traditional claims, and even those of historical criticism. One could almost see the tearful Mary of Magdala rush to the stranger, asking where the body of her Lord had been taken. In the hush of light breezes through the curling leaves above, one could almost hear the master's voice: "Mary." The case for the authenticity of the Garden Tomb, replacing ancient assumptions that dated at least to the fourth century, is an argument from fittingness, and it has been good enough for a century's worth of tidy-minded pilgrims. God comes to the beautiful places, and those who find God there become beautiful people.

But that is not Jerusalem. As this book will show, vague intuitions about the numinousness of this place — specifically, about the rock over which the Islamic dome now stands — evolved from the fertility-god cults of prehistoric times into actual incarnationalism, an idea, larger than Christianity, that the sacred shows itself not "near here" or "in the air" or "perhaps" or in "the idea" of the place, but *hic*. Here and now. In this place and no other.

The first to have this intuition were "primitives," who founded Jerusalem by choosing its high point of land as a site of sacrifice. In all likelihood, human sacrifice. Genesis tells the story of Abraham taking his young son Isaac up a mountain to an altar of sacrifice on which God has commanded Abraham to immolate Isaac. Isaac carries the wood for the fire, but wonders where the offering is. Abraham tells him that God will provide one, and then God does, sparing Isaac and supplying a ram in his stead.[31] The point of the story is that on the holy mountain God intervened to end human sacrifice — and the mountain, so the tradition says, is this one *here*. The rock of sacrifice is *this* rock.

The story dates to a period of perhaps four thousand years ago, yet that was already long after Stone Age peoples had, in all likelihood, designated the site of this rock as sacred. In the Abraham story it is called Mount Moriah, although the promontory was eventually conflated with Mount Zion, the pinnacle on which David built his house. With David and his son Solomon — a mere three thousand years ago — the sacrificial site was enshrined in the Holy of Holies of the Temple, the radioactive sacredness of which can be felt in the Haram al-Sharif to this day. The Dome of the Rock enshrines *this* rock. For Jews, Muslims, and Christians, this real estate — "holy land" — is a magnet that draws to itself, and thereby organizes, the shavings of a million impressions of transcendence.

The first to formalize their religious understandings around this *hic* were the Hebrews who, 2,600 years ago, were exiled to Babylon. Looking back from that foreign land, they recognized the sanctity of Jerusalem only when they had lost it. That recognition led to their invention of a mystical Jerusalem ("By the waters of Babylon, there we sat down and wept when we remembered Zion"[32]) and motivated their return to it. Upon return, it motivated their reconstruction of the Temple. When the Temple was again destroyed, this time by the Romans, not quite two thousand years ago, the followers of Jesus located the mystical *hic* in *him*, but Jerusalem came back big-time three centuries later, when his "True Cross" was discovered in caves beneath the pagan metropolis — Aelia Capitolina — with which the Romans had superseded (from the Latin for "sit upon") Jerusalem. Now the empire was pagan no more, ruled as it was by the convert emperor Constantine, whose mother, Helena, did the discovering. What the resurrection was to the story of Jesus, the discovery of the True Cross — and therefore the Christian revalorizing of Jerusalem — was to the coalescing of the until then disorganized Church. As Jesus had been resurrected from the dead, so was the holy city resurrected when believers made it a refuge of particularity amid the impossible abstractions of universality. Transcendental desire is built into the human condition, and so Jerusalem, as the seat of that desire, is not exceptional, but incidental, in the sense that the incident occurs here. Jerusalem, with its holiness and its violence both, is a distillation of the human condition, a purification and intensification of what it means to be alive on the earth.

And why shouldn't Muslims have felt its pull, too? That they did so is suggested by the already noted fact that the first ambition the armies of Muhammad had, even without him — or, rather, especially without him — was to take Jerusalem. Why? Because they, too, were alive to that *hic*. And so alive were Christians to it that, in a version of what the Hebrews had done in Babylon, when Christians lost the actual place to the excluding Muslim infidel in that seventh-century conquest, they invented an *idea* of it — "coming down out of heaven from God" — around which to organize the very civilization, Christendom, that was just then coming into being.

The lost city sparked the fever of an imagined city, which spiked four centuries later in the Crusades, violence fully sanctioned by the Church for the first time, since it aimed at the rescue of captive Zion.[33] And with God's permission, the devils were set loose. But Christian Europe was pushed ignominiously away from Jerusalem, once again leaving nothing but the memory and the longing, both of which eventually made the passage to America, whose eye was perpetually cast back across the sea. The idea of Jerusalem brought consolation and it brought war. The idea of Jerusalem brought hope and it brought hubris. Humans through the ages, from widely divergent starting points, seemed equally to grasp that if the challenges of native discord and alienation could be met in Jerusalem, they could be met anywhere.

Nothing else explains why so many different kinds of people, through so many insurmountable obstacles and across so many thresholds of time, kept finding ways back to this one place. They have kissed its stones, touched their foreheads to its walls, shuffled through its alleys on their knees, drenched their faces in its pools, crushed their fingers between its crevices, thrown themselves down on its dirt. And for what? Such true belief has rarely opened into truth. Jerusalem is the home base of discord, the sanctuary of sacred violence. Disillusionment hovers over Jerusalem, but the illusion refuses ever quite to die. Disappointed hope defines Jerusalem more than fulfillment, but the very disappointment confirms the permanence of desire. Thus, for all its broken promises, Jerusalem is the womb of self-surpassing. It is the school that teaches knowledge to know itself. Its complexity — no, its impossibility — is what makes it holy. And so it has always been. Until finally, at the dawn of modernity, Western Christians took the actual city back — a Jewish city, a Muslim city — reconquered in the thick of World War I. With that reversal of the Crusaders' defeat more than seven hundred years before, Western Christians unknowingly defined, through violence and hope, the rest of the twentieth century. Jerusalem!

4. A Personal Note

What is needed is a new narrative accounting for sacred violence. Old narratives are exhausted. Thucydides said that "human nature being what it is," violence is inevitable.[34] War is a given fact of the human condition. But is it true? Among individuals, even male aggression is tamed by time. Boys grow up. They see what slingshot stones can do to the forehead of a friend, and they stop shooting them. Can the human race, by analogy, come of age? The traditional narrative suggests that the solution to violence is more violence. Not only that, but violence is a source of meaning and valor. Violence can be sanctified as sacrifice and atonement, as the will of God. But is *that* true?

Violence and religion are often spoken of as if they occupy separate, even opposite, realms of the human condition. Not so for me. I, too, was a boy with a slingshot. But something changed. The prospect of nuclear war, felt as real and imminent as I came of age in the early 1960s, was my opening to the religious conviction that still defines me. The radical transience of "this life" pointed beyond itself to the "other life."[35] I chose to make myself the servant of that other life, ultimately to become a Catholic priest.

By the time I was ordained to the priesthood in 1969, at the height of the Vietnam War, for which my Air Force father carried responsibility, the poles of my inbred imagination were teetering. This life versus the other life? The Free World versus the Iron Curtain? Good versus evil? The saved versus the damned? Earth versus heaven? Time versus eternity? The transient versus the permanent? I held such tensions in balance, poised on the fulcrum of inner conflict. Though I have considered these questions before, only now do I understand the full scope of their chronology. I was born the year that the laboratories at Los Alamos opened, the year the word "genocide" was coined. I turned twenty the year John F. Kennedy was murdered, the year the war in Vietnam began. I turned twenty-five the year Martin Luther King Jr. and Bobby Kennedy were murdered, the year Lyndon Johnson acknowledged defeat in the war, the year Richard Nixon renewed it. I turned thirty the year that the American phase of the Vietnam War ended.

The years of my priesthood had the startling effect of radically uprooting me, to use a contradictory image. Without a war to oppose or an authority figure to obey, I knew the time had come for me to find a place in which to sink my roots again, and oddly, none of the natural places presented themselves as possibilities. I was losing my grip on the priesthood. Where would I go? It was out of the question to return to Washington, D.C., which I could no longer think of as my hometown. Grateful to be Irish, and beginning to fancy myself a writer, I might have gone, say, to a cottage on the west coast of Ireland and given myself to poetry. Catholic to the core despite my argument with the hierarchy, I could have gone to Rome, perhaps to rescue my priesthood by studying at the North American College. I flew to Ghana to interview for a job as a college chaplain at Cape Coast, and I visited Gallup, New Mexico, where a bishop offered me a position working among the Navajo. But none of those places drew me.

Instead, a current of anguish and hope that I unknowingly shared with my native culture pulled me to where I'd never been — a place that, until then, I'd thought of as existing only in the past. Jerusalem. As if the palimpsest of my mind were that medieval map showing it as the pivot of three continents, the holy city, occupying the center of a dream world, rooted my imagination as much as anyone's. I had never thought Jerusalem had much to do with me, but as I plumbed my unconscious, tracking back perhaps to first images in childhood Bible stories, I discovered the city as a geography of my own.

Nineteen seventy-three. One more golden summer, this one the last summer of Israel's post-1967 complacency, because the following October, at Yom Kippur, Arab enemies would nearly defeat the Jewish state. That was a month after I left Jerusalem, returning to America. My preoccupations while in the Holy Land were not with politics, however, but with belief. In a crisis of faith, I needed more than ever to think that politics and belief were different. As soon as I was settled in Jerusalem early that summer, I set straight out to the sacred sites, beginning — why not? — with Bethlehem, the place to which Joseph and Mary made their pilgrimage, and from which, as the story goes, Jesus began his. It was in Bethlehem, in the bowels of the Church of the Nativity, that I read that defining plaque on the stone floor: *Hic Incarnatus Est*. Despite what that assertion has come to mean to me, my first sight of it left me cold. From what I saw, the birthplace of the Lord was a tourist trap. And so, as I found on my own pilgrimage — "*Here* Jesus wept over Jerusalem . . . *Here* Jesus cured the leper . . . *Here* Jesus mixed spittle and mud" — was every holy site. The assertions made at the sacred places seemed glib and incredible to me.

To see below such surfaces, perhaps I needed instruction. I acquired a trustworthy guide, an elderly French Dominican priest, renowned biblical scholar, and archeologist.[36] I expected him to rescue my devotion, but to my surprise he was dismissive of every holy place he took me to — up the Mount of Olives, down to the pool at Bethesda, across to the garden at Gethsemane, along the Via Dolorosa. Everywhere, the same curt demythologizing: "They say . . . who knows . . . the legend is . . ." To him there were no certitudes in the tradition, and certitudes were what I'd come for. The pilgrim rounds with the scholar-priest turned out to be profoundly demoralizing.

I realized that the security of faith that I longed for was what he held in contempt. I learned that the original Stations of the Cross, along with the reproductions that Catholics saw in the side aisles of every church, were invented by late-medieval Franciscans to compete with the Greek Orthodox tourist monopoly at the Holy Sepulcher. Veronica's veil, the three stumbles, the weeping women — myths all. When the Dominican took me to the Holy Sepulcher, he led me to the entrance of the hut-like shrine inside the large basilica, a memento of the tomb of Jesus. Here I could not help but feel a mystical expectation, but when I ducked into the cramped space, it was not empty. A toothless Greek monk was waiting for me. He shoved an unlit taper in my face, growling "One dollar!"

My Dominican and I fled the place — the holiest place in the Christian world. Only then did he shift moods, gesturing at me to follow, as if my show of disbelief had qualified me for his trust. At a private house, he knocked on the door. A nun opened it and recognized him. We swept past the nun into a dark corridor, down spiraling stairs, into an excavation being dug beneath the house. It was well lit with construction bulbs. The French priest waved me close, saying, "Here . . . here!" His arms opened to the scene, behold! Large, rough-hewn stones of an ancient wall rose on either side of us, but it was to the gap in the stones that he brought me. He pointed to the ground, to a large stone slab about nine feet long and three feet wide. I sensed a change in the priest as he stood staring down at the embedded monolith. He said, "This was the threshold stone of the city gate in the time of Herod . . . Here you see the city wall . . ." The huge wall had been covered with mounds of debris, only recently cleared. Then he said, "It is certain that Jesus of Nazareth stepped on this stone, probably with bare feet, when he left the city to die."[37]

I reacted to that threshold stone as if finally I had been brought into the presence of something that would last. The stone had been buried when the Romans destroyed the Temple, and buried even deeper when they destroyed the entire city, in the generations after Jesus. For all these centuries the threshold stone had been lost. Now it was being uncovered, as if for me. The Dominican, who had displayed such cynicism before the pious shrines and chapels and Stations of the Cross, was now palpably moved in the presence of this rough granite slab on which Jesus had almost certainly stepped. The stone moved me, but so did the priest. I bent, knelt, and kissed the stone, touching with my lips what the skin of Jesus had touched.

This was as close to touching God as I had come. That it was impious, untraditional, and unsanctified allowed me to consciously admit for the first time that I was bound to leave the priesthood. The threshold stone took on meaning as my threshold, a crossing into the rest of my life. It meant more than I could articulate then that I found this permission in Jerusalem, as if a trumping of Rome.

Only now do I fully understand that I kissed that stone because of the gravity of its presence, not its future or its past. The Kingdom of God is *here,* Jesus had said and said again. *This* world, not some other world, was the one for which he gave himself. *This* time, *this* place. If a defining dread of war had lodged in me, it was because I understood war's meaning as the destruction of the only thing that matters: each person killed is the whole world killed. Every death has absolute significance. If the promise of heaven mitigates that significance, it is a lie. The threshold stone, when I kissed it, was the only heaven I wanted or needed.

I left Jerusalem, and Israel, at the end of that summer. I went home and, over the following months, composed a letter to my religious superiors, announcing my decision to leave the priesthood and seeking due dispensation from my vows. Not that I had lost my Catholic faith. Not at all. I believe in the presence of God in this life, what Jesus called the reign of God. That this life is the only life is what makes it God's. That stone on which Jesus stepped was the reason I gave myself, if not others, for my decision, nevertheless, not to leave the Church. Its language alone gives me a measure of God's meaning.

It has taken me all these years to reckon with the obvious fact that the threshold stone, dating to the time of Herod and therefore of Jesus, is no more a "thing that lasts" than the tongue-compressed air-burst of a spoken word. I also see that the Dominican and I shared a kind of elitist condescension toward the ordinary faith of the vast majority of believers. The first symptom of Jerusalem fever is contempt for those who feel the heat of faith differently. That rough threshold stone, precious to me because of its roughness, was my version of the prettified Garden Tomb — at a remove from the conflicted settings of normal human religiosity. More than that, I see now that the *hic* that makes Jerusalem sacred comes not from the touch of God, as if God were up there with a finger ready to zap holiness into a stone, like a blood infusion or an electric current. No, it has been countless human beings across the centuries who, with the imposition of their belief, brought to bear *hic*, have made this place holy.

That Jerusalem has for millennia been regarded as holy is the point. Humans create holiness. Now I am one of those who have done so, despite my condescension. If God is the origin of the holy, that is only because God sanctifies creation *through* creation. In this case, through us. Through our good intentions, yes, but also through our conflicted attitudes and fallible behavior. Indeed, humans who believe God intervenes directly to give them the Holy Land, whether Jews, Christians, or Muslims, have made the land a sacrilege, seeding it with mines.

My fallibility will be on display throughout this book. As I acknowledge at the outset that my first experience of Jerusalem reinforced the vanity of my assumptions of superiority toward those I thought credulous, I note also that there can be a vanity of hindsight. In laying out a history of sacred violence overwhelmingly defined by mistakes and crimes, I am not so sure that, if I knew and believed only what actors in this drama knew and believed at the time, I would have behaved differently. There is also the vanity of evolutionary thought, as if forms of belief and culture that come later are necessarily improvements on those that went before. This is the trap of supersessionism, and religious people, especially Christians, fall into it regularly. So do thinkers who take for granted that world history has been building toward doctrinaire postmodern secularism.

In reviewing sources and texts for this study, I have been limited by my knowledge and background — no Hebrew, no Arabic. I write as a Catholic, aiming to tell a full interfaith story, hoping that Jews, Protestants, Orthodox Christians, and Muslims, as well as Israelis and Palestinians, will find themselves honestly represented here. If I have an expertise, it is the grounded one of having been part of joint text study in Jerusalem with Jewish, Christian, and Muslim scholars almost every year for more than a dozen years.[38] What I know from that is all that I do not know. Yet I appreciate the hard fact that, because the history of Jerusalem is told differently by the various traditions (for example, Jews may date its origin to David, three thousand years ago; Arabs may date its origin to the Jebusites and their predecessors, going back five thousand years), or even within the traditions (Is the Canaanite rout by invading Hebrews a myth? Were Hebrews actually Canaanites with a need for a distinctive origin myth?), any work of history is inevitably problematic. Who gets to tell the story of the Temple? The Dome of the Rock? The Crusades? The 1948 war? These subjects are inevitably contentious. There is never a single explanation or a single cause. All kinds of people (Jerusalemites, pilgrims, Zionists, Bedouins, Palestinians, Armenians, believers of all stripes) feel intimately bound to this place. With their passionate attachment comes the conviction that they know its truth. Yet very few may know much that is real. Sure conviction based on the profoundly debatable is a symptom of the fever, and a source of endless discord. This book aims at a little less certainty, hoping to dampen discord.

But by writing as a Catholic Christian, an English-speaking American male, a war-obsessed soldier's son, and an outsider whose love for the city may impede as much as it helps, I claim an identity that limits me. Yet equally it gives me a place to stand. What I most value now about that transformative moment before the threshold stone of the ancient city gate is how close it brought me to the violence that was inflicted on Jesus and his people, for that slab of stone amid the rubble drew me unknowingly to the epicenter of the savage Roman war against the Jews.

Almost unnoted in Christian memory, that war defined the shape the Jesus movement took, for better and very much for worse. That war, for example, influenced Christian texts in their valorizing of Romans (Pontius Pilate as a man of sensitive conscience) and their demonizing of "the Jews," whom the Romans were out to kill. But a fuller sense of that war alone opens into the most important recognition to which a contemporary Christian can come — that Jesus died for acts of resistance against Rome, and that he did so as a Jew. Jesus was not a Christian. As a Jew, Jesus loved Jerusalem. And, acting from within his beloved Jewish heritage, Jesus rejected violence. Therefore the empire killed him. Empires still react that way.[39]

I did not know when I first went to Jerusalem that I was infected with Jerusalem fever. I thought I was simply in search of the things that last. What are they? Surely violence and religion, for starters. Violence and religion have lasted long enough to call forth this meditation on the stark revelation of religious maturity — the knowledge that nothing lasts forever. Far from opposites, as I once imagined them, violence and religion are halves of the atom we are trying to keep from splitting here, sides of the coin this book aims to flip, the brackets within which will unfold this story of holy killing, from prehistory to the nuclear age. From ancient altars of sacrifice to the "collateral" sacrifice of children today. From animists to biblical monotheists to modern atheists. From Father Abraham to Abraham Lincoln to the fathers who perennially send sons to war. From the apocalyptic lyrics of "The Battle Hymn of the Republic," to which legions of Union soldiers died in the Civil War, to William Blake's "Jerusalem," the majestic strains of which sent millions of Tommies out of the trenches and over the top in World War I. Sacrificial religion in all such instances has been used to keep the slaughter going. And sacrificial religion now undergirds the dance of death, as war threatens consequences the likes of which humans have never seen, even if that dance is occurring where King David danced when this story was far closer to its beginning than to its end.

CHAPTER TWO

Deep Violence

1. The Clock of the Past

WHERE DID JERUSALEM and all that it implies come from? In order to grasp the full significance of the holy city, and of the rituals that sanctify it to this day, as well as of the conflicts that desecrate it, the question must be pushed back. Where did religion come from? How did it sponsor violence? Who were our ancestors? And what about them prepared the way for us? As it happened, Jerusalem was close to the center of the region in which humans as we know ourselves today came into being. What makes Jerusalem a generating center of heat can be understood as predating Jerusalem, so we must begin our meditation with a kind of detour in time, to grasp more fully how our city came to be what and where it is.

Every human act has its beginning in the acts of those who lived long before us. This is true of war. It is true of religion. Can we tell time on the clock of our deep past? Was violence there at the start? When began the cult of sacrifice? When did human beings become the creatures who so oppose violence they will commit violence to stop it? Who is the God who requires such worship? Let's try to imagine, in other words, the mix of shed blood and sacred ritual at the earliest stages of human existence.[1]

Thirteen billion years ago, the hypothesis declares, all mass was concentrated into a single point, far smaller than the dot at the end of this sentence. Apart from that primeval atom, there was nothing. Then it exploded, the creation of matter and energy, hot, dark radiation moving away from what was all at once a center — an expansion of the universe that continues to this day, with all that exists still rushing away from the alpha void toward an omega void, which may amount to the same thing. So began what we think of as time and space.

Thirteen billion years ago is a mark on the human calendar. Yet the number eludes us. According to scientists at the Smithsonian Institution, the simple act of counting to thirteen billion would take the average human, counting in English, nearly 400 years.[2] Thirteen billion years of black holes, antimatter, light, velocity, force fields, liquids, gases, particles, gravity, hydrogen, oxygen, carbon, supernovas, nebulae, galaxies, stars, and planets. Four billion years ago (to which it would take 120 years to count), this process, like a potter throwing clay, threw Earth, which in turn threw earth, air, fire, water, ice, stone, soil, vegetation, fish, animals — and consciousness.

When, five to six million years ago (it would take only two months to count that high), drought replaced rain in what is now East Africa, the lakes dried up, the jungle gave way to grassy savannah, and the progenitors of present-day humans began to come into being. They learned to walk upright, to use a thumb. Over the generations, they shed much of their bodily hair, the better to dispose of heat through pores in their skin, which equipped them for sudden bursts of energy and effort, to flee or chase other creatures. Because they lost heat by expelling water from their bodies, they had to drink more than other animals. Oases became centers. They learned that melons store water. They seized every opportunity to pick and eat berries, nuts, and fruits. Soon they knew to return to abundant sources. Like all animals that are opportunistic vegetarians (for example, chimpanzees), they were competitive, did not share their spoils.

Then they began to systematically search out such foods, and went from being finders to gatherers. Instead of eating at once and alone, they carried the melons, berries, nuts, and fruits back to camps in vessels made, say, of woven leaves. They began, sporadically, to eat with others who gathered berries and nuts. When they came upon fresh carcasses of animals, they feasted. All they knew was that the meat satisfied a certain appetite. By eating this concentrated protein they could consume less bulk to achieve that satisfaction, which meant, eventually, they could spend less time in quest of food. Instead of waiting to come upon a carcass, they began to go after living animals and kill them. Because of their relatively smaller size and slower speed compared to prey, such pursuit and attack required cooperation. They grew in speed and strength. As they ran, their posture became more upright. Progenitors became ancestors.

Having cooperated, the members of the killing party, according to some anthropological speculations, would share in the relief, the ecstasy, of the kill. Their solidarity could be so powerful that it took on a significance of its own — an unseen and greater presence. The clan itself became totemic, and the practices of hunting, killing, and eating became set. Thus began what we call tradition. The vanquished prey could seem to have had magical powers, which (this, too, is speculation) one acquired by eating it. The hunters passed the meat around in a meal that reinforced their kinship. Pieces of meat took on value, a first currency. In these ways, the ancestors developed skills of collaboration, planning, and communication. They formed the habit of sharing. They learned to control desire, to put off its fulfillment. They developed patience. Thus began what we call culture. They went from being scavengers to being hunters.

Nearly three million years ago (you could count that high in only a month), in what is now Kenya, one of the ancestors sharpened a stone into a tool for use in digging up roots or slicing meat from the bones of animals. The paleoanthropologist Louis Leakey found the sharpened stone in the Olduvai Gorge in the mid-twentieth century. For one million years (eleven days of counting), so the archeological record says, such tools were hardly improved upon. The ancestors became proficient at killing animals, even mammoth ones. Yet in larger ways their lives of gathering and hunting changed very little over a long period — although the range of their searching changed enormously. Dependent on meat, they had to move when the migrating herds of animals moved. The ancestors spread out from Africa, going across the land bridge of the Arabian Peninsula into Asia and Europe. To eat, they traveled. If they did not travel, they would die of hunger. Eventually, their kind had moved across ice floes, rivers, seas, mountains, and deserts, to be found in every part of the planet. They killed and ate gazelle, antelope, mammoth, boar, seals, fish, birds, and bears. In the cold places and times, they wore the animals' skins. If there were no caves, they built shelters out of skins, leaves, trees, even ice.

Especially important when the climate became cold was fire. They knew fire from nature, as when lightning struck dry grass, igniting it. And then, at first only by carrying a smoldering brand back to camp, they began to control fire. In colder climes and times, they used fire for warmth. Cooked meat required smaller teeth and jaws, and over many generations their faces changed. Ultimately, fire would be the tool with which they extracted metals from ores, leading to copper, bronze, and, much later, steel — each offering an ever sharper edge. A better weapon. But in a far more immediate way, fire transformed experience. It is easy to imagine how, at created hearths and in caves, fire gave them lives at night. Not only light and warmth, but a way to ward off predators. The ability to communicate in the hunt, with hand signs and grunts, became a capacity for gesture and language. The images they carried in their heads prompted them to attempt expression, rendering those interior images with their hands, faces, and sounds from deep in their throats. Sitting near the warmth and safety of the fire, they spoke. They spoke of what the hunt had made them feel.

Modern people must beware of projecting contemporary sensibilities back into the minds of primitives, about whom we can know very little. Yet at some point they were not so primitive as to be indifferent to the emotional consequences of having killed other living creatures. Understanding themselves as observers of death, as perpetrators of death, and as eventual victims of it, they found themselves in the middle of death. This was a species-altering experience, and it has never left us. Having learned to carry water, food, and fire, our forebears also found a way, through the vessel of language, to carry such experience, all experience, which is a matter of interiority. Sharing food, they could now share consciousness — memory as well as worry.

Differentiation by sex took hold. The work of females was to bear children and care for them near the place of fire. The work of males was to chase, stalk, trap, and jump on animals with their flint blades, to throw sharpened sticks and pointed stones at them, to bring meat back to the camp. Archeological evidence suggests that the earliest hunters moved in bands consisting of only two or three dozen people — too small to maintain the right balance between numbers of males and females. According to the laws of statistics, it requires several hundred members living in a group to do that. Groups shy of that balance may have engaged in the deliberate slaying of infants to maintain the crucial gender ratio. If so, complications of that necessity may, unconsciously or not, have led small bands of hunters to combine with other bands, achieving that multihundred critical mass that enabled a natural balance between male and female offspring. Here began the tribe. This adaptation to multiplicity of social units — what we call networks today — would forever set humans apart from other creatures.

Evidence abounds that the deaths of band members and tribal relatives were not confronted indifferently. When one of the group stopped breathing, companions put stones on his or her body so that hyenas would not scavenge it. They pictured their own bodies laid out like that. It seemed to them that the dead ones still had power. The placing of stones became important, and across generations they found certain ways to do it. Large piles of stones took on meaning, and then monolithic stones took on majesty, perhaps because they seemed immutable, invulnerable to the terrifying change implied by death. Before such stones, with movement and sound, they performed what we might call rituals.

2. Mark Makers

Human beings sixty thousand years ago were, physically and mentally, approximately what we are. We are so close to them in time that we could count to sixty thousand in half a day. Even that impulse — to mark off time with enumeration, beginning with the fingers on two hands — is a defining characteristic. *Homo erectus* had become *Homo sapiens.* But more than that. *Homo sapiens,* knowing that he knows, had become *Homo sapiens sapiens.* Consciousness of past, present, and future defines consciousness of the unchanging self that is, through time, aware of its own awareness. "The ability to be occupied with the future," Søren Kierkegaard wrote, "is a sign of the nobility of human beings; the struggle with the future is the most ennobling."[3]

But to struggle with the future is to struggle with the self, which, while somehow unchanging, continually comes into existence. Because, unlike the apparently immutable monolithic stone, the self is forever unfinished, and the conscious human is burdened with, not mere fear as Kierkegaard insists, but with what he called angst. Fear is the dread of a known threat. Angst is the dread of the forever unknown, which is essential to becoming. The future does not *hold* danger; the future *is* danger. Because humans, in their very self-awareness in time — the source of human nobility — are forever unable to be at peace with themselves, they cannot be at peace with one another. Here, perhaps, is the source of human shame.[4]

Animals live in the eternal present. Humans live in the eternal coming-into-being. There is the difference that matters, the source of human restlessness. Angst, not fear. The question is constant: Is this all there is? But the question is its own answer. It is not a question based merely on impulses toward acquisition, as if human awareness could be reduced to mere consumption. It is, rather, a question rooted in the inevitable incompleteness of experience, a being that is always becoming. What we call intellect is compelled to record that incompleteness in its two dimensions, time and space. Time is measured against the past and future — memory and anticipation. Space is measured against the surrounding horizon, whether closed, as in a room, or open, as at sea. So intellect compulsively takes note of time, if only by scratching out a calendar on the bark of a tree or the wall of a cave — or on the pages you hold in your hand, for that is what I have been doing. And intellect takes note of space by creating representations — images, the work of imagination — of what space holds.

If all of this is true of us, it was equally true of our ancestors from a certain point forward. Making marks on surfaces — expression — was a way of interpreting what was happening to them and of giving meaning to experience through abstract representation. Interpretation was endlessly reinterpreted. This quest for meaning became the human mode of making peace — peace above all within the self, and peace, in the second place, among the group. That humans never fully succeed in making such peace means we never stop trying, which is why our marks, once we learned to make them, will define us forever.

Most of the marks made by ancestors — on trees, for example, or on the rocky faces of cliffs — were exposed to the elements and were lost, but marks made on the protected walls of caves have survived, what we call primitive cave paintings. Created by the light of torches, or perhaps of lamps that burned animal fat, the marks on cave walls were made with pigments, derived, say, from clay or berries, and rubbed onto the stone surface with mats of moss. Bits of charcoal were used, and so were liquid paints delicately blown through tubes made of hollowed-out bones. The most famous cave paintings were found in a cavernous underground network in Lascaux, France, in 1940. Cave paintings have been discovered elsewhere in Europe, as well as in Africa, Australia, and Southeast Asia. Radiocarbon dating was discovered in 1949, leading to a fuller understanding of the places the cave painters occupied in the past. The oldest, in Chauvet, France, discovered in 1994, date to about 32,000 BCE, before the end of the Ice Age, when caves were refuges from the cold.

Generally, the cave paintings show realistic portraits of large animals — bulls, horses, stags, lions, rhinoceroses. The artists were technically accomplished, capable of rendering depth and perspective, and they left behind hundreds of what we know to call works of art. Picasso, viewing the pictures in Lascaux and speaking of his own artistic tradition, said, "We have discovered nothing."

The oldest examples of cave paintings, like those at Lascaux and Chauvet, are striking for showing only animals. Plants are not rendered, and human figures are rare. The nearly exclusive subjects of the painters, that is, were the objects that they and their fellow hunters were killing. Humans had by then universally evolved to live by committing systematic acts of violence against creatures whom they would have recognized — breathing, bleeding, struggling to survive — as somehow kindred. No one can say what was in the minds of the cave painters, but the evidence of their exquisite marks suggests an interior struggle with the very idea of the hunt. Every animal portrayed on every wall of every cave so far uncovered was a victim — a creature who, at the end of the hunt, would bleed as the hunters bled, would breathe as the hunters breathed, until at last it bled and breathed no more. These hunters were predators, yes. But they were more than that.

To paint was, at the very minimum, to honor what was painted. Such lovingly rendered figures — it may not be too much to deduce — express the complicated emotion of regret at what the hunting life required. We will consider why it may be inappropriate to regard the cave paintings as religious, but they were surely spiritual — concerned, that is, with a reality as certain as it was unseen. All painting, after all, attempts to render visually what is forever invisible. After the fact of the mortal confrontation of the kill, perhaps the images of living animals — and it is living animals that overwhelmingly appear in cave paintings — were meant to restore the creatures to life, the life, at the very least, of memory. Life, not death, was the preoccupation of those images. Remembrance, humans had already learned, is the way to what we would call redemption.

Or was it the future that was the point? Perhaps by painting bulls and bears and horses, the cave artists sought to exert control over them, a magical effort to defeat the prey ahead of time. The caves may have been sites of observances we would call ritualistic, if not religious. Perhaps the painters were shamans, whose task would have been to perform actions that might influence nature, influence ahead of time the outcome of the coming hunt. Less mystically, perhaps the artists, in creating realistic portraits of the threatening enemy, were providing their band members with a way of conquering their own inevitable terror by giving the hunters a glimpse of the mortal contest ahead. Or the caves may have been centers of initiation, where young males were brought into the clan of aggression. If so, what the artist rendered was the dangerous future itself, to brace those who had yet to experience the trials of the hunt, or to reassure those who had. Through this "forward-looking imagination . . . the painter had frozen the moment of fear, and the hunter entered it through the painting, as if through an air-lock," the mathematician and naturalist Jacob Bronowski wrote. The cave paintings were "a peep hole into the future."[5]

We should not imagine that these creations were merely utilitarian, as if the cave painters did not also (*Homo ludens*) engage in art for art's sake. But whatever such activity meant to the painters, we know from beholding their work that they found images in their minds, turned them this way and that, and propelled them through their art out into the common realm, where others could match them with images drawn of their own interiority. What the cave painters did is the exact equivalent of what every serious artist—from novelist to moviemaker—does today. And for the same complex of reasons.

The carbon-dating scientists, to repeat, conclude that some of the Chauvet paintings are 32,000 years old, while others in the same region are younger by thousands of years—and yet the newer cave paintings are more or less the same as the far older ones. This is a revelation "of Paleolithic artists transmitting their techniques from generation to generation for twenty-five millennia with almost no innovation or revolt."[6] This discovery has led some scientists to conclude that the culture of the era was profoundly conservative, and perhaps for that reason satisfying. Little change over such a long period (consider, by contrast, how much the techniques of art have changed in just the last millennium, and how those developments reflected numerous cultural revolutions) suggests a kind of paradise of satisfaction with the way things were. Was that the paradise we lost?

3. Enter Jerusalem

We have already noted the even longer stretch of time — hundreds of thousands of years — during which the hunter-gatherer culture that preceded the cave painting one was relatively static, despite the migrations across vast stretches of territory. Nomadic life lacked the main engine of social change, which is a method of transgenerational learning more sophisticated than what can be spoken, the oral tradition. Some kinds of memorized lore would have come into play, as would primitive rituals. The cave paintings were a major form of intellectual and imaginative transmission over time. Yet the fact that cave artists achieved a certain proficiency of technique, and then rested there for long periods, seems static mainly by contrast with the astoundingly accelerated pace of cultural mutation that began to occur soon thereafter, with the end of the Ice Age that had made the painters' caves a refuge. With the change in climate, an ecological ripening matched the cultural readiness of humans, and an evolutionary leap followed.

In some regions, the warmer earth supplied a new cornucopia of vegetation, with plants coming into flower, offering fruits and seeds in unprecedented abundance and supporting a flourishing of animal life. One of those places is remembered as the Fertile Crescent, an area where the combination of water and seed-bearing plant life — nut-bearing trees like oak and pistachio, fruit trees, wild grains, pollen-bearing flowers — gave humans special impetus to come together there. Land and climate themselves were the appeal.

The Fertile Crescent stretches from Giza in Egypt along the southeast Mediterranean coast to the mountains of present-day Turkey, and then curves southeast into the stretch of terrain bordered by the Tigris and Euphrates rivers, and beyond. That land would be called Mesopotamia, from the Greek for "between two rivers." It was here, apparently, that humans first noticed that when some wild grains, gathered for eating, accidentally fell to the ground, they sprouted in the nutrient-rich soil. Observing this led one or more geniuses — they were probably female[7] — to drop some grains on purpose. In such a way, people went from merely harvesting grains of wild wheat or barley for food to planting those grains as seeds. These humans went, that is, from mere maintenance of wild vegetation to seed-crop farming.

Seeds may have been the clue, for once the human imagination

opened to them, other recognitions occurred. Most notably, as anthropologists now speculate, our ancestors may have realized at roughly the
same time that the harvesting of newborn babies was a result of planting, too.[8] Males and females came to see the connection between sexual intercourse, pregnancy, and, after a set period of gestation, child-
birth. Males, aware of being progenitors, discovered their relationship
to their offspring. This recognition of sexuality's biological significance
prompted the awakening to its moral meaning, with males and females
alert to paternity and maternity. Their mutual understanding of themselves as mates, jointly responsible for the well-being of their children,
led to the social revolution of family.

Perhaps at about the same time, our ever more inventive ancestors
came to the husbandry of animals, learning how to domesticate the
dog, which was instrumental in the domestication of sheep and goats.
The symbiosis of animals and humans, informed perhaps by canines
feeding off campfire scraps and finding therein a motive to help protect
the camp from other animals, may have defined that domestication.
Again, since women tended to the feeding, it was probably women who
took the lead in animal domestication. All at once,[9] humans were no
longer at the mercy of the movement of migrators. Beasts became farm
animals. These two innovations in relation to animals and plants, arrived at in some kind of synchrony during the period between 10,000
and 6000 BCE, and summed up in the word "agriculture," amounted
to a mutation in the meaning of the human condition. The changes
introduced were immediate and massive — "the most significant event,"
in Richard Leakey's assessment, "in the history of mankind."[10]

Now we were ready really to begin. Nomads became settlers. More
than that: humans became masters of the living world. Instead of
searching out edible vegetation, they grew it. Instead of following herds,
they led them. Having spent a million years wandering from one hunting ground to the next, and sometimes back again, the human species,
led by the Fertile Crescent pioneers, chose to stop roaming and settle
down.[11] The eternal sojourners became townspeople. Because they did
so, what had begun as primitive culture — with consciousness, cooperation, ritual, and language — became civilization, with even more.

The inbuilt forgetfulness of itinerant life became the social memory
of written language. The rough habit of subsistence became the easy
assumption of an abundance of food, albeit based on much fewer species of plants and animals[12] and on organized manual labor. Surplus

required, for the first time, systems of storage. Excess supply led to the new interchange of trading, as those with extra grain, say, offered it in return for meat. Symbols—beads, ultimately coins[13]—came into being as forms of currency (as meat had been in primeval times), and with this evolution to symbolic currency came wealth.

The concentration of farmers in villages led to the invention of the city, in which early forms of divided labor, cooperation, and sharing were enhanced and systematized. It is not incidental to such an evolution that the oldest extant example of written language, dating to more than five thousand years ago, is a list in abstract pictograms on clay tablets of the livestock and grain supply belonging to farmers. These were Sumerians, people who had migrated to the heart of the Fertile Crescent, in the region where the Tigris and Euphrates come together before running into the Persian Gulf, from the mountains of present-day Turkey. Sumerians were the predecessors and mythic forebears of Babylonians, Assyrians, Persians, and Semites. The important thing is that the oldest writing we know of, cuneiform Sumerian,[14] is an inventory. With the inscribed record of Sumerian farmers' possessions began what we call history, for writing is the vessel in which knowledge is carried through time. History, as the ground of transgenerational learning, with its endless accretion of detail and classifying of what is learned, is the mechanism of ever more rapid cultural change.

The mystique of the hunt—silence, stalking, wit, adrenaline of the chase, elation at the kill, something like remorse in the face of death, endless danger—gave way to a sedentary mode of being, featuring the security of hoarded necessities and expanded social networks involving much larger groups. Human population would now take off.[15] So would new forms of knowing. The cultivators developed systems for controlling the floods of the rivers and directing water onto arid land. A capacity for measuring the cycle of seasons took on importance for the planting and harvesting of crops and the herding of grazing livestock. This need for a calendar led to an awareness of the movements of heavenly bodies, which became a reliable guide both to monthly patterns—the matching of the moon to menstruation, for example—and to the annual fluctuations of heat, rain, wind, light, river flood, and wild migrations. Here was the beginning of astronomy, the birth of mathematics, the start of science.

With agriculture also came a sense of territoriality. Planting in the ground presumed the control of the ground. Harvesting through months-long planning and exertion of effort presumed control of what was harvested. Here began the idea of possession. Exclusive possession. This entailed — and at the time it could only have seemed inevitable — a new desire to accumulate, and to measure accumulation by comparison to that of others. The impulse to control what one possessed soon enough led to the urge to control those others who might desire it. No sooner had power over other living things been established than systems of power over fellow humans seemed necessary, too.

Agriculture required an endless round of mind-numbing and repetitious physical work, so it developed that those who could exempt themselves from it did. Divisions of labor became hierarchical. Because the work of farming proved cyclical, with periods of relative inactivity following the harvest, humans had time to devote themselves to the contests with each other, both within communities and outside them, that this new urge to power seemed to require. Such mutations in the social order were reflected — and extended — in stories told to account for them, the myths that tied royalty systems to the actions of gods, who could be as capricious and brutal as the lives the people found themselves living.

It is not incidental that the oldest continually occupied city on earth stands like a sentinel at the southeastern edge of the Fertile Crescent. It is Jericho, astride the valley of the Jordan River, dating to about 9000 BCE. The name is thought to derive from a primitive Semitic word for moon, suggesting that lunar gods were worshiped here. In addition to remnants of pottery, worked copper, and shaped bronze that show how settlers flourished in Jericho over twenty distinct eras, archeologists have detected evidence of the city's earliest walls and towers, which were themselves monuments to the new condition.

Jericho, long celebrated as a city of palm trees, was a settlement that nomadic peoples first saw when they emerged from the Arabian Desert, seeking the abundant realm of agriculture. Indeed, roaming bands of herders, endlessly on the lookout for pastureland for their animals, began bursting in on settled areas, disrupting the lives of farmers and city dwellers.[16] Some wanted to take up the new way of settled life, while others wanted simply to take what it produced — the theft of the fruits of the farmers' labor. So began stealing on an organized scale.

Jericho's walls were protection enough for a long time, but then another cultural leap occurred when humans, having domesticated the wild horse and turned it into a draft animal, mounted its back and bent the powerful animal to human will. Horse and rider, in communication with each other, were like a new creature altogether. Soon horses were roped to wheeled platforms, and the chariot was invented. At last the human being had a mode of physical dominance commensurate with human desire. Now the urge to power had its instrument. When systematic theft and the technology to advance it combined, something new in the human condition had begun. That happened in the plains around Jericho, when the mounded clay walls and towers were no longer enough to resist the hordes of mounted nomadic bandits and charioteers who assaulted the city.

Those assaults marked the beginning, about five millennia ago, of what we call war.[17] Its stresses were reflected — and celebrated — in the myths of Sumerian, Babylonian, and, ultimately, Semitic peoples, whose sagas were infused with defeat and conquest. Accounts of the world's creation, for example, posited mortal conflicts between gods, out of whose slain bodies were drawn the earth and heaven.[18] Intraspecies violence became so all-defining that it was assumed to be cosmic and primordial.

Jericho was a valley settlement on an east-west passage north of the body of water we call the Dead Sea. The town's vulnerability to systematic theft led settlers to a new appreciation of the natural advantages of elevation. From high up, approaching enemies could be seen, preparations for their barrage begun, and, in the conflict, their assault thrown back. Thus began the move to hilltops, the perch that humans still prefer. One of the pinnacles not far from Jericho was an especially propitious ridge, protected as it was by valleys on the east and west, which ran together like the blades of a plow, in an image we saw before for the same place, to the south. Archeologists date the first settlement of this fortified city-state to about 3000 BCE, around the time of those first mounted horses. Around the time, in fact, of those Sumerian inventory tablets that mark the start of history. Over the centuries the city would be known as Salem, Jebus, Moriah, Ariel, and, finally, Jerusalem.

4. Sacrifice

Jerusalem is built around a rock. Its most prominent feature is the Dome of the Rock. The rock, as we saw, is remembered as the launching pad for Muhammad's ascent to heaven, but more important, the rock is regarded as having centered the altar of sacrifice of the Holy of Holies in the long-gone Temple of Herod, dating to more than two thousand years ago. That Temple scrupulously built upon the same Holy of Holies rock that had anchored the Temple of Solomon, a thousand years before that. The stretches of time are real, even if traditions about the actual rock beneath the dome are mythical — no one knows precisely where the Holy of Holies was.

The holy mountain around which the city came into existence achieved its holiness as a place of sacrifice, and archeologists are agreed that, before Hebrews erected their altar there — Genesis calls it Mount Moriah — the hilltop site served as a Canaanite place of sacrifice. Indeed, evidence pushes its existence well back into the Bronze Age, suggesting that on some rock or other — and why not this one? — offerings were slain by unnamed ancestors in homage to their now forgotten deities. Those offerings included humans, which is reflected in the tradition that imagines Abraham's readiness to slay Isaac as having occurred on this rock here. *Hic.*

For us, the rock is the point. Mythologized as the navel of the universe, and as the birth bed of Adam, it came into history spattered with the blood of victims. As such, the rock ties Jerusalem to the deep past of religious sacrifice. The rock of the altar may have evolved from the monolith of the sacred shrine, which may have carried forward the protective stones of the grave, which themselves became memorials. Sacrifice, it seems clear, began as a way of dealing with death, which in turn opened into transcendence. But speculations and abstractions become specific and real when attention is focused on the place where they all touched ground. The deep past of this meditation came into the world as we know it *here,* on this hilltop. Religious sacrifice — this is not speculation — was the foundation stone of Jerusalem, and that is why, to know this city, we must know the sacrificial impulse that defines its origin.

Humans may have ritual-making in common with animals, but differently, for rituals among humans lead to ideas. Graveside actions may have begun in protection of the dead, in mourning for a particular person, indeed an affirmation of the person's particularity. But, ever generalized upon, such actions evolved into attempts to uphold a moral order by caring for the dead ancestors. The dead became the Dead.[19] And the Dead, in their absence, were felt to be still somehow present. Their absence was itself a presence, which was ultimately defined in the language of spirits or ghosts. The presence of such spirits came to be understood as Spirit; ancestors to be understood as gods; gods understood, finally, as God. The stones of the grave, that is, became the stones of altars, and ultimately of temples. Rituals led to beliefs, not the other way around.[20]

Sacrifice is the ritual par excellence, the act of making something holy by killing it. Sacrifice began as an act of ritual slaying, tied to a primordial act of slaying that preceded it. Freud, for example, postulated a preconscious murder of the group leader, a father figure, as the originating patricide out of which society drew its norms. The anthropologist Walter Burkert emphasized the hunt, asserting that prehistoric killing-to-live was crucial to the evolution of the human.[21] Emile Durkheim imagined that sacrifice was intended to recapitulate the "collective effervescence" of the killing catharsis of the hunt.[22] Theories abound. We saw earlier that the primeval killing of infants may have been at the service of gender balance in clans too small to maintain the necessary numerical ratio naturally. Such killing would likely have been ritualized, which would have amounted to an early form of sacrifice, a way of drawing meaning out of an otherwise contemptible act. From all that archeologists and anthropologists tell us, religion (a mode of meaning) was generated by sacrifice, not the other way around. Religion began, that is, in the troubling aura of violence — the violence that life inevitably required, and in the intellectual and moral reckoning that violence required.

The connection between religion and violence, embodied in rituals that have their origin in bloody sacrifice, only lays bare the foundational fact of the human condition, which is that people live by killing. Religion is how people make sense of such necessary violence, even at the risk of exacerbating it. Religion is how, in fact, people attempt to restrict violence only to what is necessary, even if religion sometimes brings about the opposite. Sacrifice is the invention that aims to make sense of, and to restrict, violence.

We cannot know precisely how or when humans came to the ritual of sacrifice. There are sociological theories of sacrifice that emphasize the communal benefits of such rituals; psychological theories that find sources of ritual and religion in the human unconscious; theological theories that see sacrifice as giving due recognition to the divine, or as a way of seeking divine approbation;[23] anthropological theories that regard sacrificial ritual as rooted in sublimations of violence; and genetic theories that see hunting behavior fixed in the DNA.[24] Both humans and animals have been victims of bloody sacrifice, and religions have evolved symbolic rituals of bloodless sacrifice, like the Catholic Mass.

Let's return to the idea of the hunt. It may be that systematic reenactments of the kill were developed by humans in the Paleolithic past of our hunter-gatherer phase — ritual as a way of reckoning with what people were doing and undergoing at the time. There would have been the real kill in the wild, and there would have been the rubrical repetition of it. But most theorists suggest that only with the invention of agriculture around ten thousand years ago — just yesterday — was there the urge to carry the foundational act of killing forward into the future by transforming it, detached from mundane and obsolete requirements of hunting, into the ritual of sacrifice.

Evidence suggests that what we call religious sacrifice began after animals were domesticated, and only domesticated animals were placed upon the altar and ritually slain. Only when humans could live without slaughter, the theory argues, did they have the impulse to enact it symbolically, whether as a way of reckoning with bloodshed's being unnecessary, or as a way of maintaining the transcendent aura of the kill — the social solidarity, the "collective effervescence," the communion with "something greater."[25] "By repeating the hunt, albeit in increasingly complicated and/or abstracted religious forms," the scholar of religion Jeffrey Carter explains, "societies define and maintain a sense of order, stability, and continuity."[26] Farmers artificially ritualized what hunters did naturally.

Ironically, as we have seen, at the beginning of the era of cultivation, when violence might have been expected to lessen (since it was no longer necessary to shed blood to eat), it seems to have escalated. Because systematic stealing, and even war, became notes of the human condition, violence was apparently directed, now more than ever, by humans against other humans. Not incidentally, with the explosive growth of population that was ignited by agriculture, intraspecies violence was a form of excess this particular gene pool could now survive. Perhaps for that reason, mitigating mechanisms faltered. Violence flourished not only between groups, but within them. This escalation was reflected in the chilling development of human sacrifice — a reifying of those primordial but necessary slayings of infants? — with religion defining itself around altars on which humans were ritually slain.

Instances of human sacrifice would be found in many cultures, even into what we think of as recent times.[27] Whatever else accounts for this, it was surely a matter of giving prerational expression to the newly acquired urge to kill those whose possessions were envied, or those who did the envying. That Sumerian inventory would have been calculated against those who could not hope to match it. Enter envy, jealousy, covetousness. Desire became dangerous.

The most influential, and controversial, contemporary understanding of the origins and meaning of sacrifice seems tailor-made for this phenomenon — human sacrifice as an antidote to a terrible escalation of violence based on rivalry and theft. René Girard is an anthropologist and literary critic whose work became so focused on the origins of religion that he is now also read as a theologian. He was born in France, but pursued his academic career in the United States, achieving eminence at Stanford University, from which he retired in 1995. His most important book is *Violence and the Sacred,* which he published in 1972. In it, he argues that religion arose in the first place through sacrificial impulses. By linking the bloodiness of ritual killing to the original human awakening to the divine, Girard accounts for the undeniable but mysterious connection between religion and violence that underlies the subject of this book. He elaborates on the reality that has already informed our observations about the way primitive human societies instinctively worked to limit violence, even while violence increased.

Humans are more violent than other animals. In mortal combat in the animal kingdom, for example, when the weaker antagonist, fearing death, abruptly goes limp, the victorious animal will usually back off. But this is not so with humans, where the passions of the fight more often carry on to the kill. Even though reasons are always offered for the use of violence, opponents in dispute universally reply with reasons of their own — "which is to say," Girard comments, "that violence operates without reason."[28] Not rational, violence is nevertheless rationalized, and as part of that mystification, it is spiritualized.[29] That occurs, from primitive times, in sacrifice, which involves projecting a generalized spirit of violence that threatens to destroy the community onto an individual victim. A particular community member is defined, first, as the source of the violent spirit, and second, once victimized and slain, as the antidote to it. The victim begins as a guilty perpetrator and ends as a source of salvation. Sacrifice transforms the victim from scapegoat to god.

Girard observes that a primal vulnerability to escalating violence threatens every society. He offers an analysis of this phenomenon, applying it to the "whole of human culture."[30] One need not accept Girard's universalizing to recognize that his thought has the quality of chilling truth. Leaving aside distinctions between hunter-gatherers and sedentary seed-crop farmers, he assumes a kind of originating violence, as if the human condition were defined by mayhem from the start. He identifies the foundational problem of what he calls "mimetic rivalry," the inbuilt inclination of humans to want what other humans want.

We are creatures who come into awareness, and self-awareness, by imitating one another. The Greek word *mimesis* gives us the English "imitate." We learn what it is to love by being loved. The infant learns to smile by offering a mirror image of the smile of the mother. We acquire language by reproducing the sounds we hear. The shopper learns what is most valuable on the sale table by seeing other shoppers reach for it. When we see what others want, we want it. The advertising industry is based on this, and so is the retail economy. We want, not what we need, but what is wanted.[31] The inbuilt restlessness of human incompleteness is channeled into the will to consume and acquire, which is fueled by the illusion that restlessness can be quieted by the satisfaction of the next desire. The trouble is made worse when the person who wants in this way is surrounded by a throng of wanters who want only what is widely wanted. Rivalry and competition become definitive.

Whether or not this social dynamic originated in the deep prehistory of the hunter-gatherers, it was exacerbated by the agricultural revolution, which created surplus, wealth, and the culture of possessiveness. What Girard calls mimetic rivalry nicely accounts for the new phenomenon of systematic stealing, as those mounted nomads swept into Jericho and the other settlements of the Fertile Crescent to raid the grain stores and the corralled livestock. This accounts for war, because the only conceivable response to the rival's violence is violence in return. Not only the stealing of grain, but the rape of women, the kidnapping of children, burning and destruction across boundaries and within them. A savage crescent of jealousy, revenge, feud, retribution. Every action in such a cycle sets violence spiraling ever more threateningly toward the ultimate obliteration of society, when every member is set against every other.[32]

This pandemonium (a Greek word meaning "all devils loose") society cannot allow. Here the communal survival instinct comes into play. Eventually, down to our own time, the structure of law[33] will be erected to deal with such human discord, but before law there is an unconscious group impulse that has its own effectiveness, when general violence is controlled by being channeled. The violent impulses of the group come to a head — what Girard calls a "sacrificial crisis" — and are projected onto a single member, who is blamed as the one responsible for initiating the discord. Typically, the designated victim is a marginal figure, one whose ties to the group are loose enough so that others are less likely to take offense at the victim's designation. "All" the devils are organized into this "one" by the spontaneous and unanimous consent of the demonizing community.

The one thus singled out is eliminated, by being killed or banished — scapegoated, a word that comes from the goat who is sent out (the "escape goat") into the wilderness to die.[34] The victim, in being aggressively rejected by all others, unites those others in the "collective effervescence" of their common rejection. We are talking about a phenomenon of prehistory here, yet this is the essence of lynching, which still occurs. That it succeeds in quieting the violent impulses of the mob — that sacrifice "works" — is taken as ex post facto proof that the victim is guilty. Like many other forms of group ecstasy, it arises with apparent spontaneity, an irrational seizure the origins of which remain obscure. For Girard, that the members of the group remain in the dark about how the dynamic works is essential. Indeed, they must be unaware that it *is* a dynamic, believing as they must that the one accused is actually guilty as charged.

Through the violence of accusation and victimizing, the threat of violence is removed. "What a relief it must have been for ancient peoples to discover that a powerful god was now in control of the violence that, as they knew so well, might otherwise rage out of control at any moment," the historian Gil Bailie observes. "Calculated and ritualized violence has a special horror, which is the source of its cathartic power, but it often warded off violence on a far greater scale."[35] It is a mistake, therefore, to think of "primitive sacrificial religion" as a mere cult of violence, as if the bloodshed were a source of delight. On the contrary, the purpose and the effect of the violent sacrifice is nonviolence, peace. And this peace is so to be valued that a way must be found to prolong it, against pressures of new conflicts. Girard suggests that the mechanism for prolonging the peace brought about by foundational sacrifice is the repetition of ritual sacrifice.

"Sacrifice" comes from the Latin for "make holy," and nothing less than holiness is what is experienced after the social peace has been restored. Because the condemned one is the source of that rescuing communion, the victim, all at once, is "something greater." The release from general homicidal violence is felt to be wondrous, what we might call miraculous. It is unable to be accounted for except by appeals to another world, a superior power. A flip occurs, and the guilty one is perceived all at once—a second ex post facto—as innocent. More than that. The victim, once despised, is taken to have been divine. Or, rather, to be divine now. The unseen realm is rendered present. Blood sacrifice has established the sacred order. The move has been made from ritual aimed at manipulating the divine to ritual aimed at honoring or expressing the divine; the move has been made, that is, from magic to belief.

This positive effect of sacrifice is the founding rationale for the universal approbation in which "sacrificial" actions are held—the hurtful giving up of something valuable out of the impulse to do good for others. Over the millennia, ideas of sacrifice have evolved and become ever more complex, and ever more ethically attuned: acts of homage, gift-giving, abnegation, atonement. There has been progress, as we shall see, from human sacrifice to animal sacrifice to symbolic sacrifice. Modern people live with the impression that blood sacrifice is obsolete. Yet we kid ourselves if we think such impulses are limited to peoples long ago and far away. Anthropology and archeology both suggest that sacrificial religion has been present wherever humans have been together—present as the generator of a positive dynamic.[36] We are defining at its most fundamental level the inner structure of culture, civilization, religion—and also postreligious secularity. Sacrifice, that is, defines the human.

Its effect is positive, of course, only as long as the point of view of the sacrifice-sponsoring community is maintained; this dynamic, seen from the other side, from the point of view of victims, is profoundly violent, ever cruel. But in the ancient world the victim's point of view remained as reliably obscure as the underlying "scapegoat mechanism"[37] of the entire sacrificial enterprise. The victim's experience remained obscure, that is, until a nomadic people forced its way into the Fertile Crescent and adopted the settled life, honoring a god who required that they, and their descendants, reverse the lens through which all of this is seen. They did this in our Jerusalem.

CHAPTER THREE

The Bible Resists

1. Wartime Literature

THE HUMAN SPECIES survives because, through violence, it found a check on violence. Otherwise, homicidal frenzy would have defined group suicide. Whether accounted for in terms of mimetic rivalry, the law of the jungle, vestigial instincts of the hunt, the anguish of contingency, or the mere lust for revenge, *Homo sapiens sapiens,* long after living solely by the hunt, found itself still to be at the mercy of the urge to kill. By channeling and ritualizing that urge, humans mastered it, and they experienced that mastery as a gift from another world — even if the channel had banks of domination and social inequity. General violence was averted by the particular violence of scapegoating sacrifice.

The meaning of sacrifice is disputed, with some emphasizing its substitutional violence, while others see it as a simple gift offering made to the divine, with destruction of the offering less important than the act of offering itself, or the consumption of the victim as food.[1] For now, the point to emphasize is that, while it is well known that the covenant the Lord made with Abraham was sealed with the sacred gift of land, less noted is that the covenant was solemnized, as described in Deuteronomy, by the sacrifice of five young animals, whose immolation marks the true start of salvation history.[2]

The paradox of violence-in-the-name-of-stopping-violence continues to inform the human condition to this day, though its religious origin has become cloaked in secular rites. Yet from a very early time, the contradiction of violence as the way to stop violence has challenged the human conscience. From the point of view of what's called Western civilization, that challenge to conscience took form in the wrestlings of the Bible.

That may seem an odd claim—the Bible as product of sensitive conscience—given the ways in which biblical themes continue even now to underwrite violence, from the slaughter of those turtledoves and pigeons in Genesis to the 1995 murder in Tel Aviv, say, of Prime Minister Yitzhak Rabin because he aimed to cede to Palestinians territory given by the Lord to Abraham. It is well known that the God of the Bible is violent, willing not only the bloody deaths of helpless animals but those of enemies, sinners—and innocent children.

The facts of the text seem definitive: the Old Testament contains six hundred passages that speak of bloody killing, by everyone from kings to empires. War—not sex, love, faith, kindness, or worship—is at the center of biblical life. And why not? Biblical Israel is a warring people because Israel's God is a warrior God. "Approximately one thousand passages speak of Yahweh's blazing anger, of his punishments by death and destruction, and how like a consuming fire he passes judgment, takes revenge, and threatens annihilation . . . No other topic is as often mentioned as God's bloody works."[3]

There is a broad (and slyly anti-Semitic) perception that the so-called Old Testament is far more violent than the New Testament—the God of Israel obsessed with revenge and punishment, the God of Jesus all-loving and merciful. "An eye for an eye" is taken to be a ruthless formula of the Old Testament, a justification for violent revenge, when in fact it was a check on *excessive* revenge, forbidding the murder of one who has taken your eye. If he takes your eye, you can *only* take his eye. Abstracting for the moment from the fact that, throughout history, Christians have made far more use than Jews of so-called Old Testament justifications for violence, the Christian scriptures themselves are also drenched in blood. While portraying Jesus himself as nonviolent, the so-called New Testament, in its dominant interpretations, puts forward a punishing, violent God—violent enough to require the death on a cross of God's only begotten son. Furthermore, in no text of the entire Bible is God's violence, and the violence of Christ himself, more powerfully on display than in the New Testament's denouement, the Book of Revelation, also (and more tellingly) known as the Apocalypse.[4]

The very structure of Israel's coming into its glory as God's chosen people is conflict, with the first consequence of that election, as the story is told, being the obliteration of people who precede the Israelites in the Promised Land: Joshua "left none remaining, but utterly destroyed all that breathed."[5] And why shouldn't that conflict over land continue until today? Location, location, location — it is the first principle of real estate and the primal source of the character of the biblical people, who found themselves — from Joshua through Jesus — living in what John Dominic Crossan calls "the cockpit of empire."[6] The Book of Revelation is sometimes described as "wartime literature," with the savage violence of the Roman war against the Jews, raging as the Christian movement was being born, enshrined in its verses. Yet the entire Bible can be read as wartime literature, reflecting a thousand years' worth of brutal conflict involving every great power from Egypt to Anatolia, from Crete to Babylon, from Persia to Greece and Rome. The lines of all these warring civilizations intersected again and again in the hills above the Jordan River, and from a certain point on, the bull's-eye of this world target was the holy city of Jerusalem.

The violence of the Bible, that is, came from the world the people who wrote it lived in. What might be called the normal violence of the human condition was in their case pushed to its extreme. Why us? they asked themselves repeatedly. And what can be the meaning of this mayhem, generation in and generation out? Sheer violence was their one absolute. It was a matter of mental and communal survival that they find a way of making sense of such experience, and the way they found was God.

2. Wars That Did Not Happen

What is the Bible? And where does it come from? We can answer both questions in one sentence: the Bible is the urtext of Jerusalem. Not only is it the city rendered, in effect, in words; the city was the context out of which the text arose. Ordinarily, we look at the scriptures as dating to the dawn of history, and its figures can seem so remote as to have little in common with us. The patriarchs lived to be hundreds of years old. The Hebrews were a nomadic throng. The kings of Israel were tribal chieftains, laws unto themselves. The high priests were guardians of purity's boundaries. The prophets were blazing denouncers. The Christian scriptures, though defining the dawn of the Common Era, seem hardly less far removed. Patriarchs, Temple priests, prophets, psalmists, Pharisees, Sadducees, disciples, apostles — all exotic, all rooted in eras about which we know almost nothing. But look more closely, and reverse the lens of time through which to perceive these events and their meaning. On the scale of the history we have been tracking in this book — going back past the first planters of seed, cave painters of Lascaux, organized hunters, shapers of tools, upright walkers, to the beginning of human life — the Israelites entered Canaan only moments ago; Jesus died just as this paragraph began. If it would take four hundred years to make a count — one by one — of the numbered years back to the Big Bang, and a month to count back to the first toolmaker in what is now Kenya, to count back the number of years separating us from the time of Abraham, which scholars put at almost four thousand years ago, would take about an hour.

We noted the domestication of horses as a chronological marker, the start of mounted mayhem and chariot-driven warfare. That occurred around five thousand years ago. By that time, the farmers at work in the hills and plains around Jericho were cultivating olives and dates, and their domesticated animals gave them milk products. Caravan trade was turning the Jordan River valley into a much-traversed route between the urban centers of Mesopotamia to the north, including Babylon, and Egypt to the south, with commercial contacts established even across the sea with Minoan Crete.

The peoples who lived in the territory of present-day Lebanon, Jordan, and Israel were called Canaanites, a word of obscure origin. Egyptian texts of the second millennium BCE refer to Canaan as one of the pharaoh's provinces. *Can* is Hebrew for "low," and the word may refer to lowlands, a relative designation of plains in contrast to the mountains that marked the northern edge of the Fertile Crescent. But *canaan* appears on third-millennium Egyptian tablets as a reference to a prized purple dye, which was produced from vegetation native to the region in question and was a lucrative product in trade. That the dye is the etymological source of the word is suggested by the fact that the Greek name for the territory of Canaan is Phoenicia, which itself means purple. The Bible's etymology is more straightforward, with Canaan being named as the son of Ham, the grandson of Noah. That the story of God's people begins with conflicts with Canaanites is evidence not of God's violence but of this people's reckoning from the start with violence as the ground of the human condition. Mimetic rivalry? Let's put it this way: Canaanites are people who are in possession of what you want. In this instance, fertile land.

Israelites were only the latest nomads who, after surviving the privations of the deserts of the Sinai and Arabian peninsulas, wanted entrance into the Fertile Crescent, what they called "the land flowing with milk and honey," which was code for the settled life of farmers and cultivators. Such assaults had occurred elsewhere, as roaming bands swept in on settled peoples from arid fringes. The aggressors were seeking pastureland and stored nutrients — Aryans in India, Luwians in Anatolia, Dorians in Greece. According to biblical accounts, the Semitic nomads simply did what others before them had done, like the Hittites and Mitanni,[7] which was to fight their way into this prized territory, beginning with the siege of the sentinel city, Jericho. To raiders, the city itself would have been the wonder, with its viaducts and drainage systems, irrigation works and paved roads, alterations of nature of which nomads knew little.

The siege of Jericho was led, in Hebrew memory, by Joshua. But scholars now tell us that the Hebrews may not have originated as an invading force from outside the land of Canaan, but may have been Canaanites themselves.[8] May, that is, have been indigenous tribal peoples who came to their distinct sense of themselves as chosen of the One God from within the multifaceted culture of the crossroads area around the Jordan River. And so the foundational belligerence of the Bible — invading Hebrews versus indigenous Canaanites, a conflict now often seen as an analogue to Zionists versus Palestinians — may be mostly or entirely mythical. It could be myth created well after the posited era of invasion by people who had come into a sense of themselves as distinct from Canaanites — as Hebrews. The question of the historical accuracy of the brutal assault on Canaanites goes to the heart of the question of Bible-sponsored violence.

According to this theory, the story later Israelites told of their alien origins — a mass migration from Egypt, an abrupt military conquest — was probably meant to posit an ethnic difference for the sake of shoring up a religious difference, once the specific cultic requirements of faith in their Lord set the Hebrews apart from their idol-worshiping neighbors. The Hebrews, that is, could well have been a Canaanite clan (not a full-blown tribe), with the story of their brutal conquest a narrative at the service of religious distinction. A very small band of Hebrews may have successfully fled from slavery in Egypt and made its way to Canaan. This group could have had its own memory of the Exodus, crossing the Red Sea, the halt at Sinai, the journey through the desert, the settlement in the plain of Moab, the crossing of the Jordan—a traumatic sojourn made meaningful by retellings over liturgical meals that came to be the Passover seder. Over the generations, other Canaanites would have associated themselves with the story of this liberation from Egypt, a story that would have served the purpose of setting the One God worshipers apart from their neighbors who worshiped a plethora of gods.

The way this would have worked is not unlike the way the American nation's sense of itself derives from myths attached to the very small band of Puritans who settled at Plymouth Plantation. The foundational event occurred in 1621, when surviving Puritans celebrated a harvest feast, which served as a rooting ritual—Thanksgiving. The harvest tradition spread as New Englanders moved west. Abraham Lincoln adopted the legend as a source of national unity during the Civil War. With Franklin Roosevelt's 1939 Thanksgiving proclamation, the handful of odd-hatted Pilgrims became officially designated universal forebears.

The span of years between the Hebraic foundational event, dated to the twelfth century BCE, and the final iteration of the "invasion" legend, dated to the Bible-generating period of the ninth century BCE, when Hebrew traditions were committed to writing, is comparable to the more than three hundred years it took for the foundational Puritan event to lodge itself in American consciousness as a source of shared national identity. In such mythmaking, an original reality can be upended—as, for example, by that turning of fiercely intolerant English sectarians into prophets of pluralism: "they came for religious freedom." In the Hebrew case, a large group of thoroughly assimilated Canaanite tribespeople were turned, by an invented association with a small group of powerless immigrants who probably arrived unnoted among them, into brutal invading aliens.[9] Brutality was not the point; difference was.

Whatever explains the account of Joshua's assault on Jericho, the Hebrew invasion of Canaan, the fact that such an act of violence is so central to biblical self-understanding remains a challenge to any conscience inclined to view history through the eyes of its victims. The violence of God is one thing, but what about the violence of God's people? If it was mandated in the past, why not the present? But the saga of the Hebrews' savaging of the Canaanites is not like other triumphal war stories. The Hebrews, whether in history or in myth, did not, after the fact, stake their claim to the land on mere force. They appealed to a prior right, insisting that their ancestor Abraham had been here before and that his heir and great-grandson Joseph had been sold into slavery in Egypt—for this was *promised* land. The Promise led to the Choice, which led to the Covenant, which led to the Land, which required observance of the Law. Out of these disparate threads, one sterling narrative rope was woven: Israel. Whatever one makes of the Abrahamic claim today—saying, for example, that it merely justifies an otherwise rapacious invasion—the point is that *these were people who felt the need for justification.* That understanding—it takes more than might to make right—itself indicates a moral sensitivity beyond what the force of arms enables. The people of Israel would be judged for their regular, and violent, failures to live up to that sensitivity—but judged by principles of their own narrative.

Joshua is thought to have led his army against Jericho—if that's what happened—in about 1200 BCE, but God's call to Abraham, with land as the sign of their compact, was understood as having occurred well before that. (Current scholarship, as we saw, dates it to around 1800 BCE.) The violence wreaked in the name of Hebrew arrival was justified not by superior power but by God's prior promise. Israel begins in violence, yes, but Israelites are already uneasy about that, which is why the promise matters. Israel's uneasiness about violence is what generates not only the Bible, but Israel's dynamic and ever-evolving understanding of God. That is why violence is so prominent in the Bible: because violence is the problem it is addressing. Across one thousand years, the human conscience began to reject what human life had always apparently required, and the record of that rejection is the Bible.

3. God's Ambivalence

Violence is the problem the Bible is addressing. We saw that from prehistoric times humans were predators with a problem, and their problem was consciousness of what killing required. Humans, that is, were predators who felt and thought. The inability to be at peace with the self, because the self was forever in the unfinished state of coming-into-being, was tied to the inability to be at peace with others. But also, since humans are forever unfinished, and aware of it, they wanted to transcend themselves. If killing provoked in the human breast a vise-like uneasiness, release presented itself in what humans already wanted. To do more. To be more. To know more. To generalize on their own tendency to generalize. Through all of this, as we saw, *Homo sapiens* had become *Homo sapiens sapiens,* the creature who knows she knows.

At a certain but undefinable point, that urge to self-transcendence through self-knowledge led naturally to what we call moral awareness. The faculty of this multivalent knowing we call conscience, which is from the Latin for "to know with." With one another, and with the double awareness of self-knowing. Conscience was the seat of the predator's regret.[10] Humans, like all creatures, suffered from things they could not control, but they *could* control their attitude toward what they suffered, and the troubled conscience was an opening to that capacity. In other words, humans could find meaning both in what they did and in what they felt about it.

Meaning is the discovery of the relationship between choice and consequence. It is the link between cause and effect. The endless quest for the primal cause is what Paul Tillich meant by "ultimate concern," which was how he defined religion.[11] Religion begins with the intuition that the better word for *what* lies beyond is *who.* This happened in line with the dynamic that had brought *Homo sapiens* to *Homo sapiens sapiens,* for just as the creature *who knew* became the creature *who knew that she knew,* that double form of knowing somehow led the creature to experience herself as *known.* Consciousness and self-consciousness, that is, pointed to Consciousness Itself as able to be related to. *Homo sapiens sapiens* became, in effect, *Homo sapiens sapiens sapiens,*[12] also known as *Homo religiosus.*

The Bible is a focused record of such a process. We speak of God's being revealed, but the revelation was a matter more of inference than flashing epiphany, a complex reflection on reflection; interpretation of what had already been interpreted — all carried out through various modes of expression that themselves defined the complexity. And not incidentally, the God of the Bible is portrayed as going through an evolution that tracks this evolution of human awareness. Thus the Bible's very portrait of God is not nearly so cleanly drawn as we have so far implied. Especially concerning the generating matter of violence.

Once the tribes of Israel were united in an understanding of their unifying leader as God the Lord, it was the most natural thing in the world for them to conceive of God's leadership in military terms, because that was the way in which cockpit leadership was defined. What leaders did for tribes was prepare them for savage war and help them survive it. The leaders knew how to surround an enemy and kill it.[13] God as warrior was a solution to the intolerable social mayhem that was a mark of life on the battlefield over which armies of Moabites and Hittites, Midianites and Egyptians, endlessly clashed. By becoming a vassal people, bound in mutual covenant to this new deity and sworn to uphold his commandments, the tribes of Israel began to coalesce, united under the kingship of a God whose very exclusivity was a form of martial dominance.

Ultimately, the highland tribes of Canaan gave expression to this transcendent kingship by imitating it. Israel's greatest leader, a "ruthless guerilla fighter,"[14] was David. He is said to have lived a couple of centuries after Joshua (about 1000 BCE). By then the Hebrews who "conquered" Canaan were understood to have divided the territory among twelve tribes, each settled in its own area. They were brought into a powerful new federation by David, who became ruler after his predecessor, Saul, refused God's merciless order, given through the prophet Samuel, to obliterate the enemy Amalekites.[15] David had no such compunction. The Psalms, which are attributed to him, are plaintive songs, marbled with pastoral imagery and elegiac nostalgia, yet they resound with cries for revenge, the thud of children's skulls being smashed in the name of the Lord, war whoops, and curses. David's was a clenched fist.

Having united the tribes of Israel under his strong-arm rule, David took over a little-noted settlement in the hills above the Judean desert, vanquishing the Jebusites who lived there. David made it his capital. Once again, violence is initiating, with a saga of conquest defining the origin of Jerusalem,[16] which became a holy city, a temple city, when a dancing David brought to it the Ark of God, thought to be a vessel holding the tablets on which the commands given to Moses were engraved, and perhaps other relics. The Ark is also described as serving as God's sedan chair.[17] Whatever the Ark actually was, it seems to have occupied a place in the early Hebrew imagination that can be compared — if perhaps not equated — to the place in which idols were ensconced in the pagan imagination. The Ark, that is, evoked the presence of Israel's deity, and like the idols of neighboring clans and tribes, it required a sacred place in which to be enshrined. The Jerusalem Temple would be like temples everywhere in the ancient Middle East, but its Holy of Holies would house the Ark.

Now to build it. But with all that blood on his hands, David is surprisingly disqualified from the new and ever more sacred task of constructing a Temple for the Ark — a task left to his son Solomon. As Saul was disqualified by his refusal of hyperviolence, David was in turn disqualified by his embrace of it. The God of this people is a warrior god, but also a god marked by ambivalence toward violence. This is not narrative inconsistency but conscientious struggle. Indeed, it is conscientious objection.

The Bible is nothing if not the record of defeat and victory, brute force the defining note of a blood-soaked world and Israel's astonishing survival in it. Therefore the violence of God, understood as the sponsor of that survival, is an essential theme. The modern liberal wish for a different God, the way critics of biblical religion are scandalized by sacred violence (or the way anti-Semites want to place unique blame on the Jewish God for the origins of holy war[18]), has nothing to do with the reality of life as lived in the midst of war. And war not only prompts horror in the human heart but also, as the ultimate generator of "collective effervescence," stimulates pleasure. Thucydides, in writing of the Peloponnesian War, as we noted, has regular recourse to the phrase "Human nature being what it is," to get at humanity's dirty little secret, which is that humans, especially males, love war as much as they are in horror of it.[19] Ambivalence defines the experience.

Even the enemy's occasional triumph over God's people is taken by the Bible to be God's purifying action, as much a signal, in the divine economy, of God's faithfulness as Israel's own victories are. God, that is, is seen as the master of war, win or lose. If the Bible can be understood as an answer to a primordial question about the source of violence, the prophets' answer is clear: God is its source! Not because God lusts for blood, but because God, like Thucydides' war, is a stern teacher. The effect of violence, understood in this way as sacred, is to prompt in God's people not the vengeful urge for further violence, but self-criticism, repentance, and return to God's way. God's way is not violence, but God's way is not foreign to violence either.

The texts that show this, as Gil Bailie has written, "are obviously troubled texts, but what troubles them is the truth. Myths exist to spare us trouble. The greatness of the Hebrew Scriptures lies in the candor with which they document a system of sacralized power and violence." Humans living three and four millennia ago may have no more sought out such portraits of a blood-lusting divinity than modern people do, but that very inhibition may be what makes the Bible unique. To believers, the book is divinely inspired, but what defines such inspiration of texts if not their revelation of "what neither their authors nor their readers wish to have revealed"?[20]

What is perhaps most remarkable about the Bible, though, is the way it brings a charge against its own interior logic by enshrining this terrible ambivalence about the violence that life as God's people seemed to require. Indeed, it is not too much to say that the Bible's subject is that ambivalence. Long before post-Enlightenment sensitivities took offense at the violence of the biblical God, the Bible itself did. Against the violent God, the Bible proposes a countervision of God, a deity whose most solemn allegiance is not to the perpetrator of violence but to its victim. *God does not sponsor violence but rescues from violence.* Cain, early in Genesis, gets the whole thing rolling by murdering his brother, yes, but the crime immediately draws God's notice and punishment: moral order is affirmed. What Cain gets rolling, God derails. A wrathful God, "repenting" of having created humans, punishes violent humanity — and all the innocent children — with the violence of the Flood, yes. But the promise God makes to Noah as the waters recede is that such divine destruction will not happen again — the source of the timeless moral imperative "Never again!" Moses begins as the slayer of an Egyptian overlord, yes. But the Exodus he leads is of a violently outcast people, and the story is told from the outcasts' point of view. From the point of view of the literally "exterminated" ones — a word meaning to be driven across the border. The "escape goat" gets its day, if not in court, in the light.

Against the violent powers of the world, the Bible's God has thrown in with the world's victim peoples. So much so that this God, as revealed in the story of Jonah, can even be said to repent of former vindictiveness.[21] The God who repented of creation is replaced by the God who repents of its destruction. *The warrior God repents of violence.* This is a vision of God that Israel arrived at only gradually — a vision that came into its own, not surprisingly perhaps, only after Israel suffered the first of its two greatest defeats.

In the usual chronology, which we have been tracking, the biblical starting point is the call of Abraham (about 1800 BCE), followed by the Exodus and the arrival at the Promised Land (about 1200), and then David's institution of Jerusalem (about 1000). The Bible itself, as a record of these saving events, tells readers that its first author (or the

author of its first five books) is Moses, but contradictions and incon-
sistencies in the texts themselves suggested to modern scholars that the
texts originate in multiple sources with numerous "authors," if that's
the word. In fact, the composers of scripture were a community of people. It's not too much to say that they were *the* people. Someone told
a story, and someone else repeated it, and someone else elaborated it.
An early interpreter read the story as a one-note signal about the Lord,
then a later interpreter found in it second and third notes. Harmonies,
melodies — a symphony. Thus myths, laws, songs, proverbs, dirges, oral
traditions, stories told around fires, rhyming and rhythmic verses, heroic legends into which youngsters were initiated in generation after
generation — all of it became scripture. A complex and multifaceted set
of narratives that began to jell as an interrelated set of texts around the
time of David, or 1000.[22]

The sources include orally transmitted tales and readily memorized
story poems and ultimately written texts, all drawn from the broad culture within which the Hebrews found themselves. Sumerian (or Uga-
ritic, or Assyrian, or Aramaic) myths accounting, say, for the primeval
transition from hunter-gatherer culture to agriculture (Adam and Eve
being expelled from the Garden, with Adam condemned to the sweaty
labor of farming), or relating foundational conflicts between farmers
and herders (Cain, whose offering is grain, against Abel, whose offering is a lamb), or recalling epic natural occurrences (the Flood), all
had what might be called normal meaning for the early Hebrews, and
formed the ground of an ever more cohesive tradition. But the glue of
the cohesion, what began to set the Hebrews apart from neighboring
peoples who might have had such myths and memories in common,
was a progressively focused idea of God — one whom the Hebrews
called Lord.

The Lord is with us. The Lord is for us. The Lord is unlike the gods
of others. Simple folk legends of the kind that animate every people
sparked the imaginations of this people, but they were conscripted into
service as elaborations of the significance of the Lord's presence. Thus
the story of Lot's wife being turned into a pillar of salt, for example,
probably originated as a tale to account for a female-shaped geological
formation with which the story's first hearers would have been familiar.[23] But now such a tale was put at the service of something besides
accounting for mere stone formations in the desert: it was saying something about the gravity of the Lord's commandments. Bible stories, that

is, began as one thing and, as an illumination of some aspect of the Lord's meaning, became something else. And that becoming was the work of anonymous editors, redactors, and interpreters. Let's call them spin doctors, and what they were spinning was revelation. They were people whose brilliant intuition — inspiration — was that the most ordinary accounts of human experience can serve as pointers to the Lord.

In all of this, the Hebrews, as they groped toward an understanding of their god, were parting ways with their neighbors whose gods were increasingly distinct. But in the larger project the Hebrews were just like their neighbors, like all humans, forever asking, How did we come to be here? What does our being here signify? Who has put us here? And how does the past reveal the meaning of the present? For hundreds of years, the self-generating process of narrative transmission (whether orally or textually), interpretation and reinterpretation, as it unfolded among the Hebrews, was haphazard.

But then a great thing happened, a traumatic act of violence in which the religion of the Jews, the religion of the Lord, should have been destroyed, but instead was born. It was born as the religion of the Book. And it began and ended with Jerusalem.

4. Conceived *in* Jerusalem, Born in Exile *from* Jerusalem

In the early sixth century BCE, the Hebrews living in King David's hilltop city found themselves under attack by armies from the northwest — the Babylonians, under the leadership of King Nebuchadnezzar. An ancient clay tablet stands in the British Museum, its cuneiform markings translated to read, "In the 37th year of Nebuchadnezzar, king of the country of Babylon, he went to Egypt to make war." Nebuchadnezzar (630–562 BCE) presided over one of the great imperial powers of history, and though Babylon, with its tower,[24] lives on in cultural memory as an image of infamy, its king was heir to one of the most humane legacies of the ancient world. Hammurabi preceded Nebuchadnezzar as Babylon's king by a thousand years, and his code of laws (c. 1760 BCE), anticipating the laws of Moses, enabled a first centralization of state authority — including a check on that authority, with law trumping lordship. This marked a turning toward what we call civilization.

The city of Babylon straddled the Euphrates River about fifty miles south of present-day Baghdad. Nothing is left of it today except a tell, a massive mound of dirt, and legends attached to the Hanging Gardens, which every schoolboy of my generation could identify as one of the Seven Wonders of the Ancient World — without having a clue to what it was. Yet in Nebuchadnezzar's day, Babylon was a teeming urban center, probably the largest city in the world, as it had been even in Hammurabi's time. It had paved roads, waterworks, public markets, great palaces, and clean abodes. In the sixth century BCE it had a population of at least 200,000.[25]

But when the mighty Nebuchadnezzar took on Egypt, he met resistance. The British Museum tablet continues, "Amasis, King of Egypt, collected his army and marched and spread abroad." The Babylonian invasion occurred in 601. Egypt's retaliatory "spreading abroad" put Nebuchadnezzar on the defensive, leading some of his vassal states in the Fertile Crescent to think him vulnerable. They rebelled. One of these was Judea. Big mistake. Nebuchadnezzar's armies turned back to territories closer to home, stamping out local resistance. In 597, the Babylonians occupied restive Jerusalem.

The third chapter of the Hebrews' own Book of Daniel (written much later) tells what happened then. Nebuchadnezzar required "all the peoples" to bow before an idol, "an image of gold, whose height was sixty cubits, and its breadth six cubits." Everyone "worshiped the golden image which King Nebuchadnezzar had set up." Everyone but three Jews. Known more through the old Negro spiritual, perhaps, than through Bible reading, the three were Shadrach, Meshach, and Abednego. "These men, O King, pay no heed to you," the Babylonians complained. "They do not serve your gods or worship the golden image which you have set up."[26] So the enraged king threw them into the fiery furnace — an act of anti-Jewish violence that would be brought to demonic pitch in the twentieth century. Unlike what happened in Hitler's fiery furnaces, an angel of the Lord protected the Jews from being burned, and the three were spared. The Book of Daniel says that Nebuchadnezzar was properly impressed with the Jewish God, but Jewish resistance to his authority continued, and finally, in the year 587, the king whom the Book of Jeremiah calls "the destroyer of nations"[27] turned his wrath on Jerusalem itself.

The last chapter of Jeremiah (in verses written not so long after the events) tells the gruesome story of what should have been the end of the Hebrews once and for all. "In the fifth month, on the tenth day of the month — which was the nineteenth year of King Nebuchadnezzar, King of Babylon — Nebuzardan, the captain of the bodyguard who served the king of Babylon, entered Jerusalem. And he burned the house of the Lord, and the king's house, and all the houses of Jerusalem; every great house he burned down."[28] The violence of the Bible had come to a climax in the cockpit of empire, although not a climax the people of God could have imagined. Their city was destroyed, and with it the house of their Lord, the Temple, which David's son Solomon had built as a shrine for the Ark of the Covenant and as the house in which the Lord had taken up residence among the chosen people. But if they were chosen, how could they now be so defeated?

And not only defeated, but kidnapped. Thousands of Jews — effectively, the elite — were "carried away captive" from Jerusalem to Babylon. "How lonely sits the city that was full of people," the Lamentations of Jeremiah begins. "How like a widow has she become, she that was great among the nations . . . She weeps bitterly in the night."[29] The carrying off of the Jewish people from their cultic and cultural center was not an act of tyrannical whimsy but a deliberate attempt to eradicate their national identity.[30] In Babylon, a city defined by altars and shrines to dozens of gods, life took its daily measure from second-nature gestures of worship. Mundane activities, from eating to copulation to bathing, involved rituals of deference to the divinities. In such a setting, the idea that a captive people could refuse to observe such cultic practice, and in so doing not only maintain but reinforce their distinct identity, was unthinkable. Yet that is what happened.

Jews in Babylon were confronted in that terrible circumstance with just how different they had become from other peoples. They did not start out that way. The similarity between the Hebrew religion and the religions of other Semitic peoples is reflected in the fact that the Jerusalem Temple and its rituals, both dating to Solomon and described in the Book of Kings, were strikingly like temples and rituals that archeologists have uncovered elsewhere in the Middle East.[31] Just as scholars now understand, as we saw, that tribal Israel came into being from within the tribes of Canaan (and not as an invading force from abroad), so the religion of the Hebrews began as a religion typical of broader Canaanite culture. But the Hebrew religion had evolved into something new. Israel's God was new.

At first the Hebrews were monolators — people who worshiped only their god without necessarily denying the existence of other gods. But as time went on the character of their god had suggested itself in ways that called into question not so much the existence of other gods, but the very idea of local, limited, narrowly understood, tribal deities. Their god, that is, had become God. In Babylon, forced into the presence of objects associated with other deities, captive Jews confronted how different their own notion of the divine had become. Their visceral refusal even to acknowledge the pagan gods, much less bow before them, was a first clear demonstration that they had become monotheists — believing not just that their God alone was to be worshiped, but that their God alone was real.[32] Their own behavior revealed this faith to them. Israel's loyalty to its God, made palpable in exile and embodied in the *Shema*, which affirms God's Oneness, defines Israel to this day.

The Hebrews' refusal to worship the myriad gods whom the Babylonians honored was combined with an unpredicted and unbreakable attachment to the idea of Jerusalem and its Temple. Instead of forgetting where they came from, as kidnapped peoples typically and eventually did in the war zones of Mesopotamia, this people insisted on its memory. The implements of memory were the texts, songs, traditions, and stories the people had carried into exile with them. Indeed, these things were all they had, which is why they were understood anew. If the Psalms, for example, had begun as verses to be recited during the rituals of worship in the Jerusalem Temple, they were now recited alone, detached from ritual, with the words themselves understood as worship. The laws of purification that had been attached to the Temple's sacrificial cult could now be observed for their own sake apart from the Temple; the laws themselves became the sacrifice. It was possible to draw close to God without the Temple, through story and law — through Torah, a Hebrew word that means teaching or instruction.

As we have been doing in this book, the impulse was to find meaning in the present by returning to the past, including the deep past of origins. In defining the character of their new God, that is, the Hebrews located God's presence in their own history, beginning with, as they said, *the beginning,* also known as Genesis. The first point to make about Genesis is the point that it makes about itself — that this creation myth is unlike others of the ancient world in that it tells of the creation not of the tribe or kingdom but of the very cosmos. Of all that is. Of no mere "god," for Genesis speaks of "God."

Not surprisingly, given the Hebrews' tumultuous recent history as a brutalized people, the various strands of the Hebrew past were now woven together to display a gradual turning away, on God's part and therefore their own, from violence. *Violence was ever the concern.* Thus the author of Genesis—and by author I mean the final redactors or editors who pulled together the various strands—defied the prevailing habit of mind to firmly reject the combative God, to place origins not on a battlefield but in a garden. In contrast, say, to the mythology of Rome, which was just then celebrating its origins in the sacred fratricide of Remus by Romulus, twin sons born of Mars, the god of war, the Genesis fratricide of Cain against Abel was not only not foundational, it was explicitly condemned by God. ("The voice of your brother's blood," God said to Cain, "cries to me from the ground."[33]) When the God of lovingkindness, fed up with human violence, became violent himself to destroy the world with a flood, he immediately repented, as we saw, promising Noah he would never do it again. ("I will never again curse the ground because of man, for the imagination of man's heart is evil from his youth. Never again will I destroy every living creature as I have done."[34]) Such was the emphasis in the narratives that came together to become defining. Oral traditions, the writings of numerous authors, morality tales, the memories of different tribes and families, codes of law, poems, rituals, etiological narratives—all of it combined in a fresh interpretation defined by the experience of exile and offering a new way of understanding God and a new way of being in the world. In exile, the people became the People of the Book, and the book, including its accounts of brutality, was emerging as an argument against the brutality in which it was born.

Amid the dozens or hundreds of idols that Jews confronted in Babylon, the exilic author firmly posited the one monotheistic Lord. "Thus says the Lord, the King of Israel: 'I am the first and I am the last; besides me there is no other god . . . I am the Lord, and there is no other.'"[35]

Ironically, this breakthrough to monotheism is regarded today by many people as an ultimate source of sacred violence, when it was the opposite.[36] Monotheism's intolerance of "other gods" is taken to be a kind of triumphalist exclusivism, a claim to possession of the absolute truth in contrast to others who possess only illusions. My God is true, yours is false! This supremacism is understood in contrast to the benign tolerance of paganism, whether Sumerian, Canaanite, or the Olympian polytheism of Greece, where various gods were enshrined to embody and enact the transcendent values of human life—Zeus over power, Mars over war, Poseidon over the sea, Demeter over fertility, Apollo over reason, Dionysius over ecstasy, and Aphrodite over sexual love. Against such a range of existential tolerance, Hebrews were understood as standing with their radical rejection: No! No to all such imagined deities, in the name of the One God of Abraham.

Are religious wars built into the structure of the religions that flow from this? That has been the main charge lodged against all three Abrahamic faiths at least since the Enlightenment. Yet ironically, this divisive notion of monotheism is, as the "ism" suffix suggests, a wholly modern idea. The word "monotheism" wasn't coined until the seventeenth century.[37] Christians affirm the Credo, Jews the *Shema,* Muslims the *Shahada* — all declaring that there is one God.[38] But what does "one" mean? In a scientific age, it is taken as a number. God is thought of as a solitary entity, standing apart from all others, and therefore, it is thought, *against* all others. If this is the meaning of monotheism, then yes, such belief is inherently a source of conflict, not peace.

Contemporary Jews, Muslims, and Christians may themselves have been influenced by univocal Enlightenment thinking, but in fact their traditions affirm the Oneness of God not scientifically or philosophically, but religiously, which is another matter altogether. Thus Moses Maimonides, the twelfth-century Jewish sage, rejected the idea that God's "Oneness" is a category of quantity. In that sense, he wrote, "the term 'one' is just as inapplicable to God as the term 'many.'"[39] Instead of a unit, the "Oneness" of God affirms a unity. Oneness in this sense means not the being who stands apart, radically different and superior, but the being who is present as the reconciliation of all oppositions. That God is One means, as Isaiah saw, that the God of this people is the God of all people.[40] Monotheism in this sense is not the source of conflict, but the source of conflict resolution.

This insight into the meaning of God is what the authors of the Bible attached to Moses, who is remembered reporting, after encountering the Lord in the burning bush, that the name of Israel's new God is "I AM WHO CAUSES TO BE." Recall that Moses has just been commissioned to lead the beleaguered Hebrews in their rebellion against Pharaoh, and it is as if Moses complains, "The Jews are going to want to know who says this." God's answer is itself the liberation. The precise meaning of the Hebrew that gives us that phrase "I am who causes to be" is in dispute,[41] but it seems clear that this God, even while noting the plight of the sons and daughters of Israel, is associated not with a clan or a tribe or a network of tribes, but with *all that is.* The Oneness of this God is not a number but a relationship with what exists. (Later, the followers of Jesus would recognize the same quality in his intimacy with the one he called Father, as in "The Father and I are one."[42] Jesus' embodiment of God's Oneness was what his followers recognized as his divinity. Still later, a desert merchant in Arabia, influenced by Jews and Christians, would come to an intuitive grasp of the Oneness of God, recognizing in it an antidote to violent tribalism. A feeling for the Oneness of God, and not violent jihad, as we will see, sparked the rapid spread of Muhammad's religion.)

This God is apart from other gods not merely in opposition to them, but in an entirely separate category of knowing. Here, to elaborate a point made earlier, is what it means to suggest that, having progressed from *Homo erectus* to *Homo sapiens* and to *Homo sapiens sapiens,* the human species had now come to be *Homo sapiens sapiens sapiens.* From "I know" to "I know that I know" to "Knowing that I know means I am known." The *being known* defined the Oneness. From consciousness to self-consciousness to self-transcendence. God is present in the world as meaning is present in knowledge. Knowledge itself is revelatory. To affirm the Oneness of God is to affirm a God who is closer to us, in a formulation of St. Augustine's, than we are to ourselves, closer to us than our awareness is. That is the Oneness that counts, and monotheism in this sense, identifying awareness as such with the holy ground of being, amounts to a magnificent breakthrough in the religious imagination.

This breakthrough unfolded over time among that obscure Semitic people, coming to clarity during and after the Babylonian exile in the sixth century BCE, when biblical writers and editors arranged and rearranged Hebrew narratives going back to Abraham and Moses (as if they had been mono*theists* and not just mono*lators*) to emphasize this newly understood aspect of the God of Israel. They understood God's Oneness, that is, by means of an act of remembering what God had meant to their ancestors, a remembering that took the form of the arranged and edited sayings and writings of the Hebrew tradition. But more than merely remembering, this was interpreting. Or, rather, every act of remembrance is an act of interpretation, and that dynamic defines the long, slow evolution of the textual amalgam that snaps into structured focus as "the Bible" only now. After the breakthrough recognition of exile, Hebrews, referring to narratives, poems, and myths that were already essential to their tradition, recalled how the ancestors heard God define himself, in foundational accounts known to us as Exodus and Deuteronomy, as "jealous" of Israel's love, exactly like a tribal deity.[43] A God who could tolerate no competition from the venerated statues, magicians, and wizards of other tribes, and who, in establishing his bond with the Hebrews, set himself against the competing gods of Egypt, and overpowered them.

But now Israel's God was perceived as of an entirely different order, a realm in which competition from, or comparison to, other deities was simply inconceivable. There was no question of this God being threatened or, well, jealous. This recognition, which is worthy of its designation as revelation, makes its significance plain in the editorial arrangement of texts that occurs now, with Exodus and Deuteronomy preceded by Genesis, in which God identifies himself as the God not of the tribe but of the cosmos — of all creation. This God, if jealous, is jealous of *everyone's* love, and offers himself, through the Israel-establishing promise made to Abraham, not to a single people but to "a multitude of nations."[44] From Babylon, that is, the Jews understood afresh both what the saga of their history had meant before and what it meant now, which is why, in exile, they recognized its permanently sacred character.

Alfred North Whitehead described such an unfolding of religious awareness this way:

> Religion has emerged into human experience mixed with the crudest fancies of barbaric imagination. Gradually, slowly, steadily the vision recurs in history under nobler form and with clearer expression. It is the one element in human experience which persistently shows an upward trend. It fades and then recurs. But when it renews its force, it recurs with an added richness and purity of content. The fact of the religious vision, and its history of persistent expansion, is our one ground for optimism. Apart from it, human life is a flash of occasional enjoyments lighting up a mass of pain and misery, a bagatelle of transient experience.[45]

The Oneness of God is the core of the religious vision of the Bible, and as such it amounts to a repudiation of God's ambivalence about violence. God is the opposite of violence. Here begins the idea that God is compassionate love.

It takes nothing away from the genius — or the "inspiration" — of the biblical authors, whose awareness came to this climax during and after the Babylonian exile, to observe that humans elsewhere on the planet were at that time grappling with similar themes, attempting to understand the great mystery of life on earth and to reckon with the ways it was threatened by violence. Religions in disparate regions began to coalesce around the idea of compassionate love, the idea that God is as near as the neighbor, and that regard for the neighbor is the surest signal of God's presence. What Karl Jaspers called the Axial Age, roughly from 900 BCE to 200 BCE, was marked by revolutions in religious awareness: Confucianism in China, Buddhism in India, Taoism in Japan, philosophical rationalism in Greece.[46] Indeed, two years after the Babylonian exile ended, as ruined Jerusalem was being restored and reclaimed as the new center of the people of the One God, the man who would be regarded as the father of Greek philosophy was born.

He was Heraclitus (535–475 BCE). His analysis of thinking led him to posit the astonishing idea that reality is itself the thinking of God. By God he meant the "one thing that arises from all things, and from which all things arise."[47] What Heraclitus called the Logos — commonly translated as "word," but perhaps better translated as "meaning" — was the underlying order of all that exists, the principle of unity in which all oppositions are reconciled. The foundation of existence is not conflict and violence but communion. Oneness in this sense is not a numerical opposition — one against two — but a source of unity in diversity, as in *E pluribus unum*. This decidedly Greek way of thinking would come to maturity across the centuries with Socrates, Plato, and Aristotle. It would influence biblical faith, climaxing in the work of Philo of Alexandria (20 BCE–50 CE), whose appropriation for Judaism of the notion of the Logos as the underlying order of existence would shape Christian attitudes. That is seen especially in the author of John's Gospel (c. 100 CE), for whom the Logos was an image of Jesus.[48] *God is present in the world as meaning is present in the word.*

5. The Empty Temple

However vague Israel's commitment to the One God had been in the past, after the Babylonian exile it was sharp as the stone before which the captive Hebrews had refused to bow. Not just Israel's world but the whole world, the very cosmos, was created in six days by this God, who beheld that creation as "good . . . very good." The first generation of humanity was peace-loving and gentle. When humans defied God, God found ways to spare them. When the ancestors were taken into captivity in Egypt, God sided with the captives and sponsored their escape. At Sinai, God entered into a covenant with that people, whose response was to be defined by observance of God's laws. For forty years the people wandered, but were then brought to the land flowing with milk and honey, the fulfillment of God's promise. So ran the account that the people told themselves now, recognizing that history itself as salvation history, a special revelation from God.

Only now, in exile, did the city from which they had been roughly taken clearly emerge in the Jewish imagination as a place of transcendent meaning. Here was born the idea of Jerusalem as the holy city. In being faithful to their God, they were being faithful to the city where they had lived with God. And it was not that God had abandoned them — here was the religious tour de force of interpretation that took place in captivity — but that God had accompanied them into exile. The condition of exile was God's gift to the people, and the obligation was to learn from it. And so exile was a place of purification. Holiness was now the duty of the people — holiness consisting in doing what was right, as defined by the commandments of God.

The religious thinkers who helped the Jews[49] come to this recognition were, as we saw, the prophets. Some of them had spoken in the centuries before the exile, and some spoke now, especially the anonymous genius known as "Second Isaiah."[50] The message of the prophets was heard as nothing less than as a message from God. Their themes prepared the Jews in exile to adjust what they believed. So, too, their own anguish, as they read, for example, of Second Isaiah's identification of suffering as a sign of God's favor (a theme that would profoundly influence the followers of Jesus in their understanding of his fate).[51] The sympathy of Israel's God, the prophets had said, was with victims, not with victimizers — and how could that not resonate with a captive people, and not firmly alter their conception of God?

Since the time of David, Israel had had its kings, or chiefs, known as judges. As multitribal people dispersed in hilltop settlements, they were suspicious of kingship, and the prophets reflected that, consistently criticizing those in power. But always the prophets refined Israel's ideas of God, gradually setting the beliefs of this people apart from the unsubtle and polytheistic religions of neighboring tribes. Prophets like Micah and Amos had criticized the rituals of Temple sacrifice, and figures like Hosea and Jeremiah had insisted that what God wanted was not cultic observance but compassion and obedience.[52] The prophets are often understood as in opposition to the priests, yet prophetic critique was always for the sake of purified Temple observance — cult always in connection with lovingkindness, but always cult. Prophets and priests, connecting compassion and ritual, were partners in affirming God's presence in the Jerusalem Temple.

The Jews were held in Babylon for nearly fifty years, until 539, when yet another wave of savage violence changed the story. Persians, under the command of Cyrus the Great, swept across the plains between the Tigris and the Euphrates, overwhelming the once invincible Babylonians. (Think of the savage Iran-Iraq-American wars of the 1980s, 1990s, and 2000s, when millions of people died on the same terrain.) The Persians, unlike the Babylonians, ruled through local vassal states and allowed subordinated peoples to maintain their own identities and cults. Thus Cyrus demonstrated his authority over the vanquished Babylonians by setting their Jewish captives free and allowing them to resettle Judea if they wished. Given how Jewish lamentation had spiraled around grief for destroyed Jerusalem, it can be no surprise that most of them — historians suggest as many as forty thousand — went home.

In returning to Jerusalem, the Jews were alive in a whole new way to its meaning. That was especially true in relation to Jerusalem's living heart, the Temple. As the place in which sacrifices were offered to God, involving the slaughter of living animals, the Temple embodied the conscientious and ongoing struggle with the very idea of violence. To begin with, the centralization of sacrificial worship in Jerusalem,[53] after Solomon, had meant that, unlike other peoples, the Jews did not have a multiplicity of temples. Before, as was true among all the Canaanites, Jews had offered sacrifices "in all their towns . . . on every high hill, and under every green tree."[54] But no more. Jewish cult had evolved so that sacrifice was enacted only in the one place. That had already meant that most Jews, living a day's journey or more from the cultic center, did not have regular experience of this kind of worship. For all of the asserted holiness of the Jerusalem Temple, its very exclusivity had long meant that sacred violence was effectively mitigated in the lives of most Jews. They maintained their relationship to God less through sacrifice than through observance of God's commands. That form of devotedness — law instead of sacrifice — had come into its own during the exile.

Back in Jerusalem, the Jews set about the reconstruction of the Temple — it would be reconsecrated in about 515 BCE — but now it was different. Most importantly, the Ark of the Covenant was gone, lost in the catastrophic chaos of the Babylonian conquest, never to be found again. That meant that the Holy of Holies of the restored Temple would be empty — an absence that, in fact, was the perfect symbol of the way this God was now understood to be present to this people. The Temple was God's house, yes, but God did not really live there. That God was said to be "in heaven"[55] merely meant that the God of Israel was of an entirely different order than other gods. They were simply not to be compared. God was beyond. God was wholly other. The God of Israel, unlike other gods, could not be represented, period.

Here was the great recognition embedded in what we call monotheism — that *the idea of God is not God.* To attribute divinity to any particular understanding of God is as much idolatry as the worship of statues. This — what the very vacancy of the Holy of Holies pointed to — was not absence, but was absence understood as the only form of presence. The single thing that can be known of God is that God is unknowable, *and this is knowledge.* It is insisted upon by the vacancy of the sacred space (where others put their statues) and by the mandated refusal even to utter God's name.

Idolatry is far more than statue worship; it is a mode of thinking toward which every human inclines, just because humans know through representation. The Hebrew breakthrough amounted to the intuition, or revelation, that God who, through God's creation and through history, can be related to, cannot be represented. Corollary to this was the recognition that the Temple's raison d'être, sacrifice, was not actually what God was after. Israel's history, a progressive moving away from the imaging of God, as reflected in the Bible, is equally a progressive moving away from the violence of God. That is shown above all in the understanding that what this God wants decidedly does not include the sacrifice of human beings.

This is a delicate point. An abstract question about "sacred violence" becomes appallingly specific when the God-commanded killing is of a person on an altar — even a child. Anthropologists speculate, as we've seen, that all religion began as sacrifice, and that sacrifice began as human sacrifice. It was triggered by the scapegoat mechanism through which the anarchic impulses of the frenzied community were channeled toward one person—a focused and limited act of violence for the sake of sparing the broader society from far more damaging violence. Against prevailing assumptions today, this was no mere phenomenon of primitive prehistory. Something basic to the play of the human psyche is at work here, even if one's glance involuntarily shifts away. The burning of children on altars was part of the culture out of which the faith of contemporary Jews and Christians comes, though one finds it almost impossible to think so.

The violence of the Bible is one thing, but violence against babies? Pagans, perhaps. But monotheistic believers? One's ancestors in the faith? Failing to reckon with this fact of our own tradition means we fail to appreciate *the present significance* of that tradition, operating explicitly and subliminally. "Without reference to the ancient myths associated with child sacrifice," the Harvard scholar Jon D. Levenson argues, "certain biblical narratives about the origins and character of the people Israel and of the Church cannot be properly understood."[56]

Human sacrifice was routinely practiced in the ancient world, well into what we think of as the early chapters of our own civilization, including among the humanist Greeks and Romans,[57] certainly among the pagan neighbors of Israel,[58] and among the Hebrews themselves far into the biblical period. It is not clear when the moral rejection of this practice took hold, but it is clear from the many condemnations of it in the Bible that human children were being put to death in the name of God by Israel's near neighbors, and, at times, by monotheistic Hebrews themselves.[59]

In the Book of Micah, for example, the question about sacrifice is put directly: "With what shall I come before the Lord, and bow myself before the Lord on high? Shall I come before him with burnt offerings, with calves a year old?" But that is not the half of it, for the questioner goes on, "Shall I give my first-born for my transgression, the fruit of my body for the sin of my soul?" And the prophet answers, "He has showed you, O man, what is good; and what does the Lord require of you but to do justice, and to love kindness, and to walk humbly with your God?"[60] In reading such clear rejection—no to burnt offerings, no to child sacrifice—it is necessary to remember that Micah would not have condemned what was not happening. Micah is dated to the late eighth century BCE, but Jeremiah and Ezekiel, writing two hundred years later, in the sixth century, are equally fervent in condemning child sacrifice.

It is clear that Israel's moral repugnance against this still common practice was permanently solidified by the end of the exile, and once again, that may have resulted from the captive Hebrews' intimate encounter during those years with the cultic practices of polytheistic paganism.

The great parable of the moral move away from human sacrifice is, of course, the story of what Jews call "the Binding of Isaac," or the *Akedah*, and what Christians call "the Sacrifice of Isaac" — Abraham hearing from God the command to kill his beloved son, only to have God spare Isaac by providing at the last minute a substitute victim, a ram stuck in a nearby thicket.[61] Abraham had already come into the narrative as a figure of God's preference for nonviolence, since his story is offered, in effect, as a correction to the story of Noah that precedes it in Genesis. In that first case, God sought to bring about a just and peaceable world by destroying it — the Flood. Abraham represents the repentant God's adjustment — the achievement of peace and justice not through destruction but through the coming of a vast new people that defines itself by peace and justice. "Instead of the just one [Noah] being preserved while all others are slaughtered," the scholar John Dominic Crossan observes, "the just one [Abraham] is chosen to bring blessings to all the 'families of the earth.'" Crossan emphasizes the contrast between "the story of Noah in which a whole population is eliminated so that one man can survive and the story of Abraham in which one man generates a whole people."[62] That Abraham represents God's turn toward nonviolence is complicated by the fact that the Promised Land with which God will seal the Abrahamic covenant is dead center in that hyperviolent and perennial "cockpit of empire,"[63] the land a source of discord to this day. God's chosen people will not know peace. Indeed, generation in and generation out, they will make war. But always they will measure their behavior against an alternative standard. They will, if only through the telling of Abraham's story, resist, in Crossan's word, the "normalcy" of war.

They begin this by resisting the normalcy of child sacrifice. The point of the "Binding" story is evident: the God of Abraham, unlike the gods of other Canaanite cults, does not desire the blood of human children.[64] Yet the impact of the story, and the various ways it has been and continues to be read, is far more complex than that. Just as the Promised Land, sealing a covenant of justice and peace, has itself been twisted into a source of conflict, this repudiation of human sacrifice has been twisted to define the inner logic of sacrificial violence among all three religious

traditions that honor Abraham as father. The entire saga of sacred violence is summed up in the Abraham-Isaac episode, as Jews read it in the
beginning and as they read it later, as Christians sacramentalized it, as
Muslims rewrote it,[65] and as it resonates to this day.[66]

6. Abraham's Kill

Recall that historical time is telescoped in these texts. As we saw,
Abraham, if he lived at all, dated to about the year 1800 BCE, but this
coherent story associating him with the end of human sacrifice is usually dated to about the ninth century,[67] with its power emphasized
three hundred years later by its inclusion in the "scripture" then being assembled by editors and redactors at work in the exilic period or
shortly after. At each of these points, the authors and editors of Israel's
texts were finding it necessary to argue by means of this tale against the
practice of child sacrifice.

"The firstborn of your sons," the God of Exodus is remembered as
saying, "you shall give to me."[68] But here the command God gives to
Abraham applies to a boy with a name: "And He said, 'Take your son,
your only son, Isaac, whom you love, and go to the land of Moriah, and
offer him there as a burnt offering upon one of the mountains of which
I shall tell you.'"[69] The Abraham-Isaac story represents the transformation of this early sacrificial practice into a symbolic offering involving
the substitution of animal for human — a transformation, in the words
of Jon D. Levenson, "that metamorphosed a barbaric ritual into a
sublime paradigm of the religious life."[70] That Abraham is praised for
his willingness to carry out this command of God's suggests that true
devotion returns all of creation to God *as belonging to God*. The most
precious creature of all, one's firstborn, is the ultimate emblem of this
piety, even if God, in all mercy — and in rejection of violence — does not
require it. The substitution of an animal for the firstborn child amounts
to what Levenson calls a "ritual sublimation," and the blood shed at
circumcision, the ultimate Hebrew sublimation of child sacrifice, is an
extension of this metamorphosis.

As a way of surviving as a separate people in exile, as we saw, Jews
codified their traditions. They observed the Sabbath, for example, as
well as dietary restrictions, with new rigor. But it was in exile that male
circumcision came into its own as the defining ritual of Hebrew reli-

gion, a development that necessarily occurred away from the Temple precisely because the cutting of the foreskin of the male recapitulated the offering of the child on the altar. In exile, amid the pagan gods, the only possible sacrifice open to Jews was the wholly symbolic, and by entering its terrain, Jews initiated a new form of religious consciousness. In all of this, the exiled Jews experienced a spiritual breakthrough. Drawing close to God was now a matter of interiority, memory, words, devotedness, contemplative prayer — and, fulfilling the already noted mandate of monotheism, of compassion for the neighbor. Indeed, it is not too much to say, as the historian of religion Karen Armstrong does, "The religion that we know as Judaism originated not in Judea, but in the Diaspora."[71] In captivity.

Apart from Jerusalem, holiness was located in a *remembered* Jerusalem. Torah replaced the Temple. So when, upon their release by Cyrus, Jews found themselves in the real Jerusalem again, in a position to resume a sacrificial cult, it was bound to be different. When, upon their return from Babylon, they "went up" to their ancient city on a hill, this *aliyah* was something new. Genesis calls the mountain to which Abraham led Isaac Moriah, and from an early time Hebrews had identified that place as the hilltop in the center of Jerusalem, the spot on which the Temple was built.[72] The Temple was restored by those who returned to Jerusalem from Babylon, but now, with this reclaimed Mount Moriah story of Abraham and Isaac as foundational, the Temple cult was understood as emphatically opposed to human sacrifice. The Temple, that is, by being associated with Moriah and therefore with the Binding of Isaac, represented a sublimation of anti-human violence into nonviolence. The Temple, having been conceived in Canaanite religious culture five centuries earlier, was recast as a repudiation of Canaanite influence, a decisive mitigation of the violence of God.

Archeologists suggest that well before David took Jerusalem, its hilltop had been a place of primitive sacrifice dating back to the Bronze Age. Human sacrifice continued to be practiced in its environs into the seventh century BCE.[73] But post-exilic Jewish piety, in emphasizing the Mount Moriah connection, saw Abraham's ascent as a kind of primeval Temple consecration. After Babylon, the Temple was rebuilt on an entirely new understanding. The imagined Temple of exile, that is, transformed the actual Temple of Jerusalem when it was restored.

The Binding of Isaac is central to Jewish religious awareness because it emphasizes two things at once: God's merciful rejection of human sacrifice and Abraham's willingness to enact such sacrifice even on his own son, if that is what God wants. The story may have originated as an etiological tale to account for the end of child sacrifice, but the authors and editors of the Bible, working right through the period of exile and after, also hold it up as an exemplar of authentic deference to God. The sacrifice is not of blood but of will. The idea of a father ready to sacrifice his son so centers Jewish religion that it will eventually also define Christian faith and, substantially, Islamic devotedness.

But by emphasizing Abraham's willingness to kill Isaac in obedience to God over God's sparing of Isaac—Kierkegaard will see that willingness as the paradigmatic "leap of faith"[74]—the well of devotion becomes poisoned. A breakthrough against sacred violence, that is, will become a sponsor of a whole new kind of sacred violence. "Uniquely among the religions of the world," the scholar Bruce Chilton observes, "the three that center on Abraham have made the willingness to offer the lives of children—an action they all symbolize with versions of the Aqedah—a central virtue of the faith as a whole. Child sacrifice is not merely a possibility: it is incorporated within the pattern of faith, not as a requirement of literal ritual, but as an ethical virtue every believer should be prepared to emulate."[75]

7. Apocalypse Then

It was violence that made this happen. After Jews returned from Babylon to Jerusalem, they became religiously centered on the Torah while maintaining the tradition of animal sacrifice in the Temple. Politically, they were still a subject people, as the tides ran in and out on one empire after another—from Cyrus the Persian to Alexander the Macedonian to the Ptolemies of Egypt. Always, the relatively powerless Jews were permitted to maintain their religious independence, and in return they declined to challenge the principalities that held sway over them. But at the beginning of the second century BCE, a Syrian dynasty that had begun as an offshoot of Alexander's regime, founded by the Macedonian general Seleucus and called the Seleucids, took control of Judea. Their ruthless crackdown extended to oppression of the religious practice of Jews—outlawing Sabbath observance, circumcision, and the reading of Torah. The Temple was desecrated. The Jews resisted and were crushed, with tens of thousands put to death. Resistance became open rebellion, led by a warrior clan known as the Maccabees, the story of whose exploits is given in the two books of that name, dating to about 100 BCE.[76]

The Maccabean resistance to the Seleucid tyranny culminated in a victory that is celebrated to this day as the feast of Hanukkah. The political-religious tensions of the conflict defined Jewish life for a century, until the Romans moved into Palestine in about 65 BCE. But in that pre-Roman period, this, the most violent upheaval in Jewish history until then, led to key revisions in what the religion meant. A cosmic dualism seized the Hebrew imagination, with satanic forces of evil arrayed against angelic forces of good. Israel's duty was no longer to purify itself through self-criticism, repentance, and rededication to the Law, but only to choose God's side in the great final battle. Here begins the bifurcation of the world — a kind of Manichaean split that is, ironically, an offense against the cosmic oneness implied by the Oneness of God. The bifurcation of the moral order: good versus evil. The bifurcation of the temporal order: time versus eternity. The bifurcation of space: earth versus heaven. The bifurcation even of the self: will versus weakness.

Most dramatically, weight thus shifted from the most ancient pillar of Hebrew religion, the prophets, to a new way of understanding the mystery of violence and the suffering it causes. One can understand the entire Bible, as we have been doing here, as the record of a people's grappling with that mystery — as that people was again and again subjected to, and at times guilty of, terrible assault. If Israel's God was omnipotent, and Israel was God's beloved, how could that God permit Israel to suffer so? In the eighth century, the brutal invasion of the Assyrians (around 722 BCE) raised the question, and prophets like Hosea, Isaiah, and Amos proposed an answer. The Assyrians are God's instrument of punishment; God himself has assembled their armies[77] to punish Israel, because "you did not return to me, says the Lord . . . Therefore thus will I do to you, O Israel. Because I will do this to you, prepare to meet your God, O Israel."[78]

In the sixth century, during and after the Babylonian assault, culminating in the destruction of Jerusalem and the exile, this note of prophecy — God using Israel's enemies to punish Israel for failing to keep God's Law — came into its own with figures like Ezekiel and Jeremiah. "Therefore thus says the Lord of hosts," Jeremiah proclaims to his own people. "Because you have not obeyed my words, behold I will send for all the tribes of the north, says the Lord, and for Nebuchadnezzar the king of Babylon, my servant, and I will bring them against this land and its inhabitants . . . and I will utterly destroy them, and make them a horror."[79] God is the agent of Israel's destruction. Destruction is the occasion of repentance and return to the Law of God. That, according to the prophets, is the meaning of violence and suffering that is otherwise meaningless and absurd. By asserting Israel's guilt, deserving of punishment, the justice of God is affirmed. I suffer, is the lesson, therefore I am guilty.

But Israel at war with the Seleucids in the second century, a war fought in defense of the Law of God against blasphemers, in defense of the Temple of Jerusalem against idolaters, was certain of its own virtue. No prophet arose to declare that the Maccabean fighters were faithless. Instead, a different kind of voice emerged, one that reversed the traditional notion. Violence and suffering were being inflicted on God's chosen ones not because they were unfaithful, but because they were faithful. The Seleucids were not instruments of God's justice, but were instead agents of God's enemy. Where before, God's sway over the creation was absolute, now a cosmic dualism meant that God was in mortal combat with an evil nemesis. The Seleucids were, in effect, the least of it, because God was at war with Satan. The people of Israel were subjected to violence because they had chosen to side with God in this transcendent conflict. This is not prophecy but a new form of Hebrew religious affirmation — apocalypse.[80]

The Book of Daniel, anonymously composed during the thick of the Maccabean war, is chronologically the last book of the Hebrew Bible (1 and 2 Maccabees are included in the Roman Catholic canon, not the Hebrew canon). We referred to Daniel earlier in reference to the war with Babylon, and it pretends to have been written then, with "Daniel" identified as one of those in exile. Daniel's visions, given mainly in the seventh chapter of the book, establish the new genre that divides creation between forces of good and forces of evil, and divides the realm of time between the present age, which is wicked, and the coming age, when God will triumph. And that age is coming soon. With Daniel, the idea of an afterlife takes root in the Jewish religious imagination, a necessary corollary to the conclusion that in the present age, God's justice is inevitably thwarted. In order for that justice to be victorious — God's judgment vindicated — there must be life after death. A religion of space — Holy Land — begins here to become a religion of time — End

Time. A time of some kind of resurrection. Israel's hope is for restoration of the kingdom not in the here and now but in the messianic age, ushered in by one identified only as the "Son of Man."[81]

Daniel sees four monsters rising out of the sea—the first is a lion with eagle's wings—and these monsters, scholars tell us, represent the four imperial powers that have ravaged Israel and Jerusalem down through the centuries: Babylon, Medea, Persia, and Greece. The "Ancient of Days," God, comes down from heaven to smite these beasts and burn them with fire. God perpetrates violence, but not, for a change, against God's people but against God's enemies, all of whom advance the cause of one who is nearly, but not quite, God's equal. Satan had made earlier appearances in the Bible (in Job, for example, where Satan is little more than God's kibbitzer), but never like this. "It is with Jewish apocalypticists that Satan takes on a different character," the scholar Bart D. Ehrman observes, "and becomes the arch-enemy of God, a powerful fallen angel who has been forced out of heaven and wreaks havoc here on earth by opposing God and all he stands for. It was ancient Jewish apocalypticists who invented the Judeo-Christian Devil."[82] Violence invented the devil.

In the Book of Daniel, God's violence is positively good—a destruction of the world for the sake of the restoration of the world. This violence, apocalyptic in the end, will rescue all those who have sided with the Holy One during this torment. And what was the surest sign of having taken God's side? The answer to that question, too, represents something new that took hold of the Jewish religious imagination during the Maccabean war. The battle was not just for Israel, not merely for Jerusalem, not even for Jewish nationhood. The battle was for cosmic order and for God. In such a battle, no price was too high to pay, which led to a new and unprecedented emphasis on martyrdom, with the expectation that faithful death would be rewarded by physical resurrection.[83] This willingness, even eagerness, to die for God was abetted by the incorporation into Jewish thought of Greek ideas of immortality, but the virtue of suffering embraced for the higher cause of good over evil had itself become an absolute.

The brutal willingness of Jewish fighters to take casualties, to die themselves, and to send their own sons into apparently futile battle—"to wallow in martyrdom," as the critic Judith Shulevitz puts it[84]—was essential to their victory over the Seleucids. This type of armed apocalyptic true belief, having led to national liberation in the second century

BCE, would make a ferocious comeback a century and a half later in combat with Rome — an ultimate instance of the cosmic war between good and evil. Once more, Jewish resisters, braced by what was then fully revered as the Bible with its apocalyptic climax, embraced martyrdom and bloody self-sacrifice to the point of mutual suicide. Alas, the Jewish zealots would learn, to their final horror, that Rome was no mere Syria.

Perhaps because the Maccabean rebellion began with a warrior, Mattathias, whose five sons were its great heroes (including Judah, whose nickname, HaMakabi, "the Hammer," gave the Maccabean movement its name), the readiness to sacrifice sons for the cause became a defining motif. The most dramatic passage in 2 Maccabees is the account of a mother who watched her seven sons being tortured to death one by one for refusing to eat pork while imploring them to "prove themselves worthy by dying." The passage ends, "The mother was the last to die, after her sons."[85] Not surprisingly, therefore, the willingness of Abraham to sacrifice Isaac became the scriptural touchstone for Jews in the midst of such persecution. Mattathias, on his deathbed, lifts up Abraham's readiness for divinely ordained filicide as the source of his righteousness before God. As Bruce Chilton points out, whereas in Genesis Abraham is "reckoned as righteous" just because "he believed in God,"[86] in 1 Maccabees, the source of Abraham's righteousness is defined as his willingness to bring the knife down on Isaac.[87] The ultimate in holiness is readiness — if not to slay a son, to see him slain.

This last large note of Jewish scriptural interpretation — the Bible as wartime literature reaching the fever pitch of cosmic conflict between good and evil — was the context in which was understood the arrival, only decades later, of Jesus of Nazareth, who is heard applying to himself Daniel's age-ending title of "Son of Man." Son indeed. Jesus was yet another beloved son, born in wartime and in whose name biblical ambivalence about sacred violence would take another deadly turn.

CHAPTER FOUR

The Cross Against Itself

1. Jesus to Jerusalem

THE STORY OF JESUS, well known as it is, seems complex only if it is told from outside his point of view. The Gospels account for his life not as he experienced it, but as it appeared to his followers *after* they had come to believe in his special status. But how did Jesus see himself as he moved through the days and years of his time? Is that an impossible question? In fact, because of the scholarly discoveries of recent decades[1] we know almost as much about the context in which Jesus lived as those who came not long after him — and more than those who followed him only a generation or two later. Scholars have begun to assimilate these new understandings of Jesus, but ordinary believers have not. Many people who follow Jesus, and most of those who have left behind any sense of his transcendent significance, are alike in failing to grasp the core meaning of his life and witness. It may seem self-serving to assert such a thing in a history of sacred violence, but sacred violence is precisely the problem against which Jesus measured himself.

For our purposes, it is enough to insist that attempting to imagine how Jesus thought of himself is not a fool's errand, and it can be crucially illuminating. Presumptuous as it might have been only a short time ago, we can say with relative certitude that Jesus' self-image did not square with the view of those who glorified him after the facts of his death and resurrection, whatever those mysterious events were in history. Looking at the markers of his life as he must have experienced them, the story is a simple one. It has a beginning, middle, and end. The story concerns violence. The accounts agree that the story decisively takes its shape from Jesus' relationship with his mentor and friend John the Baptist, a Jewish zealot whose actions made him a first victim of violence. And the story drives inexorably toward Jerusalem, which, however sacred, surfaced for Jesus as the locus of violence.

The story begins with Jesus as a Galilean peasant nobody, at the mercy of his own sense of failure and sin. That was the point of his seeking out John, whose message was, Repent, repent, only repent. The context in which all of this unfolds — a context mostly forgotten in the Christian telling — was the brutal occupation of Palestine by the Romans, who, over Jesus' lifetime, had snuffed out — mainly through crucifixion — the lives of thousands of Jews who had, in any number of ways, looked askance at the emperor's power. John's preaching of repentance was a revolutionary challenge to the spirit of acquiescence with which most Jews had come to accept that occupation — a challenge to the distant emperor and to the nearby Herod Antipas, Rome's puppet ruler. To later Christian ears, John's message may have seemed to have been "merely spiritual," but that missed how only a morally purified Israel would be able to throw off the detested imperial yoke. Throwing off the yoke of Rome was the point. There was no separating religion from politics. The most intensely personal program of spiritual purification was, in that context, a provocative political act.

Whatever his followers would make of him later, Jesus, to himself, began like every human being, each of us born with a sneaking suspicion that we are morally ugly. We typically deal with that suspicion by attributing ugliness to someone else. When we join with others in doing so, singling out a magically designated third party onto whom to unload the weight of all our ugliness — well, we have enacted the by now familiar pattern described by René Girard. The much older term for this inbred constitutional tendency is "sin." That Girard's notion defines the human condition is caught in the idea of "original sin." When we acknowledge, under the burden of an uneasy conscience, that this is what we have been doing, we may have our suspicion of moral ugliness confirmed, but also we seek a way to get out from under its weight. We look, that is, for a way to repent.

That, in Jesus' time, was what brought droves of people out into the arid valley that had been cut by the brackish river that ran from the Sea of Galilee to the Dead Sea. Shakespeare could not have chosen a more aptly symbolic setting for the public acknowledgment of the need for repentance, since the Dead Sea sits astride the tectonic plates joining Arabia and Africa. The plates are constantly shifting, with the result that the Dead Sea and its valley drops ever deeper into the earth; on average, it falls a meter every year. Already by Jesus' time, it was the lowest point on the planet.[2] How low in his own estimation does a person have to be to present himself for forgiveness to a wild man who wears animal skins and eats locusts? What drew Jesus to John the Baptist? Not the script written by God, as the Gospels are usually read. Jesus must have understood himself as needing to hear what John was preaching, as needing to have what John was offering.

The hope of Israel, in its resistance to Rome, was repentance. As a Jewish apocalypticist, John was declaring that the reign of God, triumphing over Rome, would occur when the defeated and divided people united in turning back toward their Lord — a promised triumph in history, not mysticism. John was declaring that the restoration of God's authority was a possibility in the near future, and the more who took in his message, the more likely it seemed about to come true. John was a dangerous man.

"What did you go out to the wilderness to behold?" Jesus asked his hearers about John. "A reed shaken by the wind? A man clothed in soft raiment? Behold, those who are gorgeously appareled and live in luxury are in kings' courts. What then did you go out to see? A prophet? Yes, I tell you, and more than a prophet . . . I tell you, among those born of women, none is greater than John."[3]

The story's first surprise occurred when Jesus presented himself to John for the baptism of repentance, and presumably what happened then was as much a surprise to Jesus as to anyone. The Gospel accounts say the heavens opened and nothing less than the voice of God was heard declaring that Jesus was God's own beloved son. Jesus, having assumed his unworthiness, had his assumption turned upside down: he was approved by God. There was no question of having to earn God's approbation. Jesus simply had it. This language of theophany — "This is my beloved son" — and this symbolism — the dove of God's spirit descending — intended simply to convey the epiphany Jesus experienced in the presence of John, the defining revelation of Jesus' life.

Against every human suspicion of unworthiness, his own and others', Jesus is the recipient of the unconditional positive regard of one whom, from this point on, he calls Father. And from this point on, Jesus, a Galilean nobody no longer, will preach that *everyone* is held in just such unconditional positive regard, and that *everyone* has the right to call God Father. This turns the traditional religious quest for salvation on its ear. *You don't need salvation; you are all already saved! You need only recognize it and accept it.* As others would hear this life-changing and history-changing good news from Jesus, Jesus heard it from John. What Jesus would become to those who later followed him, that is, John the Baptist was to him.

That is why the second and third turns in the story are so momentous. First came word that John was imprisoned by Herod. In the Gospels, and in the Christian memory, John's offense was his criticism of Herod's adulterous relationship with a woman to whom he was illicitly married, but clearly the issue was the political threat posed by John's popular movement. In an occupied land, every crowd can become unruly, and every public affirmation of God's reign threatened Rome's. As John was removed from the scene, Jesus took his place. He, too, preached repentance, but repentance now meant simply letting go of the mistaken conviction of unworthiness. Jesus went all over Galilee proclaiming his insight into God's abundant loving mercy. *That we are in danger of being rejected by God is our illusion, and fear of that rejection is the real content of our sin.* Every sermon Jesus preached made the point: "Blessed are the poor, the hungry, the grief-stricken . . . they will inherit everything, be satisfied, and laugh." Every parable he recounted made the point: God is the father who never stops loving the child no matter how prodigal the child is in self-destruction and self-doubt.

Yet Jesus' message was inevitably political, too. Even his message of loving the neighbor—loving the enemy!—served the purpose of calling the Jews of his time out of their sectarian divisiveness, back to the sacred unity of being God's people Israel. No mere message of sentimental affection, the love Jesus preached was solidarity, and for an empire that depended, as empires always do, on the internecine divisions of the occupied people—neighbor against neighbor—such solidarity could not be allowed to grow unchecked.

That Jesus had stepped into the imperial death zone was made crystal clear when news came that John, his mentor and inspiration, was executed by Herod—decapitated, with his head presented on a platter at Herod's banquet table. This act of violent sadism, the grotesqueness of which is lost in the familiarity of Bible stories, defined the future that awaited Jesus. Herod was waiting for Jesus, too. That Jesus knew it is clear from the simple line that describes his reaction: "When Jesus received this news he withdrew by boat to a lonely place where he could be by himself."[4] From this moment on, Jesus understood that the course on which he was set in his Jordan River meeting with John the Baptist was taking him directly to his death.

Having learned in John's presence of his being radically accepted by God, the one whom he called Father, Jesus learned from John's death that that acceptance meant there was nothing to fear in death, because death does not overturn God's love. Here was the turning point: the prospect of death is what makes humans suspicious of their moral worth, which is why humans fear death, but Jesus, with his worth affirmed by the Father, was released from that fear. *That* was what made him the transcendent figure in whom people began to recognize the Son of God. Release from the fear of death became his message, and the way he spoke of that release was to declare that the reign of God — the all-accepting, merciful God — had already begun. *The Kingdom of God is within you.*

The ultimate contradiction of that message was the blasphemous occupation of Israel by Rome, which emphasized the unworthiness of the subjugated people and played upon their fear of death. It was inconceivable that Jesus, worthy and unafraid, *not* challenge Rome, which meant, first, daring Rome's puppet, John's murderer, to take him on. When warned that Herod was out to kill him, Jesus replied, "Go and give that fox this message." Jesus put him on notice that he was casting out devils.[5] What devils? The devils that were making the people afraid. Herod's power depended on the acquiescence of a people in the demonic grip of fear. "Be not afraid," Jesus preached again and again.[6] And the more he preached it, the more people rallied to him. And the more direct, as such solidarity grew, was his challenge — not to the petty ruler but to Rome itself. There was only one place where that challenge could be fully joined, and, after the death of John, Jesus knew it. The cockpit of empire.[7] He had no choice but to plunge into it. Jerusalem. Jesus to Jerusalem. The rest of the story followed, and is well known.

2. Rome's War and Its Consequences

The Roman attack on Jerusalem forty years later, in 70 CE, culminating in the destruction of the Temple, occurred just as the followers of Jesus were coming into their own as a coherent movement. The key to that coherence had been the telling of the story of Jesus in light of

Israel's Book—a telling that became known as the Gospel. By 70, the work of Paul in preaching the Gospel in various cities of the Mediterranean was complete, the apostle having been martyred in about 64 CE. In that year, "Christians" had been scapegoated by Nero for "the great fire of Rome," a conflagration that ravaged more than half the city's districts and destroyed prominent temples dedicated to Jupiter, king of the gods, and Vesta, virgin goddess of the home.

Such temples were crucial to what happened because the Christians were singled out as a group already known for what Tacitus calls "abominations," what amounted to the conspicuous refusal to participate in the prevailing deity cults. Nero may or may not have been the mad tyrant of his reputation, although he does seem to have executed both his brother and his mother. It seems clear that he saw to history's first recorded savagery aimed at Christians as such, traumatizing a young movement that was still mainly taken—and probably understood itself—to be a sect within Judaism. It is impossible to say how many Christians were put to death, but the number was surely large and the method of killing grotesque enough to terrify most of those who followed Jesus. "A vast multitude," Tacitus reports, "were convicted not so much of the crime of incendiarism as of hatred of the human race. And in their deaths, they were made the subjects of sport, for they were wrapped in the hides of wild beasts and torn to pieces by dogs, or nailed to crosses, or set on fire, and when day declined, were burned to serve for nocturnal lights."[8] It may be that St. Paul himself was murdered during this festival of carnage, and the same may be true of St. Peter.

Excessive Roman brutality was not normally so cynically displayed as in Nero's scapegoating ploy; more typically it was used as a means of control, with any manifestation of rebelliousness by subject people being met with overwhelming force. Nero had earlier seen to the bloody putdown of a revolt in Roman-occupied Britain, for example. The point is that Roman hyperviolence was far from unique at that moment in time, and if it was mounted in response to what could be taken as sacrilege, then the gods themselves were sponsors of the merciless bloodshed.

But expressly religious offense could be taken by all sides. The great Jewish revolt against Rome began in 66 CE when pagan Greeks in the city of Caesarea, a large Hellenized metropolis on the coast of Palestine, enacted cultic sacrifices of birds on a site near a Jewish holy place. The

Jews in Caesarea objected to what they regarded as defilement, then took action to stop the sacrifices. This sparked tension with the Roman authorities throughout occupied Judea. In Jerusalem, the son of the high priest led a successful attack on the Temple garrison. Jewish zealots, acting in the spirit of the Maccabean rebels of a century and a half earlier, successfully occupied the Temple Mount and its environs. A broad population rallied to them, perhaps half a million Jews crowding in to join in Jerusalem's defense.[9] This sent the Romans into retreat. The zealots held the Temple Mount and its surrounding area for more than three years.

Why did such a vast throng rally to the defense of the Temple? Modern categories of nationalism, ethnic identity, or anti-imperial resistance fall short of grasping what was at stake for the Jewish people when it came to their Temple. This was the place where God lived, even in God's absence. And it was the place where the most sublime experiences of their individual and communal lives occurred. It was in the Temple that they made their thanks offerings, full of awed gratitude for the Lord's gifts of children, health, prosperity, and Torah. It was in the Temple that, after days of purification, the majestic rite of atonement occurred, when guilt or impurity was transferred to a blemish-free bird or lamb, which was handed over to the priests, blessed, brought to the flaming altar, its throat slit, and its body offered up. Afterward, portions of the meat of the sacrificed victim were shared with family and friends in a joyous and sacred meal. These rituals, commanded in every detail by God, were an unsurpassed source of meaning, consolation, awe, and holiness. The awareness of every Jew, including those living too far from Jerusalem to have the direct experience of sacrifice more than rarely, was centered on the Temple. God was present there as meaning was present in every word and gesture required in the Law.

It was when that central institution of religion, nationhood, and meaning itself was under threat that the text we know as the Gospel of Mark, the earliest of the four Gospels, came into being. Mark was assembled from various sources, mainly catechetical and oral, by an editor-author who was probably attached to the Christian community in Rome. The heat of Nero's persecution would barely have cooled among such Jesus people in the imperial capital, and word would have reached them and other Jews of what was happening in Jerusalem. In the next handful of years, as the composition of the Markan Gospel reached its final form, the fate of the Jerusalem Temple was sealed.

Thus when the Gospel has Jesus "prophesy" that the Temple will be destroyed ("Do you see these great buildings? Not one stone will be left upon another"[10]), the editor-author is not reporting a vision that Jesus foresaw in the year 30 or so, but is reflecting on the disastrous fate of Jerusalem and its Temple that was either unfolding as "Mark" wrote or had just occurred. Likewise, the lament that is attributed to Jesus — "O Jerusalem, Jerusalem . . . how often would I have gathered your children together as a hen gathers her brood under her wings"[11] — reflects both the catastrophe that befell the city long after Jesus died there and the love for the city that defined Jesus and every Jew.

Once the zealots had taken control of the inner city, men, women, and children took up the cause of a fight to the death. That was what they got. As Romans seized Jewish fighters, each captive was turned into a harbinger and a warning by being grotesquely executed. This display of Roman sadism was probably counterproductive, because it obliterated among Jews any thought of surrender. By the conclusion of the Jerusalem siege, the rotting corpses of tens of thousands of Jewish resisters would hang from crosses all around the core city. Crucifixion was general.[12]

The Romans were teaching the stiff-necked Jews a lesson, a lesson not lost on the Rome-centered Jesus people who had just been so traumatized under Nero, the same Nero who defined the response to the Temple Mount takeover.[13] A brutal war between the Jews and Roman legions would continue intermittently for seventy years, leading to the deaths of perhaps more than a million Jews.[14] This included most of the Jesus-believing Jews who were prepared to understand Jesus in a fully Jewish context — those centered not in distant Rome, from which Mark's Gospel likely came; not in Damascus, from which Matthew's Gospel probably came; not in Antioch, from which Luke's Gospel likely came; not in Ephesus, from which John's Gospel probably came; but in Jerusalem, from which — only because of this violence — no final version of the story of Jesus was preserved or canonized.[15] With the disappearance of Jerusalem's Jesus people, the Christian movement would be quickly dominated by Gentiles and Hellenized Jewish Christians who had little feeling for the Judean Jewishness of Jesus or his message, an accidental turn that had, to say the least, dark consequences.

The point to emphasize is that the most savage Roman violence against the Jews and their homeland — from Rome's point of view, a religiously motivated violence — occurred during the decades when the Christian movement's Gospel texts were taking shape, when the movement's decisive understanding of Jesus was being fixed. That context defined the text. The figure of Jesus, who occupies that text's center, was himself firmly opposed to violence, an opposition rooted not in some abstract ethics but in his sense of the Oneness of God, of God's Oneness with him and with every creature. ("That you may be sons of your Father who is in heaven, for he makes his sun rise on the evil and the good, and sends rain on the just and the unjust."[16]) Yet the Gospels were composed as a literature of violence, as wartime literature. Despite the probable intentions of their editor-authors, they were composed in such a way, in narrative form and in theological meaning, as to serve as a hospitable niche for the self-nurturing virus of war — although not war with Rome.

The followers of Jesus in 70 associated with the violent impulses of revolutionary Jewish zealots no more than Jesus himself had in his time, around 30. And while they surely valued the Temple — as Acts makes clear, Jerusalem Christians continued to worship there long after Jesus;[17] as Paul makes clear, Christians from far-off cities, including Gentiles, continued to send the annual Temple tax to Jerusalem[18] — they did not regard the provocative occupation of the Temple Mount by the zealots as their fight. A sizable number of Jewish Christians left Jerusalem for Pella, across the Jordan, while others went to Syria (Antioch), Asia Minor (Ephesus, Smyrna, Pergamum), Greece (Thessalonica, Corinth, Philippi), and North Africa (Alexandria, Cyrene). Deflecting any sense that their movement was part of a militarized Jewish rebellion, they wrote their Gospel in such a way as to distance Jesus from the anti-Roman antagonism of, say, the insurrectionist figure Barabbas, who is put forward in Mark by the Roman authority Pontius Pilate as Jesus' foil.[19] Indeed, in the story of Jesus' death as given in Mark and subsequent Gospels, the cruel Pilate is portrayed benignly, a perversion of historical fact, since other sources (especially including Tacitus, Philo, and Josephus[20]) show Pilate to have been brutal even by Roman standards. The Gospel texts did this, first, for the straightforward reason that vulnerable Christians, simply to survive, had to insist that they were not Rome's enemy. Otherwise they were dead, period. But that wasn't all. To emphasize the innocence of Jesus, which seemed important to his meaning, it was necessary to emphasize the guilt of his antagonist, who hates him "without a cause."[21] If that was not Rome, who was it? To second- and third-generation Christian Jews and Gentiles whose claims for Jesus were being disputed by other Jews, an obvious answer presented itself: the Jews rejecting *them* between the years 70 and 100 were put into the Passion story as rejecting *Jesus* in 30 or so. The innocence of Jesus assumed the guilt of "the Jews."

Tragically, this immediately exacerbated conflict with a second group of Jews who, like the Christians, did not support the violent actions of the Temple-occupying zealots — a second group of Jews, that is, who sought to distance themselves from bloody mayhem. These Jews were no friends of Caesar, but they regarded the frontal assault on the Roman legions as suicidal[22] and refused to participate. They began as a party of Pharisees, who, while honoring the Temple and participating in its cult, may already have been less inclined than Sadducees, or the priestly caste, to define the Temple as the only and absolute center of Israel. Recall that some Jews, like John the Baptist, perhaps, or like the sectarians of Qumran, altogether disdained Herod's Temple as a Hellenized blasphemy: there were varied responses to the Temple as a flashpoint of war with Rome. Indeed, at times that diversity sparked war *among* the Jews.

The Jesus people were far from the only ones refusing to rally to the zealots. In the year 68 or 69, as the siege of Jerusalem was approaching its bloody climax, this Pharisaic party petitioned the Romans to be allowed safe passage out of the blockaded city, and the request was granted. To protect their leader, Rabbi Yohanan ben Zakkai, from fellow Jews who had to regard such abandonment as betrayal, he was smuggled out of Jerusalem in a coffin. With Roman permission, the Pharisees established themselves in Yavneh, a town near the Mediterranean coast north of Caesarea.

In the summer of 70, the Romans breached the walls of Jerusalem and set about ransacking the city and slaughtering its defenders. Many thousands died in this assault. When the Romans took control of the Temple Mount — an event commemorated in the Hebrew calendar as Tisha b'Av, the ninth day of the month of Av — they set it afire. The Temple, one of the world's greatest buildings, was reduced to ruins. The victory was so significant for Rome that the general in charge, Titus, was soon named emperor. That the horror of Jerusalem was his claim to fame can be seen today on his monument in Rome, the great Arch of Titus near the Colosseum, which is engraved with scenes of legionnaires looting the Temple. Titus decreed that his victory meant that the Jews were "a people forsaken by their own God."[23]

It could seem so to Jews. The utter loss of the Temple, together with the instant elimination of the religious traditions and communities most associated with the Temple, sparked an immediate identity crisis among Jews everywhere. What is it to be a Jew without the Temple? What is worship without sacrifice? How is God present to God's people if the house of God in their midst is gone? The community of Pharisees that had escaped to Yavneh on the coast became the center of reflection on and adaptation to this new situation. Having narrowly escaped the Temple, they became its chief mourners—and as Jews had done in the past, they used their grief as the ground of fresh interpretation and religious invention. In effect, the great exile had begun again. What was started at Babylon five hundred years before was completed at Yavneh.

Jews around the Mediterranean were at risk, with brutal Roman assaults against them occurring in North Africa, on Cyprus, in Mesopotamia. Everywhere, once more, the lost Temple was reimagined and a devastated Jerusalem was brought back to life in memory. "Next year in Jerusalem," they swore, as their progeny would forevermore, but the city was necessarily spiritualized, and so was the Temple. Indeed, the rabbis held Jerusalem in mind as a present-tense phenomenon, a symbol of all the ways God comes to God's people. Jerusalem, as a city from which they were banished, became a living emblem of the God who went with them into banishment. As close as God was, so close was the imagined city: in the shtetls of Poland centuries later, rabbis would still be intoning prayers for Jerusalem's weather. That the city had to be imagined defined the Jews' sense of loss.

This religion-sparking grief would become a permanent feature of Jewish faith, when the Roman war concluded in 135 CE with the final destruction of Jerusalem and the Rome-legislated banishment of Jews forever. The religion that had come into being around a particular place and its highly contested past would be transformed as that place was projected into the indefinite future, with a heavenly Jerusalem[24] as the designated center of hope. The Temple would be rebuilt and Jerusalem restored—but only at the end of time, when God's Messiah would come. Meanwhile, holiness required not the physical reconquest of the earthly city and its house of God, but studious contemplation of its past meaning for the people Israel as the sign of God's enduring covenant. The Temple cannot, for now, be recovered; it can only be remembered and imagined. A new experience of waiting for the Messiah, and longing for the fulfillment of God's promise, transformed the unfinished future into a vividly fulfilling (if never fulfilled) present.

From this point on, prayer and atonement were accomplished through the study of and obedience to Torah rather than through animal sacrifice, since the one altar of sacrifice, and its priestly caste, were lost. This "observance of the Law" went far beyond mere subservience before a set of commandments, as Christians imagine. Law involved a way of life, a structure of thought, a source of personal identity. Most compellingly, for example, the Sabbath became, in the formulation of Abraham Joshua Heschel, a Temple in time.[25] "The Temple is to space," the scholar Jon D. Levenson wrote, "what the Sabbath is to time."[26] The Sabbath was a Temple at home, too, with a core religious ritual brought weekly to life within the family around Shabbat symbols of bread, wine, candlelight, and table talk — the telling of the stories of salvation.

The interpretation of ancient texts in the light of recent experience enabled these Jews to make sense of the trauma they had just been through: the destruction of Jerusalem and its Temple was no betrayal by God, but was God's purification of the chosen people. Such interpretation was the new meaning of revelation. This was the beginning of what came to be known as the Talmud, accomplished by the first of what the tradition would now call rabbis, who replaced the priests as Jewish leaders. The rabbis "transformed a temple-based religion suited to a pastoral and agricultural people into a ritual-based religion suited to an urban and far-flung one."[27] But the replacing of priests was key, because in this religion the ancient cult of sacrifice, which was essential to every form of piety in the ancient world, would become spiritualized as Torah study and the performance of *mitzvot*, requirements of the Law, and the ritualizing of mundane experience. "There are blessings for waking up, for washing the hands, for eating bread or water, for going to the bathroom . . . The rabbis demystified holiness; they democratized it, making it less a function of spiritual genius than of personal self-discipline."[28] Most importantly, the rabbinic leaders of a traumatized people affirmed that suffering itself could accomplish the atoning that once had been the work of sacrifice. Suffering was sacralized. That Jews from this time forward did not participate in the ritual slaughter and offering to the deity of animals marked them as atheists among their pagan neighbors.

Despite the traumatic loss of the Jerusalem Temple, the fact that the synagogue — not a place of cultic sacrifice but of study — already existed as a Jewish institution throughout the Mediterranean world meant that the religious imagination of Jews apart from Palestine was already prepared for this spiritualizing of the Temple. That the Palestinian Jews, with regular access to Jerusalem and the Temple, were not similarly prepared ceased to matter when so many of them were simply killed. The Temple would be glorified in memory and in hope, but as a place of literal bloodiness, it would be implicitly disdained. The replacing of the slaughter of animals with the more esoteric "sacrifice" of thought and interior prayer was taken by the rabbis as an improvement — a fulfillment at last of Hosea's prophecy: "For I desire lovingkindness, not sacrifice; obedience to God, and not offerings."[29] As Abraham's sacrifice of the ram in place of Isaac represented progress from human sacrifice to animal sacrifice, the rabbis argued, so the shift from a literal Temple to an imagined Temple represented the next stage of progress. It was symbolized in the most ordinary of ways: "When the Holy Temple stood, there was no rejoicing without meat," the Talmud says, reflecting the ubiquity of animal flesh in the altar cult. "Now that the Holy Temple is not standing, there is no rejoicing without wine."[30] The Sabbath cup and challah loaf would be sanctified and sanctifying in the way that Temple-cooked meat once was (a transformation that would likewise inform the Christian sacramentalizing of wine and bread).

This Phoenix-like reinvention of the Jewish faith braced what survivors there were in Palestine, but it profoundly energized Greek-speaking Jews throughout the Mediterranean, who recognized in this Torah-centered, biblically structured way of carrying forward the covenant of Israel an adaptation of what, in their synagogues apart from Jerusalem, they had already been doing. In such memory, interpretation, imagination, study, and observance of the Law, that is, began the religion known to the world from then on as Judaism.

3. The New Temple

But was this new Judaism, so distinct from the lost religion of the high priests, the true Israel? Many other Jews, out of loyalty to the Temple, would surely have said no, but most of them were dead, or soon would be as the Roman war continued. What was the point of arguing for a literal Temple religion when there was no Temple? Among those who survived to register a competing claim to the legacy of the true Israel was the other group of Jews and their Gentile companions (from the Latin, "to break bread with") who had declined to join in the violence of insurrection against Rome. For them, the answer to the Roman-forced question — What is it to be a Jew without the Temple? — was simple. The "new Temple" was Jesus, and in their Gospel they made the claim explicit. Indeed, they recognized in the destruction of the Temple a kind of replay of the crucifixion of Jesus.[31]

Like the rabbis in Yavneh, these Christian Jews and their companions argued that such destruction was God's will, God's purifying deed, a necessary consequence of Israel's failure to properly observe the Law and recognize God's saving actions.[32] But these Jews went further, turning their interpretation against the rabbis by saying that it was precisely *their* refusal to acknowledge Jesus that caused God to wreak judgment on Jerusalem.[33] For Christians, the Temple's destruction was proof of the claims they made for Jesus, and in telling his story they highlighted the Temple's role as a point of conflict between Jesus and his contemporaries. And they emphasized the Pharisees as Jesus' main disputants more because of their own conflict with the Yavneh-based Pharisees than because of anything that transpired in Jesus' time.

Thus, despite the fact that his crucifixion — a method of execution reserved for troublemaking resisters — identified Jesus as an enemy of Rome, the Gospel of Mark, and subsequent Gospels, named his foremost enemy as "the Jews," as if Jesus were not one of them. Here is the tragic irony: as the followers of Jesus sought to distance themselves from one violence, they laid the groundwork for another. As the Passion narrative was being written, highlighting "the Jews'" preference of violent Barabbas over nonviolent Jesus, against whom they cried "Crucify him," trumping the Romans as protagonists of the execution, no one could foresee what it would lead to. Defining itself as a religion of love, over against Judaism as a religion of Law, Christianity prepared for an ultimate betrayal of love. Gospel fictions about "the Jews" would turn out to be the casus belli of yet another war against the Jewish people, one that would, across centuries, prove even more devastating than the Roman war.

There is much debate about the distance between the theologically motivated inventions of the Gospels and the actualities of the historical Jesus, but one issue looms above all the others. The Gospels, beginning especially with Mark, portray Jesus as opposed to the Temple, as if he objected in principle to the bloody sacrifice of pigeons and lambs; as if he rejected the priests' obsession with purity; as if, in Mark's formulation, he opposed love of one's neighbor to "burnt offerings and sacrifices."[34] Liberation theology, a twentieth-century Christian (primarily Catholic) movement, is indifferent to questions embedded in Temple cults, and still sees Jesus' opposition to the Temple as a primal — and licensing — instance of anti-institutionalism, as if the Temple priesthood were the equal of any and every power structure. But this has little to do with who Jesus really was.

In the narrative of all four Gospels, the dramatic nub of Jesus' conflict with "the Jews" is his attack on the Temple,[35] the "cleansing" in which he drives animals away and overturns tables and scatters coins. Those coins especially gripped the anti-Jewish imagination, and the Gospel characterization of "moneychangers" was eventually read as if what Jesus opposed were usurious Jewish interest rates.

That cleansing of the Temple, an act of coercive force, has always troubled the Christian conscience. "Righteous indignation," the nuns explained to us in religious class, a justification I never understood. Anger is wrong, they taught us, and violence is wrong. But what Jesus did was "zeal." In the Gospel, Jesus' violent overturning of the tables, complete with cracking whip and a claim on the Temple as "my father's house," is the event that generates the murderous rage of his enemies — the high priests who are in charge of the Temple and have reason to take his assault there personally. The Temple, quite simply, is what Jesus holds against his people, and the Temple is what makes "the Jews" move promptly to bring about the execution of Jesus.

But this Gospel report cannot square with the man Jesus was. It was constructed as part of the Jesus followers' making sense, two generations later, of the present-tense fact of the Temple's destruction. To have Jesus railing against burnt offerings and the purity requirements of the sacrificial cult was one thing when both had been made irrelevant by the Roman action in 70. It would have been another when Jesus was alive, and a man so devoted to Temple worship that his followers diligently continued to practice it long after his death. If Jesus launched a protest demonstration at the Temple, it was more likely to have been a protest *in favor* of purity regulations than against them; a protest in defense of the proper way to sacrifice animals, and against inroads of carelessness that had come into Temple practice during the Hellenizing project of Herod; or a protest against adjustments made by a collaborationist priesthood too beholden to the Roman occupiers.

Thus, to suggest only one other way of reading the "cleansing" protest, Jesus, as the scholar Bruce Chilton proposes, might have

been attacking the selling of pigeons and lambs, prior to their being offered in sacrifice, because the sacrifice of Israel was supposed
to come from within Israel, from within the owned resources of the
sacrificing believer. It might have been convenient for a pigeon seller
to provide pilgrims with the offering they needed to participate in
the sacrificial cult in exchange for money to cover his costs and a
little extra. But such a practice violated the requirement that the pilgrim make an offering out of his own possessions, an animal out of
his own herd or flock, or fruits of his own agricultural labor. This
may have been the point Jesus was making, and if so, such a preoccupation would show him — against common Christian understanding rooted in the Gospel slant — to be intensely concerned with strict
cultic regulation, not indifferent to it, much less hostile.[36] To repeat,
the historical Jesus was more likely to have been a defender of the
Temple and its cult than a critic of it.

Those who, after the fact, denigrate the Temple customs as too
bloody, or too concerned with form over substance, or too concerned
with money — whether it is Christians doing the denigrating or the descendants of the rabbis at Yavneh — miss the point.[37] The Temple was
a center of justice, commitment to the poor, welcome to non-Jews (the
Court of the Gentiles was the most spacious area of the Temple Mount),
and authentic worship of the God of Israel. The Temple priests, so detested in Christian memory, conducted themselves as heroes at the
end, in the teeth of Roman violence. The historian Josephus reports
that they "carried on their religious service uncurtailed, though envel-
oped in a hail of missiles. Just as if the city had been wrapt in profound
peace, the daily sacrifices, the expiations and all the ceremonies of worship were scrupulously performed to the honour of God. At the very
hour when the Temple was taken, when they were being massacred
about the altar, they never desisted from the religious rites of the day."[38]

Twenty-first-century religious sensibility — what both rabbinic
Judaism and Christianity with their spiritualized notions of sacrifice
planted in the Western imagination — takes offense at the work of such
priests, how they stood up to their ankles in a flow of blood in gutters, wielded knives at the throats of helpless creatures, shoveled ash
from altars, distributed the remains of burnt offerings to penitents and
supplicants. All of this amounted to interactions of the flesh, the most
profane activity imaginable rendered into something sacred. Twenty-
first-century meat eaters rarely look so squarely at the products of flesh

or the requirements of flesh, but sacrificial religious rituals of all types, and certainly those of the Jerusalem Temple, reckoned directly with the central fact of human life — that animals are a prime source of essential protein. They are sustainers of life. To eat an animal is to engage in a moral act, one that should be reckoned with as such.

Animals on which humans depend for food are dignified when the first portion is ritually handed over to the Holy One who creates life in the first place. In other words, the Temple was the place Jews went to have their meat-eating blessed. A vestige of this ritual lives on in kosher regulations. The point is that the sacrificial enterprise, far from being primitive, enshrined common sense from start to finish. Strict concern for cultic purity, for example, was rooted in the necessary practice of good hygiene, much as the priestly art of butchering protected both the dignity of the slaughtered animal, killing as painlessly as possible, and the health of the people who consumed what remained of the offering. Even now, when it comes to killing and eating, purity is a beautiful thing, and nothing is less pure, it could be argued, than the methods of industrialized slaughter that bring meat to modern tables.[39] To imagine that Jesus — or God — was opposed to the rich culture of sacrifice, with its meaning for religion and for nutrition, is to ignore a basic fact of what life on earth has required since *Homo erectus* learned to hunt.

But the Gospel interpretation of Jesus-as-the-New-Temple involved a slide back into a kind of violence-as-willed-by-God that had long before been left behind. The idea of animal sacrifice, which the Temple so humanely enshrined, and which originated in the mists of prehistory as a way of substituting animal victims for human victims, was subtly reversed when, as the Jesus story was told, a human was put on the altar once again. It would be wrong to see in this theologizing of the crucifixion as a God-pleasing sacrifice a simply "Christian" innovation, since Jewish preoccupation with martyrdom themes dated at least to the Maccabees. As we saw, that was when the sacrifice of Abraham had been reinterpreted to emphasize the idea that faithfulness to God can require an acceptance of the death of the beloved son after all. And we saw that this upended the original point of the Abraham-Isaac story, which was that God does not will the death of the son.

This reversal was embodied in the way the loving mother of 2 Maccabees rejoiced to see her sons slain — "Prove yourselves worthy by dying!" — for their refusal to eat pork, before being slain herself. When

Jesus of the Gospels was repeatedly proclaimed by a divine voice from heaven to be "my beloved Son,"[40] beginning with the epiphany before John at the Jordan, it could seem a corollary that his death was foreordained by the Father above. His beloved status put him in danger, for there was only one way to prove himself worthy. Martyrdom.

The dramatic structure of the Gospel of Mark has Jesus going from Galilee to Jerusalem — but Jerusalem equals death, and, as we saw, Mark's Jesus knows it. To prove himself worthy, he has to die. That Jesus, because of his Father's affirmation, has overcome his inborn fear does not undercut the Gospel's character as a terrifying journey to perdition, from Galilee to Mount Moriah. Yet whatever Jerusalem was for the historical Jesus, it was an emblem of death and carnage for the Gospel writer Mark simply because that is what Jerusalem really was, as Mark wrote.

The *interpretation* of Jesus — overwhelmingly shaped by violent events that occurred decades after he died — is not Jesus, as the *text* about his life is not his life. The burden on Christians is always to return to what can be known of the man himself.[41] Jesus was a man of peace, and his message was one of peace between God and God's creation, a Father whose only attitude is love. But we look at Jesus mostly unknowingly, through the lens of a savagely violent war — decapitations, limbs lopped off, women of all ages raped, corpses stacked in pyramids left to rot, disease rampant, blood clogging the gutters — and not surprisingly what we see is distortion born of violence.

The Passion and death of Jesus was related as a narrative of ultimate submission: "Yet not my will," Jesus is remembered by three Gospels as praying, "but Yours be done."[42] At the most basic level, as the story is told, Jesus submits not to Romans, not to antagonistic high priests, not to "the Jews," but to a God whose economy of salvation requires the ultimate victim. God wants a sacrifice of such efficacy — and such brutality — that it is offered, in the decisive phrase of the Book of Hebrews, "once and for all,"[43] obviating the need for any further sacrifice. That assumes the disappearance of the Temple, which has already occurred as this theology develops. That assumes, further, that the ultimate victim undergo the ultimate in suffering. *No one ever suffered like Our Lord suffered.* In the Christian memory, the thousands of crucified Jews whose corpses hung during the Roman war as savage ornaments of defeated Jerusalem, *even as the Gospels took shape,* were less forgotten than deleted. Jesus alone, taking the sin of the world upon himself, suffered insult and anguish of that extremity because only infinite suffering could atone for the infinite offense suffered by the infinite God. The economy of this salvation was soon enough understood to mandate that, to balance such a scale of justice, the offered victim had to be as divine as the one receiving the offering. Hence the victim is God's only begotten son. The victim is the Son of God. The victim is God. This theological progression has roots in the primitive sacrificial turnabout we have already noted.

In the Akedah story in Genesis a lamb was provided to take the place of the son; in the Passion, which occurs at the Passover festival of slain lambs, a beloved son is provided to take the place of the lamb. In this transcendent reversal, Jesus willingly becomes the Lamb of God. "Behold the lamb of God, who takes away the sin of the world," John the Baptist is remembered as having said when Jesus first appears on the scene.[44] But the one "remembering" that proclamation is the other John, the author of the Gospel, written around the year 100, by which time the post-Temple theology of Jesus as the final sacrificial offering had taken hold. There are consoling implications in this understanding — consolations that would unleash the imaginations of suffering millions among the underclass of the Roman Empire, but there are troubling implications as well. What kind of God requires the death on the cross of God's beloved son?

4. Scapegoat Mechanism

Humans threatened by violence oppose it with violence. That ancient dynamic threads through the entire Bible, and can be seen to have been powerfully recapitulated in the way the followers of Jesus made sense of the violence that had been inflicted on him, and in the way they understood the violence Rome inflicted on Jerusalem. In both cases, it was taken to be God's violence. Where does that leave us?

Recall that sacrifice itself was at the service of the mitigation of violence, a particularizing of forces of destruction so that generalized forces threatening the survival of the group could be thwarted. The peace of the community results from this particularizing act, the escalation of violence is checked, and the bond of shared negativity aimed at the victim resolves all kinds of social discord. René Girard, as we saw, calls this the scapegoat mechanism, and sees in it the very origin of religion. But this positive reading of sacrifice never quite dispels a perennial human uneasiness with it, as one sees in the way religion has developed.

Religious evolutionists tend to read the history of salvation, dating back to the patriarchs and prophets and culminating with Jesus, as a gradual interiorization of sacrifice. According to this scheme, the movement begins with the sacrifices of Cain and Abel, when the latter's was preferred over the former's because of a lack in Cain's attitude. The tenth-century-BCE Genesis text is clear in affirming that the outward act of sacrifice is not enough to please God; the right internal disposition is also required. By the fifth century, after the Babylonian exile, when sacrifice at the Jerusalem Temple was impossible, pleasing God was a matter less of enacting the sacrificial cult than of doing so in submission to Torah. Torah and sacrifice were joined. The cultic ritual was less the magical act that changed God's disposition than the external symbol representing the changed internal disposition of the person making the offering. But after the Temple was destroyed in 70 CE, for the rabbis, obedience to Torah alone replaced sacrifice; for the Christians, the internalizing of sacrifice was a matter of loving the neighbor in the name of Jesus.[45] All of this amounted to a progressive turning from physical bloodletting to a spiritual form of self-denial, either for observance of Torah (which included compassion for the neighbor) or for the sake of compassion as such—the kind of sacrifice, say, that Catholics observe during the penitential season of Lent. ("The sacrifice of God is a broken heart," the psalmist prays. "A heart contrite and humble God will not despise."[46])

This may be evolution of a sort, but the shift from Temple sacrifice involves not only internalization but a change in the emotional content of sacrifice, from the essentially joyful celebration of closeness to God in God's house to the grim act of propitiating God at a far remove. That is, from the Temple before which David danced when he installed the Ark in its Holy of Holies to Golgotha, the hilltop on which dancing was unthinkable in the presence of the worst suffering in history. This is why, as the theologian Robert J. Daly comments, "in the highly religious world of ancient Western civilization the term 'sacrifice' was associated with a rich variety of positive connotations, while in the highly secularized modern Western world, the term is laden with a broad range of negative connotations."[47]

If Jesus represents an internalizing of sacrifice, it matters whether he is understood as acting within the Jewish tradition or against it. The Christian memory is offended by Jewish sacrifice and cannot imagine Jesus as respectful of it. Christians want to see an essential criticism of violence in the Jesus story, and that aims to include the violence of sacrifice, which is why the story features Jesus' assault on the Temple.[48] But Christians must reckon with the fact that that same story justifies violence. Sacrifice is the motif within which sense is made of the fate of Jesus. ("Without the shedding of blood," the Book of Hebrews says, "there is no forgiveness of sins."[49]) And the shedding of blood, in this instance, belongs to God. Christians, affirming love, imagine that they have left all affirmations of violence behind, which prepares them, willy-nilly, to be violent anew.

In the Christian revelation as constructed in the Passion story, the tragic fact of the human condition — that universal human inclination toward violence shows up even in opposition to violence — is once more laid bare. But this has happened before. Conceived in the crucible of the violence that defines its subject, the Bible is itself infected with the violence it resists. The life and message of Jesus, which can be understood (not only through numerous references in the Gospels to his message of peace, but also through the work of historians of Jesus who locate him in his Jewish milieu) as having been essential celebrations of nonviolence, took second place to a particular telling of the bloody denouement of Jesus' death.

Today most Christians want to defend the Church's origins as wholly innocent. If violence was later affirmed in the Passion's name, that resulted from mistakes and misunderstandings of the primal revelation, not from the primal revelation itself. Believing, with the orthodox Christian tradition, that the "apostolic age" lifted those who knew Jesus — or knew those who knew Jesus — above the human condition, both in the way they recorded their experience in scripture and in the way they themselves replaced violence with love ("See how they love one another"[50]), such innocent believers cannot fathom the possibility that violence so defines the human condition that it also defines Christianity at its source.

The Bible, as we have seen, tells the story of a God who sides with the victim against the victimizers — first, in Exodus, the victim Hebrews, and finally, with Jesus, the victim Son of God. "All of the world's great religions," the scholar Gil Bailie has argued, "urge their faithful to exercise compassion and mercy, as does the Judeo-Christian tradition.

But the empathy for victims—as victims—is specifically Western and quintessentially biblical."[51] Girard argues that the sacrificial mechanism can work only when scapegoating communities are ignorant of this dynamic, and he argues further that, with the New Testament, the hidden structure of such violent victimization is finally and fully revealed. Once revealed, it is rendered obsolete and can be left behind. For Girard, that is the Good News. "The gods of violence were disenfranchised," he wrote, "when the God of love was revealed. The machine has gone out of order. The mechanism of violence no longer works. The murderers of Christ acted in vain, or better yet: their deed was fruitful in that they helped Christ to record the objective truth of violence in the gospels."[52]

In this reading, the story the Gospels tell is one of stark and transforming simplicity: the sacrificial nature of the human condition was not invented by God; rather, God is murdered by it. God is absolutely the God of the victim, not the victimizer.[53] Not only is the victim innocent, so are the texts that tell his story. The cross is innocent. Any use of the cross to elevate God-willed violence is a perversion. Such perversions are the theologies—from St. Paul in the first century (as he is commonly understood), to St. Anselm in the twelfth century, to Cotton Mather in the eighteenth century, to Billy Graham in the twentieth century—that put "substitutionary atonement" at the center of hope, the idea that Jesus, like that lamb, takes the place of sinners on the altar of sacrifice, appeasing an angry God, atoning for sins of which Jesus himself is wholly innocent. This valorizing of suffering, and the sacralizing of violent retribution, according to defenders of the texts, are distortions of the Gospel.

Thus the violence of the death of Jesus, like the violence of scripture generally, exposes the great deception that God in any way wills violence. Regarding violence, there is no ambivalence in God. Ambivalence about violence—violence to stop violence—is wholly human, and undivine. Sacred violence is, therefore, a contradiction in terms. In the people Israel, and in Jesus, God has all along been exposing God's own rejection of violence. Violence has a name in this story, and it is Satan.[54]

Unfortunately, this celebration of the innocence of Christian origins is upended by nothing so much as the fact that the Gospels themselves identify Satan with a people, not with an abstraction. Now we can see the full significance of that early opposition between the two groups of post-Temple Jews and what it led to. The harsh fact is that the defining conflict of the Gospels is the bipolar antagonism between Jesus and—not Rome, which murdered Jesus, but his own coreligionists, who, in the Passion narratives, are shown forcing the reluctant Romans to their act of murder.[55] But the anti-Jewish lie of the Passion ("His blood be upon us and upon our children"[56]) only brings full circle the anti-Jewish lie of the whole life story ("He came unto his own, and his own received him not"[57]). Elaine Pagels has famously tracked the progression in the Gospels: how in the earliest, Mark, the antagonist of Jesus is an embodied Satan who has possessed a man;[58] in the middle Gospel Luke, the antagonist is still "the evil one" but is now identified with "the chief priests and captains of the temple and elders";[59] and finally, in the last, John, the identification of Satan and "the Jews" is complete.[60]

The assertion that the Gospels expose and therefore disarm scapegoating[61] is attractive, but it seems disingenuous in the extreme, given how the scapegoating of Jews—whom the Gospels explicitly indict for scapegoating Jesus ("It is better for one man to die for the people," the high priest Caiaphas is reported to have said, pronouncing the death sentence, "that the whole nation not perish"[62])—is central to the story. "The perverse innovation" of Christian anti-Judaism, as the scholar Mark Heim puts it, "is to make scapegoating itself the charge by which to scapegoat."[63] And so the Gospels, reacting more to the destruction of the Temple than to the crucifixion of Jesus, tell the story of that crucifixion in order to declare an end to sacrifice. But in doing so—and here is how we know the story is not one Jesus himself would tell—the Gospels sacrifice Jews. This self-contradiction in the heart of Christian foundational texts has come to be much noted, especially in Christianity's post-Holocaust reckoning with the roots of anti-Semitism.[64] But the fatal character of this structure—Christianity born of and nurtured by the same scapegoating violence that killed Jesus—has yet to be fully faced.

5. The Violence of Christians

Within weeks of the September 11, 2001, attacks on America, Britain's Prime Minister Tony Blair declared that those responsible for the attacks were "no more obedient to the proper teaching of the Qur'an than those Crusaders of the 12th century who pillaged and murdered represented the teaching of the Gospel."[65] Blair's motive here—to protect the vast majority of Muslims in the charged aftermath of 9/11—was admirable, but the hard and fast line he draws between the foundations of the religions and the violent acts of their zealous believers may be blurred by the inquiry we are pursuing here.

How did we get from Jesus, the "man for others," to the Crusaders who killed in his name? A thematic summary suggests an answer. The Christians who had declined to join in the violent Jewish resistance to Rome continued to eschew violence, at least in principle. But the ideal was affirmed in its being out of reach. The time, the place, and the people were universally wracked by war-sparked sectarian strife between and among Jewish zealots, pietists, moderates, and the Jewish establishment. The Jesus people, too, were at the mercy of a generalized spirit of war and civil war. Christians knew they needed to be forgiven for their acts of violence (Peter's drawing the sword), but they began to think of themselves as more forgiven than other people, especially than the Jesus-rejecting Jews, who refused to admit their need to be forgiven. Because Jewish rejection went to the core of Christian self-understanding, violence against Jews could be justified as self-defense.

But what about violence among those who revered the Lord? Acts of the Apostles reports physical assaults by "the Jews" on St. Paul and other followers of Jesus, a dispute usually taken to be between identifiably distinct "church" and "synagogue." Yet not only was such a distinction impossible at that point, but there is reason to conclude that "the Jews" referred to as Paul's antagonists were actually Jewish followers of Jesus who objected to Paul's liberal-mindedness in relation to Torah and Temple, at least in regard to the Gentiles to whom he was preaching the Gospel.[66] In fact, it is likely that the vast population of Jews, having ignored Jesus when he was alive (Jerusalem at Passover when Jesus died would have been a city of hundreds of thousands of residents and pilgrims), took little notice of his post-resurrection movement, and was probably indifferent to Paul's preaching. In that case, the New Testament itself would be reporting, at least in part, acts of violence occurring *within* the Jesus movement—notwithstanding the remembered nonviolence of Jesus, who rebuked Peter for pulling that sword. That memory served as an ethical standard against which to measure Christian behavior. The baptized were forbidden to serve in the Roman army, which modern-day antiwar Christians point to as support for their pacifist position, but it is likely that such a prohibition of military service had as much to do with avoiding the routine honoring of the emperor's divinity that was required of soldiers as with a strict rejection of armed force. There was no idyllic Quaker pacifism of the pre-Constantinian church, in other words, but there was still a general disavowal of killing in the name of God.

Early Church fathers, from Justin Martyr in the early second century to Tertullian and Origen in the early third century, were emphatic in saying no to *any* Christian's committing acts of bloodshed. In the neighbor, Christians were instructed (and often inclined) to see nothing less than God. The Oneness of God, which was the decisive insight of monotheism, was understood as the joining of humans to their Creator—and therefore to each other. In that oneness, a blow struck against the neighbor was struck against God. Monotheism, tied to an understanding that Jesus and his Father were One, was an ultimate source of peace.

But when the emperor Constantine converted to Christianity in 312 CE, the empire that had killed Jesus decisively changed the meaning of Jesus. The Constantinian era *was* different. Up to that point, for example, the dichotomy between church and synagogue had yet to become hard and fast, with Jewish Christians still honoring Torah, and Christian Jews, in addition to observing Shabbat, still celebrating Sunday Eucharist. The bifurcations of Old Testament–New Testament, law–grace, and church–synagogue had yet to be canonized in texts, doctrine, and creed. But now bifurcation took hold, even to the divide between life and death. For the first time, with the "discovery of the True Cross" in Jerusalem by Constantine's mother and the construction of a great basilica on the discovery site—the Martyrium—the tomb of Jesus was valorized. Christian piety took on characteristics of ancient pagan tomb cults. This was in direct contradiction to Jesus' own denunciation of the practice of celebrating burial places, which he dismissed as "whitewashed tombs."[67] Karen Armstrong observed, "Three hundred years earlier, Jesus had risen from that tomb. Now the tomb itself had risen, as it were, from its own untimely grave, just as Christians were witnessing an unlooked-for resurgence of their faith."[68]

But what kind of faith? The empire-wide celebration of the discovered burial place of Jesus was a reversal of the "empty tomb" ethos of the Gospel, and led to a fixation on death in popular piety.[69] The Christian Holy of Holies would from now on be a sepulcher—the Holy

Sepulcher. Like the Holy of Holies of the post-exilic Temple, this one would also be vacant, but soon enough the tomb would weigh more in the imagination than its emptiness did. Thus was the seed planted for Christianity's enduring mistake: reducing itself to a solution for the problem of death. Jesus was understood as having come not "to bring life, life to the full," as he put it, but to die a grisly death for the sins of the world. Only now was the crucifixion of Jesus given more emphasis as a source of redemption than either his teaching or his resurrection. The death of Jesus came to the fore. The cross, which is nowhere found on the walls of second- and third-century catacombs, replaced what is found there: symbolic renderings of the cup, the fish, the loaf of bread. It cannot be emphasized enough that the cross became the central Christian symbol only with the imperial conversion.

Constantine was saluted as a new Moses, leading the Church into the triumph it had been promised. But he was also hailed as a new Abraham, as if he were to be the progenitor of a new religion — which, in a way, he proved to be.[70] But there was an unintended implication in the emperor's identification with the father of Isaac, for Constantine had found it "meet and just" to put his own son, Crispus, to death. Crispus was killed on order of his father during the course of palace intrigues, perhaps as a would-be usurper. The important point, however, is that the filicide occurred in the same year, 325, that Constantine, with his mother, valorized the "True Cross" — and the same year that Constantine, an archmythmaker, first reported his having been converted back in 312 by, yes, a heavenly vision of the cross, which he reported seeing as a sword.[71]

It was psychologically satisfying, and perhaps inevitable, that such a killer-father would see to doctrinal emphasis on the idea that God the Father, as a heavenly ruler who "so loved the world," had found it necessary to require the death of *his* beloved son. In a reversal of Abraham, here was the father who had actually killed the son — and how could it *not* have been God's will? Indeed, the myth then grew up among Christians that the place where Jesus was put to death, Golgotha, had been the site of Abraham's nearly killing Isaac.[72] Abraham's willingness to bring the knife down, if God had not stopped him, came to the fore as the supreme example of Christian faith. *Back to child sacrifice.* Death was centrally salvific. And from now on, instead of by mass attraction from below, the Catholic religion would spread mainly, as with the emperor himself, by conversion of elites from above, who then forcibly converted their subjects. Coercion replaced persuasion as the main mode of evangelization.[73]

So, too, with the content of faith. For more than a hundred years, the followers of Jesus had remembered him in diverse ways, as the multiple texts of the New Testament themselves suggest. In 180 CE, the Lyon-based bishop-theologian Irenaeus wrote *Against the Heretics,* a five-volume indictment of nearly two dozen heretical groups. His disciple Hippolytus, in Rome, went further, censuring fifty heretical sects — an astonishing proportion of the unorthodox in a population that at the time numbered no more than about one hundred thousand Christians of any kind.[74] This suggests how multifaceted in belief, and probably cult, the Jesus movement continued to be. But all that changed. With the emperor-commanded definition of the Nicene Creed in 325, orthodoxy began to be enforced by the power of the state.

Indeed the state, a vast, uncertain sovereignty stretching from the isles of Britannia to the southeastern corner of the Mediterranean, depended on that orthodoxy as its one overarching source of cohesion. In 384, an Iberian named Priscillian, noted for preaching a severe asceticism, was put to death for heresy — the first recorded instance of the Catholic Church formally executing anyone for wrong belief. Scapegoating was back. More Christians would die at the order of Christian emperors than had died at the order of pagan emperors, although these dead would be "heretics," not "martyrs." In 391, while executing heretics, the emperor Theodosius I outlawed the pagan sacrifice of animals as inhumane. Temples and sacrificial altars disappeared, but not their cultural significance.

In the same era, Christian cultic practice shifted decisively, with the Eucharist, which had been a joyous meal shared over tables in home churches, becoming "the sacrifice of the Mass."[75] A reinvented ritual was now celebrated on altars in large basilicas, which replicated the temples of antiquity and rescued their aesthetic. This Christian reclaiming of sacrifice, and the core institution of priesthood it assumed, served the needs of the newly empowered hierarchy. The sacrificial Mass empowered the priest above the laity and infected Eucharistic theology with magic, resuscitating "many of the characteristic abuses of a material sacrificial cult."[76]

Violence against the Church's enemies (which meant the empire's enemies), whether Jews or barbarians, was approved by late-fourth-century figures like St. Ambrose, the bishop of Milan. Indeed, with Ambrose a crucial change was brought to the primordial tale of the Binding of Isaac, for now Abraham, instead of threatening his son with a shepherd's knife, according to a sermon Ambrose preached in 390, wielded a warrior's sword.[77] But Ambrose was powerfully rebutted. His protégé St. Augustine, in the early fifth century, tried to mitigate the violence of the now Christian empire with his groundbreaking theory of the just war. In later years, the just-war theory would mainly be used to sanction state violence, but Augustine had set out to restrict it. The point is that theology here was following politics. There would have been no question of a need to offer a rationale in defense of imperial violence, even if to limit it, if the empire was still pagan. Augustine's theory justified Church-sanctioned violence that was already under way, albeit without benefit of the ethical underpinning. The Gospel was being spread. Praise God.

Even more important than his abstractions about *jus ad bellum* and *jus in bello,* Augustine came forthrightly to the defense of Jews. He insisted against those, like Ambrose, who wanted to kill Jews (since, after all, Christian heretics were being killed for denying mere details of orthodoxy, while Jews rejected the whole of it), that Jews should be permitted to survive *as Jews* within Christendom. They would be the "witness people" whose survival as impoverished wanderers would always drive home the truth of Christian claims. This defense of Jews, backhanded though it was, may have prevented a Final Solution from occurring in the fifth century.[78] But, less as Augustine intended than as later Christians understood him, it was a defense with a terrible price. Not only were Jews to be in mortal danger whenever they surpassed "surviving" by thriving, but the Western imagination would be permanently braced by the positive-negative bifurcation that infected the Gospels. A religious denigration became a civilizational structure of mind, with a negative "other" required as the counterpoint of cultural identification. The Jew would remain the quintessential other, but that slot in the polarized consciousness of the Christian West would also be filled by the woman, the Muslim, and ultimately the "savage" of colonial lands, the Communist of the Cold War, and the "Islamofascist" of the present War on Terror. In the post-Constantinian and post-Augustinian institutionalization of anti-Judaism can be found the roots of the peculiar forms of racism, misogyny, and ideology that polluted the culture; "the origin," in the Palestinian scholar Edward Said's words, "of white Christian Europe."[79]

When Christians went to war after Augustine, the war was always "just" and Christian soldiers were always mobilized by the idea of their own virtue. They lustily waged "just wars," for example, in the East against the Persians, who conquered Palestine in the early seventh century. Once again, in 614, Jerusalem was leveled as the Persians took the city, slaughtering tens of thousands of Christian defenders.[80] This time, such savage destruction was taken as an offense, especially, against the cult of the tomb of Jesus. As Jews had twice (after Babylonian and Roman destructions) turned their grief and distress over a violated Jerusalem into a new attachment to the city — an imagined city — so Christians did now. But the infidel assault was against the Lord himself, victimized once more. That the Persians stole the True Cross enflamed all Christians who heard of it, and so did the Persian alliance with the Jews.

Jews had been banished from Jerusalem by the Romans in the first century, an exile that was reinforced by the St. Augustine–inspired fourth-century theology of Jewish dispersal as the "witness people." The Jewish Christians and Christian Jews whom we noted earlier now wholly disappeared from history, as the "rule of the excluded middle" took hold. Jewishness itself was moral — and physical — pollution. Thus, when the victorious Persians promptly installed Jews as rulers of Jerusalem, a tenet of established Christian theology was violated, and so was the very structure of the Christian mind. Jewish dispersal from Jerusalem was a corollary of faith.

The Christians rallied and were able to reconquer Jerusalem in 629, rescuing the True Cross. Jerusalem now came fully into its own as the anchor of the Christian religious imagination, with its holy places taken as sacraments of God's presence — "unassailable proofs," in one pope's words, that God had come.[81] As such, the holy sites became magnets of mass pilgrimage. As the myth of St. Helena and her Holy Land discoveries took fresh hold, the cult of relics, many associated with her — the crown of thorns, the staircase up which Jesus walked to judgment, the robe he wore, the shroud he was buried in, the nails that pierced his hands — became a pillar of the European imagination. The True Cross had preeminence, but the supreme relic of all was Palestine itself. Jerusalem would be placed at the center of the primitive world maps that began to be drawn. Indeed, cartography, in the West, came into being in part to valorize Jerusalem, and the holy city occupied the center of European maps — and imagination — for more than a thousand years.[82]

But the Jerusalem of this dream, the "New Jerusalem," was by definition and by theology devoid of Jews. Therefore, after rescuing the city from the Persians, Christians promptly and forcibly rid the city of Jews once more, most of whom fled to Arabia. The material Jerusalem, now exalted by Christians as sacrosanct in just the way they had deplored when Jews so regarded it, was restored as a Christian pilgrimage destination, although not for long.

6. Apocalypse Now

As if resolving the great biblical and Gospel ambivalence about violence, the last word, and last book, of the Christian Bible is the Book of Revelation, also known as Apocalypse, the Greek word for "unveiling." Although a marginal reading of the Christian story (neither Orthodox Christians nor Martin Luther affirmed its place in the canon), Revelation represents one of the most powerful reactions to the Gospel, and it taps into a much broader apocalyptic stream that runs from Jewish antecedents like Daniel (as we already saw) to the movement sparked by John the Baptist to the first impulses of St. Paul — all the way forward to millenarian movements in the Middle Ages and Pentecostalism in the modern era. The apocalyptic imagination gives expression to the experience of crisis. Uncertainty, physical fear, social disorder, a radical sense of alienation, these are the seeds of the apocalypse, and the canonized Christian example of the genre is a masterpiece. In the faith of terrified believers, Revelation has always held a place of primacy.

It reads like a battle manual, ordering "a spasmic paroxysm of divine violence by the returning Christ."[83] Famine, earthquake, mass slaughter, rivers of blood, lakes of fire, a cosmic showdown between armies of good and forces of evil — ultimately the catastrophic end of the world. Never has violence been more vividly portrayed. But all of this was not the product of a fevered imagination. Dream-like visions, yet it was no dream. Revelation was written in the 90s, nearly halfway between Jerusalem's first destruction by the Romans and its final and total obliteration in 135. We have referred to the Bible as wartime literature, but as an example of that genre, this book is in a class by itself. War — real war, as experienced by raped women and orphaned children and maimed fighters and enslaved survivors — is its ground. Its meaning. Its alarm.

Revelation seems to reflect the preoccupations of Jesus communities in the cities of Asia Minor.[84] Written by one who identifies himself as "John," living on the Greek island of Patmos,[85] the text was addressed to those Christians as a promise and a consolation, an assurance to people on the losing side of a violent struggle that they would ultimately win. The decisive victory would be at a battle between God's armies and Satan's at Armageddon, which refers to a plain outside Jerusalem. In Christian memory, Roman persecution of the late first and early second centuries was for the most part aimed at the baptized, especially under the brutal Domitian, who rivaled Nero for psychopathic violence. Domitian's reign of terror ran through the period of Revelation's composition in the 90s. In effect, the battle of Armageddon had begun — the battle of Christian life in an empire that hated Christ. In fact, though, Domitian targeted Jews as much as Christians, and probably failed to draw much distinction between them. This emperor nurtured the antipathy toward Jews that his predecessors had indulged in a more or less unending war, which would soon reach its savage climax. Throughout the time of the Palestine-centered Roman war against the Jews (70–135), Jewish communities were targeted, as we noted, by Roman legions across the Mediterranean, from Mesopotamia to Egypt to Cyprus. Expressly Christian martyrdom surely took place in this period, but that violence paled in comparison to the ongoing campaign that the empire was waging against the Jews wherever they had significant settlements.[86] With Revelation, the Roman war against the Jews, which is astonishingly absent from the Gospels, makes its explicit entry into the Christian narrative, even if later Christians fail to read it that way.

Twentieth-century scholarship mainly emphasized that Jesus himself was an apocalypticist — the point of his being identified, or identifying himself, with the "Son of Man" from Daniel.[87] Surely his vision assumed a great struggle between God and God's enemies, centered in the blasphemous imperial occupation of Israel. But Jesus as portrayed in the Gospels resisted a good-versus-evil dualism, upending such categories by criticizing the pious and befriending the ignominious. Jesus was historically minded, not mystically minded.

Picking up the theme of his mentor John the Baptist, he expected that God's reign would transform the situation of God's people, not in some far-off future or a distant heaven, but in the near term — a transformation of Israel on the earth that meant the actual defeat of Rome. *Jesus was wrong,* but his first followers picked up the theme, with Paul especially giving expression to an urgent apocalyptic hope, defined as the expectation that Jesus "the Christ" would return soon to establish God's reign. *Paul was wrong.* In these disappointments began the transformation of Christian meaning.

Jesus was understood as affirming the *present* reign of God, and as defining his purpose as one of bringing life, life to the full, here and now. "The time is fulfilled" was his watchword.[88] "Blessed are your eyes, for they see; and your ears, for they hear. Truly, I say to you many prophets and righteous men longed to see what you see."[89] What you see in front of you — here and now in his own person and in his ministry. The technical term for what Jesus preached is "realized eschatology," the End Time having broken into the present time. As such, in the words of the scholar James D. G. Dunn, this teaching "forms a decisive break with the apocalypticism of Jesus' time"[90] — a break, probably, even with his mentor John the Baptist. The present is absolute because God is present. Jesus preached nothing but the immediate nearness of God.

In this preaching, therefore, earth was not devalued in favor of heaven, fleshly life was not devalued in favor of spiritual life, nor was "this" life devalued in favor of afterlife. This can be seen in the one pronounced difference between Jesus, who loved socializing at banquets, and John, who renounced sumptuous fare in favor of locusts. But as the years passed and the various traumas inflicted themselves on those who followed Jesus — from his brutal death to his failure to return after the resurrection; from the destruction of the Temple two generations after Jesus to the obliteration of Jerusalem yet another two generations later — those followers found it impossible to cling to what had to seem a facile belief in the immediate nearness of God, in the good things of life. Indeed, God had never seemed more absent, and that is why the spirit of a flesh-denying (present-denying) apocalypticism informed their recast hope. After Jesus, and despite his carefully recorded preaching of the present reign of God, the religion that was formed in his name partially carried the characteristics of an eschatological sect within Judaism. That shows itself in parts of the Christian scripture (for example, in the way the destruction of Jerusalem is "foretold" in Mark 13, and in the earliest writings of Paul, 1 and 2 Thessalonians), but where it really finds expression is in Revelation.

As the violence of the Roman war destroyed the mother community of the Christian movement in Jerusalem and threatened other communities elsewhere, an urgent apocalypticism once more seized the religious imaginations of Christians, as it had seized the Jewish religious imagination in such crisis. (Even though the books of Daniel and Revelation are the only two clear examples of the apocalyptic genre in the canonical Bible, there were dozens of such works circulating among Jews and Christians in the biblical era.) And central to that religious vision, in the 90s as much as two and a half centuries before, was the warrior God, engaged in a dualistic cosmic struggle, a final battle, against God's enemies.

War is the problem to which the apocalyptic vision responds, but it does so as a justification and celebration of war as the proper answer to war. It is as if the thousand-year-old biblical struggle against the tragedy and cost of brutal coercive force as experienced at the militant crossroads of so many empires and armies has been distilled to an essence of killing. Revelation offers a formulaic summary of the human condition as defeated in the long struggle against violence: the human race doomed to a mass suicide from which it can be rescued only after the fact, and magically.

The first coming of Jesus was as a Lamb, but, having been slaughtered, in Revelation the Lamb comes as one bearing wrath, a killer Lamb.[91] The Lamb, so the book says, summons 144,000 armed fighters to Mount Zion, and the Lamb is named as the target of the armies of evil.[92] The vision is notable for combining the historical Jesus, the anointed Christ, and the Lord who will come again soon—but this complex affirmation is mainly accomplished in the language of symbols. None is more pointed than Jesus as the Lamb. The scene of the Lamb's appearance is expressly sacrificial: a temple, an altar, the killing table. This Lamb is victorious precisely in being put to death; the victim is the victor. And his victory extends to all who have been victimized. The book's author stands before the sacrificial altar and writes, "I saw under the altar the souls of those who had been slaughtered for the word of God and for the testimony they had given; they cried out with a loud voice, 'Sovereign Lord, holy and true, how long will it be before you judge and avenge our blood on the inhabitants of the earth?'" And the promise comes in reply that the enemy is "soon to be killed."[93]

The Bible began, as we saw in Chapter Three, when exiled Jews reinvented their religious identities in Babylon, in reaction to the destruction of the first Temple in Jerusalem. Monotheism came into its own then, with the Oneness of God experienced as a principle of unifying peace among all nations. With this sense of God's Oneness, humans had a deity against whom to measure their own impulses and work to change them. Hebrew religion was revivified as a religion of compassion and empathy, its god a God to be honored in acts of loving-kindness toward the neighbor. But that memory of Babylon is reversed in Revelation by a present experience of a "new Babylon" — a reference to Rome, the destroyer of the second Temple. Babylon One and Babylon Two: the twice-ravaged Jerusalem brackets this ultimate revelation. And, against the great insight into the Oneness of God, and therefore the Oneness of all that exists, the first effect of this new revelation is to see the cosmos itself as broken in two. With apocalyptic literature, dualism — the idea that creation is split between equally powerful forces of good and evil — takes the religious imagination hostage.

The more humane notion is that experienced oppositions represent an interior self-alienation, not the structure of a bipolar reality. But such self-alienation is a first consequence of violent threat, never more than when a war has entered the death zone where a people are fighting for survival. In the death zone, it is kill or be killed. Of course, in a situation of such life-and-death peril, the enemy is experienced as evil, and of course, in that extremity, the experience is magnified from the local to the cosmic. That magnification is built into the survival mechanism: this is all there is, and if God is on our side, it is inconceivable that God can be on the enemy's side. Consequently, there is no Oneness. At the heart of existence there is radical conflict. *This* conflict. Kill!

Those who lived through the Roman destruction of Jewishness in Palestine, centered on ravaged Jerusalem, naturally understood what happened as having happened to the whole world. To them, that is what Jerusalem was. And this was experienced not only by the Jews living in besieged Jerusalem but by all who understood themselves in its terms — certainly including the post-Temple rabbis and Jesus people. For their heirs, Jews and Christians both, *the destruction of Jerusalem is what gives us our religion, and the destruction of Jerusalem, despite all else, defines the heart of our religion.* In Revelation, this is made explicit when the destroyer emperor Nero, who launched the Roman war against the Jews and first ordered assaults on Christians in Rome, is specifically identified as "the beast whose number is 666."[94] But Nero is named as one on whom revenge must be inflicted. War requires war. Here is the irony for Christians, though: this clear, apocalyptic demonizing of the imperial beast morphed quickly into a demonizing of the Christians' fellow victims of that beast, with other New Testament texts resolutely refusing to portray Romans in a negative light—even the Passion narratives, with Romans rendered as supremely reluctant executioners.

Within a few years of Revelation's anti-Roman division of the cosmos between the forces of God and those of Satan, the fourth and final Gospel, also attributed to John and composed a decade or so later, reproduced this dualism, but did so, as we saw, by defining as the "sons of Satan" not Romans, but Jews.[95] Good-versus-evil apocalypticism was conscripted into the argument between Jesus-believing Jews and those Jews who rejected Jesus, which is why the Gospel of John represents the most extreme denigration of "the Jews" in the New Testament. Again, the bipolar structure of the Christian imagination, especially once Gentiles dominated the Church after the Roman war eliminated most Jewish Christians, defined the cosmic struggle as against Jews, who were cast in the role of the paradigmatic negative other against whom the Church affirmed its positive identity.

Against God's enemy, in Revelation, Jesus himself is seen setting the avengers loose, for the Lamb's function, in John's vision, is to open each of seven seals on the fate-defining scroll that God holds in his right hand.[96] With each opened seal comes a savage assault, culminating in the ghastly "four horsemen" of conquest, war, famine, and plague.[97] But it is not only Rome against whom this fury is brought—"Babylon the Great"[98]—but the entire sinful world. The cosmos-destroying Jesus, treading the grapes of wrath, "the winepress of the fury of the wrath of God Almighty,"[99] transforms all creation by its destruction. Redemption comes through violence, and this, finally, is what makes violence sacred.

Christians of tender conscience have wanted to reject Revelation as not being truly representative of their religion.[100] But this unambiguous sanctification of revenge and doom only proves the truth of biblical inspiration—biblical inspiration bound by what is true—"human

nature being what it is," in our mantra from Thucydides. The apocalyptic mindset, with its dualism, carries this pessimism to a whole new
level with the division of time into the present age of wickedness and
a future age of glory; its division of space into the doomed world here
"below" and the joy of heaven "above." Temporal dualism and spatial
dualism combine to denigrate the here and now, a denigration that has
proven to be history's most potent source of violence against the earth
and its inhabitants—violence carried out in this world in the name of
another world; life assaulted for the sake of afterlife. Only in the hereafter does God's reign of justice, mercy, and peace apply. In the by-and-
by, therefore, anything goes.

Revelation makes explicit the perversion that implicitly infects the
other foundational texts of Christian faith, especially those that end
scapegoating by scapegoating. Revelation's inclusion in the New Testament gives the lie to Christian claims to be only a religion of love, and
forecasts the bloody mayhem that will be the mark of Christian sway
almost everywhere it holds—certainly including the Crusader kingdom, but also including, centuries hence, the republic whose "grapes of
wrath" battle hymn is drawn from this text.

The Jesus who rebuked Peter for drawing his sword[101] now arrives
with a sword coming out of his mouth, and while that image had a
symbolic reference to scripture, which is elsewhere called a "two-
edged sword" for being just and merciful,[102] Christian readers of Revelation saw a weapon pure and simple, not a symbol. Indeed, the text
has Jesus giving up his tender role as Lamb to come down from heaven
on a white warhorse, assuming the role of grand marshal in the transcendent battle of good against evil.[103] And the sword of Jesus swings
not just against Rome but against every living thing. This is the apocalypse gone berserk. The consummation of history, which in Isaiah was
to be God's heavenly banquet, "a feast of fat things, full of marrow, of
wine on the lees well refined,"[104] has become, in the ultimate Christian
vision, a feast for vultures encircling a vast smoldering ruin: "the lake
of fire that burns with brimstone"; a wasteland of corpses, "and all the
birds are gorged with their flesh."[105] And where does this eschatological travesty take place but in an otherwise golden city that is expressly
defined by the absence of the Temple: "I saw the holy city . . . and in
the city I saw no Temple, for its Temple is the Lord God the Almighty
and the Lamb." And what is this fire-purified, sword-swept place but
our "New Jerusalem"?[106]

CHAPTER FIVE

The Rock of Islam

1. No god but God

MUHAMMAD DIED IN 632. The next year, only two years after the Byzantine Christians had reconquered Jerusalem (and rescued the True Cross) from the Persians, a mounted force of Bedouin fighters who revered the Prophet's memory invaded the Byzantine-controlled territory of Palestine, near Gaza. The attackers moved rapidly in clustered units, with their faces covered against sand and sun, their white desert robes flying in the air behind them. Those mounted on horseback formed the avant-garde, but the main body rode camels, normally ungainly beasts that, when galloping, take on the fleetness of gazelles. The Byzantines retreated, though they carried banners of the Eastern Roman Empire, whose control of the region went back six centuries.

Their hold on the territory had been weakened by a series of brutal wars, with Persian armies from the northeast and with the Sassanian Empire, centered in Baghdad, extending from the Caucasus Mountains into parts of present-day Turkey and sweeping, along the ancient crescent, across to central Asia as far as present-day Afghanistan. During the previous decades, in battles from Constantinople to Antioch to Armenia, the Byzantines and Persians had exhausted each other, making both vulnerable to the unleashed military power of the heretofore unnoted camel riders coming up from the Arabian Peninsula.

These nomads, whose first claim to culture had been defined by merchant activity in oasis settlements that marked the Levant caravan trade with the East, had a second claim that depended on the exploitation of that trade, whether as hired navigators of the vast ocean of sand or as raiders and thieves. Only recently had the Arabs found it possible to put aside their age-old tribal rivalries to form an invading front unprecedented in its unity and in the fervor with which it carried out assaults. Formerly their social contacts, including conflict, had been mainly internecine, but recently united, they found it natural to seek connection — and plunder — beyond their traditional territory. Out of a barren emptiness that had hardly registered in the centuries of late antiquity, no one saw them coming.

They called themselves "Muslims," a participle form derived from the verb "Islam" and meaning those who submit to God. Their Prophet was Muhammad ibn Abdullah (born 570). He began as a shepherd and merchant in the oasis center of Mecca, but by middle age (he was forty when God's revelation first came to him) he was recognized throughout Arabia as a mystic, philosopher, and military leader. By those who followed him, he was understood as calling for a purification of the revelations of Abraham, Moses, and Jesus, although Jews and Christians took him to be the founder of a new, and fallacious, religion. The region's tribal elders and proprietors of traditional cults, involving representations of various deities — idols — had reason to reject Muhammad's teaching too, but large numbers of Arabs instinctively responded to his core insistence, which was on the immateriality of God. That, paradoxically, was the precondition of intimacy with God, and that intimacy became widely felt, and universally available. A twenty-first-century Muslim, the writer Reza Aslan, observes that Muhammad "launched a revolution in Mecca to replace the archaic, rigid, and inequitable strictures of tribal society with a radically new vision of divine morality and social egalitarianism." At first this "tore apart the fabric of traditional Arab society," but under Muhammad, a vision of God's Oneness became an unprecedented Arab oneness.[1]

In effect, it was a repetition of the union-beyond-uniformity phenomenon that had spawned Judaism and inspired the Jesus movement — far more, as we saw, than a merely numerically conceived monotheism. For Muslims, submitting to God and submitting to the *ummah*, or community, amounted to the same thing. That God rewarded their submission seemed clear from the astonishing fact that already, within a year of their Prophet's death, their numbers had grown exponentially. The tribal bands of Arabia had become a well-coordinated fighting force. But military prowess was based on a social revolution. The move from clan loyalty to the affinity of belief created an unparalleled scale of organization, but the key enabling factor was the character of the affinity, not the content of the belief.

Whatever the Oneness of God meant in the abstract, it was made concrete in that oneness of social enterprise launched in the name of that Oneness: "There is no god but God." Now Muslims were battering at fortifications from the far side of the Nile delta to the banks of the Euphrates, rattling what remained of the greatest empires in history. Those being rattled were quick to misunderstand what they heard defined as jihad. To Muslims, *jihad*, the Arabic word for "spiritual effort," had the meaning less of holy war than of what Christians were already calling "just war," a set of principles that rationalized violence and limited it, rather than simply unleashing it. Jihad might involve military action, but that would be only one manifestation, and not the most important. Muslims distinguish between "lesser *jihad*," meaning defensive war, and "greater *jihad*," meaning moral struggle with oneself in front of God.[2]

The Prophet had taught that jihad required, for example, that punishment be in proportion to the offense. And once punishment was exacted, all conflict in the matter was to cease. Blood feuds were defined, indeed, *by blood*, with only immediate relatives given license to avenge an offense. The concern to limit violence is the source of the well-known Muslim prohibitions of alcohol and gambling, both of which, in Arabia as elsewhere, were explosive stimulants to feuds. That the preconceptions of Islam thus displayed attempts to control violence only demonstrates how severely constrained by violence was the culture into which Islam was born. And that culture's religious assumptions were no more immune from generating conflict than were its other features, whether trade or turf or conceptions of honor.[3] We have seen this before, how religious violence emerges from a human impulse to quell violence. That tragic arc is what connects the many parts of the human narrative we are recounting, and Islam showed itself to be like other religions in being readily brought into the fight.

Europeans who, much later, sought to explain the remarkably successful march of the Prophet's armies, solely emphasized Islam's violently religious and religiously violent character — ". . . spreading by the sword the faith he preached"[4] — as if holy war in the name of the deity were an innovation. Indeed, group brutality regularly exploited the religious aspect in the ancient world, whether it was devotees of Vishnu against those of Shiva in India, or Buddhists against Taoists in China, or Byzantine Christians versus Persian Zoroastrians in what had been Mesopotamia. But however defined at the time, these were wars over territory, trade routes, and plunder more than over ambitions of religious conversion, and so were the campaigns of Islamic battalions.

Muhammad, in fact, thrived in a very rough milieu. Like everyone of his era, he would have taken brute contention for granted — massacres in combat and the enslavement of the vanquished, including their women. What is remarkable is that the revelation given to him was explicit in forbidding coercion when it came to belief.[5] That principle was rooted in a breakthrough sense of the radical inviolability of the autonomous interior life — what a later age would call conscience — of even the most humble camel driver. The simplest illiterate could grasp the sacred character of the immaterial realm of his own consciousness when the Prophet insisted on the singular immateriality of the deity. The preaching of God's Oneness, that is, was just as much a message about the sacredness of one's inner life, which was experienced as a sanctuary, as it was about Allah. That is why, from the start, the central Islamic act, in contrast to the external rituals of most ancient religions, has been the cultivation of interiority in prayer, expressed in an uncomplicated obeisance repeated five times a day.

"I became more than ever convinced that it was not the sword that won a place for Islam in those days," Mahatma Gandhi wrote. It may seem odd to offer an Indian Hindu's interpretation, but Gandhi's world was as defined by hostility to Islam as medieval Europe, and his perception offers a corrective. No, he said, "it was the rigid simplicity" of Muhammad's "absolute trust in God and in his own mission. These and not the sword carried everything before them and surmounted every obstacle."[6] Submission to God, made physical in that bowing, was the condition of felt union with God, a participation in Oneness itself, which became manifest then in what could only seem a miraculous felt union with others who had submitted. Practice, not theory,[7] marked this religion from the start — a way of behaving more than a way of believing, and its main effect was to give the practitioner an experienced hint of what God's Oneness was like. God's Oneness opened into Islam's. This kind of critical mass drove newly energized Islamic armies out of Arabia, and it was the most natural thing in the world that they should have directed their campaigns along the extended routes of trade that had so long found in their desert wasteland nothing but watering holes and tent-made shade. But the first goal of Muslim conquest was no mere trading center. In Palestine, moving from Gaza, they quickly laid siege to the fortified city on an unassailable — and mythic — mountain ridge. It was the myth that drew them. Coming out of Arabia, that city was their first ambition, their first mark as, and claim to, the world power they would soon become. That city was Jerusalem.

In the beginning, perhaps around 610, when Muhammad prayed to the One God, Allah, he faced Jerusalem and instructed his first followers to do so as well. He did this for the simplest of reasons, understanding his revelation as coming from the God who had made a home in that city, in its Temple. Thus "the earliest Arabic name for Jerusalem is Madinat Bayt al-Maqdis . . . 'city of the Temple,' taken from the Hebrew for Temple, *Beit HaMikdash.*"[8] Muhammad seemed to sense that the apparently miraculous cohering that was even then making a people out of a rough set of nomadic clans and raiding parties was a replay of what had transformed a dispersed group of exiles into the first People of the Book. Muhammad is said to have been illiterate,[9] but he was exceptionally intelligent and had become well acquainted with that people's narrative tradition. Only when the Hebrews, in Babylon a full millennium before, had finally grasped the meaning of God's Oneness did the meaning of Jerusalem as God's home become clear. And only in their returning to Jerusalem did the now necessary vacancy of the Holy of Holies — recall that the Ark of the Covenant was lost during the exile — adequately represent the immateriality of God. It was the Jewish sense of, and commitment to, that immateriality that entranced the young Muhammad. The God of Israel could not be represented because any single image of God would insult God's true character as the transcendence of all imagining. Only the story of God — the Book — could represent God, but that story was overwhelmingly the story of a place. Just as the vacancy of the Holy of Holies was its revelation, so the loss of that place had been the key to discovering its meaning.

The story kept repeating itself, and Jerusalem emerged as a classic instance of René Girard's principle of mimetic desire, as each of the varied groups felt the irresistible pull toward a city that others either possessed or coveted. Like those shoppers at the sale table we saw earlier: You have it, therefore I want it! Some of the Jews who had been banished from Jerusalem and its environs by the Romans in the first and second centuries CE, and whose exile had then been enforced by Byzantine Christians, had made their way to Arabia — but, as we saw, they never ceased their open longing for Jerusalem. Next year in Jerusalem! they prayed, like Jews everywhere, with nostalgia and grief, hope and desire. The unforgotten city lodged itself in the innermost circle of the Jewish imagination. Presumably, that longing, witnessed by Muhammad in Arabia, had imbued him with a reverence for the place.

Jews were joined in Arabia by some of the Christians who, guilty of "wrong beliefs," had likewise been expelled from Byzantine Palestine or had fled from it for their lives. These were "heretics" — at first, the Jewish Christians who were denigrated by Gentile Christians, and whose commitment to Torah continued to define their understanding of baptism. Like Jews of old, their religious life owed more to practice than theory — observing Shabbat on Saturday, the Lord's day on Sunday — even as an increasingly Hellenized Christian faith redefined the practice-theory tension as contradiction. Scorned by Jews and Christians alike, these Jewish Christians remained apart from the communities whose understandings of Jesus were shaped in the first generations by Greek philosophical categories, and ultimately into doctrines of God's triune nature and Jesus' divine personality. Jewish Christians, probably above all other Christians, maintained a loyalty of longing for the place that defined their faith, that Jerusalem which was the site of the tomb of Jesus, from which every promise arose, but which had first been made holy by their Temple, and from which they, too, had been driven by Romans and forbidden return by Byzantines. Jewish Christians occupied the forbidden middle ground between two groups, each of which had rejected them.

Arabia provided refuge to other "heretics" as well: those Byzantine Christians who, accepting the divinity of Jesus, lost out in the great theological arguments that said how such a thing could be true — especially Monophysites and Nestorians.[10] Yet for them, too, Jerusalem, site of their Lord's death and resurrection — and True Cross — defined their heart's desire. Among the pagan Arabs, such renegade Jews and Christians could believe and worship as they chose. In some ill-defined way, Muhammad had come under the influence of these people. Necessarily attuned to what separated Jews from Christians, and probably aware of the Church-splitting arcane arguments over the "natures" and "persons" of God and Jesus, he was nevertheless gripped by their central vision: a particular consciousness of God that had braced Israel after the Babylonian exile, a consciousness that had set Jesus apart as manifesting the communion of all in the One whom he called Father.

Far more seized this Arab visionary than the dry ideology implied in the Enlightenment word "monotheism." To say there is only one God, or that God is One, or that God alone is to be worshiped, is to say only part of what this vision means. It may be that Muhammad encountered a crude Trinitarianism in the Christians of Arabia, or an equally unsubtle notion of what it meant to believe that Jesus was the Son of God, but both affirmations left this desert seer, and therefore his movement, with an unnuanced contempt for central Christian tenets as idolatrous. Byzantine theologians had spent generations refining the Christian faith, conjuring language to account for the extraordinary impact and ongoing felt presence of Jesus, and allowing for a plurality of manifestations of the Creator's presence to the creation, all the while protecting the central insight of biblical faith that God is One. As the numerous violent conflicts among Christians themselves showed, doctrines of the triune God and of the Incarnation squared this circle with enough imprecision to protect the divine mystery and to guarantee human misunderstanding and argument.

But at bottom, Muhammad joined his fellow monotheists in taking a feel for God's Oneness as the opening to an understanding of the cosmos, and as a demand for a new relationship with all that is. God's Oneness says as much about human experience as it does about divine sublimity. It is a solution to human alienation, an existential stance that requires not only worship of the Creator but regard for every creature as the Creator's trace.[11] The unity of humankind and the equality of every human with every other are corollaries to God's Oneness, which is why the long legacy of monotheism, however imperfectly realized, has been positive. Whatever Muhammad's revelation was — and we will see how it was eventually articulated as the Qur'an — he understood it as coming from the God whom the Jews and Christians worshiped, even if they did so inadequately. It may be that at first Muhammad expected the Jews and Christians of Arabia to recognize his religious program as a purification of theirs, and in all likelihood some of them did.

The ancient religions of Arabia, meanwhile, were defined by a multiplicity of deities, each tribe or clan having its own god, represented by figures — idols — that were kept in a sacred shrine at Mecca, the central Arabian settlement. The shrine was a cube-shaped structure made of wood and stone, the size of a house. The Arabic word for cube is *ka'ba*, which gives the structure its name. The main religious ritual involved circling the structure seven times, a repetition of the course the sun made around the earth. Nothing better symbolized Muhammad's innovation than the fact that, upon taking control of Mecca late in his life, in 630, he cleared the Ka'ba of idols, leaving only the sacred black stone, which may have originated as some kind of meteorite, but which, according to his revelation, had been chosen as the structure's cornerstone by the Ka'ba's originator, Abraham.[12] From Muhammad's cleansing, the very emptiness of the Ka'ba, with all the idols gone, was a sign of the ineffability of the One God, much as the empty Holy of Holies in the post-exile Temple of Jerusalem had been a sign of the absence that alone defines God's presence. This monotheism is apophatic: a knowing that knows by what it cannot know.

In the twenty-first century, the cliché about Islamic terrorists has them crying "God is great!" before detonating their explosive vests in crowded markets or on buses. But that line in English is a mistranslation of the common Arabic affirmation of faith, *Allahu akbar*. Each of the five daily calls to prayer begins and ends with the phrase, yet it is better translated as "God is greater" — greater than any conception of God, or any way of knowing God.[13] The terrorist's act, carried out with a monumental self-obsession that itself betrays the mandated humility, is a perversion of the real meaning of the phrase and what it requires. "God resembles nothing," Reza Aslan writes, "either in essence or in attributes."[14] God is greater than greatness. It was Muhammad's genius to grasp this idea that is beyond ideas, and to convey it in a way that the simplest person could shape his life around it. God's immateriality, therefore, was the most important revelation of God's Oneness, and before it, all a believer could hope to do was submit.

The claim to connection with Abraham was essential. Genesis understands him as the ancestor of Hebrews and Arabs both, with his son Isaac most famously the progenitor of Israel — but Isaac was second. Abraham's first son, conceived with his wife's Egyptian maidservant, Hagar, is Ishmael, who became the chief of tribes living "to the east of Egypt."[15] In Arabia, that is. Not only is Ishmael thus the father of Arabs, but Abraham himself, having been the first to submit to the One God, was regarded as the first Muslim. That lineage was central to the kind of religion Islam would be. That Abraham stood before God, encountered God, understood God as "other," defined Islam as a religion of relationship *to* God, rather than of selfless union *with* God. Islam, like Judaism and Christianity, and unlike the religions of India and China, would not be a religion of mystical union with the divine, a union in which the self is subsumed in the all. Rather, Islam, like Judaism and Christianity, would be a religion of loving friendship with the divine, in which the self is fulfilled in relationship. A corollary of such relationship is that this religion also assumes God's actions in history, not in some mythical — and mystical — realm. This religion expects an end of history, not an eternal return. It is likely that, instead of imagining himself as the founder of a new religion, Muhammad thought he was leading an Arabian awakening to the most ancient religious impulse of humanity, which is what the connection to Abraham would have meant.

But by claiming the tie to Abraham, who knew God before either the Torah or the Gospel existed, Islam was also laying claim to the legitimating precedence implied in the birth order given in Genesis. That primacy would qualify Islam to rival the other monotheistic religions. Abraham, after all, was chosen of God long before Israel had come into being, much less the Church. The distinction between Ishmael and Isaac took on barbed importance — and the ancient theme of sibling rivalry reasserted itself — when the main Jewish tribes in the area aligned themselves with Muhammad's rivals in the early struggle for control of Mecca.

The Jews of Arabia rejected Muhammad's revelation as coming from their God, showing — so Muslims concluded — that Israel had betrayed its revelation. It was only after that rejection that Muhammad changed the direction of prayer, facing toward Abraham's *ka'ba* in Mecca instead of toward Jerusalem. To this day, the prayer niche of every mosque in the world is notched in the wall nearest Mecca. But in this most basic impulse, Islam claims its orientation as much by what it turns away from as by what it turns toward. Jerusalem was God's first city. Girard's mimetic desire was made absolute in this: because God longed for Jerusalem, each of the people who honored God did so as well. Thus it was inevitable that, when those who had submitted to God began to cross the boundaries of their known world, they would go to Jerusalem as directly as they could. And so they did.

2. Al Quds

Muhammad was succeeded as leader of the Muslim movement by Abu Bakr, his closest companion, but that reign was brief.[16] After Abu Bakr's death in 634, Umar ibn al-Khattab, also an intimate of Muhammad's and the father of one of his wives, became successor, or caliph.[17] The first to style himself as "Commander of the Faithful," Umar led Bedouin tribal bands as one army, quickly taking control of lands from Iraq to Egypt. As soon as 637, only five years after Muhammad's death, Muslim forces laid siege to Jerusalem, which was ruled by the Orthodox patriarch Sophronius, who, though an influential theologian in the Byzantine/Hellenistic debates over the meaning of Jesus, was himself an Arab. To Sophronius, as to Umar, Jerusalem was Al Quds, "the holy" or "the sanctuary." It was the site of some seventy monasteries and churches. After a long siege, the patriarch agreed to surrender Jerusalem on the condition that Umar come personally to negotiate terms. In a gesture of humility, Umar entered the city on foot instead of as a mounted victor. With the exception of a relatively brief period in the twelfth century, this Muslim rule of Jerusalem would last one and a third millennia, until 1917, when Britain's General Sir Edmund Allenby imitated Umar by dismounting when he entered the city as its conqueror.

Umar is said to have met Sophronius at the Church of the Holy Sepulcher,[18] and when the patriarch invited the caliph to pray in the place where Jesus was revered, Umar declined, explaining that if he did so, his followers would turn the church into a mosque. Umar asked to be shown the site of the Jewish Temple, which the Christians (venerating Jesus as the New Temple, and taking the visibly denigrated Jewish Temple as proof of Christian claims) had turned into a garbage dump. This was emblematic of the way in which Christianity had defined itself positively against the negative of Judaism — a bipolarity of which Israel knew nothing, conceived as a people *among* nations, not against them. Islam, too, at this point was given more to that Abrahamic multiplicity than to Manichaean negation, which is why Umar took offense at what Christians had done, and ordered the plateau to be cleaned up.[19]

Against the Christians, who saw in Jewish exile another proof, Umar invited Jews to return to the Temple Mount. When a dramatic outcropping of rock was pointed out to Umar as associated with the ancient place of Jewish sacrifice, in a further show of ecumenical sensitivity he ordered Muslims to construct their place of prayer at a respectful remove.[20] This was the origin of the Al Aqsa Mosque, on the far edge of what to all concerned was still the Temple Mount. And so the Islamic arrival in Jerusalem was marked by a refusal of the supersessionist impulse, in relation to both Jews and Christians. It may be that Umar was giving simple expression to knowledge that the cult of Jerusalem, dating to the Psalms, insisted on righteousness as the precondition of holiness. Indeed, Umar may have known that in the Bible's first mention of Jerusalem, David's followers were living in harmony with the vanquished Jebusites who had preceded them there.[21] The city itself tempered the mood of an otherwise merciless conqueror.

Recall that at this early date there was no written Qur'an. Muhammad's revelation is regarded to have been dictated to him (*Qur'an* means "recite") by the angel Gabriel over a period of years. Muhammad, in his instruction — however it came to him — was responding to the many challenges that faced his followers as they confronted opposition from the Mecca establishment and grappled with the implications of his innovations. As he recounted that revelation, his literate companions jotted down his sayings on pieces of hide, bone, palm leaves, or rough tablets. The sayings of the Prophet, which achieved the character of sublime poetry, were passed among first- and second-generation Muslims as oral tradition, creating a class of memorizing Qur'an reciters. It may be that Umar, in Christian Jerusalem, was made aware of the potency of venerated written text as an organizational foundation. Mimetic rivalry again, this time in relation to the Book. Thus, around the time of his conquest of Jerusalem, Umar seems to have ordered the compilation of the Prophet's words. Over the next couple of decades, an ad hoc set of primitive memory aids was transformed into a formal sacred text. The text was organized into *surahs,* or chapters, arranged not chronologically or by theme, but according to length.

This was an Islamic version of the collating and editing that had produced, among Jews, the Torah, the prophets, and the "writings" (Psalms, Job, Song of Songs, etc.) from the fifth to the third centuries BCE; and among Christians, the Gospels, Acts, and Epistles in the late first century CE. Early forms of the Qur'an showed up in the second half of the seventh century, within a generation of Muhammad's death. "With its content and the beauty of its language, this is a unique miracle, *the* sign of the revelation of God and the credibility of the Prophet."[22] The incarnational center of Islamic religion is not Muhammad but the text — the mystical presence of God. What Jesus is to Christians, that is, the Qur'an is to Muslims.

In the same period, understandings of the Muslim relationship to Jerusalem evolved as well, taking off especially from an enigmatic Qur'anic reference to Muhammad's mysterious "night journey," which was an initiating mystical experience traditionally dated to the start of the Prophet's revelation in 610. One brief *surah* declares that he was spirited to a place identified only as "the farthest mosque."[23] By the reign of the caliph Abd al-Malik in the 680s, the belief was taking hold that that journey had carried Muhammad, in Gabriel's company, to Jerusalem, and the mosque that Umar had constructed on the Temple Mount began to be referred to as the mythic "farthest mosque" — Al Aqsa, as it is known to this day.[24] Whereas Umar had revered the place for its association with the Jewish Temple, and through Jewish mythology with Abraham, now Muslims revered it for its association with Muhammad.

It was Caliph al-Malik who ordered the construction of a shrine over the rock of sacrifice, that stone outcropping that Umar had honored by staying away. Soon the rock would be revered by Muslims as the spot from which Gabriel, in the culmination of the "night journey," elevated Muhammad to the heights of heaven. This is the origin of the magnificent Dome of the Rock, completed in 691, an enduring symbol of the supersessionist claim that Islam imposed, albeit only over time, on the Jewish holy place in what had become the Christian Holy Land. The rock itself was resoundingly mythologized: "The Rock of Foundation: Precious Stone. Rock of Atonement. Adam's Sepulcher. Navel of the Universe. Stone of Stumbling. Rock of Sacrifice. David's Rock. Holy Rock. Rock of the Holy of Holies. Zion's Rock. Rock of Calvary. Rock of the Ages. Jacob's Rock. Peter's Rock. Rock of the Church. Rock of Salvation. Stone of Consolation. Rock of Fear and Trembling. Rock of Judgment. The Rock has many names."[25] And its shrine would be worthy of them. Glazed tiles of infinitely subtle blues, ochers, and mauves were overlaid with intricate calligraphic renderings of Qur'anic verses. The interior was so perfectly proportioned as to elevate architectural design to an expression of divine harmony. "Not since the Greek temples," Amos Elon observes, "had anyone so deftly infused space with spirit."[26] As for the Temple Mount on which it stood, its name would be, for Muslims, Haram al-Sharif, the Noble Sanctuary.

In sponsoring this transition of the ancient Jewish holy place into an Islamic one, it may be that al-Malik's motive had less to do with a rivalry with the monotheistic religions than with fellow Muslims. Al-Malik introduced expressly Islamic currency, art, architecture, language, and, momentously, a martial ethic that transformed ad hoc raiding parties and roving nomadic bands into a well-ordered military. Its operations were marked by the mobility of small, swift-striking units and by the overall leadership of tacticians adept at improvisation. No one was forced to fight in the Muslim armies, and conquered peoples were invited to assimilate with the conquerors, which soon enough led to the collapse of distinctions between Arab and non-Arab manifestations of Islam.

Caliph al-Malik, that is, was presiding over a shift from charismatic movement to institution, from desert patriarchy to imperial potency. In 684, he had moved the center of his caliphate from remote and desolate Mecca to the empire-worthy Damascus. As tribal culture rapidly gave way to a pan-Arabic elite, traditional limits of geography — and imagination — had to be overcome. By elevating the religious meaning of Jerusalem for Muslims, he may have been downplaying the religious significance of the sacred center he had dared abandon in Arabia. Especially noteworthy is the design of the Jerusalem Dome's interior, which accommodates the ambulatory circling — sun around earth — that had so long defined the devotional ritual of the Ka'ba in Mecca.

Even as the Dome of the Rock emerged as a symbol of the religious argument based in Jerusalem, the city remained overwhelmingly Christian, which is the surest evidence of the broad spirit of tolerance with which the conquering Muslims arrived. They denigrated Christian belief in the Trinity — "Say not 'Three'!" is inscribed on the tiles of the Dome[27] — and in Jesus as the Son of God, but they also protected the space within which Christians maintained those beliefs. The Qur'an, just then taking form, includes a verse addressed to Jews and Christians: "Let us come to an agreement on the things we hold in common: that we worship none but God; that we make none but God equal; and that we take no other Lord except God."[28] While Muslim commanders, beginning with Muhammad himself in the 630s, did not hesitate to enforce Christian and Jewish (and Bedouin) submission to the military and political dominance of Islam, a submission defined over time by taxation, they left religious submission to the side.[29] There was generally no question of Christians, much less Jews, being forced to convert to Islam.

Indeed, for the first time in its history, Jerusalem began a period in which members of the two now distinct religions, Judaism and Christianity, lived together in peace, while Muslims developed traditions about Jerusalem's centrality for Islamic belief. For example, as Syria replaced Arabia as the locus of the Islamic empire, Jerusalem's religious importance was further enhanced by sayings (Hadith) attributed to the

Prophet. He was remembered as declaring that on the Last Day the Ka'ba would be moved from Mecca to Jerusalem: Jerusalem would be paradise. This, too, was an ecumenical vision, an End Time ingathering not just of Muslims, or of People of the Book, but of all humans.[30]

3. The Masterpiece Relic

A world empire was born. A handoff occurred from Damascus to Baghdad, which quickly became the largest city in the world, with a population of between 300,000 and 500,000 people.[31] By 712, Muslim dominance had spread as far east as the Punjab, in present-day Pakistan, and as far west as the Iberian Peninsula. A single caliph was regularly revered as the symbolic head of the *ummah,* the House of Islam, though separate regions were governed by different rulers: Baghdad would rule Persia and central Asia; Cairo would oversee Arabia, North Africa, and Syria; Córdoba would be the hub of Islamic Iberia. Local languages survived, but Arabic emerged as a lingua franca. The spread of Islam involved an unprecedented cultural mixing, with elements of the classical, Arab, Persian, Hellenistic, Byzantine, Latin, and Zoroastrian coming together to form a rich brew out of which inventions of science, mathematics, art, philosophy, and theology would reverberate across the next three centuries. Where Christians felt intimacy with their crucified God in the experience of suffering and defeat, Muslims sensed God's approving nearness in triumph — and triumph abounded.

Success redoubled the Islamic esprit, yet the motives of Muslim forces remained defined by the mundane — and, among empires, universal — quest for plunder and subdued populations on whom taxes could be levied. It cannot be emphasized enough that, however braced by a sense of God's favor it was, Islamic expansion was not driven by expressly religious ambition. Yet when a putatively Christian force, led by a minor Frankish warrior in 732, held the line against Muslim raiding parties near Poitiers,[32] a decisive line was drawn — perhaps in the real history of Islamic dominance, but certainly in the imagination of Europe. The warrior's name was Charles, and after this battle, he would be known as Charles "the Hammer," or Charles Martel. His success was overwhelmingly understood as a religious one — as the enemy was understood, too, in exclusively religious terms.

Edward Gibbon offered a typical interpretation of Martel's victory by saying that, had it not occurred, the Qur'an would be taught to the "circumcised" at Oxford instead of the New Testament. Gibbon does not imagine that, had the battle gone the other way, Oxford itself, or an equivalent, might have come into existence far earlier than it did.[33] The preeminent British university traces its origins to 1167, more than a century after the death, to name only one Muslim genius, of Ibn Sina (Avicenna, died 1037), whose *Canon of Medicine* emerged as the basic medical text for medieval Europe. As Oxford was getting going, another, Ibn Rushd (Averroës, died 1198), was already doing his greatest work as a synthesizer of Aristotelian and Neo-Platonic metaphysics. A nascent university was taking shape in Cairo as early as the eleventh century.[34]

Whatever was made at the time in a rough region of the Frankish kingdom of a battle that may have been little more than a skirmish, it was soon mythologized, at least on one side. Charles Martel, in *chansons de geste,* was seen as the champion of Christendom, the hero who held the line against an infidel enemy, which was hell-bent on replacing faith in Jesus Christ with the "Mohammadan" faith. And who was Muhammad? An eighth-century Christian source, explaining the importance of Poitiers, portrayed the Prophet as nothing less than the Antichrist and devil's disciple.[35] Islam, violating the natural boundary of the Pyrenees, was taken to have its sights set on the whole of Christian Europe. Never mind that Europe, in anything like what is meant by that word today, did not exist; nor that, religiously, the Franks, Visigoths, Normans, Celts, and other tribal peoples in that time before Charlemagne (Martel's omni-baptizing grandson, of whom we will see more later) were hardly what one would call Christian.[36] And never mind that Islam, extending from the Pyrenees to the Himalayas, had probably reached, as every empire does, the outer limits of what its sources of supply, communication, and cultural cohesion could sustain. In Islamic historiography, Charles Martel is hardly noted. In Europe, he is nothing less than the founder of civilization, the progenitor of a continent-wide dynastic tree that still honors his descendants as royalty. The point is that the Christian European imagination — as Christian, as European, and as imagination — jelled around the idea, regardless of the fact, of the near defeat at Poitiers by Islam.

In any event, Europe became "Europe" in reaction to the perceived

threat from an external enemy that was understood as denying everything — not that Europe was just yet, but that it soon would be. And it
shaped the perception of the next 1,300 years that the threat was understood, again regardless of what the fact was, as expressly religious. Islam's astounding military success was crudely misunderstood as resulting from the holy war esprit of jihad, when to Muslims, as we saw, the
concept included ethical *limits* on warmaking. In the European mind,
though, sacred violence here found its most basic and enduring point
of reference.

Spurred by this mythology, the Franks, under the Carolingians, went
on to dominate central and northern Europe. Indeed, it is not too much
to say, with Hans Küng, referring to Charles Martel's grandson, that
"Muhammad made Charlemagne possible."[37] And whatever "holy war"
meant to Muslims, it became an overriding fact of life among the con-
testing Franks and Latins. In the West, violence in the name of God
was brought to a fever pitch in the late eighth century by Charlemagne's
wars of conversion against the pagan Saxons. Priests accompanied his
armies to enact mass baptisms of the conquered Germanic tribes. This
was Constantine's evangelizing-from-above par excellence (and such
proselytizing by the sword suggests why Continental Christianity never rid itself of a substratum of pagan superstition[38]). Yet bishops also
protested Charlemagne's tactics of forced conversions, and soldiers still
understood their acts of killing in these battles as mortal sins. Priests
accompanying armies were there not only to baptize the forced converts but also to hear the confessions of soldiers whose hands were
bloodied in the very acts of forced conversion.

But the popes, competing with Frankish and other kings, found it
useful to emphasize the religious nature of the "infidel" threat, as if
it required a unified religious response, keeping Rome on its leading
edge. Against Muslims, popes themselves became warriors. And why
not? Muslims, it was said, were after nothing less than the souls of believers. Power shifted away from the East, where borders with Muslim realms spawned insecurity, especially once the Seljuk Turks took
Baghdad in 1055 and began to move west through Anatolia and the
Balkans. But how was the Islamic threat to be made palpable to the
mass of illiterate and village-tied dwellers of the dark, impoverished,
forested, and isolated lands beyond the Alps, up the Rhone, and to the
Rhine — a population with little or no idea of the scale of geography
involved in Muslim conquest, and for whom the ubiquitous threat of

locally based violent brigandage made the horrors of turbaned armies of dark-skinned scimitar wielders seem remote?

The answer was the violated home territory of Jesus Christ. A blasphemous interloper had taken illicit possession of the Christian Holy Land, a sacred legacy that had been bequeathed to the followers of Jesus by God, who had banished from its precincts the Jews who had rejected Jesus *because* they had rejected him. God's old enemy, the "perfidious" Jews, had a new ally, the "infidels." The connection between the two is crucial.

For hundreds of years, religious anti-Judaism had insisted that, because the Jews had killed Christ, and in killing Christ had killed God himself, Jews were properly punished by degradation, impoverishment, and powerlessness. Indeed, their sorry state was witness to the truth of Christian claims, and every baptized serf, no matter how lowly, could feel superior to the Jews, whether he knew any or not. But now came news of infidels—not Jewish precisely, but somehow like Jews in their rejection of Jesus—who were far from powerless. Scripture-licensed and Constantine-empowered anti-Jewishness had already seen to the bifurcation of the Christian imagination, but when the "other" was suddenly perceived as powerful instead of weak, the bifurcation, as it were, became armor-plated. Jews were mere victims, in the Christian mind, but Saracens (from an Arabic word meaning "eastern") were a mortal threat.

Muslims were so powerful, in fact, that they had been able to wrest control of God's most sacred acreage—not from God's Church, but from God himself. Jerusalem properly belonged to Christians, as was proven by the Rome-enforced but God-ordained exile of Jews from Jerusalem, an exile that had theological weight since the time of St. Augustine. As Muslim forces moved west and north, religious concern for the holy city came to the fore. Only in the ninth and tenth centuries, that is, did the European imagination begin seriously to reckon with the seventh-century occupation of Jerusalem by Umar. The relatively benign character of that occupation, and the fact that, under a tolerant Islam, Jerusalem had subsequently remained a predominantly Christian city, with its shrines respected, were forgotten.

We saw how, beginning with fourth-century myths associated with Helena, the mother of Constantine and first patroness of the Christian connection to Jerusalem, Christian piety was marked by an attachment to relics, especially those related to the Jerusalem events of the Passion and death of Jesus. But this morphed into fetishism in the Latin West, as barbarian subjects were coercively brought into the Church by the conversion of their rulers, with little or no attempt to replace pagan superstition with authentic religious instruction. Among Franks, Visigoths, Normans, Germanics, and Lombards, ancient death cults meshed with the morbidity that emphasized the agonies of the death of Jesus and the imitative deaths of those "martyrs" who followed him.[39] Morbidity was the point, and for the mass of believers, rationality was irrelevant. When competing Frankish churches each claimed possession of the decapitated head of John the Baptist, for example, pilgrims could contentedly visit both shrines in the belief, as a monk instructed them, that one church had custody of the saint's head when he was a youth, while the other preserved his head as it was when he was an old man.[40]

Until the Jerusalem-sacking Persians had "stolen" it in 614, a full generation before Muhammad, the masterpiece relic — Helena's greatest discovery — had been, as we saw, the True Cross, grandly displayed in the Church of the Holy Sepulcher. After its much-touted but historically dubious recapture by Byzantine forces a few years later, pieces of the True Cross had begun showing up in churches across Europe. So the True Cross had become ephemeral — much spoken of and universally venerated, if in slivers and splinters that were housed in golden reliquaries in churches minor and major.[41] Catholicism is a sacramental religion, rooted in matter and sensation, but something perverse occurred when primitive believers focused on emblems of God's mortality. Their lust for relics could not be sated. It was then that all sorts of tokens of the Passion were made available to the credulous faithful — those sanguinary stairs, cloths, robes, thorns, nails, lances, every bloody thing.

But once Christians were confronted with an infidel threat near at hand, as legends attached to Charles Martel at Poitiers were spread by troubadours and mythmakers, the infidel insult far away seized the nascent consciousness of Europe. The most sacred token of all was the very place where Jesus died. And this the Muslims had, even if those far-off Christians had little idea of what, exactly, the infidel-dominated city amounted to. From the seventh-century conquest on, caliphs of various dynasties, whether operating from Cairo or Damascus, guarded the holiness of Jerusalem and its ever-empowering aura.

The fortunes of the actual city in this period ebbed and flowed, with the population hovering around 100,000. Combinations of factors, from earthquakes to the power struggles, and even madness, of the caliphs, cast an occasional pall and caused conflict. But balancing such negative pressures was the steady current of devoted pilgrims of all three faiths, an ongoing stream of refreshment — and revenue. Among Jerusalem's Christians it was said that the Byzantine emperor himself made secret visits to the Holy Sepulcher. One needn't idealize Jerusalem under the Muslims to note that Jews and Christians mainly thrived, with the former being the most literate in the city and the latter being the richest.

But from the vantage of Frankish and Latin Europe, Jerusalem might as well have been cast in amber, a city in which nothing of significance had happened since the cosmos-redeeming death of Jesus. Jerusalem had become the masterpiece relic. Around an imagined city controlled by an imagined enemy, the imagination of Christendom came into being. Jerusalem occupied the geographic as well as the theological center of the world.

All of this was heightened at the millennium, with a multisymptomatic hysteria that peaked in a "mimetic desire/rivalry/violence/scapegoat" dynamic defined by René Girard,[42] which gave us our starting point. Here we see how, in coming together in the founding dream of European culture, an untethered spiritual and material anxiety found its anchor in a place. Jerusalem would be the stage upon which to reenact the most primitive drama of all. Ironically, this would reverse the great spiritual insight that had come to humans in that selfsame Jerusalem a millennium and a half before — that scapegoats who are held guilty for human violence are in fact its victims. That is why the narrative born in Jerusalem, the Bible, insists on seeing history from the victims' point of view.[43]

But not here, not now. Freshly aware that an "other" was in exclusive possession of the city, the newly cohesive Christendom wanted Jerusalem more than ever, and the violence required to obtain it would be someone else's fault. And so Jerusalem was the solution to Europe's terrible problem — a problem of identity, of internecine mayhem, of unbelief, of a center that was not holding. The problem would be solved as such threats of social breakdown had been solved since a primeval band of hunters had singled out a marginal figure from within, or an enemy from without, as the source and therefore the target of all disorder.

And hadn't the fullness of time arrived when just such longing and rage could be openly expressed? Ordinary people were little aware of the calendar, but preachers, especially when faced with plagues and other disasters, emphasized hidden meanings of the year 1000, as if it marked the dawn of the End Time. As noted, the Book of Revelation offered a way of explaining pestilence, war, famine, and death, and its timetable could seem to suggest that the end was near.[44] Indeed, Revelation now came into its own.

A kind of millennial fever swept in waves across Europe throughout the tenth and eleventh centuries, and as Girard's theory postulates, the fever broke in violence. Penitential cults, seeking to deflect the doom of God's merciless judgment, took the form of sadomasochistic flagellation, dances of death, and other kinds of self-punishment. Violence was brought to the altar, where knights were dubbed and where a martial ethic was given liturgical significance. The oath these warriors swore was the means by which their bloodshed — whether the blood of their own bodies or of an enemy's — was joined to the shed blood of the Lord. The sacred consecration "This is my blood" took on a whole new significance. Such holy hysteria promoted, in turn, an emphasis on the grotesqueries of the suffering of Jesus, the scapegoated victim divine.

Superstitious conflations of time and space spawned a vivid sense of the Roman-inflicted brutalities as if they were happening now, which only reinforced the fixation on the site of his suffering, Jerusalem. It was the city of the Savior's doom and of the salvation earned by his suffering — the city of God's judgment and the celestial city. By the late eleventh century, overlaying both beatific and apocalyptic mysticism, Jerusalem had become the new incarnation of the Lord by virtue of being the place of his captivity. Those who loved Jesus were summoned to his rescue by being called to his city's liberation.

4. Jerusalem Agonistes

Jerusalem was, in fact, far away from the realms of Latin Christendom that became obsessed with it. Far closer were the lands below the Pyrenees, which were equally under infidel control. Out of Africa, Arabs and Berbers had crossed the Strait of Gibraltar within two generations of Muhammad's death, and a great caliphate had been established in Córdoba, in southern Spain, as early as 756.[45] Córdoba was soon a city of unparalleled brilliance, a flourishing spawned by its fluid exchange with the thriving Islamic capital of Baghdad, probably the most highly developed city in the world. Nothing in Europe would compare to Córdoba for hundreds of years, and it would anchor a rare *convivencia* among Muslims, Jews, and Christians. The latter were welcome, for example, to hold their own worship services in the Great Mosque, and often did so. At Córdoba was founded in the tenth century, around the time of Al Azhar in Cairo and well before Oxford, what is ranked by some as Europe's first university.[46] There, scholars of the three traditions entered into collaborations that would ignite the intellectual life of the entire continent. One of these scholars would be Moses ben Maimon, Moses Maimonides. This, the most revered of all Jewish sages, wrote mainly in Arabic, not Hebrew.[47]

Yet north of the mountains, bigoted contempt for Muslims as the hated other flourished. The contempt was thoroughly theological. Against the violent brigandage that was a mark of nascent European culture, and also to rein in sanctioned combat between landholders and feudal lords, each carrying blessings from regional abbots and bishops, popes began to unconsciously enact the primordial scapegoating drama by lifting up an ideal of battle as a form of piety, but only if conducted against God's enemy — outside. The object was to stop Christian princes from warring with each other. And just when popes and other rulers needed it, God's enemy came clear.

By the mid-eleventh century, as European awareness of the Islamic infidel was peaking, and as the coherent power of Latin Christianity under a powerful papacy was coalescing, the time arrived for a military move against the Muslims. Nearby Iberia, where Spanish Christians were struggling to launch a *reconquista,* was obviously the place to make it. To grasp the strength of the lock that Jerusalem was clamping on the imagination of European Christendom in the millennial era, it helps to see what happened in 1063 when Pope Alexander II called for a major Crusade, carrying the reward of indulgences, against the infidel enemy south of the Pyrenees: neither Europe's princes nor knights nor common people took note. Nothing happened. When Pope Gregory VII repeated the call for an Iberian Crusade in 1073, with the added incentive of papal license to keep all conquered property and plunder, still no one responded.[48] Such broad European indifference to a fight with the infidel is emphasized by the fact that, in 1091, the Byzantine emperor, Alexius Comnenus I, pleaded with the pope for help in defending Constantinople — yet nothing came of it.[49]

But only four years later, when Urban II announced the Crusade for Jerusalem — "The bastard Turks . . . shed blood like a river that runs around Jerusalem. Upon whom does the task fall to avenge this, upon whom does it fall to relieve this, if not upon you?"[50] — it was as if an electric pulse shot through the Continental psyche, with an equivalent in today's population numbers of more than a million people of all classes and stations dropping everything to take up the cross and go. "They decorated themselves prominently with their signs," a contemporary Jewish chronicler wrote, "placing a profane symbol — a horizontal line over a vertical one — on the vestments of every man and woman whose heart yearned to go on the stray path to the grave of their Messiah. Their ranks swelled until their number of men, women, and children exceeded a locust horde covering the earth."[51]

Why nothing for Iberia or Constantinople and a horde from all classes for the Holy Land? In the eternal present of the liturgical cycle, Jesus Christ was not being held captive in Córdoba, was not dying in Toledo, was not longing to be rescued by his faithful followers in Constantinople. But in Jerusalem he was. And, according to near-contemporaneous accounts, it was Jesus himself who asked for the rescue.

As reported in a history by Albert of Aachen, composed within four decades of the event, the influential preacher of the Crusades known as Peter the Pilgrim was asleep in the Church of the Holy Sepulcher. In a dream, he had a vision of Christ, who ordered him "to rouse the hearts of the faithful to come out and purge the holy places at Jerusalem, and restore the holy offices. For through dangers and diverse trials the gates of Paradise shall now be opened to those who have been called and chosen."[52] With this authority, Peter went to Rome and, so Albert of Aachen says, successfully sparked the martial ardor of Urban II, who agreed to preach Peter's Crusade for the sake of the Lord in Jerusalem. "For this reason," Albert asserts, "the Pope crossed the Alps" to Clermont, where "bishops of all France and the dukes and counts and the great princes of every order and rank, after hearing the divine commission and the Pope's appeal, agreed to God's request for an expedition at their own expense to the sepulcher itself."[53]

Urban's summons, channeling universal violence onto a particular object, amounts to a scapegoating classic. "Christian warriors," he pleaded, "who seek without end for vain pretexts for war, rejoice! For

you have today found true ones. You who have so often been the terror of your fellow citizens, go and fight against the barbarians! . . . Let
therefore hatred depart from among you. Let your quarrels end, let
wars cease . . . Enter instead upon the road to the Holy Sepulcher; wrest
that land from the wicked race."[54] No surprise that scapegoating happens here, and according to the primordial pattern. In the Christian
millennial fantasy, Jews were solidly joined with Muslims as the defil-
ing enemy. "We desire to combat the enemies of God in the East," the
Christian chronicler Guibert of Nogent wrote, "but we have under our
eyes the Jews, a race more inimical to God than all the others. We are
doing this whole thing backwards."[55] Now we see why the first violence
of the Crusaders, mobilized against the Saracen, was launched against
Jews — a savage slaughter in the Rhineland in the spring of 1096, resulting in the deaths of thousands.[56] "A beast was set loose," one theologian
commented about this attack on Jews, "and it would never be completely caged again."[57]

The Christian paranoid fantasy gave pride of place to Jews, especially when it came to the holy place, which the Christian imagination
still tied far more firmly to Jewish perfidy than Muslim. Recall that a
central tenet of Augustine's theology of Jewish "witness," as commonly
understood, was the diaspora, the idea that Jews were never to return
to Jerusalem. That they had been allowed to do so under the Muslims
was essential to the Muslim desecration of the Holy Land. Anti-Jewishness was already hard-wired into the Christian imagination; now the
wiring was expanded to include Muslims. And the knot tying all the
wires together, firing nothing less than the mind of Western civilization, was Jerusalem. And this was just the start.

The material and the spiritual Jerusalem became confusingly inter-
mingled, but in the crudely superstitious minds of northern Europeans,
that confusion produced a fierce longing. The fact that a specific place
called Jerusalem, the very place where Jesus walked, could be reached
by the mere act of walking put the heretofore unachievable goal of salvation within reach of any peasant. The Crusades built on the already
established, and now irresistible, tradition of pilgrimage. These travelers would carry weapons, but before they were warriors, they were pilgrims. Indeed, decades before they were called *croiserie* or *crucesignati,*
the Crusaders were called "peregrine," pilgrims of the cross.[58]

Going to Jerusalem in the millennial age was experienced as nothing
less than going to heaven, "a place of glittering and magical splendor."[59]

Killing for this Jerusalem was not only permitted; it was holy. Legions of priests would accompany the Crusaders, but not, as in Charlemagne's time, to hear confessions or baptize the vanquished (since few of the infidels would be allowed to live). No, priests were there to send warriors into battle with a blessing. For the first time in Christian history, the act of violence was the source of salvation. Murder in the name of Jerusalem was just, even if, ultimately, it was Jerusalem being murdered. For the first time in salvation history, Jerusalem, which had so often been attacked by God's enemies, was now attacked by God's friends.

5. 1099

It took Crusaders until 1099 to reach Jerusalem. Here is one's account of their assault:

> On Friday at dawn, we attacked the city from all sides but could achieve nothing, so that we were astounded and very much afraid. Yet when that hour came when our Lord Jesus Christ deigned to suffer for us upon the cross, our knights were fighting bravely on the siege-tower . . . At that moment one of our knights called Lethold succeeded in getting on to the wall. As soon as he reached it, all the defenders fled along the walls and through the city, and our men went after them, killing them and cutting them down as far as Solomon's Temple, where there was such a massacre that our men were wading up to their ankles in enemy blood . . . [Crusaders] rushed round the whole city, seizing gold and silver, horses and mules, and houses full of all sorts of goods, and they all came rejoicing and weeping from excess of gladness to worship at the Sepulcher of our Savior Jesus, and there they fulfilled their vows to him.[60]

And this from a Muslim account of the same 1099 siege of Jerusalem:

> The Franks stormed the town and gained possession of it. A number of the townsfolk fled to the sanctuary and a great host were killed. The Jews assembled in the synagogue, and the Franks burned it over their heads. The sanctuary was surrendered to them on guarantees of safety . . . and they destroyed the shrines and the tomb of Abraham.[61]

Before the Crusaders had arrived, Muslim defenders had sent nearly all the Christians out of the city for fear that they would serve as a kind of third force attacking from within. (Ironically, these mainly Greek Christians, later seeking to return, would also be regarded by the Latins as an enemy.) The population of the city was nevertheless swollen by refugees who had fled ahead of the advancing Frank army, and it amounted to something like sixty to seventy thousand people, mostly Jews and Muslims, two groups to whom the Crusaders showed no mercy. Ten thousand Muslims took refuge in the Haram al-Sharif, the Noble Sanctuary on the site of the Temple Mount. They were killed.[62] As the Muslim witness suggests, many hundreds of Jews crowded into the main synagogue, which was set afire. All died. The Crusaders killed nearly everyone they came upon, raped women, and made slaves of those who lived.

In doing all of this, the Franks, or "Latins," as they were also known, repeated the pattern of the two previous assaults on Jerusalem, by the Romans in 70 CE and 135 CE. For their part, the Romans were repeating the pattern set by the Babylonians in 587 BCE and the Syrians in 100 BCE. Each of these five apocalyptic attacks on the city had far-reaching consequences for politics, religion, and culture. Assaulting Jerusalem, that is, proved again and again to be an epoch-shaping act. We already saw how the Babylonian assault on the Jewish city and the subsequent kidnapping of its residents — the Babylonian exile — led to the coalescing of biblical faith, centered on a remembered Jerusalem and the firm recognition of the Oneness of God, which served in turn as the breakthrough revelation of God's will for the earth — peace and not violence. After the exile, the religious imagination of Hebrews was tethered to two poles: Jerusalem, with the Temple (its vacant Holy of Holies) at its core, and the Book, which was the living record of their struggle with the problem of violence.

But humans have a constitutional inability to hold on to the revelation of peace over violence. Again and again, humans see the source and justification for their own ambivalence about violence — violence as the solution to violence — in ambivalence attributed to God. When the *idea* of God is taken to *be* God, and a warrior God at that, beware. Again and again, that is, humans say of slaughter and mayhem, with Pope Urban, "God wills it." Still, something new was happening here.

On the Islamic side, despite the blood that flowed then and later, the Crusades would amount to a marginal episode on the less important edge of a vast empire. Islamic control of Jerusalem would be reestablished in a matter of decades, not to be forfeit again until the twentieth century. But that next Christian loss of Jerusalem, in 1187, would only redouble its significance for Europe, with its reattainment emerging, as we shall see, as a foundational ideal. Indeed, the Crusades themselves were foundational for Europe in every way—culturally, religiously, financially, politically, and mythically. What the 1099 siege of Jerusalem launched was nothing less than a permanent esprit, lasting not just the nearly three hundred years of the Crusading era, but throughout the history of the West.

The violence of the Crusaders' "victory" in 1099 defined Christendom's core purpose as an endless act of "malicide"—the killing of those designated as the evil ones. And who were they? All who opposed the God-commanded and universal missionizing of Christian faith. "Holy Christendom was created," as Tomaž Mastnak put it, "through holy war."[63] But this simple formulation does not go deeply enough into the mystery we are considering here. At one level, the Church was simply trying to stem the tide of violence, looking to replace the banditry and thuggery of a primitive world with order, law, and even peace. But the Church was swamped by that tide, with its penitential ethos drowned by the cult of war. Alas, there were theological reasons why this happened. In a way, all the themes we have been considering in this book, since those cave painters rendered beasts on torch-lit walls fifty thousand years ago, come together in what happened at the Crusades—from ancient themes of sacrifice to biblical ambivalence about God's violence to apocalyptic hope to notions of atonement to the way the followers of Jesus, for contingent reasons, misremembered his death. Many staunch defenders of Christian revelation have been thrown from their moral high horses by reckoning with its perversion in the Crusading era. Every good intention of the Jesus movement was twisted by the tragic quartet of inbred human impulses—the movement from desire to rivalry to violence to scapegoating, all of which, in combination, achieved critical mass in the Jerusalem centrifuge. Jesus Christ began as one defined by the unconditional acceptance of the God whom he called Father; now those who bore the name of Christ defined themselves, and therefore him, by the doctrine of God's wrath.

Even René Girard, who wants to claim Jesus Christ as putting an end to the desire/rivalry/violence/scapegoat dynamic, sees how it escalated in his name: "I believe it is possible to demonstrate that historical Christianity took on a persecutory character as a result of the sacrificial reading of the Passion and the Redemption. All the features of the sacrificial reading cohere. The very fact that the [Christian] deity is reinfused with violence has consequences for the entire system . . . in the apocalyptic destruction that traditional readings project upon the deity."[64] In other words, theological readings have consequences, from ideas of foundational sacrifice to End Time purification.

Ironically, this very human turn in Christian history can be understood as a consequence of the Church's alienation from its own Jewish roots, for what was lost was nothing less than the inbuilt biblical mode of constant self-criticism, which was the prophetic tradition. Because the prophets appeared again and again to demand it, Israel was prone to take its troubles, whether defeat in battle or the failure of leaders or exile from Jerusalem, as the occasion for examining how Israel itself had proven an unworthy covenant partner to God. Though the Jew Jesus also manifested this self-critical way of interpreting history — seeing the Roman occupation as the condition that called for repentance more than revolution — Christianity, beginning with its Jew-scapegoating texts, developed a different instinct. A more ancient instinct; one could say a more human instinct. Instead of self-criticism, self-justification. *Troubles are caused by someone else. Therefore, attack!*

This is the measure of the Church's embrace of the ethos of violence. That it took hold slowly, over the course of a millennium, culminating in a total war waged under the sign of the cross, does not change the fact that it was a profound betrayal of the cross's true meaning. The cross, not as a cultic token of Jewish or even Roman villainy, but as a reminder that every human sin bore down on Jesus, remains the true source of Christian self-criticism. The cross is the Church's prophet, or should be.[65] Jesus was put to death by his own: there was Peter himself, duplicating Judas by abandoning his Lord to the executioners. But misremembering the meaning of the cross, his own imagine otherwise.

6. Knights Templar

The military ethos that stamped the Latin Church might have receded after the bloody climax of the 1099 assault on Jerusalem, but instead it became institutionalized in the ideal of the warrior monk. That such a figure should have appeared on the scene just then, given the theological and cultural forces that had been unleashed by the Crusade, seems inevitable in hindsight. The saga of the Church-consecrated soldier would rewrite the meaning of heroism, of sanctity, of the Temple, and of Jerusalem.

It began when the Frankish knights, having occupied the Temple Mount, converted the Dome of the Rock into a church, mounting a cross on its pinnacle. No sooner had they cleared the nearby Al Aqsa Mosque of the hacked and dismembered corpses of the slain than they turned the mosque into the headquarters of the newly declared king of Jerusalem, Baldwin of Boulogne.[66] But Baldwin soon furnished himself with a proper castle, away from the Temple Mount, near the ancient Tower of David, and from there he solidified the Latin hold on territories from Gaza to Lebanon. The sanctity of Jerusalem was protected by the Latin refusal to allow the readmission to the city of Muslims and Jews. Jewish banishment in particular resumed its place as a proof of Christian claims, with Crusaders leaving the Jews to their settlements in Galilee and allowing them to approach Jerusalem only as far as a nearby hill, where they tore their garments and prayed for the "deliverance of captive Zion."[67]

The commodious Al Aqsa Mosque was taken over by a group of knights who dedicated themselves as pious soldiers, in the manner of sworn religious under vows of poverty, chastity, and obedience. They may have acted out of spontaneous devotedness, after "liberating" the tomb of Jesus, in the presence of which they took their vows. But they were giving perfect expression to the currents of martial religiosity that had been steadily flowing since Clermont. Their knightly zealotry was chastened by the transcendent meaning of what their combat had accomplished, with an exceptional modesty implied in the name they took: "Poor Fellow-Soldiers of Jesus Christ and the Temple of Solomon." Without benefit of historical knowledge, they regarded Al Aqsa as the remnant of the Temple built by Solomon (they apparently knew nothing of the Temple of Herod), and they therefore became known as Knights of the Temple, or Templars. They were formally chartered in 1119.

The papal bull that established them as a core institution of the Church compared them to the Maccabees, those Jewish resisters a millennium earlier who were prepared to defend the Temple to the death, and ultimately did. "The Knights of the Temple of Jerusalem, new Maccabees in the time of grace . . . ," Pope Celestine II wrote, "have taken up their cross and followed Christ. They are those through whom God liberates the Church in the East from the filth of the pagans and attacks the enemies of the Christian faith."[68]

Equally devoted to prayer and to war, they embraced a monastic discipline, observing the hours and the rule of silence even as they wore armor, sharpened blades, and honed their skills as fighters and horsemen. Ultimately there would be more than four hundred knights of the order stationed in Jerusalem alone, with each drawing on the support of many more "sergeants" and "brothers" — a set of ranks that empowered the knights as heavy cavalry, the sergeants as light cavalry, and the brothers as foot soldiers and supporting fighters. The caverns below Al Aqsa would accommodate ten thousand horses, and the warrior monks cared for the animals with a devotion that would later be associated with the beast-loving Franciscans.[69]

The idea of the Templars immediately struck a chord within the broader monastic movement, and soon they had the sponsorship of a powerful new religious foundation in Europe, the reformist Cistercians, then being led by the most famous theologian of the age, Bernard of Clairvaux. The Knights Templar adopted the white robes of Bernard's Cistercian order; white was a deliberate contrast to the black of the Cluny Abbey — its cloister chapel was the largest church in the world at the time — and to the wealth and corruption to which Bernard's order was a reaction. The knights' habit was emblazoned with a dramatic and distinctive red cross.[70] Bernard wrote a treatise that effectively canonized the Templar movement, "In Praise of the New Knighthood," which included the encomium "For if those are blessed who die in the Lord, how much more blessed are those who die *for* the Lord."[71]

The risk of that was real enough. The recovery of the holy city sparked a new pilgrimage movement, and the rush of pious travelers from Europe was threatened by bands of marauding "Saracens." The Templars were self-appointed protectors of pilgrims. Indeed, they became the sponsors of a pilgrimage renaissance, a longing for transport to the Holy Land that quickened every heart, even of those who could never make the journey. Pilgrimage became a discipline of contemplation, and the new cathedrals that began cropping up in Europe featured labyrinthine patterns in the stone floors of naves, circuits penitents could make on their knees — for example, the *"chemin de Jerusalem,"* as the labyrinth in Chartres was called.[72]

Knights Templar served as guards of caravans hauling Crusader loot back to Europe, and of return shipments of money to fund further Crusader adventures. Sea routes were soon preferred to overland ones, and the Templars developed powerful fleets, beginning a tradition of seafaring expertise. Driving a rod into European consciousness, Palestine would be referred to simply as Outremer—"overseas." Known for taking their vows of poverty and chastity seriously, the religious knights represented something wholly new: men of power who could be trusted. Because their vows were to the pope, they avoided having to choose among rival kings and princes, all of whom could therefore work with them. Before long, like an early Wells Fargo, their financial transport function grew into a kind of multinational banking system, as Templars were entrusted with treasures in the Middle East, the value of which could be redeemed at Templar centers in Venice, Paris, and London. Royalty began investing the Templars with their wealth, and benefactors left their estates to the order.[73] Popes exempted them from restrictions against usury and from taxes, and granted them the power to levy taxes in realms they controlled. Though individually poor, the order of warrior monks quickly amassed vast wealth.

As a fighting force, they soon surpassed every other, as monastic discipline created, in effect, the first true military chain of command since the ancient Roman legions. They functioned as a kind of elite fighting force, what a later age would label as storm troopers or rangers. They established outposts throughout the Latin Kingdom in the Middle East, devising a fortress architecture that combined unassailable exterior walls with interior cells and cloisters that encouraged contemplation. But Europe itself became a Templar realm, with the whole continent, from the Balkans to the Baltics, from Gibraltar to the Thames, divided into commanderies, which were controlled by warrior abbots who had become, at a remove from the battlefields, banker monks. The Templar chapel defined the commercial, if not the spiritual, heart of the cities that were just then coming into being, from Lisbon to Toledo to Venice to Paris to Vienna to London.[74] The typical chapel was built around a rotunda that repeated the forms of both the Holy Sepulcher, where the warrior monks took their vows, and the Dome of the Rock, which they maintained as their mother church, believing it to have originated as a church in the time of Jesus. (They left untouched the Dome's Qur'anic inscriptions rejecting the Trinity and the divinity of Jesus because they did not understand them.[75]) The rotunda sanctuary would be a mark of Templar structures everywhere, and the mason brothers (*frères masons*) who presided over what became an architecture of mystification—fortified sacred spaces—would be honored members. Emphasizing the importance of their impregnable battlements (and also treasuries), the

Templars' seal would combine a sword with a trowel. Another of their symbols, a six-pointed star, would be adopted centuries later by unknowing Jews as the Star of David.

The Templars were harbingers of an age to come: self-made individuals whose destiny was shaped by will (those vows), not fate; men of the frontier at war with savages in the wilderness (and the war would be genocidal); sponsors of a nascent colonialism, as their "pilgrims" traveling to wild country, and failing to return, became settlers; bringers of Christendom to the infidel, as later white adventurers would bring "civilization" to dark-skinned natives; motivated by the Gospel and its promulgation, yet finding themselves, willy-nilly, up to their eyeballs in untold wealth, they were the inventors of capitalism. It may not be too much to say that the Templars invented the next millennium.

If the Templars' story seems overemphasized here, it is because through the fact and mythology of this peculiar institution over the two hundred years of its formal existence, not to mention the subsequent seven hundred years of its multiple aftershadows, the legitimized tradition of sacred violence found its way into the genetic core of Western civilization, forming a metaphorical double helix with what was already there, and was now reemphasized: the idea of Jerusalem. Culture is a story of the mind according to which, across time, humans are able to make sense of what they undergo — and what they do. The key myths of culture, which is partly a matter of the facts of history and partly the way those facts are continually reimagined, tell people how to behave and how to think. About themselves. And about others. The Western imagination took root in classical antiquity, amid traditions according to which the epic hero — perhaps Odysseus above all — is tested by contests and journeys that he survives by himself, and only then is proved worthy of the common life, whether with the mate — Penelope — or with the polis. The Templars' story continues this tradition, though it reverses its important components. Not solitary, the warrior monk is vowed to fraternity. Individual heroics count for nothing; the triumph of the group is all.

What is true in combat is true in the sleeping chamber. The consummated sexual love that was, among the ancients, the sign of, and reward for, victory remains forever unconsummated for the warrior monk. Rather than challenging the gods and conquering them, he submits to God. All of this amounts to a decidedly partial *imitatio Christi* (partial because, what about the nonviolence of Jesus?). The Knights Templar were warriors par excellence, yet victory for them came through an interior disposition more than through physical prowess, through an aligning of the will with the will of God. Virtue, manliness, reined-in sexuality, unleashed power, courage, and the capacity for endless hours of contemplation — these were considered the epitome of holy knighthood. Against the brigand knights and feuding princes who had wreaked such havoc in early feudal Europe, Bernard defined the military order as "the living ideal of Christian chivalry."[76] Chivalry — a new virtue, tied, as the word suggests, to the man on horseback.

The result of this ethos? Violence is no mere evil to be tolerated when unavoidable, repented of when committed. Rather, violence is essential to what is admired and aspired to. The religious knights appear as the beau ideals of medieval epics and romances from the twelfth through the sixteenth centuries, the period when European civilization was defining itself. Courtly love, with its dehumanizing fantasy of woman as the forever unattainable object of desire (a counterpoint to the unsung and far more prevalent rape victim), was directly related to the image of the erotically charged but celibate knight. In twin ironies, the ultimate dehumanization of the woman is her disembodiment, as when she is reduced, in a kind of sacred pornography, to the figure of the imagined, yet forever unreal, lover. That all of this is organically connected to an ever-longed-for and eroticized Jerusalem could not be more to the point.[77]

The defining classics of constructed male and female identity spiraled around the Templar legends, from Tristan and Iseult to Parzival and Condwiramurs to Lancelot and Guinevere. As those references remind us, of course, the chastity of soldiers under vows is less a matter of lifelong celibacy than of mounting passion indulged for one night only (one night's mounting). Passion, a word heretofore attached to the suffering of Jesus, took on a new meaning here, attached to sexuality. Thence came the license for the admired promiscuity of the Western male: self-indulgence that requires no commitment (marriage is forbidden), no forethought (how, for example, to avoid conception), no facing of consequences (pregnancy not a male problem), and no sense of shame at a promise broken. On the contrary, consecrated martial masculinity required the abandonment of the woman after consummation (male orgasm), either because a battle had to be fought or because the knight belonged to God or because the spoiled woman — spoiled by passion — was now unworthy of the knight's still unsullied virtue. The woman's sorrow, according to the script of courtly love, informed what passed for female pleasure, which was the ecstasy of hurt longing.

This was a characterization of female passivity that would drive women into the one arena of action open to them: the monastery, where sisters, too, could be invested with a kind of spiritual knighthood.[78] All of this was stamped in fire on medieval culture by the iron brand of the Templars, often implicitly but sometimes quite explicitly. Lancelot's son Galahad was, in every iteration of the myth, a Knight of the Temple — white robes, red cross. That King Arthur's knights famously convened at a round table had less to do with an egalitarian-minded nobility than with the traditional rotunda form of Templar sanctuaries — a reference that went back, ultimately, to the Dome of the Rock. Camelot was Jerusalem carried north and west, but the main geography it occupied was of the Western mind.[79]

In 1182, the master general of the Knights Templar, Reginald of Chatillon, led a campaign from Jerusalem to Mecca, with the purpose of capturing the Muslim holy city and stealing the body of Muhammad — an imagined Christian equivalent to the theft of the True Cross. Reginald moved with armies, attacking Arab caravans, but also with a sea force, dispatching a Templar fleet to the Red Sea. Besides displaying the imaginative consequences of the Crusaders' own necrophilic cult of the tomb of Jesus, this adventure embodies the transformation of Christian missionizing into conquest. For most of the previous century, Islamic caliphates in the Middle East had been in open conflict with each other — a divisiveness that Christians, at the mercy of a univocal fantasy about the "infidel" enemy, had failed to perceive. Partly in response to the unforgotten extremity of the Crusader slaughter of Muslims in Jerusalem and the insult to Muslim shrines there, but more urgently in reaction to this fresh aggression against the Arab heartland, the emirates of Damascus, Aleppo, Cairo, and Mosul found new grounds for unity. The ancient principle of external threat as the source of internal cohesion applied. The charismatic leader who, by force both of personality and of arms, brought the dispersed Muslim realms together was the Kurdish intellectual and warrior Salah al-Din Yusuf, known in the West as Saladin. Having united the emirates, he exercised authority from Cairo. He moved against Reginald of Chatillon, who was forced to retreat from Arabia.

Saladin launched a sea force of his own, sending a fleet of galleys against Beirut. His forces besieged Templar fortresses in the Jordan Valley. At the climactic battle at Hattin, in July 1187, near Tiberias, the city on the shore of the Sea of Galilee named for the Roman emperor under whom Jesus was executed, Saladin's forces resoundingly defeated the Templar army—the decisive rollback of the Crusader assault. When Reginald was captured, Saladin personally saw to his swift beheading. Seeing the frightened look on the face of another Crusader prisoner, Saladin is said to have reassured him, "It is not the wont of kings to kill kings, but the man had transgressed all bounds, and therefore did I treat him thus."[80] There are reasons to regard Saladin as a relatively benign military commander, but brutality was universally a mark of warfare, and given the provocations that had preceded it, the victor's violence at Hattin was unsurprisingly extreme. The Templars were simply annihilated. While Islamic soldiers had never been tame, it seems clear that, after successive twelfth-century confrontations with Christian warriors, their methods had hardened. For one thing, expressly religious motivation had never been the driving force of Islamic wars, but Muslims were made to understand that for their Latin Crusading antagonists, religious motivation was supreme.[81] This, too, had its effect. At Hattin, more than two hundred captured Knights of the Temple were offered the chance to deny Christ. When they refused, they were decapitated.[82]

In short order, Saladin's army besieged Jerusalem. In October, the city's defenders capitulated. It was a replay of Umar. Saladin took Jerusalem without slaughter. "Christians everywhere," he said, "will remember the kindness we have done them."[83] In fact, many of the captured Latins were ransomed, and others were simply allowed to leave. Those without status were probably enslaved. The cross was removed from the Dome of the Rock. The Templars were driven from Al Aqsa Mosque, which was then reconsecrated with an elaborate ceremony highlighted by chanting from the Qur'an, the installation of a new pulpit, and the sprinkling of rose water. One of the next things Saladin did was to invite the Jews of Galilee to return to the city. They did so, establishing a presence in Jerusalem that would never again disappear.

The pope immediately called for a new Crusade to reverse this blasphemy, ordering a universal tax of 10 percent on all revenue, the so-called Saladin tax. At the head of the promptly mounted Third Crusade was the dashing figure of Richard the Lionheart, who would forever occupy the center of English Crusader mythology. Thrilling the hearts—and chronicles—of Latin Christians, Richard defeated Saladin at Arsuf, just north of Jerusalem, in 1191. But after many battles and skirmishes he could not retake the holy city itself.

Richard's legend benefited from, and reinforced, Saladin's. The two warriors were romanticized for their gallant mutuality. When Richard lost his horse in the midst of combat, Saladin sent him two steeds in replacement. Finally, in 1192, Richard, with his forces exhausted, came to terms with his now admired nemesis. At the Treaty of Ramla, the Englishman and Saladin agreed that Jerusalem would remain under the control of Muslims, but that Christians would be permitted access to the holy city as pilgrims.

Not even Richard's prestige made this deal palatable in Europe, where the longing for a reconquest of Jerusalem only intensified. As leadership of the Crusader initiative shifted to Germans, Muslims gradually relented, focusing on the only part of Jerusalem they actually cared about — the Haram al-Sharif.[84] In fact, after the reconquest in 1187, Muslims had been slow to repopulate Jerusalem, while Jews and those Christians whom the Latins had expelled — Syrians, Greeks, and Armenians — had returned in numbers. Thus, a generation after Ramla, in 1229, the Holy Roman Emperor (and grandson of Frederick Barbarossa), Frederick II of Hohenstaufen, reached an agreement with Saladin's brother according to which Christians could resume rule of Jerusalem, but with the Temple Mount/Noble Sanctuary reserved to Muslim control. This treaty was resoundingly rejected by the Knights Templar, who wanted their "Temple" back, and Muslims retained control of the whole city.[85]

The Templars were never able to regain Jerusalem, and their cavalry was in the forefront of the final defeat of the Latin Kingdom in 1291, a trauma that capped a century of free-floating European uncertainty. The loss of Jerusalem was felt as the source of Christendom's displacement of itself, even as Crusades were now launched within the world of the Church, with a Fourth Crusade against "schismatics" in Constantinople and the Albigensian Crusade against the "heresies" of the Cathars in southern France. As a way of establishing political and social order, none of it worked. Between 1252 and 1296 there were thirteen popes, and soon the papacy would be moved (or kidnapped) to Avignon, a second "Babylonian captivity" that would last for seventy years and seven papacies. The rulers of Christian Europe went at each other with a vengeance worthy of the worst of the Dark Ages. That a breakdown seemed universal only brought the universal — and now

unattainable — dream of Jerusalem more to the fore. In a kind of socie-
ty-wide parody of courtly love, the holy city became Europe's infinitely
out-of-reach object of desire.

So why should a new instance of savage scapegoating surprise,
and why should it surprise that its victims were none other than the
Knights Templar themselves? After all, hadn't they failed in their God-
given mission of protecting Jerusalem? Hadn't they brought about
the ultimate defeat of the Latin Kingdom, at Acre in 1291, when they
were finally eliminated by the Saracens as a powerful fighting force?
So, within a few years, Europe's kings, especially Philip IV of France,
moved against the Knights Templar, as did the Inquisition.[86] Their Paris headquarters, the Donjon du Temple, was seized for a prison, with
the knights themselves its first captives.[87] The Templars were charged
with various heresies and perversities, and their vast wealth and land-
holdings were confiscated. To take one example, its London headquarters was given over to the adjacent Royal Courts of Westminster for the
training of barristers. To this day, those two Inns of Court are referred
to as the Inner and Middle Temples, names that go back to the order.
The Templars' London precinct had been an enclosed "liberty," outside
the jurisdiction of the king, and access had required passing through a
raised pike, or bar — the Temple Bar. To be admitted to the courts as a
barrister continued to be referred to as "passing the bar," an instance of
how deep the Templar legacy goes.

Not only wealth was targeted; so was leadership. Across Europe,
from Paris to Venice to Vienna, the order's masters were brought to
trial and many were individually condemned. Dozens of Templars, if
not hundreds, were executed as heretics — this the payback to an order that, whatever its faults, had sent tens of thousands of members
to valiant deaths in defense of Christendom. In 1310, Pope Clement V
officially suppressed the order, and in 1314, its last master general,
Jacques de Molay, was burned at the stake on an island in the Seine.
His last desperate attempt to save himself and his order had involved
the proposal for a major new Crusade against Egypt — a final resuscita-
tion of the old dream of retaking Jerusalem. That dream did not die
with de Molay, however. Through these dislocations of the fourteenth
and fifteenth centuries, Jerusalem remained the still point of the wildly
spinning mind of Europe, even as the Saracen was replaced by the Turk
as the despised enemy.

Thus when St. Catherine of Siena passionately sought to heal the

Avignon schism, she imitated Pope Urban II when in 1095 he linked Church unity with the ideal of the captive city. "What a shame and disgrace it is for Christians," she wrote in 1376, "to allow the base unbelievers to possess what is rightfully ours. Yet we act like puny-headed fools waging wars and campaigns against one another . . . The wars Christians wage against each other ought to be waged against . . . the wicked, unbelieving dogs who have possession of what is ours."[88]

The wicked dogs were not intimidated. A decade later, in 1386, Turks defeated an army of Orthodox Christians at Kosovo, the deepest Muslim incursion into Europe since Poitiers. The trauma of Kosovo would so live in the consciousness of Serbia that Slobodan Milosević would invoke it with inflammatory power in 1989, igniting the Balkan wars of the 1990s.

Sigmund Freud would illuminate the ways in which a ruthlessly suppressed experience — repressed feeling — could live on in the unconscious as an irresistibly powerful drive of personality. The excoriated Templars lived on like that in the unconscious of the West, surfacing periodically in ever more bizarre manifestations. After the Reformation, for example, Protestants, especially in France, would not only look back on the Inquisition's war against the Templars as prima facie evidence of Catholic villainy, but would resuscitate weird aspects of the military order's tradition as an antipapal form of resistance. Hence the *frères masons,* the Templars' brother masons, architect monks, reemerged in the Enlightenment era, through a misunderstanding of the original linguistic reference, as the Freemasons.[89] With little or no understanding of its provenance in Jerusalem, the Masons embraced the Temple as the ubiquitous sanctuary of their esoteric rites — and as an express counterimage to the Catholic basilica. In post-Revolution France, the Catholic Church routinely identified its enemies with the dyad "Freemasons and Jews." Nostalgically recalled commanderies would establish secret societies that, by flaunting the secrecy of handshakes, initiation rites, passwords, roundtables, tomb cults, decapitation myths, and membership roles, made a mockery of the heretical secrets of which the Knights Templar had been accused. Such oddball reductions to the absurd would inspire cults as diverse as frat-boy clubs (Skull and Bones), businessmen's charitable groups (Shriners), organizations of wine connoisseurs (La Commanderie de Bordeaux), and, always, military elites — including savage ones in Prussia, which gave the Nazis their cultic insignia.[90]

Prussia, where the Order of Teutonic Knights would thrive, makes the point that the suppression of the Knights Templar was not the end of military orders. Warrior monks, fighters under the religious discipline of vows, survived in Europe for at least another two hundred years. After the formal suppression of the Templars in 1312, they reappeared in a somewhat different form in Portugal, beginning in 1318, where they were known as the Military Order of Christ. In fact, Portugal had been the first site of a Templar establishment on the continent of Europe, its ports providing safe harbor for Templar fleets. The headquarters in Portugal had been in the interior city of Tomar, on the Nabão River, where the twelfth-century fortress was constructed around an octagonal church that was a replica of the Dome of the Rock. When the Inquisition suppressed the Templars, the king of Portugal was in the midst of a struggle to drive out the Moors. Instead of shutting down the order and confiscating its property, as happened elsewhere in Europe, he welcomed the warrior monks and navigators as the spine of a renewed *reconquista*. Fugitive Templars from elsewhere found refuge and a new cause in Portugal. As members of the reconstituted Military Order of Christ, they took the traditional vows of poverty and chastity, but their vow of obedience was to the king of Portugal, not the pope.

Portuguese royalty so dominated the order that in 1417 one of the king's sons, Prince Henry, became its grand master.[91] The Moors having been driven out of Portugal by the Order of Christ earlier in the century, Henry, in effect, carried that holy war across the sea, capturing Ceuta, a town on the African coast across Gibraltar. An autonomous part of Spain to this day, the Portuguese settlement at Ceuta amounted to the first permanent colonial outpost by a European power — the beginning of an era. Known to history as Prince Henry the Navigator, the grand master understood that the sea was the route to Portuguese supremacy — and also to the ultimate reconquest of Jerusalem, which, true to the roots of his order, explicitly defined his purpose.

Henry established the famous navigators' school at Sagres, and he initiated the great Portuguese adventure of exploration, with a special focus on Africa. His navigators began a steady movement south along its west coast, the white sails of their caravels carrying the distinctive Templar cross of red. The Azores, the Madeira Islands, the Canary Islands. The sailor monks were on the lookout for sources of gold and ivory, and always for a sea route to India, for spices, and the Levant, for Christ. An ocean passage to Jerusalem became more urgent than ever after 1453, when, fulfilling what had been "for six centuries a vain Arab dream,"[92] the great gateway city of Constantinople fell to the Turks.

By the time of Henry's death in 1465, navigators of the Order of Christ had mapped the west coast of Africa. To take only the most famous example of the order's success, one of its religious knights was Vasco da Gama, the first European to round the Cape of Good Hope and complete the sea voyage to India.

But before that, in 1471, in one of the decisive turns in the order's history, the sailors discovered what would be called the Gold Coast, present-day Ghana, at the point — Cape Coast — where the landmass of the continent turns eastward. In 1482, the Portuguese built a castle on the coast there, the first of hundreds of commanderies the order would establish in Africa. The castle took its name from what the Portuguese were already exploiting — the area's lavishly productive gold mines — Elmina, "the Mine." Soon a large percentage of the gold making its way to Europe was coming from there. Elmina was the first permanent settlement by Europeans on the African continent below the Sahara Desert. It sent gold northward for two centuries, but before the gold was played out, it became the site of a new source of riches. At Elmina, in the early seventeenth century, the Portuguese launched the Atlantic slave trade, and the castle was transformed into a prison where Africans were held while waiting to be loaded onto slave ships. Elmina would serve this function until the nineteenth century.

7. Christopher the Christ Bearer

One of the lay seamen who learned his skills on Military Order of Christ caravels exploring the African coast was an Italian called Christopher Columbus. Even though he occupies a place of primacy in the American pantheon, little is known about his driving motivation or interior life, despite ample testimony on both fronts, from his contemporaries and from his own writings. Columbus, as every American schoolchild knows, was on the make for gold, spices, and commercial routes to India, whatever that was. All true. But none of that touches what, to the man himself, mattered most. And that was Jerusalem.

Chief sponsor of the narrowly secular assessment of Columbus, in a rationalist nation made uncomfortable by overt expressions of spiritual purpose, was his most important twentieth-century biographer,

Admiral Samuel Eliot Morison. "My main concern is with the Columbus of action, the Discoverer," Morison declared. "I am content to
leave his 'psychology,' his 'motivation' and all that to others." Yet even
Morison, aware as he was of what Columbus wrote in his voluminous
journals and of what was written about him, especially by his near contemporary Bartolomé de Las Casas, had no choice but to acknowledge,
if only in passing, "all that." One can sense the begrudging undertone
in Morison's condescension: "Christopher Columbus belonged to an
age that was past, yet he became the sign and symbol of this new age of
hope, glory and accomplishment. His medieval faith impelled him to a
modern solution: expansion. If the Turk could not be pried loose from
the Holy Sepulcher by ordinary means, let Europe seek new means
overseas; and he, Christopher the Christ-bearer, would be the humble
yet proud instrument of Europe's regeneration."[93]

In Spain, as Columbus set sail, regeneration seemed tied not to expansion but to expulsion. In January 1492, Ferdinand and Isabella conquered Grenada, the last Muslim enclave in Iberia. Finally, the Moors
were driven out of Spain—and western Europe. Now the time for a
full purification had arrived, and in March the rulers issued their infamous order "that all Jews and Jewesses of whatever age that reside in
our domain and territories leave with their sons and daughters, their
servants and relatives, large and small, of whatever age, by the end of
July of this year."[94] The great exodus culminated on August 2, with the
last Jews of the more than 300,000 expelled clambering aboard vessels in every Spanish harbor. Given the shape of this history, can it be
reckoned mere coincidence that that day was Tisha b'Av, the day on
the Jewish calendar marking the anniversary of the destruction of the
Temple? One of those witnessing this mournful expulsion at close hand
was Christopher Columbus, who—again, can this be reckoned a coincidence?—set sail on his momentous voyage the next day, August 3,
1492.

Coincidence or not, the juxtaposition had significance for Columbus, who later wrote, in his report to Ferdinand and Isabella, "And thus,
having expelled all the Jews from all your kingdoms and dominions . . .
Your Highnesses commanded me that I should go to the said parts of
India." Columbus referred to his exploratory journey as Empresa de
las Indias, the Indian Enterprise, but as the scholar Abbas Hamdani
points out, the word "India" had an imprecise meaning in Europe, with
its main connotation being the realms that lie to the east beyond those

controlled by Muslims.[95] Achieving those realms by going west defined
Columbus's purpose — and the freedom from Islamic control was the
point. Yes, Columbus wanted to circumvent the Muslim chokehold on
European trade with the East, the glories of which had been sung by
Marco Polo and other Venetian explorers. Columbus held the common
view that rulers in the East — Cathay — were friendly to Christians and
ready to form an alliance against Muslims. Such alliance was also the
point.

In his journals, Columbus's report to his sponsors continues:

> And Your Highnesses, as Catholic Christians and Princes devoted to
> the Holy Christian Faith and the propagation thereof, and enemies of
> the sect of Mahomet and of all idolatries and heresies, resolved to send
> me, Christopher Columbus, to the said regions of India, to see the said
> princes and peoples and lands and the disposition of them and of all,
> and the manner in which may be undertaken their conversion to our
> Holy Faith, and ordained that I should not go by land (the usual way)
> to the Orient, but by the route of the Occident, by which no one to this
> day knows for sure that anyone has gone.

As for the gold that Columbus hoped to find for his sponsors, he knew
that it was not merely for their enrichment. He wrote, "I declared to
Your Highnesses that all the gain of this my Enterprise should be spent
in the conquest of Jerusalem; and Your Highnesses smiled and said that
it pleased you."[96]

Columbus makes many such references to Jerusalem, and the reconquest of the Holy Sepulcher, in his diaries, including entries written
during the voyage of 1492.[97] It was the most natural thing in the world
for the white sails of Columbus's caravels to carry the red cross of the
Order of Christ, and for him to have as navigators Sagres-trained warrior monks who were members of the order. However much the mumbo-jumbo of secret societies and frat-boy esoterica would trivialize the
Templar legacy, this was one real, and world-historic, way in which
lived on the Poor Fellow-Soldiers of Jesus Christ and the Temple of
Solomon.

Morison makes reference to the semantic meaning of the name
Christopher, yet Columbus himself gave that meaning emphasis by
signing journal entries "Xpo-ferens." Columbus "had come to believe
he was carrying Christianity across the sea as his namesake, St. Christopher, carried Christ across the waters."[98] For Columbus, achieving

Jerusalem was not merely a matter of releasing the Holy Sepulcher from the age-old Muslim bondage. Like millenarians before him, he seems to have come to believe that the final restoration of the Holy Land to Christian dominion would usher in the messianic age. "God made me the messenger of the New Heaven and the New Earth," he wrote in about 1500, "of which he spoke in the Apocalypse of St. John . . . and he showed me the spot where to find it."[99] An apocalyptic impulse informed the New World project at its birth. On the day before his death in 1506, Columbus affirmed his last will and testament, including the provision for a sum of money to be used in the liberation of Jerusalem.[100]

And is it a final coincidence — or only testimony to the depth of these unconscious currents — that when the "spot" of the founding step off a vessel named *Mayflower* onto what would become the United States of America was trod upon little more than a century later, it would be commemorated ever after as "the Rock."[101]

City on a Hill

1. Reformation Wars

WE THINK WE KNOW what the Reformation was. We see a theological disputation, yet it was the capstone of an epochal cultural mutation. Not since the Neolithic revolution, unfolding, as we saw, between 8000 and 2000 BCE, did humanity undergo such a massive change as occurred in Europe between 1000 and 1500 CE.[1] What Martin Luther set loose would surpass his virtuous intentions — a coming to climax of the forces of sanctified violence that had been gathering for centuries.

We've seen that, in the prehistoric period, the invention of seed-crop farming and the domestication of animals led to the demise of the hunter-gatherer life. The hunt, however, had left humans with a taste for the "collective effervescence" of the kill, which they then resisted with cults of sacrifice, channeling mayhem by ritualizing it. Religion grew from this: religion salved a multiplicity of longings, but it began as a way of resisting violence and controlling it. The settlement of nomads led to cities and civilization — writing and history — but also to food surplus, class distinctions, theft, and the organized looting known as war. Nutrition through systematic agriculture led to reliable and abundant sources of protein, which sparked further human physical and mental development. The cycles of planting and harvesting depended on close observation of natural phenomena, like tidal flows, seasonal weather patterns, and variations in light and dark — observation that led to science. The same cycles meant that periods of intense activity were interspersed with times of relative leisure, which made new forms of intellectual work — and play — possible. Society was organized around divisions of labor, with the large majority being forced into the slavish serfdom of tilling and reaping while an elite minority exercised power. Categories of victim and victimizer were institutionalized. Violence at the service of despotic control invoked divine sponsorship. The human drive toward violence, that is, co-opted the opposite religious impulse. Religion could be used to bless bloodshed instead of oppose it. God could be imagined as a warrior.

All of this occurred in the Fertile Crescent. In a certain place there, Jerusalem, the transcendent meaning of the region for the human project became clear.[2] The Bible came into being as an act of resistance to god-sanctioned inequity—with its God evolving from potentate to friend, loyal not to one tribe only but, in Oneness, loyal to all humans everywhere. The Bible thus presented the social narrative from the point of view of the less powerful, a narrative that itself created a people, and supplied that people with a principle of self-criticism—prophecy. The Bible warned the victimized people of its own temptation to victimize. The God of the Bible, seen as tempted to violence, rejected it. After once destroying the earth with a flood, this God swore, "Never again."

Beginning in the Middle Ages, the people living in Europe underwent another vast cultural, economic, and religious change, but this one was a reversal of the narrative of "Never again." We saw how Christendom had defined itself positively over against a Jewish negative, and then how the Continent cohered as a unitary culture in opposition to an Islamic enemy abroad. Once again, human nature being what it is, a religion that began as a peace movement— "Love your enemies"—became a sponsor of war. Millennial fervor launched many movements, the most decisive being the Crusades, and the related Crusading spirit. Jerusalem reemerged as a center of meaning, and contention. As noted, the various military encounters between Latins and Arabs, as well as between Latins and Byzantines, caused massive transformations. The Middle Ages grew into what we call the Renaissance, an explosion of genius.

But in part, the European revolution was a simple matter of technical innovation: the wheeled plow enabled farmers to turn over the denser soil north of the Alps, and led to the use of draft animals—oxen and dray horses. Larger and stronger horses led to the military dominance of the mounted knight. Vast forests were cleared. Monasteries were centers of learning, and therefore of invention. Crop rotation (one field for winter grain, one for summer, one fallow) increased food production, which supported population growth. Gradually, machines like the water wheel and the windmill replaced animals and humans as sources of energy. The windmill enabled large tracts of wetlands to become arable, transforming especially the northern lowlands — the "nether lands." Networks of rivers became a highway system, causing trade to flourish. River towns became cities. Once the Great Schism of 1054 — the theological break between Rome and Constantinople — reified the East-West split, Europe found its footing to the north. As the cultural and political center moved away from the Mediterranean, where power concentrated around the inland sea had defined Persia, Crete, Athens, Carthage, Egypt, and Rome, European despotic control broke down. Competition between church and empire, with neither able to impose absolute authority, created openings for lesser powers, and for individuals. Indeed, individuals became aware of themselves as such. Serfs demanded emancipation. Townspeople became their own locus of power, and their towns — eventually city-states — became centers of further technical and social innovation, creating everything from markets and guilds to mechanical clocks and, ultimately, movable type and the printing press.

Only seventy years after Johannes Gutenberg published his Bible in Latin in Mainz, Martin Luther published a New Testament in German in 1522, which sold hundreds of thousands of copies — history's first bestseller.[3] The equivalent prophet of English translation was a priest named William Tyndale, whose version of the New Testament appeared in 1526. The Latin word for "translator" shares a root with "traitor," and Tyndale was burned as a heretic simply for that text.[4] Within a few decades, much of Europe's previously illiterate population was learning to read. The thrill of language, and the play of the mind that written language set loose, is reflected in the fact that during the second half of the sixteenth century, hundreds of separate editions of the Bible in various vernaculars were published across Europe, selling millions of copies.[5]

Catholic orthodoxy — and Latin scripture — held firm on the Iberian Peninsula, yet that place had been a first engine of profound change. Its long-established centers of learning, translation, and intercultural mixing had laid the groundwork on which the new thinking built. That flourishing was made possible by the *convivencia* of Jews, Muslims, and Christians, and the intermingling of languages. When Arabic, Hebrew, Latin, Greek, and nascent vernaculars influenced one another

("influence," from the Latin for "flow together"), culture was transformed, even if the new currents flowed mainly to the north. Linguistic
abundance sparked an explosive growth of knowledge. With Iberia as a
threshold, Europe was the beneficiary of Islamic learning (mathematics, Arabic numerals, architecture) and, through Arabic preservation,
of classical learning (Aristotle, Hippocrates, Ptolemy). Ironically, Islamic culture, which had inspired the literary majesty of Avicenna and
Averroës, Maimonides and Cervantes, was itself then channeled into a
literary backwater when Muslim reverence for the divine calligraphy
of the Arabic Qur'an — recall that God was regarded as present in this
text and could not be otherwise represented — led to the rejection of the
movable-type printing press. That amounted to a rejection of all that
the press ultimately enabled, especially mass literacy, a path to liberation as much for women as for men.[6]

We saw how Portugal and Spain had dominated the new sciences of
marine navigation (knowledge of celestial bodies, ocean currents, me-
teorology, mapping technique), which put them in the forefront of oceanic exploration. Prince Henry the Navigator embodied this. Therefore
Spain and Portugal were first to exploit the importing of gold and silver
from mines in the Americas and Africa, like Prince Henry's Elmina
in Ghana. But such mines were so labor-intensive as to require the
enslavement of aboriginal peoples on both continents. Whatever religious motive drove those first seafaring warrior monks — spreading
the Gospel? finding a sea route to Jerusalem? — the economic motive
determined the most important outcome. Chattel slavery, that is, inevitably followed from the European quest for treasure, and the long slave
history of the Ghana outpost emphasizes that.[7] Since it was forbidden
to enslave the baptized, natives were neither forced to convert to Christianity nor invited to. They were needed to bring lucre out of its hole,
and by the tens of thousands they did. So much for "Go forth and baptize all peoples." Religion once more turned against itself.
    Yet, in an unforeseen twist, the rapid importation of silver and gold
so enriched the Spanish and Portuguese that their economic motive for
home-based manufacturing and agriculture was undercut. The windfall
of mineral wealth enabled them to simply purchase what they needed
from beyond the Pyrenees. And so the financial success of Iberian exploration and discovery carried the seeds of a coming Iberian economic

impoverishment. Iberian *cultural* impoverishment would follow the abolition of *convivencia*, the final replacement of a mutually enriching tripartite culture with a stagnating univocal culture of an intolerant religion. Not unity so much as uniformity. The year 1492 would eventually prove, in its association with Columbus and with the banished Jews and Muslims, to have been Iberia's historic double-barreled disaster.

More immediately, the European encounter with the New World spawned the so-called Columbian exchange,[8] with Europe receiving stupendous benefits like corn and the potato, uniquely fertile crops that provided crucial new sources of nutrition for a burgeoning European population. Indeed, the soon ubiquitous potato accelerated that burgeoning. In exchange, the native peoples of America received, to take one bitter example, horses, which served mainly as military machines in contests they lost. America also received cattle and sheep, which — another bitterness — required the fencing of vast tracts for grazing, the European introduction of landownership. Mostly what Western Hemisphere indigenous populations received in the Columbian exchange, however, were viruses against which their immune systems were undefended, with the result that tens of millions of them died within the first generations of European arrival. The population of Mexico fell from 25 million in 1517, when Europeans first came there, to 1.5 million a century later.[9] Viruses notwithstanding, what gave the Europeans overwhelming dominance over aboriginals wherever they went was the technology of the gun, which enabled them to kill from a distance. (This in contrast to the success of Islamic armies that had extended sway from the seventh to the fifteenth century not through technological superiority but through focused motivation, their all-encompassing sense of oneness with God.)

In contrast to the Spanish and the Portuguese, the dominant motive of competing English and Dutch adventurers was not the acquisition of gold but the establishment of trade. Their colonial enterprises, still supported by the gun, were continually enriching — stimulating home economies instead of squelching them.[10] But that difference brings up the great cultural shift that occurred as all of this was climaxing in the sixteenth century: Europe's north-south schism, also known as the Reformation. The pursuit of trade, as opposed to the mere acquisition of gold, was reinforced by expressly religious ideas, especially those associated with John Calvin, whose thought had as much significance for economics as it did for theology. Where Luther had seen the sinful world as abandoned by God — *Deus absconditus* — Calvin saw the world as God's workshop, with God's people as the workers, whose task was, in diligence, to redeem it. So work, and not just the wealth it produced, was the point. Work and wealth together were the manifestation of God's favor. That the importation of gold into Catholic Spain involved little or no work for those enriched by it (as opposed to those whose labor dug it out of the earth) was itself a reason for the Calvinists of the north to disapprove it.[11]

The religious revolution — the "Protestant" break with Rome that began with Martin Luther in 1517 — was only the most blatant aspect of the profound recasting of the human mind occurring just then in Europe. Again the story could be told as one of religion's attempts to resist violence, suggested nowhere more dramatically than by Luther's fervent critique of the Catholic oppression of Jews, which, with the Inquisition, was then reaching a crescendo. Anti-Judaism had long defined Christianity's betrayal of its founder, and now, with a new emphasis on "blood purity," religious prejudice was being transformed into racism. Anti-Judaism was becoming something more venal yet — later to be called anti-Semitism. Luther saw that Christian attitudes toward Jews were wrong and dangerous. In 1523, he published "That Jesus Christ Was Born a Jew," rebutting the common notion that Jesus was not himself Jewish. Luther denounced preachers who blamed the death of Jesus on Jews, and he repudiated the idea that Jews were inferior to Christians. Remarkably, he argued that Jews were right to have resisted Christian efforts to convert them. Of all the Catholic sins he lambasted, none was second to the Church's sponsorship of anti-Jewish violence.

But in a classic instance of a by now familiar dynamic, all of this was reversed when Jews did not return the favor and embrace Luther's version of the Gospel. Pure rage was the result. In 1543, he published "On the Jews and Their Lies," one of the most anti-Semitic texts ever written. Luther advocated the burning of synagogues and declared that Jews should be "forbidden on pain of death to praise God, to give thanks, to pray, and to teach publicly among us and in our country."[12] Luther's "our country," of course, was the nascent Germany, and nowhere did his anti-Jewish demonizing fall more forcefully — and permanently — than there. In fact, Luther was repeating the age-old pattern. His diatribe came shortly before the Council of Trent, convened in 1545, which solidified the Catholic rejection of his reforms, a final defeat of his initial purpose, which had been to change the whole Church, not to splinter it. In defeat, he sought a scapegoat, and in the Jews he found one. Once more the religious impulse had moved from nonviolence to violence.

Luther gave intensely personal expression to a broader cultural ferment that, as in his case, began as an overwhelmingly positive manifestation of human creativity. The geniuses whose lives and thought overlapped in that critical period included Nicolaus Copernicus (1473–1543), who theorized that the earth moved around the sun, not vice versa, suggesting that humans were not the center of the universe; Michelangelo (1475–1564), who nevertheless located the spark of divine grandeur (the outstretched finger of God) in the human imagination; John Calvin (1509–1564), whose trade-igniting ideas would promote individualism, capitalism, and representative democracy; Giordano Bruno (1548–1600), a monk whose belief that the cosmos is infinite meant that God's omnipresence transcends the Church, and even the earth; Johannes Kepler (1571–1630), whose mathematical formulations supporting Copernicus developed a universal language of physics; Galileo Galilei (1564–1642), whose telescopic observations proved Copernicus's theory; William Shakespeare (1564–1616), for whom moral order was created not by God's judgment but by the dramatic ties of personal choice, its consequence, and a next, even graver choice; Thomas Hobbes (1588–1679), who saw self-interest as primal and proposed self-interested cooperation as a new ground of politics; Benedict Spinoza (1632–1677), whose rejection of God-sanctioned violence, in his groundbreaking *Theologico-Political Treatise,* recast both politics and religion; John Locke (1632–1704), whose faith in human reason was infinite, and infinitely catching; Isaac Newton (1642–1727), who combined observation, experimentation, and deduction into a systematic scientific method; René Descartes (1596–1650), who affirmed the self-aware person as the be all and end all of truth.

Of that litany, perhaps Spinoza, with his rejection of sacred violence *as sacred,* is key. He introduced the idea that the power of the magistrate and the conscience of the citizen were of distinct realms, which is why he separated them with that momentous hyphen in the title of his treatise. Spinoza's solution to the tension was to give primacy to state power over religious authority,[13] but the idea embedded in that hyphen would come to flower in liberal democracy and its linchpin, the separation of church and state. But the idea did not come to Spinoza out of thin air. Rather, it came to him out of the experience of an omni-directional magisterial abuse in the name of religion.

Born in Amsterdam, Baruch Spinoza was the son of Jewish refugees of the Inquisition in Portugal. His father's mother had been burned at the stake. He was himself investigated (and therefore threatened) by Inquisition spies. But Catholics were far from his only problem. He was regarded as an atheist by the Calvinist governors of the Dutch republic, which, not satisfied with banning his works, banished him. A synod of the Reformed Church denounced him as "a renegade Jew and the Devil." But then, his affirmations of God's immanence in nature, and his dismissal of the anthropomorphic God prevalent among Jews as well as Christians, made him persona non grata among his fellow Jews, some of whom denounced him as a pantheist, while others agreed with the Calvinists that he was an atheist. The Amsterdam synagogue, censuring his "evil opinions and acts," excommunicated him (which prompted him to change his name from Baruch to Benedict).[14]

Everywhere Spinoza turned, some state-sanctioned religious power imposed on his conscience. His rejection of that imposition was a one-man dress rehearsal for what a later age would call human rights. Spinoza was a palette of all the colors of intolerance, and his response to clashing absolutes, each of which claimed divine sponsorship, was to see through them all. In an age learning to be obsessed with fact, Spinoza's concern began and ended with what was left over after all the facts had been catalogued and defined. He refused to treat God as a fact, and equally refused to treat the mystery of his own inner life as a fact. *Mere* fact. These refusals made him a heretic — what the scholar Karen Armstrong calls "the first person in Europe to live beyond the reach of established religion"[15] — but also made him the most truly religious man of his age.

In a way, modernity's critique of religion began with Spinoza. What modernity would forget, though, was that its critique of religion, like Spinoza's, drew on the core values of the biblical tradition in which both came of age. Modernity invented an idea of religion of which the Bible knew nothing: a distinct human reality that exists in isolation from social organization, the power of the ruler, the cultural shape of daily life. The Bible assumes that God subsists in everything, but the Bible simultaneously so insists on the otherness of God as to define the piety of image-making as temptation to idolatry. Modernity's idea of religion, as we shall see, yields to that temptation.

That the human condition is rooted in mystery is its strength, not its weakness. Therefore every picture humans have of God, including the Bible's and the Gospels', falls short of God. This was the good news that, in Spinoza's day, the warring religious factions, each with its claim on God, did not want to hear. Similarly, the Bible so insists on the infinite innerness of conscience as to make it the place in which God meets each individual. Therefore, individual identity is sacred. The Bible assumes that history is going somewhere, which generated the peculiarly Western — and invigorating — idea of progress. That idea, in turn, led to innovations in social organization and technology that made progress real. And a biblical predisposition toward reason itself — since the Bible is nothing but reasoning about God — led to the triumph of reason both in politics (ultimately, self-critical democracy) and in the economic order (capitalism). Modernity's most fervent denouncers of religion, flying flags of "rights" and "reason," operated within an intellectual and ethical framework that was itself the product of biblical religion. But modern critics forgot this. That prophecy became secular did not make it less prophecy for that, even as the abuses of religion made prophetic critique more urgent than ever.

Post-Reformation Europe, in its clashing absolutes, was the assault on Spinoza writ large and made bloody. Overwhelming all of the era's creative invention was the brute reality of the most savage religious wars in history — or, rather, what are remembered as religious wars. Christians, as we saw, remember the story of Jesus and the early Church without the hyperviolence of the Roman war against the Jews — a war that in the first phase killed Jesus, and in the second forced church and synagogue to split. We saw how that Christian amnesia distorted the meaning of the Gospels, especially by casting Jesus' own people as his mortal enemy, with the Romans, by comparison, as his friends. Western civilization, that is, deflects its gaze from its primal source in violence and in the confusion about what that violence involved. As the Gospels tell a story of the Jesus people against "the Jews," as if the Romans were not a party to the violence, the modern memory does something similar in the way the Reformation conflicts are remembered.

In the post-religious era in which "enlightened" liberal states distinguished themselves from the primitive theocracies that had been overthrown, emphasis was always given to the religious element that defined so many of the savage European conflicts of the sixteenth and seventeenth centuries. Thus, the Bible-based polemic, with mutual excommunication and the odd martyrdom — or preacher-sanctioned massacre — thrown in, meant the wars were about irrational doctrine, not reasoned dispute over values that mattered. The murderous Reformation wars were taken to be fueled by abstract, if rude, theological disputation: abuse of indulgences, grace versus works, predestination, the proper number of sacraments, the celibacy of the clergy, the primacy of scripture as opposed to tradition, and so on. Wily Jesuits at lecterns in argument with Geneva divines in flying pulpits. Above all, the religious wars were between Protestants and Catholics.

Is that so? In fact, those wars were as much about shifting centers of economic enrichment and about emerging state powers — secular powers — as they were about doctrine. Catholic realms, like Cardinal Richelieu's France, fought side by side with Protestant ones, like Lutheran Sweden. The Thirty Years' War (1618–1648) reached its climax as a war between the Hapsburg Empire and the Bourbon dynasty, the two most powerful Catholic forces in Europe.[16] If the "religious" wars were thus misremembered, it served the interests of those doing the misremembering — mainly rulers whose discrediting of *all* churches served their own reach for power in what a later age would recognize as the birth of nationalism. By the nineteenth century, this dynamic would lead to claims that the modern state, freed from religious primitivism, had left irrational war behind. If a modern state went to war, whether it was the Union against the Confederacy, democracies against the empires in World War I, or, for that matter, the Soviet Union against its own people, it was a rational war of necessity by virtue of its being secular, not religious.

But modern memory fails to do justice to the threshold "religious wars" of the sixteenth and seventeenth centuries for other reasons. For one thing, the agony and despair of those years transcended the capacity of any language to convey it. The wars were not remembered as they really were because no vocabulary existed to match the scale of suffering. An instinct for denial overcame the culture of multifaceted misery, yet the fact remains: the scale of violence was unprecedented. Beginning almost immediately after Luther's posting of theses, with the so-called Peasants' War in Germany (1524–1525), which resulted in the deaths of about 100,000 disenfranchised people, the Reformation involved an interminable series of brutal clashes.[17] Not only peasants, but princes, kings, queens, emperors, abbots, bishops, popes, and the rising burgher class all found justification for savagery in sanctified appeals to the will of God, even if implicitly the conflict had more to do with the incubation of new power centers than the defense of a fading Christendom.

In the popular memory, yes, on one side, Thomas More was beheaded for opposing Henry VIII's divorce, and yes, on the other, a goodly number of French Huguenots were massacred on St. Bartholomew's Day,[18] but those famous instances were neither exceptions nor particularly notorious. (Who today has heard of the 1631 Sack of Magdeburg? Yet that caused the slaughter of thirty thousand men, women, and children.) In fact, mayhem was general. A new social order was coming into being, with the nation-state, the market economy, manufacturing enterprises, the scientific method, and cross-border financial institutions. The political, social, and economic revolutions so underwrote the violence that it is shallow and misleading to think of these conflicts simply as "wars of religion."[19] But of course, doing that, emphasizing the villainy of religion, means that the political, social, and economic factors can go uncriticized.

But look. If the supremacy of the pope was questioned, so was the divine right of kings. If clergy could challenge bishops, tithing farmers wanted to challenge landlords. If the Bible could be printed in the vernacular, why could its evident standard of social justice not be applied among the literate believers who could now read it for themselves? For that matter, if Almighty God could become subject by entering into a covenant with God's people, why could a mutually agreed covenant not define the relationship between worldly ruler and ruled? If priests and kings were subject to the law, who was to rule over the newly empowered lawyers (like More and Calvin)? And what happened when those claiming the right to dissent from orthodoxy were then confronted with dissenters within their own ranks? When the state defined itself in terms of religious denomination (as after the Peace of Augsburg in 1555 and the Peace of Westphalia in 1648), what used to be mere heresy had become treason. An old hegemonic order (centered in the Hapsburg vestige of the Holy Roman Empire) was yielding in this era to a new, dispersed, and multifaceted order — which was inevitably perceived as a kind of disorder. Coming out of the Middle Ages, when all self-understanding was somehow religious, it was certain that the steaming fissures caused by these tectonic shifts in the cultural ground of Europe would fuel much conflict. Perhaps the last vestige of the way the medieval religious view shot through everything lies in how that conflict is remembered merely as "the religious wars" when they were about so much else.

The larger point is that the conflict that shaped modernity was un-relentingly extreme. Where before wars were a matter of the armies of princes fighting it out on the hilltops, while civilian populations kept to their chores in the valleys, now entire societies were enlisted in the fight, and the battlefield was everywhere. In the French Wars of Religion (1562–1598), Protestants fought Catholics and between two and four million people died. In the Thirty Years' War, usually defined as having been fought between the Protestant Union and the Catholic League, and raging from the Baltics to Spain and from the Netherlands to Austria, between four and seven million people died. In the British civil war (1641–1652), nearly 200,000 died in England, more than 50,000 in Scotland, and between 400,000 and 600,000 in Ireland. In related Polish and Ukrainian pogroms (1648–1654), more than 100,000 Jews were murdered in the name of Christ. The witch-hunting wars against women roiled Europe between 1560 and 1670, with sanctioned executions totaling between 40,000 and 100,000.[20] These numbers of violent deaths in the sixteenth and seventeenth centuries, accomplished mostly with knives, axes, pikes, and nooses, make the even larger totals of mass killings of the twentieth century seem almost benign.

When the religious element did come to the fore, the wars were noth-ing if not personal. Catholics stuffed pages of the Geneva Bible into the bowels of gutted Protestants.[21] Where they could, as in Ireland, Prot-estant armies engaged in what a later age would call genocide, killing hundreds of thousands of Catholic peasants village by village, one at a time — highlighting the peasants' loyalty to the Antichrist in Rome as jus-tification. The warrior God was said to be back, not only by the denomi-national disputants, but especially by those disapprovers who eventually would claim to be leaving God behind, which also enabled them to claim that, by comparison, their own, secular exercise of power was benign.

2. Separatists

And why would devout believers not want to get away from all of this? In March 1630, nearly halfway through the Thirty Years' War, a small fleet of vessels carrying about seven hundred people set sail from Yar-mouth, England, bound for the New World. Their flagship was called the *Arbella,* named for the wife of one of the group's leaders. These were so-called Puritans, and while they were dissenters from the prevailing practice and belief of the Church of England, their motive was not to reject it altogether. Rather, by establishing an exemplary community in an unspoiled land apart, they meant to offer an image of what the purified church should be. In this they differed from their predecessors, the so-called Pilgrims who had sailed into Massachusetts Bay a decade earlier aboard the *Mayflower,* a contingent not merely of separatists but also of rejectionists, zealots who aimed to have nothing further to do with the corruptions of the Church of England. What consciously offended both groups was not England's complicity in the orgiastic European violence of Christian against Christian. Indeed, the scale of wars waged across the continent depended on the nearly universal conviction that, however complex the hidden sources of political and economic dislocation, the social chaos was simply God's own chaos, the mode of God's redemption. But was there an unconscious impulse behind separatism?

The dissenters' overt objection to the Church of England, in fact, was that it was insufficiently reformed — in a word, too popish. Though Anglicanism had broken with Rome — famously beginning about a century before with Henry VIII's divorces — it had not broken with Canterbury. During the reign of Elizabeth I (1558–1603), Canterbury had found a kind of middle ground between the extremes of the Geneva radicals and the influential elements of the British aristocracy that remained more or less loyal to Rome. The English Church was understood to be "Protestant," but in its polity (the rule of bishops), its liturgy (sacraments, including belief in the real presence of Christ in the Eucharist), its prayer book (set prayers instead of spontaneous utterance), even its Bible (subject to episcopal interpretation instead of each believer being free to interpret for himself), Canterbury was all too Roman: impure.

This was not, as it is usually remembered, a simple matter of anti-Catholic prejudice, as if the Puritans were an oddball sect whose religiosity had spawned an untoward demonizing of the pope and all that smacked of his influence. As the midcentury civil war between Roundheads (for the short hair Puritans favored) and royalists would demonstrate, Puritanism was a mainstream English movement. Between 1620 and 1640, ahead of the civil-war showdown, around twenty thousand Puritans made the arduous journey to the Massachusetts Bay Colony,

a pilgrimage made out of profound conscientious objection. In this religious motivation, the New England settlers, traveling in family units
and making the break with their homeland, differed from the English
adventurers — mostly unaccompanied males — who were simultaneously establishing outposts in Virginia as traders and entrepreneurs.
The Virginia English, intending not a break but continuity, sought to
reproduce the way of life and culture they had left behind. The Church
of England, for example, would be firmly established there. With early
prosperity, and the eventual arrival of their families to Virginia, came
powdered wigs, satin breeches, and porcelain tableware, a necessarily
primitive aping of Elizabethan opulence that would have no equivalent
in bare-bones New England.

The Puritan objection to all things Roman was rooted in the single
most powerful, and least understood, current of the Protestant Reformation: toward the millennial fulfillment of God's purposes. And here
we come to the important point. The reform of the Christian Church
was nothing less than the precondition of the Messiah's return and the
prelude to the End Time and God's reign on earth. Protestant defiance
of an old order that, for nearly one thousand years — since Constantine,
even if Protestants were only vaguely aware of that history — had been
understood as willed by God was so dangerously extraordinary as to
require a compensating sanction, some testimony that this sacrilegious
revolt was itself God's will. That sanction was found in the first act of
Protestant rebellion, which was *to read the Bible.* The book that not
only justified but mandated the sacrilege, first, of Martin Luther, and
then of the mass of his followers, carried the decisive clue to God's new
will — and wasn't the clue exactly that span of one thousand years?

The Book of Revelation served as the Protestant handbook and military manual. "Then I saw an angel coming down from heaven holding in his hand the key of the bottomless pit and a great chain. And
he seized the dragon, that ancient serpent who is the devil and Satan,
and bound him for a thousand years; and threw him into the pit, and
shut it and sealed it over him, that he should deceive the nations no
more till the thousand years were ended. After that he must be loosed
for a little while."[22] With its bifurcated narrative of the cosmic war
between the forces of God and those of Satan, with Christ himself in
command of a slaughtering army, Revelation proved to be the justification that the rampaging rebels needed. The chronologies of the
text are mysterious and confusing — a thousand years here, a thousand

years there — but the timetable could be adapted to match tumultuous experience.

What needed more precision was the identification of the "ancient serpent," "Antichrist," "Whore of Babylon," "Beast of the Apocalypse" — and the Protestants knew exactly who that was. Luther had been quick to come to such polemic, especially in his masterpiece diatribe "On the Babylonian Captivity of the Church."[23] Both the Geneva Bible and the Westminster Confession explicitly identified the papacy as the Whore of Babylon. But when such epithets were hurled at Rome, they were not, as the modern ear hears them, mere insults, assaulting various corruptions. They were designations of a Bible-predicted Satanic presence in the world, the goal of which was to deceive Christians and lead them to eternal perdition. Roman Catholicism was the devil's strategy for "deceiving the nations" and defeating God. As such, its defeat justified every measure of blood, every scale of destruction, every act of slaughter. The Protestants were freeing the Church from its captivity, and each Christian from his or her damnation. The Reformation, then, was a redemption in and of history, accomplished by a new chosen people who, as of old, were summoned to wage the war of God.

John Calvin found the same justification in the Book of Daniel, which he called a mirror to the age. Daniel, as we saw, preceded Revelation by foreseeing an apocalyptic war, with the "Son of Man" in command of angelic armies. Calvin began as a man hoping for peaceful resolution to the Reformation's disputes — his *Institutes of the Christian Religion* is devoid of violent references — but his impulses, too, were ultimately defined by war. He called on his followers to be ready to die "to vindicate God's glory." And to kill. Calvin's idea of mitigating sacred violence was eventually epitomized in his preference of beheading heretics over burning them at the stake.[24] And the ever-growing mass of heretics deserved it. That "so great a multitude should willfully perish ... need not disturb us," he finally wrote with sanguine equanimity.[25] The apocalyptic impulse had once more come to dominate the religious imagination.

To the Protestants, with their devotion to the newly available (because of printing and reading) apocalyptic texts, "as of old" meant the time of Jesus, the time of his imminent return, but in fact they were giving expression to the millennial fever of redemptive violence, as the Crusaders had done a mere half a millennium before. As in the Crusades, such rivers of blood as the Reformation wars set flowing could have run on as they did only if sanctioned by God. A thousand years of violence would be followed by a thousand years of peace, and that very turning point had arrived. The destruction itself was both the necessary precondition and the signal of the Church's long-overdue purification and of the final establishment of divine justice and peace—the true millennium. The destruction itself therefore—to hell with all restraint!

This was a decidedly Protestant vision, but the Catholics, defending not the Whore of Babylon but the Bride of Christ, were more than ready to match the stakes of violence and raise them. And so it had been going for most of a century. But that led to an expressly Protestant problem: if this was the cosmic battle joined at last—angels against demons—why, after all this time, had the demons not been vanquished? That papal iniquity lived and continued to infect the whole Body of Christ was precisely the charge the seventeenth-century Puritans brought against the English Church. Canterbury's prayer books, sacraments, and mitered bishops were not just theological lapses; they were snares of the devil, and *that* was why they had to be rejected. The Puritans could also perceive the savage, if still indecisive, religious wars wreaking havoc across Europe as yet another act in the apocalyptic drama. If the four horsemen of the apocalypse—conquest, war, famine, and plague—had ever been set loose, it was then, and the brutalities of those horsemen were themselves prelude to and signal of the final coming of millennial peace.

In the Puritan vision, that climax of history would be accomplished by God's designation of yet a new chosen people, a biblical category that could animate and sanctify John Calvin's notion of the Elect. That theology was a far version of Luther's rejection of "works" for "faith," a conviction that certain persons are set above others by virtue of God's mercy—to be "holy and spotless and irreproachable in his sight."[26]

This Calvinist idea of election, when politically defined in the New World, would forever inform America's self-understanding, for better and for worse. But the first consequence of election was the vocation to a literal reenactment of the Exodus, a pilgrimage out of captivity, across the sea, into the wilderness from which they would come, at last, into a new Promised Land, which in God's providence had *just then* been made available. Once again, land was the seal of the covenant, the proof of election. The hook of land at the tip of Cape Cod, the verdant forests across the bay at Plymouth, the hills sloping down to a perfect harbor at Boston, the open expanse of unclaimed territory to the infinite west: "the land that I will give you." The Puritans could read the signs of the times, read them not as typology or analogy, the way earlier Christians might have, but as lived reality. They knew their scripture well enough to recognize that this chosen people, with the redemptive mission of saving the impure Church by rescuing its faltering Reformation for the sake of establishing God's reign on earth at long last—that this chosen people were themselves.

The New World was there for them. And the millennium went from being a mere phenomenon of time to being the place in which time would be fulfilled. *This place.* The New World Puritans were the remnant whom God had decided to pluck out of the "exterminating havoc" of Old World religious conflict, or as one of their leaders put it, the remnant whom God had decided "to save out of the general calamity" of Europe's savage wars—just as in the biblical age the Lord had rescued Noah and his clan by setting them afloat on the Ark.[27] "*This* is the place," the leader said, "where the Lord will create a New Heaven and a New Earth."[28] That leader was John Winthrop—another lawyer—and he was in command of the small fleet of vessels in train with the *Arbella.*

To enter into the imagination of those people, after months of crossing a storm-tossed sea, making for an untamed and threatening continent, what could possibly have given them the mettle to persevere? Only a transcendent purpose, a divine vocation—and that was what they had. In June 1630, shortly before they made landfall at Salem, Massachusetts (from which they would soon decamp south, to establish Boston), Winthrop probably delivered his famous sermon: "For we must consider that we shall be as a city upon a hill. The eyes of all people are upon us."[29] For Winthrop and his hearers, the "eyes" they hoped to edify included those of their fellow Christians back in England. They intended their settlement as a model of purified reform, aiming to be imitated at home. But the stakes of their mission had risen higher than that, and "all people" were its object now.

The "city upon a hill" was no mere metaphor for the Puritans. A citation of Jesus,[30] the image refers to Jerusalem—the paradigmatic city on a hill. Twenty-three hundred years before, the idea of Jerusalem, recalled by Hebrews from their Babylonian exile, had redefined the meaning of Israel, for whom, from then on, Jerusalem was home to the One God. When, sixteen hundred years before the Puritan voyage, Jerusalem was destroyed by the Romans, Jews reconstructed their faith around a remembered Jerusalem of the past, and Christians defined their hope as the heavenly Jerusalem of the future. In St. Augustine's fourth-century formulation, Jerusalem became the mystical, hidden "City of God," but in the Middle Ages, as we saw, Augustine's allegory gave way to the literal, with the earthly Jerusalem revealed again as the actual site of the death, resurrection, and return of the Lord. A cohesive Europe, aflame with millennial fever, came into being around the hoped-for recapture of infidel-occupied Jerusalem. The Protestant imagination was quickened in just this literal way.

If Islam never developed a spiritualized cult of the city to compare with what Jews and Christians did, that was because, after Saladin, Muslims never lost control of the physical place. Earthly dominance, in effect, meant the city, while remaining holy, could also remain mundane. Islamic consciousness jelled far more around Córdoba, Baghdad, Damascus, Cairo, and, ultimately, Istanbul than it did around Jerusalem. Mecca with its Ka'ba, around which worshipers swirled and toward which the Prophet had directed prayer—away from Jerusalem—formed the permanent center of Islamic religious imagination.[31] But for Christendom, Jerusalem, after being definitively lost to Islam in the twelfth century and repeatedly unrecovered by a succession of failed Crusades, emerged as the goal and goad of European longing, shaping the purpose even, when it dawned, of the Age of Discovery. As is evident from the already noted journals of Christopher Columbus, no one knew any longer where the physical city ended and the fancied one began. All they knew was that Jerusalem defined their every hope.[32]

Age in and age out, Jerusalem presented itself as the golden object of desire, until finally the Catholic vision was transformed into a Protestant program of action. Augustine's mystical scheme for the City of God, and his allegorical reading of the Apocalypse, were abandoned in favor of God's literal intervention in the city of man. The fullness of time had come.[33] The Puritans understood themselves, in stepping ashore at Massachusetts Bay, to be opening nothing less than the final chapter of salvation history. Their arrival meant the New Jerusalem would be established in the New World, an understanding that would serve as a permanent pillar of the American imagination.[34]

3. The God of Peace

American self-understanding gives pride of place to the Pilgrim myth, from Plymouth Rock to the City on a Hill, as a shining image of tolerance, pluralism, religious freedom, and liberalism. Oppressed for their beliefs in England, they came to America to assert the primacy of freely exercised conscience — the ground of democracy. In part, the myth braces the American imagination for the simple, mundane reason that New England intellectuals, who claimed biological and emotional connection to *Mayflower* and *Arbella* antecedents, dominated the nation's historiography for its first two centuries, drawing a straight line from the Puritan settlers to American democratic liberalism.[35] But the myth took hold, celebrated with Pilgrim rituals every Thanksgiving and serving as the most important expression of the nation's cultural consensus. And why not? The myth, featuring generous friendship between Europeans and native peoples, is irresistibly humane, while also being somehow divine.

The settlers' self-image as the new chosen people retracing the Exodus sojourn from oppression to liberation informed even the deist imagination of Thomas Jefferson, who, when asked to design a national seal in 1776, proposed the figure of the Red Sea parting ahead of God's people.[36] "We Americans are the peculiar, chosen people," as Herman Melville would put it with rare succinctness most of a century later, showing how deeply into the American psyche this goes, "the Israel of our time."[37] Reflecting such God-commissioned destiny, John Adams wrote in 1765, "I always consider the settlement of America with reverence and wonder as the opening of a grand scene and design in Providence for the illumination of the ignorant, and the emancipation of the slavish part of mankind all over the earth."[38]

The contradictory clue there, of course, is the word "slavish." The first African slaves arrived in North America in 1619, brought by Dutch traders to Virginia a year before the *Mayflower,* and nothing in what those first English dissenters believed would inhibit the denigration of either Africans or the heathen native peoples who welcomed them. Indeed, the ancient pattern, much noted, repeated itself as the Pilgrims solved the inevitable problem of discord among themselves by means of external projection — the scapegoat mechanism. That first generation of New England settlers had to be a frightened, insecure company, given the threats that surrounded them in that wilderness. Previous New World settlements had failed and disappeared precisely because what Thomas Hobbes called the "war of all against all" had gotten the better of them. But the Puritans found it possible to do with their fear, and their own violent impulses, what surviving human societies had been doing since prehistoric times. They channeled such fears and impulses onto some "other."

John Winthrop was a master at nurturing the cohesion of his beleaguered company by identifying the surrounding Indians as God's enemy. "God hath cleared our title to this place," he wrote, justifying anti-Indian violence.[39] When a devastating smallpox epidemic, caused by European viruses, struck the Pequot people, Winthrop happily defined it as God's intervention. In 1636, when four hundred Pequots were massacred by a Puritan raiding party, its commander, William Bradford, said, "It was a fearful sight to see them frying in the fire . . . but the victory seemed a sweet sacrifice."[40] Sacrificial violence, as of old, was being rediscovered as a path of renewal. Matching the infidel Indian "enemy outside," Winthrop was quick to identify heretical enemies inside, targets within the Pilgrim community onto whom a generalized spirit of tense hostility could be thrust — and discharged. This was less *E pluribus unum* than *Contra pluribus unum*. Once again, uniformity trumping unity. Contrary to any notion that Winthrop was leading an experiment in religious tolerance is his record of brutal enforcement of Puritan orthodoxy among the settlers who repeatedly elected him as governor. Indeed, religious dissent in Boston was soon defined as a capital crime, and the heart of Boston Common was given over to a gallows — in effect, the place of paradigmatic sacrifice.

In the estimation of the great historian of Puritan New England Perry Miller, John Winthrop "stands at the beginning of our consciousness."[41] But so do those who resisted him. The strong countercurrent to Winthrop's apocalyptic messianism was begun rather quickly. Of tremendous importance for the present narrative is the fact that it was started by women. The first was Anne Hutchinson, who arrived in Boston with her husband and eleven children in 1634, only four years after the *Arbella*.

Every sectarian movement, born in the absolute claim of righteous dissent, must face the built-in problem of its own dissenters. In that era, perhaps it was no accident that among the first challenges to Massachusetts Bay Company authority came from members who had no share in it — females. As Bible believers, the Puritans blamed the woes of humankind on the wife of Adam. Women were the font of sin. Some divines wondered if women even had souls. Anne Hutchinson said yes. She objected to the ways in which Puritan preachers interpreted scripture and began to bring her own Bible to the otherwise mundane gatherings of women. So while women, in their chore circles, shared the tasks of butter-churning, child-tending, spinning, weaving, and sewing, Hutchinson invited them to think aloud about their own religious beliefs. Informal and accidental, these sharings soon took shape as Bible study groups, which the male establishment immediately condemned. The contest between Puritan leaders, especially John Winthrop, and Anne Hutchinson was conducted as if the questions were religious. Yet there were two equally determinative questions: the place of women and the role of power. In 1637, Winthrop condemned Hutchinson for conduct "not befitting her sex," and in 1638, she was formally tried for the crime of "traducing the ministers."[42] Guilty as charged, she was banished from Massachusetts.

Hutchinson's fate in Boston might have been different — even more woeful — if the rigidness of the Bay Colony had not already been challenged by one of its most powerful members. Roger Williams had been a prominent Puritan in England. He was trained as a minister at Cambridge, had served as a tutor to John Milton, and had defied his prominent Church of England father over religious questions. In 1631, he made the journey to America, settling as the minister at Plymouth Plantation. But his preaching was informed by reactions to what he found, and was immediately controversial. If the Bible began as the rare narrative told from the point of view of the powerless, the scapegoated, and the sacrificed, Williams instinctively reclaimed that legacy, rejecting religious violence on religious grounds. In that, he embodied the momentous character of religion as a mode of resistance to violence that echoes throughout the history in this book. He condemned the use of violence against native peoples, and also argued that they should be compensated for the land that had been appropriated from them. When challenged over such views by the plantation magistrates, he denied that they had any authority over his inner religious convictions, or over any member's. "Soul liberty" was his watchword. He argued that the Church existed to protect this liberty for each individual. He wanted "a hedge or wall of separation between the Garden of the Church and the wilderness of the world."[43] Soon enough, Williams was insisting that the Indians, too, had souls — and, heathen or not, they had the right to liberty of their own.

In 1633, Williams was forced to leave Plymouth, and he went to Salem. But his assertions in favor of Indians and of the rights of conscience were no more welcome to the north of Boston than they had been to the south. Further, the defense of his own soul liberty had become expansive, as he saw ever more clearly that the rights he was claiming for himself belonged to every person. He took what had to be received as a truly outrageous position: "I commend that man, whether Jew, or Turk, or Papist, or whoever, that steers no otherwise than his conscience dares."[44]

In 1635, the ruling council of Salem condemned him for having "broached and divulged diverse, new, and dangerous opinions."[45] Indeed. Williams was not so much a prophet of what might be called, anachronistically, civil liberties, as he was an objector to intrusions on conscience of *all* public authority, without offering prescriptions of how that authority could defend conscience. His omnidirectional objections to magisterial command took on the flavor of anarchism, and so his banishment is not surprising. Nevertheless, he planted seeds of more than he knew. With a dozen friends, Williams left Massachusetts, heading south. Once clear of the Bay Colony's authority, following the principle he had already preached, he purchased land from the native peoples he encountered and established what would be the Providence Plantation and the colony of Rhode Island.

In 1644, the year Rhode Island was formally established, Williams published the work that would make him immortal in America, a treatise entitled "The Bloody Tenent of Persecution." Our theme finds its summary and significance in the opening proposition: "First, that the blood of so many hundred thousand souls of Protestants and Papists, spilt in the wars of the present and former ages, for their respective consciences, is not required nor accepted by Jesus Christ the Prince of Peace." Williams goes on to argue, through a dozen similar propositions, that persecution for "the cause of conscience" is never justified; that "officers of justice" are "not judges, governors, or defenders of the spiritual"; that the "permission of conscience" is granted to all; that the "sword" is not to be used against them. Williams seemed to understand both the implications and the dangers of the nascent American self-identification as the new chosen people, which led him to declare that "the state of the Land of Israel" is merely "figurative and ceremonial, and no pattern" for any "civil state in the world to follow." Nor did he shy away from the great theological implications of his argument, acknowledging first that "God requireth not a uniformity of religion," since, as history was even then showing, that would require the "destruction of millions of souls," and, second, that Christians must therefore "disclaim our desires and hopes for the Jew's conversion to Christ." That renunciation, for reasons made clear in Chapter Four of this book, cuts to the quick of every kind of Christian intolerance and violence.

Enforced religion, in sum, violates God's will. Violence in the name of God is unholy. Magistrates or civil powers who act otherwise "sin grievously against the work of God." The implication of all this could not be clearer: the civil and the religious realms must be kept distinct. "Magistrates as magistrates have no power of setting up the form of church government . . . and churches as churches have no power of erecting or altering forms of civil government." The magistrate owes even false religion "permission and protection," if not approbation, because what the magistrate is protecting is not the falsehood but the person who, in conscience, believes it. Civil authority exists to protect the conscience of citizens, period. All of this Williams asserts in the name of "the God of Peace."[46]

That Roger Williams understood the full meaning of what he wrote in 1644 is implied by a detail of the charter establishing the colony of Rhode Island that was granted in that same year. He had accepted as his partner in applying for that charter the fugitive from Boston Anne Hutchinson, whom he had welcomed to Rhode Island in 1639. Alas, before the charter was granted, she had moved on to territories farther south, where Dutch settlers were in vigorous conflict with native peoples. Hutchinson and all but one of her children were slain by Indians in 1643, in the area around the present-day Bronx.[47] But because of her partnership with Roger Williams she is the only woman credited as a founder of any of the American colonies.[48]

Indians were not alone in killing English women. In 1641, a law was passed in England making witchcraft a crime punishable by death, setting up the war against women that would arrive in Salem a generation later. But first, expressly anti-female violence came to Boston, in the story of what happened to one of Hutchinson's fellow Bible studiers, Mary Dyer. She, too, had been banished from Boston and had found refuge with the Williams settlement in Rhode Island. But in 1652, she had returned to England, where her life was turned upside down by the preaching she heard. The preacher's name was George Fox: "When the Fox preaches, then beware your geese!"[49] To Mary Dyer, the compelling

Fox was expressing all that she had already been through. From Fox, Dyer heard nothing less than a new language.

The English civil war had climaxed with the regicide of King Charles I in 1649, and was now approaching its bloody denouement. Hundreds of thousands had been slain over the previous decade, and Fox was giving vent to a visceral rejection of all that had made that possible. The mass killings were politically charged, royalists versus republicans, but the river of blood was driven by questions of religious cults and sacraments, prayer books, the authority of clergy, and the ownership of churches. The sheer scale of carnage led Fox to reject it all, no matter how it was justified or explained. Instead of arguing over which sacraments were valid, he said no even to baptism. Instead of a ministry, he proposed that every member was the minister, including every woman. Against controverted texts in worship, Fox declared that the only worship God wanted was silence. In silence each member could be attuned to his or her "inner light," what an admiring Walt Whitman would call "the deepest, most eternal thought latent in the human soul."[50]

Religious questions inevitably opened out into political ones. Fox and his followers made their repudiation of religious violence plain by rejecting all forms of war and committing themselves to refuse any service in war. Where other Christians made appeals to the warrior Christ of the Book of Revelation, Fox preached the Jesus of the Gospels — not a milquetoast, but a man strong enough to turn the other cheek. "All bloody principles and practices we do utterly deny . . . ," goes the Fox movement's formal Peace Testimony, originating in 1660, "with all outward wars, and strife, and fightings with outward weapons, for any end, or under any pretence whatsoever, and this is our testimony to the whole world . . . The spirit of Christ, which leads us into all Truth, will never move us to fight and war . . . neither for the kingdom of Christ, nor for the kingdoms of this world."[51]

The Fox critique of power was made real by the refusal of his followers to bow, salute, doff hats, take oaths of allegiance, or make any other gesture of subservience. Those who responded to the preaching of George Fox called themselves the "Friends of the Truth," which soon — because the operative rule was "Simplify! Simplify!" — was shortened to the "Friends." Fox regularly opened sermons by calling his listeners to "tremble at the word of the Lord," which led to their designation as "Quakers." Not surprisingly, they were often arrested, condemned, and beaten. When they were seen answering such abuse with the resolute nonviolence of a turned cheek, their movement only grew.

Mary Dyer carried the message of the Friends back to Massachusetts, returning in 1658. When the Bay Colony outlawed the Friends, she protested. Banished, she refused to stay away. She returned to Boston and preached the Friends message of peace and inner light on the Common. In 1660, for defying the law, she was arrested, tried, and convicted. She was escorted by the authorities back to the Common from which they had chased her, only this time it was to be hanged. John Winthrop, who had personally presided at the trial of Anne Hutchinson, deriding her as "an American Jezebel,"[52] was dead by the time of Dyer's execution, but he'd have approved, and would have welcomed the "eyes of all" who beheld it. Such was the City on a Hill.

But the Friends movement did not end, either in England or America. In England, one of those drawn to the Quakers was a man of immense wealth and influence, William Penn. He befriended George Fox and protected him, calling him "civil beyond all forms of breeding." Penn had been a close-up witness to, and even a perpetrator of, the religious violence of the civil war, serving as a young soldier in Ireland, where Catholics, having been slaughtered by the hundreds of thousands, were still in need of subduing. His role in a brutal occupation army unknowingly prepared him for his attraction to the illegal meetings of Friends that were taking place not far from his barracks in Cork. It was there that, at age twenty-two, in 1666, Penn declared himself a Quaker.

Like others, he was arrested, and disowned by his family. Eventually he and his father reconciled. The elder Penn, having guessed right in whom he backed during the civil war, had influence once the restoration of the king had taken place. When, with his father's sponsorship, William Penn proposed a mass emigration of the troublemaking Quakers, King Charles II promptly agreed and gave him the land grant in America to make it possible. Penn was named the "absolute proprietor" of a vast, unsettled tract of interior territory, West New Jersey, which would become known as Sylvania, and then Pennsylvania, named not for Penn but for his father.

What Penn called the "holy experiment" of the Quaker settlement, dating to 1682, differed markedly from the Puritan settlement of New England.[53] In Massachusetts, the so-called King Philip's War — which one scholar has dubbed "America's forgotten conflict" — was only recently concluded, with thousands of the children, grandchildren, and cousins of those natives who had welcomed the first Puritans to Plymouth having been slaughtered.[54] Like Roger Williams, William Penn did not accept the Calvinist principle that only those who "cultivated" land and "improved" it could count as owners, and so the Indians in Pennsylvania were compensated for territory the Europeans began to cultivate. There would be no significant violence between Europeans and Indians while Quakers controlled the territory.[55] That territory was so large (45,000 square miles) that, when violence among settlers threatened ("human nature being what it is"), a solution could be found in the simple act of moving west—an example of geographic nonviolence among Americans that would form a powerful pillar of the national imagination, providing assurance to America's founders that they could escape the curse of European-style border wars.[56]

Unfortunately, the Quaker commitment to treat Indians fairly would not make the journey west, nor would the American sense of infinite expanse—what a later age would call *lebensraum*—as the solution to war. Yet for a time something golden happened. In Pennsylvania, persecuted minorities, war rejecters, and dissenters of all kinds were welcomed. They included Huguenot refugees from Catholic France, Mennonites from Switzerland, Amish from Germany, Jews from Catholic Brazil, and even Catholic refugees from various Protestant realms. A city could be named for "brotherly love"—and left deliberately unfortified—and no one would laugh.[57] The Friends would continue to generate an American countercurrent, marked by nonviolence and tolerance. Its tide would rise and fall over the years, but it would never cease to flow. It was at the Quaker meeting in Philadelphia, to take the most potent example, that the movement to abolish slavery in the United States began, a full century before it spread to and picked up force in New England.[58]

By far the most lasting legacy of the reaction to the Puritans' City on a Hill theocracy, however, was Roger Williams's notion of the strict distinction between the magistrate's power and the citizen's conscience. Williams's notions would only slowly define an American consensus: a hundred years after his death, the president of Yale College would refuse the donation of a library from a Rhode Island merchant because the colony founded by Williams was "schismatic."[59] Yet the separation of state power from religious belief as envisioned by Roger Williams, eventually taking form in the Bill of Rights provision that the federal government "shall make no law respecting an establishment of religion,"[60] is the single largest turn in the story of sacred violence in the West since the partnership of state and church, always implicit in the unitary cultures of premodernity, was established by Emperor Constantine in 319 and institutionalized in the Crusades.[61]

Indeed, the magistrate's first duty is to protect the citizen's freedom of conscience, which means the magistrate must of necessity be religiously neutral. No state coercion of conscience, period. Ultimately, this breakthrough in polity traced back to Augustine's distinction between the two Cities; to the *convivencia* of Jews, Christians, and Muslims in Iberia; to Galileo's insistence that faith must be subject to experience; to Spinoza's Amsterdam escape from religious oppression by Catholics, Protestants, and Jews alike; to John Locke's revolutionary idea of "toleration" as "the chief characteristic mark of the true Church"[62]; and to Descartes' affirmation of individual selfhood. For all such European antecedents, and numerous others, however, it was in America that something new took flight: a critique of religion *in the name of religion* that led to unprecedented political structures. The American creed began, after more than a thousand years of religious wars, with the long-overdue promise of being a religion of peace. All that is properly cherished as the American idea began here. Once again, humanity had come to a hopeful and unexpected turn in its story, as a nation began to provide the coherence and even the transcendence — God's mode of acting in history — that had once belonged to the now disqualified Church.

But the story yet again showed its tragic aspect as, ironically and equally unexpectedly, America's exceptional idea then aggrandized itself as an exceptionalism that would make it more millennial, more utopian, and more dangerous than ever. America, that is, joined Christianity itself in a condition of self-contradiction when the chosen people became the chosen nation.

4. Return to Jerusalem

What was it that they wanted? Those English settlers, and their ever more "American" progeny, swore, in effect, that they would not give up until, this time, the heavenly city was built on earth. Jerusalem had long been a defining point of reference for apocalyptic Christians — but that would nowhere be more so than in the New World, where at first the *New* Jerusalem had seemed so close. The reenactment of the Exodus journey, an entry into a new Promised Land; the purification of the Reformation impulse, and the act of separation from the religious wars of Europe; the establishment of a model community of faith, which, by its example, would bring about God's kingdom on earth. The name for all of this was — Jerusalem!

Even before John Winthrop's 1630 "City upon a Hill" sermon, this was reflected in the name those who preceded him had given the harbor settlement toward which the *Arbella* sailed as Winthrop declaimed the vision. Upon arrival four years earlier, they had adopted the Indian name for their settlement, Naumkeag. But in 1629, they had rechristened it Salem, which is how Jerusalem is first referred to in the Bible.[63] This was no mere memorializing of an Old World city, as the 1620 naming of Plymouth had been, but a gesture toward the literal realization of the Puritan vocation. *The covenant of God had passed from the Hebrews to the English colonists.* As the colonists fell to disputing among themselves the meaning of their vocation, that covenant kept passing, and so did the name. Within a few years another, purer town named Salem was established not far away, in present-day New Hampshire. Some who followed Roger Williams to Rhode Island made the point of their departure from Massachusetts by naming their community Jerusalem, showing that they meant to build it right.

But what was to follow when, despite every attempt at purification, it did not happen? The old apocalyptic problem showed up again. Recall that Christianity began in the disappointment that Jesus — identified with the "Son of Man" in Daniel — did not return to establish the reign of God. Periodically across the centuries, millennial hopes were dashed, and if America was conceived in such hope, it makes all the difference that America was born in reaction to the defeat of millennial hopes. Decades passed after the Puritan city was first set upon its hill, and as the early discord with dissenters showed, and as a later decline in apocalyptic fervor — what Puritans called "declension" — continued to display, Jerusalem was not built. Nothing dramatized this more than the way Christians back in England, far from being edified, ignored or denigrated the New England colonists. But even in Boston, within a generation of its founding, more than half of the citizens were not affiliated with the church.[64] By the end of that first century, about a hundred years after Winthrop's sermon, preachers took up the question of what could only seem like a religious failure. The new Exodus had decidedly not led to the New Jerusalem.

But instead of adjusting the primal idea, the preachers returned to it. God had not failed to keep the new covenant. Like the prophets of old, the preachers chastised the people with the harsh fact of *their* failure to keep the covenant. Typical of such preachers, and greatest among them, was Jonathan Edwards (1703–1758), who is remembered mainly as the maestro of hellfire and brimstone.[65] His work, including the significantly titled "Notes on the Apocalypse," was central to a dramatic revival of fervor in the colonies, the so-called Great Awakening, what Perry Miller characterized as "a social revolution that profoundly modified colonial society."[66] If there was a religious return here, however, there was also a political reversal, for the biblical theocracy of the Puritan settlers was now reimagined, in part because the well-educated ministers were steeped in the classics, in republican categories that owed more to Greece and Rome than to ancient Israel.

After a century of the devotional and aesthetic restraint of Puritan Congregationalism, religious gatherings convened by bevies of traveling preachers took on the heat of ferocious emotional extremity — the felt dread of hell, the intimate nearness of the redeeming Christ, the absolute power of individual conversion, all of it undergone in the presence of others who were likewise being transformed. This was an outbreak of an American version of the old fever. *God is coming! The end is near! Our common response to this call will enable it to happen! This is not just about the Church, but about the nation we are founding!*

Such a group experience far outweighed individual piety, and a new form of purposeful American ritualism was born, one that would be reflected as much in political rallies and national festivities as on the sawdust trail of Christian revivalism. A felt experience of something higher — God, the commonwealth, the nation — enabled individuals to surrender themselves to a group loyalty, a loyalty felt as both political and sacred. "The traditions of Protestant covenant theology and republican liberty," as Robert Bellah observed of the phenomenon, "were joined together."[67]

As the Great Awakening spread west from New England to New York, Pennsylvania, and the Western Reserve of Connecticut (later known as Ohio), and south along the Atlantic seaboard to the tidewater colonies of Virginia and the Carolinas, this fresh manifestation of the ancient phenomenon of "collective effervescence" would prove to be a crucial element in the unification of diverse American colonies. A refreshment of apocalyptic expectation meshed with the growing disenchantment the colonials felt with the mother country, and soon the urge to break the tie with Britain was taken to be a divine command. The defeat of the tyrant king began to be discerned as defeat of the Antichrist. London was joined to Rome as the Whore of Babylon.

In this preacher-promulgated religious expression, the American Revolution began. Its ideology was more complex than what clergy invoked, yet this fervor was central. Once more, a sense of God-sponsored violence for the sake of an ultimate and lasting reign of peace — "republican eschatology"[68] — took hold of what was now becoming the *national* imagination. American colonists embraced, as if for the first time, the providential mandate to change world history, but they did so in a way that broke free from the narrow denominational identity of their Puritan forebears. Still Christian, and still apocalyptic, this religious-political current, which the historian Nathan Hatch has called "civil millennialism,"[69] prepared the heretofore divided colonies to come together in a broad-based public piety that prepared them not only to break with England, but to set out on the road toward what, a priori, had to be reckoned a suicidal war against the king.

Even adjusted in this way, the original Puritan understanding of a New World messianic vocation continued. The chosen people, the chosen nation, the millennial saviors of mankind — this would be America, and what pointedly symbolized that destiny was the way in which the idea of Jerusalem remained the touchstone of the greatly awakened American imagination. If in the seventeenth century a handful of Puritan settlements were named for the holy city, in the eighteenth and continuing into the early nineteenth century, as the redeemer nation expanded, more than twenty towns and cities were named Jerusalem, from Vermont to Georgia (each of those states has to this day two Jerusalems); from Ohio (three Jerusalems) to Maryland (four). New York has a town named Jerusalem Corners, while Ohio and Pennsylvania each have a place called New Jerusalem. Across the United States today, 61 towns are called Zion (from Zion City in Alabama to Zion Crossroads in Virginia), with dozens of simple "Zion"s everywhere else. Meanwhile, 127 towns and cities, in more than half the states, are called Salem, almost certainly the most common place name in the nation.[70] If today's residents of the various American Zions and Salems are vague about the connection to their namesake in Israel, that was decidedly not the case with the revival-minded founders, most of whom, from 1628 to the early 1800s, chose those more than 200 surviving American place names to declare themselves, in a new manifestation of Jerusalem fever, as servants of God's decisive intervention in history.[71]

5. Temple Roots

In the pre-Revolutionary period, in addition to the great religious awakening, the American colonies were also alive to the thought of Locke, Hume, Hobbes, Rousseau, and Voltaire, even if it was mediated through a relatively small intellectual elite. The founding scriptures of the new nation, from the Declaration of Independence, to the Constitution and Bill of Rights, to the Federalist Papers, would be rife with Enlightenment ideas that included a resounding critique of the "malignant influence," in James Madison's phrase, of religion-based intolerance. As these thinkers broke apart the ancient union of religion and the broader commonwealth of which it was an inextricable part, they were, in effect, inventing the divide between secular and sacred. Indeed, they were inventing a standalone phenomenon called religion. The purpose of this invention, naturally, was to hem religion in, or even to reject it. But the purpose of *that* was to imbue the thus liberated state with the transcendent significance that formerly belonged to the Church.

"Miracles or Prophecies might frighten us out of our wits; might scare us to death," John Adams would write, "might induce us to lie, to say that we believe that 2 and 2 make 5. But we should not believe it. We should know the contrary."[72] The intellectual and religious compromise between the new rationalism and the old religion was deism, affirming a supreme being but without theology, claiming the virtue of belief but without a creed to define its orthodoxy. Thomas Jefferson would edit the superstition and irrationality out of the Gospels, and would be left, in his *Life and Morals of Jesus of Nazareth,* with a banal handbook of moral uplift.[73] The "Creator" to whom Jefferson deferred in his Declaration of Independence was the undefined God of nature, not Adonai, Yahweh, or the Holy Trinity. New England Congregationalism, what was left of fierce Puritan belief, was spawning the offshoot Unitarianism, which would be caricatured as the denomination that believes in "at most" one God. The continuing influx of settlers from the various and distinct cultures of Europe meant, equally, that in America, as nowhere else just then, faith was becoming *faiths*. In a marketplace of religions, individual choice — "conversion," "born again" — emerged as decisive, which further glorified the invented self over the received community. In strict opposition to the Old World, religion in the New World was less given than chosen. And American religions responded to this new condition with active proselytizing and missionizing. The circuit-rider preacher was born, and so were the "astonishing varieties of religion created in America and duplicated nowhere else."[74]

The skeptical rationalist Thomas Paine could sell half a million copies of his *Common Sense* in the years immediately before the Revolution.[75] Yet not even deist skeptics were ready to jettison God, nor were they prepared to forgo affiliation with an institutional tradition that offered language and ritual for the mystery of life. They liked to emphasize that the religion of old from which they were liberating society was a source of irrational and wicked violence, while they took for granted that the violence of the nonreligiously defined state was, by virtue of its distance from religious justification, virtuous.

A curious form of the dual impulse to reject old doctrinal forms and continue the self-aggrandizing engagement with life's mysteries emerged in a shadowy new group that took shape in the early eighteenth century in Scotland, England, France, and ultimately across the European continent. Known as the Freemasons, they associated themselves with the ancient builders of the Temple of Solomon. God was the "Great Architect of the Universe," and the prescribed dimensions of the Jerusalem Temple, given in Exodus, Leviticus, and Deuteronomy, display God's engineering expertise. That the Temple rooted the imagination of what amounted to an anticlerical attempt to break free of traditional Christian religion demonstrates the power of the subliminal currents we have tracked in this book. Jerusalem fever, in effect, went secular.

The Masons drew connections to the medieval Knights Templar, who, as we saw, had been suppressed in the fifteenth century. The secular resurrection of the Freemasons was a facet of the broad cultural war against the Roman Catholic Church, and the Templars' suppression was of great importance to the Freemasons. The last grand master of the knights, recall, was Jacques de Molay, who'd been burned at the stake in Paris, and now de Molay emerged as a Freemason hero. The French king banned the Freemasons in 1737, and a year later the pope announced that any Catholic who joined the order would be excommunicated.[76]

The secret society, embraced by men who identified with reason, nevertheless embraced all manner of illuminati mumbo-jumbo, beginning with its name. The Freemasons claimed to be descended from the free or superior guild of masonic craftsmen, those entrusted in ancient times with cosmic secrets of creation's primal architecture. The elaborate symbology[77] of the Masonic movement — compass-and-square, eye-and-pyramid, geometric forms — implied a claim to mystical knowledge of the inner structure of the cosmos, the custodians of which were those "free masons," a medieval elite. (No matter that, as we saw earlier, the name is a mundane corruption of *frères masons,* the brother masons, a rank among the warrior monks who supervised the building of Templar fortresses.)[78]

Boston and Philadelphia became Freemason centers, and the secret society took hold among American aristocrats and Revolutionary leaders, including Benjamin Franklin and George Washington. At the latter's direction, the District of Columbia, precisely ten miles square, was originally laid out according to Masonic formulas. It may be that the Boston Tea Party was a Masonic adventure. Perhaps a third of the signers of the Declaration of Independence and Constitution were Masons. Supreme rationalists and rejecters of revealed religion, disdainful of the revivalist awakenings that were sparking such enthusiasm among the less lettered colonists, the Masons nevertheless had their occult rituals, secret handshakes, oddball vestments, headgear, and "temples." The initiation rite required new members, in a parody of Jesus' resurrection, to undergo a death and rebirth, blindfold and all. A man (and Masons were only male) could feel simultaneously liberated from superstition and licensed to engage in it — an irresistible self-contradiction. In the decades after the Revolution, the movement took off, with something like 100,000 men joining Masonic lodges all over the United States.[79] Without knowing it, these fraternal chums were paying tribute to the power of the very stream of culture — religious, violent, primitive — that they prided themselves on having left behind.

Ironically, the Enlightenment aggrandizing of the individual, and its essential alienation from the core intellectual history of western Europe, centered in Christian theology, philosophy, and iconography, would have its counterpart in the revivalist religion that swept America during and after the Revolutionary period.[80] Revivalism, of course, was a reaction against the modernizing forms that openly denigrated or even demonized religion, though revivalism could be seen to confirm the rationalist critique. We saw that the Great Awakening began before the 1776 Revolution, but its second phase opened around 1800, when solitary frontiersmen took to gathering at revival campgrounds. In such isolated places, rituals of orgiastic spirituality salved the rough-hewn men and women whose backwoods lives had left them desolate and lonely. People had begun crossing the Appalachians by the tens of thousands, and then by the hundreds of thousands — a mass deracination. Enthusiastic religion, characterized by an ultrasupernaturalism,[81] proved to solve the American problem. Revivalism, often led by farmer preachers, became a national form. Commonly called "exhorters," these preachers were ordained not by churches but by their own ecstatic enthusiasm — not for the Gospel, exactly, but for the creedless idea of it. By 1840, there would be more than 40,000 such preachers at work, one for every 500 people.[82] They would invent a peculiarly American form of the sacred, and, owing to the untamed context within which it arose, violence would be essential to it.

The more preachers turned the Bible into what Harold Bloom calls "an inerrant icon, the limp leather Bible as object, hardly even as Scripture,"[83] the more pious believers were set adrift, on their own, in sects more than in churches, relating mainly to the friendly, risen Jesus with whom they could go for walks. In campy hymns they could chat with their Lord. The friendly Jesus was the solution to frontier friendlessness. "A religion of the self burgeons, under many names, and seeks to know its own inwardness, in isolation. What the American self has found, since about 1800, is its own freedom."[84]

Here is the true origin of that peculiar freedom that defines the national ideal — a freedom from social obligation, from history, from orthodoxy, from the requirement to submit fresh experience to the test of what humans have learned before. This was a religion that could brace a nation that was constantly rediscovering itself in the poignant solitude of the next frontier. Because the frontier was as physically dangerous (involving, among other hazards, the retaliating Indian populations that were being moved ever westward by the tens of thousands) as it was emotionally trying, it helped that the quickened religious esprit included a cult of God-licensed self-defense. God and the gun would find each other, a uniquely American sacramentalism that engendered what Bloom dubbed "the troubling near identity between the religion of violence and the violence of religion."[85] It is this combination that made the American soul, in D. H. Lawrence's phrase, "hard, isolate, stoic, and a killer."[86] In most parts of America, God and guns are together still.

6. Jerusalem Marchers

The public show of devotedness, in combination with an increasingly private understanding of what it signified, became the mark of American religion, and it stamped nothing so much as the political doctrine of the separation of church and state. The virtues of that separation are evident, and in our appreciation of Roger Williams's innovation we have already noted them. State power and religious zealotry, joined in coercion, make a deadly combination. But for all of the virtues of church-state separation, this tradition would have two profoundly negative consequences.

Because matters of religion would be kept in a realm apart, the zone designated as private, the kinds of human development nurtured in the public square would not find a hospitable niche in religion. In America, for example, the task of education would increasingly belong to the consciously nonreligious sphere — a good thing in itself, but unintended outcomes followed. Public schools and publicly supported institutions of higher learning set the tone and standards for education generally. In fact, public education in America would have an unmistakably Protestant stamp until the mid-twentieth century, but that, too, would be purged for the important reason that the consciences of pupils must not be even implicitly coerced by government-sponsored initiatives. All instruction in religion, as well as exercises of religion like prayer, would be banned from public classrooms.[87]

Meanwhile, church-sponsored religious education — Sunday school — would be overwhelmingly focused on children, resulting in an infantilization of belief. Bible stories yes, biblical criticism no. This would lead to a widespread religious illiteracy,[88] and not even those educated in religiously affiliated private (parochial) schools would be exempt from it, since they, too, would suffer from the corrupting sacred-profane dichotomy. Most secular Americans would be too ignorant to know how this lack in their education would undercut them, while relatively few American believers would ever be offered significant religious instruction by their faith institutions. Thus church-affiliated people, to take only one example, would accept too easily the canard that science and religion are necessarily in conflict, while scientists would condescend to religious traditions that produced science in the first place (Copernicus was a priest).

The result of all this would be a population that takes for granted the methods of historical and critical thinking in all other areas of life while remaining intellectually immature when it comes to religion. The unconscious assumptions of belief would go forever unexamined. Science, meanwhile, would regard ethics as a subspecialty instead of as an all-encompassing way of thinking. The a priori assumptions of science would alone be exempt from the obligation to submit all knowledge to the test. Such bifurcated thinking is why the core subject of this book—how religion and violence advance each other—has been so far beyond the competence or interest of most public criticism. That biblical ideas of apocalypse, to stay with a key motif, have underwritten most American warmaking is neither understood nor addressed to this day. Religion as an invented realm apart is understood to be a source of intolerance and violence, while the nation—and all things secular—are seen as intrinsically tolerant and, unless unjustly provoked, peaceful.

But the separation of church and state had a more immediate, and more immediately negative, consequence—and that consequence would be apocalyptic. Because the private realm of church was taken to be exempt from public challenge, represented by the authority of the state, the single largest moral question of the new American nation went unasked—that of the claim of some persons to have ownership of other persons. The explosive growth of intensely private religiosity, leading to singularly American religious forms, matched the growth of chattel slavery in the United States. The uncontested individualism of the pietist denominations—especially Baptists, Presbyterians, and Methodists—reinforced the frontier nation in its refusal to intrude on the individual or the individual's conscience. That sacred, fenced-off interiority was increasingly described not in the theological or philosophical categories of tradition, but in terms of each believer's personal relationship with Jesus. The most sacred realm of that refusal, as American selfhood was literally defined by the act of staking claims to pieces of the ever-expanding supply of land on the frontier, had to do with what came to be known as property rights.

In 1780, there were 2,500 Christian congregations in the nation; by 1860, that number had grown to 52,000, vastly outstripping population growth.[89] The number of slaves in the United States, meanwhile, went from around 600,000 in 1780 to about four million in 1860. Christians were divided on the morality of slavery, but slave owners readily found justification for ownership in their creeds.[90] For Thomas Jefferson and other slaveholders, the "wall of separation" between church and state meant that the government had no business in regulating, or passing judgment on, the private affairs of property owners, which is why he could argue during the 1789 Constitutional Convention for the continuance of chattel slavery.

Jefferson reckoned slavery as wrong ("I tremble for my country when I reflect that God is just, that his justice cannot sleep forever"), but he could not bring himself to support a government-mandated end of it when, compared to what followed, it would have been relatively easy to do so. The tragedy of timing, of course, is that slavery was not fully embedded in the economy of the South before the invention of the cotton gin by Eli Whitney in 1793. That unpredicted leap in the technology of cotton processing required a much larger number of manual laborers. Once the entire economy of the cotton-growing South — and the textile manufacturing North — was dependent on the institution of slavery, it could not be changed by the mere votes of lawmakers.

In 1831, an apocalyptic Christian took the matter into his own hands. A Methodist "exhorter," or lay preacher, he had been carefully instructed in the scriptures by his grandmother.[91] The rhythms and imagery of the Book of Revelation were second nature to him, and, as it happened, the millennial enthusiasm of what would be called the Second Great Awakening was at full tide across evangelical America. From Oberlin, Ohio, to Rochester, New York, to Nashville, Tennessee, the evils of alcohol, penal abuse, and corruptions of the government's spoils system were roundly denounced by preachers, but the heretofore avoided beast in the American sanctuary, chattel slavery, was finally drawing notice as well.

Had slaveholding America lost its status as God's new chosen people? Had it gone the way of the faithless Israelites? Was the Armageddon reckoning at hand? Could the United States, in which so many individuals were undergoing the rebirth of a new baptism in the spirit, itself be reborn? As this particular Bible-preaching exhorter saw the thing, the corruptions of the mystical Babylon were now epitomized by the brutalities of the slave nation, and the time had come when an avenging messenger of God would bring about slavery's end. For him, the question went beyond morality or politics; it was a matter of life and death. He, too, sensed the imminence of the End Time and felt compelled to act on it.[92]

He was a broad-shouldered man in his thirties, marked with scars from the kick of a mule and the whip of a slave master. The vision that was to make him the scourge of the abomination of slavery could not have been more explicit. "I heard a loud voice in the heavens," he reported, "and the Spirit instantly appeared to me and said . . . I should arise and prepare myself, and slay my enemies with their own weapons."[93] The first of those weapons was the broadax with which he had done his work in the fields, and the first against whom he swung it was the sleeping Travis family in Southampton County, Virginia. Striking in the middle of the night on August 22, 1831, he killed the Travis mother, father, and children, including the twelve-year-old boy who was his legal owner.[94] Then, accompanied by perhaps a dozen other slaves, armed with hoes and axes, he set out on the Barrow Road, heading for the county seat, where he believed there was an arsenal of the guns and ammunition that would enable their rebellion to succeed. Defeat was unthinkable.

"I saw white spirits and black spirits engaged in battle," he had prophesied, "and the sun was darkened—the thunder rolled in the Heavens, and the blood flowed in the streams—and I heard a voice saying, 'Such is your luck, such are you called to see, and let it come rough or smooth, you must surely bear it.'"[95]

It came rough. Along the Barrow Road, he and his comrades fell upon other farms, killing families as they slept—including some of the Turners, his original owners, the family that gave him his name. The plan was that the rebels would gather recruits to their band from among other slaves as they went, but as many slaves resisted them as joined them. The leader knew only that once they reached the county seat, they would be victorious. But white militias sprung up to stop them, blocked the roads, forced the rebels into hiding.

The revolt was quickly over, but rumors and reports of a slave insurrection went wild and wide. Panic spread among whites throughout Southampton County and beyond. Hundreds of slaves who had nothing to do with the rebellion were whipped and even killed for imagined acts of insolence. White women and children fled farms and plantations to take refuge in the county seat, huddling in and around the courthouse. In the end, about sixty Negroes had joined the revolt, and about as many whites were killed. The rebels may have had no real plan beyond their mystical sojourn on the road toward the main town of Southampton County, as if arrival there would be enough. In fact, there was no arsenal, no store of guns. Even if there had been, it is likely that few of the rebels would have known how to load and fire the muskets.

By the end of August, the rebellion was fully quashed, and the leader holed up in the woods. He eluded capture for two months. "It was plain to me," he reported, "that the Savior was about to lay down the yoke he had borne for the sins of man, and the great Day of Judgment was at hand."[96] At the end of October, he was captured. He was brought at long last to his fated destination — but in chains. While awaiting death in his cell, he dictated his "confession" to a white lawyer. He was hanged on November 11. His name was Nat Turner. The town toward which he set himself and where he was executed, the county seat of Southampton, Virginia, was Jerusalem.[97] And how could he not have believed?

After Nat Turner's rebellion, laws were passed across the South further restricting slaves, especially forbidding their education. Reading was proscribed, notably including the Bible, which, sanctioning the victim's point of view, had again proven to be subversive. Nat Turner was the strange fruit of the Reformation and its biblical literacy. Some states required that white ministers be present whenever slaves gathered to worship. The combination of involuntary servitude and millennial Christian enthusiasm was explosive, and in 1831 it was far from disarmed. The African-American historian and civil rights activist Vincent Harding sums up what the Nat Turner rebellion, and the subsequent attention paid to his "confession," set in motion: "So black struggle and black radicalism had no choice but to continue as an active, moving, relentless sign, forcing the issue of the nation's future, never allowing any of our God-driven, freedom-seeking, Jerusalem-marching fathers to have died in vain, pointing the way."[98]

CHAPTER SEVEN

Messiah Nation

1. Jerusalem and Exile

SO IN 1492 Christopher Columbus set sail with the hope of reaching a fancied Jerusalem by traveling west. And in 1492, practically on the same day, Jews were expelled from Spain, a reiteration of their ancient banishment from Jerusalem. More than a century later, English Puritans understood their New World settlement project as if they were Hebrews, establishing a New Jerusalem, the City on a Hill, transforming the Jewish curse of wandering into the virtue of American mobility.[1] At the time of those events, the real Jerusalem was a small, neglected backwater of Damascus, which was itself a province of the Mamluk sultanate at Cairo. The shrines of the holy city were neglected. Rampaging Bedouin tribesmen made trade and pilgrimage routes dangerous, choking off the city's economic lifeblood. The distant Mamluk overlords were indifferent to the place.

Originating as a military caste at the service of Saladin, who so famously routed the Latin Crusaders in 1187, the Mamluks had grown in power through subsequent Crusades, turning the Latins back every time they tried to retake Jerusalem. The Mamluks then consolidated their dominance of the House of Islam when they defended the Arabic realm from Mongol invaders in the fourteenth and fifteenth centuries, so that, as the sixteenth century dawned, Jerusalem, such as it was, remained theirs.

Something like 13,000 people lived in Jerusalem in 1500 (compared to between 80,000 and 100,000 when the first Roman war began in 70

CE[2]). Of that number, 10,000 were Muslim, with the rest about evenly divided between Jews and Christians. As it had been since the Latins were driven out by Saladin (and as it would be for most of a thousand years), Jerusalem was a predominantly Arab-Islamic town. The Christians of Jerusalem were mostly Arab also, adherents of Byzantine Greek Orthodoxy. The Christian community was organized around caring for the decrepit shrine of the Holy Sepulcher, commemorating both Calvary and the empty tomb — devotions carried out by the Orthodox in competition with small contingents of Latin Christians (mainly Franciscan friars), Ethiopians, and Armenians. Jewish observance consisted of gatherings at the Temple remnant, while Muslims made obeisances at the similarly neglected Al Aqsa Mosque and the Dome of the Rock. All three groups were dependent on the financial support of far-off religious sponsors. Jerusalem was affirmed as the center of the earth by one of Islam's most influential medieval mystics, Ibn Ali Ibn Arabi, but he offered that valorization from Damascus.[3]

Apart from the minor trades attached to the pilgrimages that survived banditry, Jerusalem had no viable economy of its own, which was why it was more or less left alone by the distant sultans. As long as the minority communities of Jews and Christians paid their taxes to the Muslim authorities, they were left to administer their own affairs, even as those taxes guaranteed their ongoing impoverishment. Jerusalem's Jews, Christians, and Muslims were alike in being less intimidated by one another than by the unchecked Bedouins, whose raids on the town were carried out without regard for religious affiliation.

The Jewish population of Jerusalem had increased somewhat when Sephardic refugees expelled from Iberia in 1492 ("Sephardic" comes from the Hebrew for Spain) had made their way back to Palestine. But relatively few Jews settled in the holy city itself, where Muslim and, especially, Christian hospitality remained constrained. Instead, a spiritual renewal of Judaism took hold from a nearby center in the hills above the Sea of Galilee, a town called Safed.[4] There, a trickle of refugees grew into a river, as thousands of uprooted Sephardic Jews arrived, and found it possible to stay. Through the sixteenth century, these Jews accomplished an intellectual transformation of the experience of exile by turning it into a metaphor for God's own experience. Exile from Spain, and other European realms from which Jews were increasingly expelled,[5] or the internal exile of urban ghettos into which they were then steadily corralled throughout Europe, gave Jews a renewed sense of their primordial condition as exiles from Jerusalem.[6]

For centuries, as we've seen, no matter where they were, Jews had prayed "Next year in Jerusalem," sustaining their religious identity around texts that kept King David's city rooted in the Jewish imagination. Indeed, those texts had coalesced as the Bible around the first experience of exile. "By the waters of Babylon," as Psalm 137 crystallizes it, "there we sat and cried as we remembered Zion." Every year on Tisha b'Av Jews fasted, shunned all comforts, and tore their clothing, signs of permanent grief at the final loss of the Temple and of Jerusalem, which was the seat of God's presence to Israel. But now the Temple was no longer the center of sacrifice and atonement, but of lamentation.

During the Crusades, when thousands of Jews were slaughtered in the Rhineland by cross-bearing mobs, the observances of Tisha b'Av were expanded to commemorate that catastrophe as well. Angels wept at the destruction of the Temple, and every destruction was folded into that one. Lamentation had replaced sacrifice in the Jewish religious imagination — but lamentation focused on the place of sacrifice. Longing for the return to Israel defined piety, and the daily prayer of Jews, from Poland to England to Arabia to North Africa, included prayers for rain across the hills of Judea, so that the olive trees would flourish while their tenders were away. Ever since St. Augustine, Catholic theology permanently mandated the absence of Jews from the Jewish homeland, their "wandering" as proof of the truth of claims made for Jesus, and Jewish religion had spiritualized that absence, turning grief into the pulse of devotion.

But now that changed. Jewish communities throughout Europe, especially west of the Danube, were forcibly dispersed again, and in one of the great — if not quite unprecedented — twists of Jewish history, the brutal condition of exile was reimagined as blessing instead of tragedy. Dispersal was taken as a new mode of God's presence to God's beloved people. Instead of the center of holiness being lost in the home that was left behind, holiness was understood as consisting in the condition of homelessness. Animated by this reversal, Safed came alive in the sixteenth century with dozens of synagogues and schools, an intellectually vibrant religious renewal that was propelled by a broad literacy enabled by the recently invented printing press.

In fact, Jews in Safed may have been the first people outside of

Europe to make systematic use of Gutenberg's movable-type device, a technique that allowed them to make widely available texts of Torah, Talmud, and the new commentaries. The printing press was regarded as holy; it was compared by Jewish sages to an altar.[7] The activity of study expanded, through printing, from an elite clique to the whole community, just in time for the massive theological innovation. The idea was that God himself had accompanied his people into exile—lately from Iberia, before that from Jerusalem, but even in the prehistory of a primordial catastrophic fall, known as *tsimtsum*. This theology made exile itself into something positive, the existential ground of the human condition. Thus the very creation was, as Harold Bloom summarizes it, "God's catharsis of Himself, a vast sublimation in which His terrible rigor might find some peace."[8]

This speculation was most associated with the figure of Isaac Luria (1534–1572), and it changed the meaning of Jewish hope by seeing life in banishment as a way to approach the self-banished deity.[9] God's exile, in Luria's scheme, consisted in the Creator's having been "splintered" into the material world. All that exists, exists in exile, and that "all" is nothing less than the Holy One, whose new home is the diaspora. Now, as Luria put it, God's people were charged with restoring God to the primal wholeness with which God had begun. God, renouncing omnipotence, had put himself at the mercy of what and whom he had made. God's creatures were his partners in God's own rescue.

This adjustment in the tradition posited not a single Messiah as the source of hope. Instead, the messianic renewal of the world—simultaneously the rescue of God—was the redemptive work of the whole Jewish people. *This* was what they were chosen to do. Peoplehood was never more to the point, which meant that even the scattering of the Jews became a condition of cohesion, not dispersal. Beyond tribalism or ethnicity, this spiritual bond became the basis for solidarity among Jews wherever they were. And now what made them a people was the study of Torah and Talmud—hence the importance of that printing press.

Rabbis had always studied the Torah, and the early commentaries that resulted from that study had been compiled in the Talmud and its self-multiplying interpretations. But beginning about now, "unhoused in the world [but] at home in the word," the Jewish people themselves had direct access to the sacred texts and great commentaries.

They broadly experienced their vocation anew. Jews would find, in the phrase of George Steiner, their homeland in the text.[10] At last the ancient People of the Book would become just that for the first time, as a new literacy and the availability of the printed book enabled Jews to prefer reading to plotting any actual return to the Holy Land. "Any place there is a library," as Steiner puts it, is "an 'Israel' of truth-seeking."[11] Jerusalem was still not forgotten, but it was reimagined. A Jew could return to the holy city and reenter the Temple by studying.[12]

Of emphatic importance is the way in which this positive vision overturned the apocalyptic vision, first articulated, as we noted, in the books of Daniel and Maccabees, which foresaw destruction as a path to cosmic redemption. Lurianic Kabbalah, as it came to be known, foresaw not destruction but healing, rooted in the study of Torah and Talmud and in acts of loving mercy. Each such act of faithfulness (*tikkun olam*) would contribute to the reconstitution of the shattered cosmos, an ingathering of the shards of creation to enable nothing less than the return to the wholeness of God. This affirmative religious vision spread from Safed and, through books, took hold of the Jewish imagination throughout the diaspora (especially in Poland and Ukraine), and eventually came to flower in the rich religious tradition of Hasidism in central Europe. Still, the memory of the homeland and the promise of return to "terrestrial Jerusalem" somehow remained a "linchpin of the axis mundi."[13] God remained the God of Israel, and Israel remained centered in the unforgotten Temple and its city. But for the first time in a millennium, the prayer "Next year in Jerusalem" could be uttered without grief.[14]

The Jewish cult of Jerusalem had been mystified and also detached, for the Jewish people now understood their epic of return as contingent not on some external breakthrough by a savior figure, but on their own works of study, kindness, and justice. Thus even the Messiah took second place to Torah, the lighting of Shabbat candles, the observance of mitzvot, and prayer — all of which defined the Jewish home here and now as the home of God. Such spirituality lessened the pain of being separated from the remembered city, and eased the longing for return. And its affirmation of the created world as composed of sparks of the divine stood in marked contrast to the contemporaneous, ever more apocalyptic visions of Protestants and Catholics, both of whom — Reformation and Counter-Reformation — saw the world in negative terms, as an occasion of sin to be fled, worthy of its being doomed.

2. The Printing Press and Ottoman Jerusalem

The instrument of Reformation, and all that followed from it in the West, was Gutenberg's invention — the decisive technological breakthrough that enabled the new knowledge of the Renaissance to spread rapidly and widely through Europe.[15] Luther would not have been Luther without it. In October 1517, he nailed his provocative "95 Theses" to the cathedral door in Wittenberg, a traditional way to publicize academic argument at the time, but given the limits of who would pass by the cathedral door, such argument was always local. What made Luther's act Continental, and therefore revolutionary, was the fact that the theses were immediately reproduced as broadsides on printing presses, with thousands of copies in quick circulation.

Luther published a New Testament in German in 1522, sparking a revolt against Latin, undercutting the clerical monopoly on scriptural knowledge, and making the sacred text widely available, beginning the era of popular literacy and vernacular languages. In the five years between Wittenberg and the German New Testament, hundreds of thousands of copies of Luther's works in German were sold, and his movement was launched. It was unstoppable.[16] The printing press was an empowerment machine, ultimately producing democracy as well as broadsides, pamphlets, and books. In a last-ditch effort to maintain control of sacred texts and clerical power, the papacy attempted to require the licensing of printing presses, but it was too late. In short order came William Tyndale's New Testament in English (1526), which, as we saw, was taken over more or less whole by the King James Bible (1611), which was itself nothing less than the language of William Shakespeare.

For Protestants, the Bible superseded the Church as the ultimate authority, but Catholics, too — which is to say all of Christendom — were changed by the sudden democratization of knowledge, which would, among so much else, bring about the end of Christendom. When the Catholic Galileo's observations of celestial bodies were published in 1613 as *Letters on the Solar Spots,* they bore out the heliocentric theory of the Catholic Copernicus, who had written his *On the Revolutions of the Heavenly Spheres* in 1543 — but the point is that the work of Galileo, despite the papacy that tried to squelch it, was truly published — made public, given to the people. And at issue in the Church's dispute with Galileo was less a question of astronomy than the people's right to read, and understand, sacred texts for themselves.[17] The scientific era began when many people embraced the new thinking that had previously been the thinking of a few. And not just thinking, but reading. The train of thought then left the station, headed for modernity—Copernicus to Kepler to Galileo to Newton to Descartes to Hobbes to Kant to Locke to Jefferson to Darwin to Freud to Einstein. Europe's cultural, artistic, political, religious, intellectual, economic, industrial, scientific, and imperial explosion was ignited by the printed book.

If 1517 was decisive for Europe, it was also decisive for Jerusalem, for that was the year the Ottoman Turks conquered the city, wresting control from the Cairo-based Mamluks. Beginning when Luther began, the Ottomans would rule Jerusalem for exactly four hundred years, until 1917. That beginning was bright with promise. The Turks—having captured Constantinople sixty-four years earlier, their climactic sweep into Syria and Palestine, and from there down to Arabia, and across North Africa as far as Algeria—represented what might have marked the start of a Muslim version of the European Renaissance. Under the Ottomans, after an Islamic decline embodied in Egypt's narrow Mamluk militarism, the Arab-Muslim genius that had long shown itself, from Baghdad to Córdoba, in inventions of mathematics, astronomy, language, and philosophy, could be revivified.

The Turks had burst upon history in about 1300, a warrior tribe moving west from the far plains of Anatolia. For more than two hundred years their expansion had gained in momentum, sophistication, and, in absorbing Islamic fervor, the spiritual energy that had made the continuous spread of Islam the most important fact of history since the fall of Rome.[18] The Turks mastered the latest in military technologies—artillery had enabled that victory at Constantinople—and naval science. By the sixteenth century, Ottoman slave galleys and corsairs dominated the Mediterranean. When this formidable power turned toward Palestine, it seemed at first that a reinvigorated Islam would sponsor an *actual* New Jerusalem.

The first Turkish ruler of Syria and Palestine was Selim I (sultan 1512–1520), who also took control of the holy cities of Mecca and Medina. Selim was nothing if not an innovator. After centuries during

which the various sultanates[19] had rejected a unified spiritual authority, he, and then his son, restored the universal caliphate under the Ottomans (recall that "caliph" means "successor" to Muhammad). Islam
had a spiritual center once again, symbolized by the sacred sword and
mantle of the Prophet, which Selim brought from Mecca to Istanbul
(where they can be seen today at Topkapi Palace). Selim's consolidation
of power was so thorough that the dynasty he established would rule
the Ottoman Empire, and the caliphate, for four hundred years, an unbroken succession of thirty-six of his descendants.[20] Yet Ottoman rule
turned out to be what one historian calls "a profound tragedy for all the
Arab-speaking peoples of the Middle East."[21]

Of all of Selim's successors, the most competent was his son, Suleiman I, also known as the Magnificent (1520–1566). Inheriting the title and power of sultan at the age of twenty-five, he wore the turban,
small beard, and thin mustache that became the clichéd image of the
Turkish ruler, but there was nothing ordinary about him. Suleiman was
well educated, and taking off from his father's triumphs, aimed to repli-
cate the sway of Alexander the Great. Suleiman personally led military
campaigns against the Serbs, Bulgarians, and Hungarians, pushing into
Austria, where he began a long siege of Vienna. Only in 1529 were his
armies decisively defeated there, and, as it would turn out, that defeat
marked the high-water mark of the Ottoman Empire in more ways
than one.[22]

Ruling from Istanbul[23] through a palace bureaucracy, and depending on an elite corps of janissaries, the sultans would maintain an or-
derly hold on their vast empire for centuries. The Ottoman system
of governance reflected a humane ministering to the basic needs of
subjects, but it also involved the funneling of tax revenues from the
far distance to the Sublime Porte, as the ruling elite became known, a
name derived from one of the lavish gates in the Topkapi Palace, which
perched above the most storied stretch of water on the globe. Lavish-
ness, more than power, became paramount, and the sultan's rule was a
matter less of sovereignty than suzerainty.[24] Subdued opponents, like
the Mamluks in Egypt, became vassal subjects, maintaining limited
power in their locales. With the empire organized according to ethnic
and regional divisions of labor and power, intended to produce taxes
rather than economic, political, or technical innovation, what began as
the vital center would become stultified. Minorities would survive, or
even thrive, as long as they paid their taxes. One notable consequence

of this policy was that the Ottoman Empire, over the centuries, would be uniquely hospitable toward Jews.

But Ottoman leadership would be detached from the sort of intellectual and industrial inventiveness that was then changing the shape of European trade, craft, science, and culture. The Sublime Porte was attentive to the latest technology in weaponry, but in little else. Suleiman's descendants would be as close to omnipotent in their own sphere as a ruler could be, but that sphere would grow ever narrower. A small patrician elite would dominate a vast population of the powerless — the opposite of what would occur in Europe, where a creative middle class was beginning to emerge. The sultans became notably uneducated, increasingly isolated, and therefore easily manipulated by courtiers and janissary leaders who became the real rulers of the Ottoman Empire.[25]

It did not begin that way. Suleiman's main object, in addition to military conquest, was to reinforce the spiritual legitimacy of his Istanbul caliphate. His religious motive was authentic, but it had a practical aspect. He understood very well that his political sway as caliph over rival sultans depended solely on his religious standing. Istanbul itself embodied the reach of his ambition, his sights set westward across the Balkans and northward beyond the Black Sea, but the city posed a problem for the tradition-bound House of Islam. To have transferred the sacred heart of the Prophet's faith from Mecca to Damascus or Baghdad or Cairo — as had occurred over the centuries — was one thing, but to move it, as Suleiman's father had, entirely away from the Arabic world, to the seam between Asia and Europe, to a metropolis that had teemed with infidel excess and idolatry for more than a thousand years, was quite another. Radical as Suleiman may have been politically and militarily, he had to be conservative when it came to the forms of Islamic devotion.

This explains his interest in Jerusalem. The fact is that Suleiman's most lasting achievement was also the most dramatic improvement in the physical makeup of the holy city to have occurred since Omar built the Haram al-Sharif, the Noble Sanctuary, in the eighth century. This was Suleiman's massive fortified wall with which he encircled the whole of Jerusalem. Two miles long, forty feet high, braced by thirty-four towers, and broken by seven gates, the city wall was built with remarkable speed, between 1537 and 1541. It still stands today, and after the Dome of the Rock, it is the most magnificent feature of the golden city. Indeed, the crenelated wall defines its most fantastic aspect. Offering protection to the residents of Jerusalem from the Bedouin bandits who had periodically caused them problems, the monumental fortification was nevertheless a folly, a construction suited to a bygone era. As a defensive battlement protecting against rival empires (as opposed to bandits), it was obsolete even before being completed — made so, as Suleiman would well have known, by the artillery that the Turks themselves had used to breach the similar walls of Constantinople. But that did not matter to Suleiman, whose purpose was more sacramental than military. His wall was a glorification of Jerusalem, pure and simple, proclaiming his piety for all the House of Islam to see.

So was his glorious restoration of the Dome of the Rock. It was Suleiman who, in the same years, transformed the octagonal façade of the Dome with the installation of the blue faience tiles and azure Iznik porcelain that make the structure shimmer to this day. The metallic glaze of heavenly blue, ringing the golden dome, still dominates the impression the structure makes from a distance, a sublime and otherworldly finish to the already renowned architecture. (The same tiles and porcelain would make the Sultan Ahmed Mosque — the Blue Mosque — in Istanbul legendary around the world, surpassing the Dome of the Rock's beauty, but that would be constructed more than fifty years later, when the legitimacy of the caliphate in Turkey was well established.) Suleiman also saw to the restoration of the ancient aqueducts supplying water to Jerusalem — and especially to the Noble Sanctuary, which was glorified with numerous fountains. These were not mere decorative embellishments, but essential for daily prayers, which began with ritual ablutions. Fountains were sacraments.[26] The entire Islamic world soon knew that Suleiman, the caliph from Istanbul, had raised the most important Muslim structure to a new magnificence.

Beginning with Suleiman and through most of the rest of the Ottoman era, "Jerusalem remained a focus of devotion, and was the recipient of considerable largesse from the central authorities" in Istanbul.[27] That largesse was a claim on religious legitimacy, and the reconsecrated (and bandit-protected) city did, in fact, begin to grow again.[28] As always, matching the actual city, the fantasy prospered, too. The golden image of Jerusalem gloriously enclosed by crenelated walls of gleaming white stone, with majestic gates and towers, abounding in fountains (where one could always see Jesus, as if sitting by the well), was precisely the picture that Puritans in America would soon conjure as the shining icon of their sacred purpose. What the Puritans did not know, nor did those who, as if by holy virus, caught their vision heading west across the American continent, was that this primal Jerusalem was created not by David, not by Herod, not by the Crusaders, but by the Turks.

Suleiman had another way of displaying piety worthy of the caliph, a far less fortuitous one for Islam, as it turned out, than his sanctification of Jerusalem. During his reign, and almost certainly under his influence, the Muslim world made what can be reckoned, from the point of view of the West, as its greatest mistake: the rejection of the movable-type printing press, the revolutionary significance of which we have noted. Other factors directed Islam down its distinctly different path into the modern era, like its adherence to the strict prohibition against usury, which blocked the economic flourishing of capitalism. But the rejection of mechanized printing was momentous.[29] This occurred in part because of the simple fact that the alphabets based on Latin and Greek—and, for that matter, Hebrew—are made up of block letters, while Arabic is a cursive script, depending on tiny dots for distinctions between vowels and consonants, making Arabic far more difficult to transform into type. But an even more important factor in the initial Muslim rejection of printing was the determination to defend the Qur'an from sacrilege.

A traditional understanding of the sacred text elevated the verses of Muhammad's "recitation" (recall that "Qur'an" means "recite") above all other expression. God is present in the words as they are spoken. Just as the Qur'an, as the eternal self-revelation of God, cannot be translated from its original language,[30] neither could the words of the Qur'an be rendered on the page mechanically. Recitation is the act of bringing God alive in the congregation, which is why Qur'anic reciters hold positions of prestige and power, but the spiritual power of the Qur'an is also conveyed through highly developed Islamic calligraphy, which is "more than just an art form; it is the visual representation of the eternal Qur'an, the symbol of God's living presence on earth."[31] Calligraphic representations of the sacred text were (and are) ubiquitous in the Muslim world, inscribed everywhere from the walls of mosques to mundane objects like rugs and lamps. God's speech is everywhere. Calligraphy and the typeset page were, in effect, from different planets, and it was the most natural thing in the world for the *ummah*, beginning with Suleiman the Magnificent, to reject the mechanical press. It would not have been lost on the caliphate that for a century after Gutenberg, the most commonly printed book by far was the Bible. No such vulgarization — sacrilege — would be allowed to happen to the Qur'an.

We saw that the democratic revolution that followed on the heels of the Reformation depended on printing, with Luther leading the way into the new world of expanded literacy. As Bible reading became the province of each believer, the authority of the clergy was undermined — which accounts for the papacy's early (failed) attempt to control the printing press through licensing. Revolutions in science, commerce, medicine, precision instruments, politics, philosophy, art, technology, and agriculture were accelerated, if not sparked, by the printing press. All that we mean by the Enlightenment and the Industrial Revolution followed — and so, too, Europe's ascendancy.

The year 1517, with Luther, marked the start of all this; it also, as we saw, marked the start of Ottoman rule in Jerusalem. But because, from that year, the unlettered Islamic world cut itself off from the new knowledge by what one historian calls "a self-imposed archaism,"[32] it would gradually slide into political, technological, and cultural backwardness. Jerusalem, even with its splendid wall, would once again become a backwater town in a minor, ever more impoverished province.

3. The Peaceful Crusade

And so it went until 1798, the year that Europe made its long-in-coming countermove against the House of Islam with the invasion of Egypt by a French force led by Napoleon Bonaparte — the first shot in what would be a drawn-out colonial war. Included in the vast store of supplies that Napoleon brought with him, besides icons of the Enlightenment like a portable scientific laboratory and a library of recent political and philosophical books, was a printing press with type in Arabic script.[33] Napoleon would not be the last European aiming to improve the culture and education of the "backward" Middle East.

But with Muslims throughout the region rallying to the Ottoman sultan, Napoleon's expedition would fail. His infantry would reenact the Crusaders' decisive defeat at the coastal city of Acre, in the far north of Palestine. The arrival of the French in the region sparked rage and fear in Jerusalem, with long-buried memories suddenly aroused. The city was ever more insecure, as well it might have been. Its decline matched the "decline of Faith and State"[34] that, apart from defensive military prowess, marked the Ottoman regime through the seventeenth and eighteenth centuries, when Suleiman's successors were most remarkable for their mediocrity. Where the population of Jerusalem had burgeoned after Suleiman, in the recent century it had fallen off to, by 1800, about nine thousand. Of that number, about half were Muslim, with Jews and Christians each making up about a quarter.[35]

The only notable religious violence to have occurred in Jerusalem for a long time had been violence among and between Christians. As if carrying on a Middle East version of the Protestant-Catholic wars that rent Europe in the sixteenth, seventeenth, and eighteenth centuries, Catholic, Armenian, and Greek Christians had, in the same era, bloodied each other periodically in disputes over the Holy Sepulcher—clashes that climaxed in 1757 in all-out intra-Christian warfare in the streets of Jerusalem. The Ottoman sultan, Osman III, imposed an agreement on the Christians, a division of turf and responsibility for the holy sites that holds to this day.[36] But the subsequent arrival of the French was taken by Muslims, accurately, to be a European avant-garde, and though Napoleon bypassed Jerusalem for the more strategic port city to the north, its riled Muslim citizens attacked churches and monasteries, and took monks as hostages.[37] That violence was short-lived, however, as the Jerusalem Muslim authorities ordered such assaults to stop. In fact, Christian and Jewish minorities were consistently protected in Jerusalem, even as European pressures on the weakened Ottoman Empire increased.

In 1821, for example, rebels in the Greek provinces, centered in Peloponnese and Crete, launched their war of independence against the Ottomans. As the Greeks pushed the Turkish line back toward the Bosporus, the Greek Orthodox Christians in Jerusalem, however much they might have sympathized with their coreligionists, were protected by Muslim authorities. "Do you not disturb the subjects, for they are faithful," the Jerusalem Islamic court decreed. "Evil done to them is a sin and an injustice against our God and our Prophet."[38] The pattern of Muslim tolerance in Jerusalem, that is, remained consistent despite the passage of time and regardless of conditions.

The vulnerability of the Ottoman Empire was inviting pressures not just from European powers but from within the House of Islam. On the Arabian Peninsula a Bedouin tribe, the Saudis, ousted the Turks to take over Mecca and Medina. The Saudis were practitioners of a puritanical form of Islam called Wahhabism,[39] and the campaign against agents of distant Istanbul was grounded in the religious project of restoring Islam to an imagined original Arab zealotry. The Saudis slaughtered thousands of their fellow Muslims as infidels, and it was not clear what Istanbul could do about it.

No sooner had the Greeks successfully established their independence than the Ottoman viceroy of Cairo began to imitate Athens, pressing Istanbul for regional autonomy in Egypt, if not outright independence. His name was Muhammad Ali, but he was no zealous fundamentalist. Wahhabism (like other fundamentalisms) can be understood as a reaction against the first signals of modernity, but Muhammad Ali's response to such signals was to try to understand them. No Wahhabist, he wasn't even an Arab. Born in what had been Greece, he was an ethnic Albanian, and as a young officer in the Ottoman army, he was sent to Egypt with the infantry that reestablished control after Napoleon was forced out. That the Egyptian populace was leaderless and dispirited offered an opening to a man of Muhammad Ali's spark and ambition. He took it, and his ascent to power in that fluid situation was swift.

Muhammad Ali was typical in having been raised as an illiterate, but he was unusual in understanding his ignorance as a handicap. At age forty, he learned to read. Whether in agriculture or industry or medicine or the military and naval sciences, he saw how far the Arab world had fallen behind what Europeans were achieving. He set out to correct that, and Egypt was where he would begin.[40]

He had seen firsthand the weaknesses of Istanbul's approach. His own delayed education was an illumination, and he systematically promoted education among his officers and soldiers in Cairo and Alexandria. He built on what the French had begun, and dispatched senior officials, and eventually young people, to Paris to study. He ordered the publication — through printing — of his government's proceedings, which would evolve into the first Arab newspaper. He took control of Egypt's disorganized agriculture, setting the stage for a Nile Valley boom in cotton (the word derives from the Arabic *qutn*) that would eventually rival production in the American South.[41] He laid the groundwork for a modern industrial economy. And he set out to expand the frontiers of his own suzerainty.

Muhammad Ali moved first against the Wahhabist Saudis in Arabia, and he defeated them, restoring the nominal authority of the Ottoman sultan over the holy province. He captured the Saudi tribal leader and sent him to Istanbul, where he was beheaded.[42] Next, Muhammad Ali moved against Syria, which meant that he first took over Gaza and Palestine. In 1831, he gained control of Jerusalem, which, because he was a modernizer and not a Wahhabist, would lead to the most significant changes in the city's character since the Crusades. Palestine would become a separate political entity, centered in Jerusalem and independent of Damascus or Beirut, for the first time in a millennium.[43] Embodying Muhammad Ali's wish for openings to Europe, the British were allowed to establish a consulate in Jerusalem, and other European powers followed. These diplomatic arrivals defined themselves as protectorates, European nations as self-appointed protectors of Jerusalem's religious minorities — as if they needed protection.[44] Even more momentously, with Muhammad Ali's permission, the first Protestant missionaries from America were given a foothold in Jerusalem, with the American consul coming in train as their protector — the beginning of what would be called "the peaceful Crusade."[45]

Without his anticipating it, Muhammad Ali's modernizing and Westernizing purposes backfired in two ways. First, for the people of Egypt and the Middle East generally, the experience of modernization would prove not liberating but profoundly alienating.[46] Second, Muhammad Ali's openness to the West intersected with — indeed unleashed — a force he could never have foreseen, which was the boomeranging return to the holy city of European and, especially, American religious zealots whose ambition was to reshape the city according to the Revelation myth. The first step in their goal of bringing the world to Jesus — or, better, of bringing Jesus to the world in his fiery Second Coming — was to return Jerusalem and Palestine to Jewish sovereignty.[47] Setting in motion a transformation in the physical character and religious meaning of Jerusalem that would define its politics and spirituality from then on, these evangelical Christians were "told by God" that the time was right to make real the apocalyptic fantasy of the heavenly city that was already reflected in the names of dozens of American towns, including Nat Turner's and Abraham Lincoln's.

4. Restorationism

The so-called restorationists got their name from the goal of restoring the Jews to their Bible-decreed role as rulers of Palestine and Jerusalem. "There still exists in the breast of every Jew an unconquerable desire to inhabit the land which was given to the Fathers," an expedition-launching preacher declared in Boston's Old South Church in 1819. With the return of the Jews to Jerusalem, and the reestablishment of the polity that reigned in Jesus' own day, the last condition for the return of the Messiah would be fulfilled, and everyone — Jews, Christians, Muslims — would see the light. "Every eye," the preacher said, "is fixed on Jerusalem."[48] A literal reading of the Bible spawned the belief that the Messiah's return would begin in the city, and that it was contingent on the prior return of Jews to their homeland — and their overdue conversion: *Salvation will come from Zion.*[49]

The preacher was Levi Parsons, a twenty-seven-year-old, well-connected New Englander, whose nephew and namesake would later become vice president of the United States. Taking off from Boston, Parsons became a leader of a Jerusalem movement ignited by the Second Great Awakening. From New England to the land beyond the Appalachian Mountains to the American South, wherever pioneers were naming their settlements for Jerusalem, Zion, or Salem, the idea of Christian missionaries commissioned to travel to the holy city, hastening the Second Coming, was irresistible. Thousands identified as restorationists, and sent Parsons off. Equipped with bundles of evangelical pamphlets and Bibles in numerous languages, and carrying bona fides supplied by Secretary of State John Quincy Adams (who declared, "I really wish the Jews again in Judea, an independent nation"), Parsons went to Jerusalem in 1821. Forbidden by Islamic law from proselytizing Muslims, and ignored by the Jews of the city, he was reduced to evangelizing the Catholics, Greek Orthodox, and Armenians. No one listened. Jerusalem shrugged. His fantasy punctured, Parsons fled Jerusalem for Alexandria, where, within months, a fever killed him.[50]

But Parsons had unleashed a missionizing current that would run from the United States to Jerusalem for much of the nineteenth century, influencing developments in the city but also transforming American religion, and American politics. The United States was a "spiritual hothouse,"[51] and we have already noted how explosively the congregational life of various evangelical denominations grew in the first half of the century. This hothouse produced a crop of attitudes that overgrew all boundaries of religion.

That the idea of the Jews being restored to Jerusalem appealed to the vast majority of American Christians is only part of the story. For one thing, this notion contradicted the ancient understanding, dating at least to St. Augustine, that Jewish banishment from Jerusalem was willed by God, with Jewish exile ("wandering") being a sign of the truth of claims made for Jesus. That this tradition was essential to Roman Catholic "replacement" theology—the unbelieving Jews having forfeited all claims on God's promises—made it all the easier for virulently anti-Catholic Protestants to repudiate.[52] For another, the idea of restoring Jews to their homeland squared with an ongoing Christian ignorance of the real situation of Jews, few of whom wanted to physically resettle Palestine, and an ignorance, for that matter, of Palestine, which was assumed to be practically unpopulated.[53]

But the most important aspect of restorationist thinking was its apocalyptic urgency, a bringing to fruition of the majestic sense of mystical purpose with which the Puritan settlers had arrived in the New World. These believers seriously assumed that the End Time was approaching, and that the American replay of Exodus was a divinely appointed instrument to bring it about. There is a direct line from the utopian higher calling of the City on a Hill to the idea of Manifest Destiny, a slogan coined in the 1840s[54] and usually associated only with westward expansion across the continent. But the American destiny, forever defined by Revelation, went eastward also, to the original City on a Hill. *Americans, that is, shared with a thousand years' worth of Christian forebears an irresistible, if by now almost wholly unconscious, urge to go to Jerusalem.* In numbers that would steadily increase in the course of the century, they did so—not mainly as tourists, but as agents of the End Time. Jerusalem was where the American-sparked end of history would first manifest itself. Restorationist missionaries who actually moved from the United States to Jerusalem began their days by ascending the Mount of Olives before dawn, so that at first light they would be ready to greet the Messiah when he arrived.[55]

In 1860, the number of Americans who voted in the presidential election was about one quarter of the number who went to church every

Sunday. Between a third and a half of all Americans were evangelical Christians—more than ten million people. They made up, in the words of Drew Gilpin Faust, "the largest and most formidable subculture in American society."[56] Apocalyptic restorationism was a mainstream American idea, and so was the obsession with Jerusalem. "So much has been said for generations of the Jews regaining possession of Jerusalem," a *New York Times* editorial commented in 1866, "that it is agreeable to think that they are likely to do so at last. They certainly deserve Jerusalem." Not only preachers were obsessed with the holy city. Leading figures in politics (William Henry Seward, William Tecumseh Sherman, Ulysses S. Grant) and the arts (Mark Twain, Herman Melville, Washington Irving, Ralph Waldo Emerson) would line up to make the pilgrimage. "America's Palestine mania," one historian dubbed it.[57]

And the greatest politician of the age felt it, too. Restoring the Jews to their national home in Palestine, Abraham Lincoln said in 1863, "is a noble dream and one shared by many Americans."[58] Lincoln, as is well known, was not a conventional believer, and he was certainly no evangelical Christian. But the very air he breathed was infused with motes drifting in the light of this religious vision, and it informed what he believed about his nation, what he did, and what he said, even if unconsciously. He had begun his adult life in New Salem, Illinois, one of those places named, whether he knew it or not, for Jerusalem. And that was only the start.

5. Abraham's Altar

The religious fervor of evangelicals was an essential part of the burgeoning movement toward the abolition of slavery, and as the crisis of 1860 built, a primary source of understanding and interpretation was the text of Revelation—the moral life defined by a deadly struggle between good and evil, building to a final battle. Preachers were the great articulators of the apocalyptic vision. In the North particularly, and in the border regions of Appalachia, there developed a sense of America needing to be born again, with the impending conflict culminating in the transcendent fulfillment of the nation's founding promise. The war would be Armageddon—the elimination of sin, the quickening of the American mission.[59]

But first, the war would be for Union. In order to recapture the mystical resonance of that word "Union," it is necessary to imagine the rush of the new national spirit that was gripping the century, or soon would be, not only in America but across Europe, from the French republic to Garibaldi's Italy to Bismarck's Germany to the subdividing Scandinavian realms. The nation-state itself was the great cause, the source of meaning, an ultimate value for which to live and die, and kill. That such a firm nationalist purpose had gripped Americans — in the North, to be sure, but also west of the Alleghenies — is surprising because of the intense regionalism of the ever vaster country and because less than three generations earlier, "secession" was taken to be an "inalienable" right. When, in 1776, thirteen colonies seceded from Britain, it was high patriotism, and a principle might be seen to have been established. But when eleven Confederate states declared their independence from the United States of America in 1861, the action was declared illegal, and a cause for war.

To be sure, Lincoln loathed the institution of slavery ("If slavery is not wrong, nothing is wrong"[60]), but to go to war over it? Britain had outlawed slavery in 1807 without violence. The importing of slaves to the United States had been made illegal in 1808. In subsequent decades, slavery would be eliminated by acts of legislatures of the European colonial powers and by Latin American nations. (Only in Haiti would it take a war to free slaves. Brazil, to which more Africans were brought as slaves than any other nation, would abolish slavery by law, not war, in 1888.) The month before Fort Sumter, Tsar Alexander II had issued an emancipation manifesto freeing the Russian serfs. It is impossible to know precisely what Lincoln's awareness of global trends toward slavery's waning amounted to, yet he would likely have understood that history was turning a page on involuntary servitude. However gradually and through whatever mechanisms of compensation, it was reasonable to expect that slavery in the American South would end. If it could be kept out of the new territories as the country expanded westward, there was hope that the existing institution would become uneconomical and morally untenable — which is why Lincoln had run for president in 1860 on a platform of limiting slavery, not eliminating it.

Lincoln was explicit in declaring that the purpose of the war was the restoration of the Union, not the abolition of slavery. Indeed, his administration welcomed the Crittenden-Johnson Resolution which said exactly that, passed by Congress within weeks of the war's beginning.[61]

But that changed. Within a year, since the moral horror of slavery was not at issue in the war, France and England, which were otherwise opposed to slavery, were lining up to support the Confederacy. Young Northerners made plain their reluctance to join a fight that would leave slavery intact. And Lincoln's generals wanted to recruit freed Negroes for the fight.[62] Factors all, but none of them were the reason that Lincoln's war aim shifted from the cause of Union to abolition. The reason was simply that, by the summer of 1862, the level of bloody carnage had risen higher than anyone ever anticipated, and Lincoln could see that, because of orders he was issuing, the violence was soon to grow even worse. The enemy was intractable, Lincoln's generals (especially George McClellan) were unreliable, and his own frustration was growing unbearable.

At the war's start, there were 300,000 men in the two opposing armies; a year later, that number had grown past 1 million. By the end of 1862, there would be 1.4 million men in arms, and more than twice that number by war's end.[63] As the numbers of the uniformed living increased, so did the numbers of the uniformed dead. At Shiloh, in April 1862, there were 24,000 casualties. In July, at the second Battle of Bull Run, where the Yankees were routed, there were 20,000 casualties (compared to about 7,000 at first Bull Run the year before). Then, at Antietam in mid-September, came the bloodiest day in American history, when 24,000 casualties were suffered in twelve hours, a slaughter that changed the meaning of the war. A week after Antietam, Lincoln issued the Emancipation Proclamation.[64]

Emancipation was more a moral symbol than a political act. As such, it was joined in Lincoln's mind with the scale of the war that was yet to come, for he saw that only a higher purpose would justify the total war that would be required if the United States were[65] to prevail over the Confederacy. Some historians argue that Lincoln simply seized upon Antietam as a politically efficacious moment to issue the emancipation decree he had long intended, but Antietam changed the meaning of the act, whatever Lincoln's purpose was. The Yale historian Harry Stout sees the ethical context of escalation as crucial. "By Lincoln's calculation," Stout writes, "the killing must continue on ever grander scales. But for that to succeed, the people must be persuaded to shed the blood without reservations. This, in turn, required a moral certitude that the killing was just." Mere nineteenth-century nationalism — Union — was not enough. For Americans, the nation was becoming sacred, but it was not yet that sacred. "Only emancipation — Lincoln's 'last card' — would provide such certitude."[66]

The abolitionist fervor from which Lincoln had kept his distance, but which he now needed to enlist to brace the Union for massive suffering, was rooted in the evangelical zealotry of which we have already taken note. Recall that the number of religious congregations in the country had grown from 2,500 in 1780 to 52,000 in 1860, growth by a factor of 21 at a time when the population grew by a factor of 8.[67] And most of the congregations were enthusiastically "awakened," Bible-believing apocalypticists ever alert to the dawn of a millennial contest between the forces of good and evil. The North-South splits in the evangelical denominations over the issue of slavery (Presbyterian in 1837, Methodist in 1844, Baptist in 1845) were a dress rehearsal for the political secession of 1860, with each side fueled by righteous indignation.[68] Abolitionism was overwhelmingly an evangelical phenomenon, little involving less enthused denominations like the Roman Catholic, the Episcopalian, and the Unitarian.[69] In the North, slave masters already embodied the Beast of Babylon, while in the South that role was amply filled by the hated Yankee. Preachers on both sides had been taking the lead in defining the conflict in cosmic moral terms[70] — and it was into that realm that the heretofore detached Lincoln finally stepped with the Proclamation.

America, North and South, may have been "awash in a sea of faith," in the phrase of historian Jon Butler — but Lincoln himself was not. He was a figure of the Enlightenment, a man whose God was more like Jefferson's than Jonathan Edwards'. But that God, however removed from doctrinal specificity (no Jehovah, no Trinitarian Father, no hypostatic Jesus) and however unworshiped in Lincoln's congregation of one, soon loomed large in Lincoln's psyche. A God of fatalism, not approbation. A God whose ways were mysterious. And a God who was invested, as one scholar put it, in the "salvation of the nation and the nation's soul, not individual salvation."[71] It was not his own state of grace Lincoln fretted over, but America's.

And how was the fall from grace to be redeemed? For that, Lincoln drew from the deepest well of the biblical tradition, passionately embracing the idea that God was invested in human suffering, could even be appeased by it. Lincoln found that he was suffering's maestro. Replacing the blood-averse McClellan with Grant and Sherman at the head of a lethally equipped army, Lincoln began to inflict hurt on human beings that, because of its industrialization, was unprecedented in the annals of war.[72]

Presiding over the war's carnage no doubt had a profound spiritual effect on Lincoln, a spiritual*izing* effect that was reflected in a shift in his mood and in his public utterances. Lincoln, as he began to think of the war in moral as opposed to merely political terms, became a mystic, and the war took on a meaning Lincoln himself could no longer glibly explain. Once emancipation entered the equation, Union took on transcendental purpose. Slavery was all at once an issue involving not only the fate of the Negro but the hidden depth of the human condition. The war, which began as a strict matter of coercive enforcement of legality, with pragmatic limits in its aims, became, in its escalation beyond all pragmatism, a crusade.

The code word for Lincoln's morality, his mysticism, and now his political purpose was "freedom." He defined this scale of significance himself a few months after the September declaration of emancipation, in the State of the Union address of December 1862 when, breaking with his previous position, he argued that the only way to save the Union was to free the slaves, and *their* freedom was essential to freedom itself. "In giving freedom to the slave, we assure freedom to the free — honorable alike in what we give and what we preserve." And suddenly, in an astonishing rhetorical leap, the American mission defined by this grant of freedom was no longer a matter of concern merely for the United States, but owed itself to the entire human race. "We shall nobly save or meanly lose the last best hope of earth."

It falls short to imagine that Lincoln here is thinking of republicanism as such a universal hope, or constitutional democracy — political ideals that were indeed proving all too contingent in mid-nineteenth-century Europe, and needed the shoring up of America's success. No, that wasn't it. In fact, the United States was, as we saw, among the last nations to free its slaves (not mentioning its recent illegal seizure of vast territories from Mexico, or its soon to intensify campaign to exterminate native peoples, both of which troubled Lincoln), and therefore could hardly be seen as representing a global ideal. No, it was not emancipation that was making the difference in Lincoln's mind at that point, but the scale of suffering that he and his nation were prepared to undergo to achieve it. That suffering itself defined the nobility of which he was speaking.

The shocking move into the savage killing of total war that occurred in 1862 led to a sanctification of the nation that alone could justify it. Categories of political analysis were replaced by ancient tropes of sacrifice, substitutionary atonement, redemption, resurrection, and apocalyptic moralism, all for the sake of a reinvention of the United States of America. Or perhaps *invention,* since what is meant by America came fully into existence only now. "Lincoln knew," as Stout puts it, "that total war would demand even more blood on the fields and far more suffering in the civilian homesteads, and this realization incarnated in him a growing mystical reverence for the Union as itself something sacred and worthy of sacrificial worship."[73]

In his second inaugural address, in 1865 not long before he died and when the war was all but won, Lincoln would humbly declare, "God cannot be for and against the same thing at the same time. In the present civil war it is quite possible that God's purpose is something different from the purpose of either party."[74] But at the end of 1862, when he was launching a total war, he saw it differently, concluding his State of the Union address by firmly asserting that what he had just initiated for the sake of freedom and Union was "a way which, if followed, the world will forever applaud and God must forever bless." God *was* on his side.

The immediate consequence of this mysticism was to reinforce the readiness of Union supporters and fighters to sacrifice their sons and themselves for this transcendent cause. It would not be freedom that saved—or, rather, created—the mystically elevated new Union, but death. Two weeks after emancipation was proclaimed, Charles Sumner of Massachusetts declared, "To die for country is pleasant and honorable. But all who die for country now die also for humanity. Wherever they lie in bloody fields, they will be remembered as heroes through whom the Republic was saved and civilization established forever."[75] There would be bloody fields that could be crossed without touching ground, treading only upon the rotting flesh of fallen soldiers.

The Confederacy had its version of this brutal devotion. The Civil War would simply not have occurred the way it did except for the heavenly-city piety that gripped the imaginations of North and South alike. The war was an ultimate instance of sacred violence, tied to a sacred reward. Fired by their evangelical certainty that Jesus awaited them in the evening garden, and that their sacrifice would hasten the fulfillment of God's plan, soldiers threw themselves into open fields, charging ramparts, thinking of God but also of the Union or of Dixie. "Sacrifice and state became inextricably intertwined," Drew Gilpin Faust comments, noting that the approximately 700,000 Civil War dead, as a percentage of the U.S. population, would amount today to nearly seven million.[76]

"Death created the modern American union — not just by ensuring national survival, but by shaping enduring national structures."[77] Chief among these is the structure of the American conscience, for now, after such a sacrifice — Frederick Law Olmsted dubbed America "the Republic of Suffering"[78] — the nation became, to itself, wholly unlike any other nation. Indeed, beginning now and because of the dead, America rose above the human condition to proclaim itself immortal. Or, as Lincoln put it in November 1863 at Gettysburg — the July battle there had involved the war's largest number of casualties at 50,000 — the only way that "these dead shall not have died in vain" is if "this nation, under God, shall have a new birth of freedom — and that government of the people, by the people, for the people, shall not perish from the earth."[79]

So here arrives the peculiarly American turn on the old connection between religion and violence, for with the Civil War, in effect, they become the same thing. After the long gestation that began at the Puritans' City on a Hill, American religious nationalism and American political spirituality were born at Gettysburg as twins joined at the hip. When the phrase "under God" was appended to the Pledge of Allegiance in 1954, as an expression of fervor in the struggle against "atheistic communism," few noted that it originated with Lincoln, at Gettysburg. The legions of dead soldiers, valorized for the ages by Lincoln's brief burial ground address, were taken as one cosmic Christ figure, and, like Christ in his suffering and death, they accomplished eternal life for the nation. In his second inaugural, Lincoln would define the suffering of the war as a sacrificial atonement for slavery, which was the nation's sin: "As it was said three thousand years ago, so it still must be said, 'the judgments of the Lord are true and righteous altogether.'"[80]

If 1862 was the year when the war took its transcendent turn, both in the scale of bloodshed and in its significance in Lincoln's mind, the transformation was symbolized by the lyric that then began to lift the Union's heart, "The Battle Hymn of the Republic."[81] The words penned by Julia Ward Howe, set to the tune of a preexisting campfire song, were first published on the cover of the *Atlantic Monthly* in February 1862. Two noteworthy things about the anthem are that it literally defines the republic's battle as the cosmic Armageddon out of the Book of Revelation, and that, as the North-South conflict shifted to total war, it became the marching song of every Union regiment. By handing its sons over to the maw of death, the nation was sealing its chosenness by battling none other than the Antichrist. America was finally coming into its own as the instrument of millennial fulfillment — not just for itself but, as Lincoln was asserting, for all the earth's people.

In Howe's lyric, the violence heralded the coming of the Lord, who *himself* was trampling out the vintage of the grapes of wrath, was loosing the fateful lightning of his terrible swift sword, was sounding forth the trumpet that never calls retreat. The hymn described its own being sung at watch-fires of a hundred circling camps. And above all, the hymn defined the new American piety — sacrificial death for the sake not of holiness but of freedom, with the verses building to the conscripting climax, "As He died to make men holy, let us die to make men free." And note that, hereafter, American sacrifice, especially as demanded by politicians, would not mainly involve activities of life (the giving up of money through taxes, or of time through, say, mandated community service). American sacrifice was about death. "A new rationale of national mission was constructed," Ernest Lee Tuveson observed, "and epitomized for all time in 'The Battle Hymn of the Republic' . . . The struggle to eliminate slavery came to be explained as both a judgment on national wickedness and a way in which the chosen nation, by *sacrificing its own sons*, dealt a fatal blow [against] the power of darkness; it seemed to validate the millennialist hopes. Perhaps, even, Armageddon had been fought"[82] (italics mine).

Jon Butler observes that "Howe's hymn was a proselytizing instrument." Proselytizing for the messianic Jesus, but also for the high moral certitude that would enable young men willingly to sacrifice themselves, and their parents to feel edified when they did so. "Few people better symbolized the continuing need for this proselytizing than Abraham Lincoln."[83] It is not cynical to note that the formerly agnostic president had come rather desperately to depend upon, and even to exploit, the naïve credulity of the American majority, with their simple faith — "In the beauty of the lilies Christ was born across the sea / With a glory in his bosom that transfigures you and me" — that Lincoln himself had no part of. Might even have disdained.

This freedom for which the war was at last being justly fought was an abstraction, of course, and would be betrayed at war's end when

the freed slaves were promptly resubjugated. Indeed, the "re-enslavement of black Americans," to use Douglas Blackmon's phrase for what
happened after the Civil War, puts the contested question of the war's
purpose back on the table.[84] It began for the cause of Union, but once
the killing reached an unspeakable level, that aim lacked moral gravity.
Therefore the emancipation of slaves was proclaimed, and the war's
purpose became freedom. When that purpose was betrayed by "black
codes," white supremacy, Jim Crow, and widespread lynching in the
South, and by legally sanctioned segregation and incarceration in the
North, one is left to ask the ignominious question: Had savage violence
become not a regretted means to a virtuous end but its own end? Except in recalcitrant parts of the American South, the Civil War is remembered as an unambiguously just war, but was it? When it became a
total war, was a totalitarian spirit set loose in the American breast, with
killing having no larger meaning than the killing?

But the betrayal of blacks — and therefore of the war's claim to moral
order — took place without Lincoln, and it is impossible to know how
Reconstruction would have unfolded had he lived. Perhaps his full
greatness had yet to show itself in a balancing of "malice toward none"
with real justice for the freed. We will never know. In the evening of the
very day on which the flag of the United States was once again raised at
Fort Sumter — five days after Grant ceremoniously received Lee's sword
at Appomattox — Lincoln went to the theater. It was Good Friday, and
his assassination on that day made it all but impossible for the nation's
tens of thousands of preachers, throughout that Easter weekend, not to
equate the president's martyrdom with the vicarious sacrifice of Jesus
Christ. "He [Lincoln] has been appointed . . . to be laid as the costliest
sacrifice of all upon the altar of the Republic," one set of clergy eulo-
gized, "and to cement with his blood the free institutions of this land."
As with Jesus, "the man dies, but the cause lives."[85] What had become
the Messiah nation under Lincoln now had its Messiah, and the Lincoln cult soon reinvented the American religion. Citizens began to put
the *h* in uppercase when referring to Him,[86] and they did the equivalent in referring to their country.

But if Lincoln was an American Christ, he was also an American Moses, who was refused entry into the Promised Land of a nation at peace.
And above all he was an American Abraham, who had, reversing Genesis, presided over the slaying of sons because that was what his lonely
God told him he had to do. We saw early in this book that the site of the

sacrifice of Isaac, who was spared at the last moment, was nevertheless mythologized as the rock on which the Temple of Solomon was built, and over which the Dome of the Rock stands to this day. America, too, has its temple, the Lincoln Memorial in Washington, with the hall holding the great Daniel Chester French sculpture as its holy of holies. In a symbol of the Union that was preferred, after the war, to justice for blacks, the adjacent Memorial Bridge joins Lincoln to Robert E. Lee, directly across the Potomac River in Arlington. What was once Lee's plantation is now, in the shadow of his mansion, the National Cemetery, on the rolling hills of which only dead soldiers may be buried.[87]

The Lincoln Memorial is a replica of a Greek temple of the Doric order, and the sculpted Lincoln presides just as Zeus would. In such structures long ago children were put to death. But Greek architectural style of this kind marked the whole of the later Hellenized world, including King Herod's Temple in Jerusalem. That biblical resonance makes Lincoln's temple an echo chamber, as the lost voices of this long history bounce off one another. The rock on which this memorial stands is the sacrificial death of sacred war, from Agamemnon's to the Maccabees' to the Masada resisters' to Constantine's to Urban II's to Christopher Columbus's to Oliver Cromwell's to John Winthrop's to Lee's and Lincoln's — right up, as we will see, to Woodrow Wilson's. Indeed, the Lincoln Memorial was constructed, beginning in 1914, through the precise course of World War I, which for all parties, including America, was a sacred war for empire.

In the afternoon, as the sun sets behind the ridge of Arlington, Lincoln's becolumned structure takes on the character of the National Cemetery's master mausoleum. The majestically enthroned president is flanked by marble tablets on which are engraved the Gettysburg Address, which defined American sacrifice as a source of national immortality, and the second inaugural, which, with its "malice toward none," gave American warmaking its Great Absolver. The stone Lincoln, facing away from the cemetery, gazes out over the National Mall, perhaps less like Zeus than like a pantocrator Christ beholding the chapels of his open-air basilica. But the side altars in this case are the bronze, granite, and marble memorials of a dozen foreign campaigns — all his sons offered in sacrifice through the wars that followed. And why should his name not have been Abraham?[88]

All of which implies what was in Lincoln's mind as he spoke his last words on April 14, 1865. He and Mrs. Lincoln had gone to Ford's Theatre to see a play, a much-longed-for bit of relaxation. But the president was preoccupied. While the play was in progress, he was in whispered conversation with his wife. Now that the war was over, husband and wife had been discussing their careless dreams of what they would do when at last they were free to travel. We have already noted the context out of which the desire Lincoln then gave voice to might have arisen, yet the statement seems ripped from history's unconscious. Lincoln's mouth was close to his wife's ear. "There is no place I should like to see," he confided, "so much as Jerusalem."[89] Then John Wilkes Booth fired.

6. God's Right Arm

The joining of sacrificial understandings of America's purpose and the readiness to express them through apocalyptic violence marked the epistemological tipping point that occurred in the Civil War, a permanent change in how the nation viewed itself and the world. Jerusalem fever implicitly fired the national imagination, even as otherwise marginal restorationist Christian missionaries were planting the American flag in the actual city, beginning *its* transformation. Through the mass suffering of the war, the American nation was born again, and despite the orgy of killing that had cut down so many of its bravest and most resourceful young men, a spirit of hope and energy informed a new sense of communal purpose. We saw how one of the cherished consequences of primitive acts of sacrificial violence was the "collective effervescence" that united the community after the victim's blood was shed. Something like that happened after the war's end and Lincoln's death, as the country embraced its new condition with a passionate enthusiasm. After its historic sacrifice for Union and for freedom, America was, as Ralph Waldo Emerson put it, "a last effort of the Divine Providence in behalf of the human race . . . the beginning of a new and more advanced order of civilization."[90]

Most obviously, the burst of post–Civil War esprit ignited the next phase of westward continental expansion, with the concomitant climaxing of the war against native peoples — which, since it was commanded and executed by veterans of both sides, amounted to the total war continued. "While Lincoln passed tragically from the scene," Harry Stout comments, "Grant, Sherman, and Sheridan remained to carry the new moral logic forward."[91] Indians were all at once considered an obstacle

both to the newly felt homogeneity of the nation and to its destinar-
ian territorial mandate, so their mere transfer to the hinterland was no
longer the point of military action; elimination was. What was happening around the globe, as European imperial powers violently laid
claim to colonies on lands occupied by inferior peoples — "exterminate
all the brutes!"[92] — happened in the plains, deserts, and mountains of
the American continent. The new sciences of eugenics and pseudo-
Darwinian racial ranking joined with an ancient religious impulse to
"save" heathens, civilize them, and, where necessary, kill them. By 1891,
when the Indian wars drew to a bloody close at Wounded Knee, the native population of what is now the United States had been halved since
1800, not mainly through disease, which is what had decimated Indians
beginning in the sixteenth century, but through military action. In the
end, 5 percent of the aboriginal population survived.[93]

The vast stretch of the continent was open at last, which unthrot-
tled the long-implied American vocation and brought it into the open.
"Here upon these plains," Washington Gladden, the founder of the Social Gospel movement, preached in 1890, "the problems of history are
to be solved; here, if anywhere, is to rise that city of God, the New Jerusalem, whose glories are to fill the earth."[94]

This is familiar territory, and the point is not to moralistically rehash the revisionist history of America, "the last best hope," as having
been every bit as much an imperial power as the wicked Old World
nations were. (No sooner had the dust settled at Wounded Knee — and
the frontier closed in 1890 — than American military forces were taking
over Hawaii, Wake Island, Guam, Cuba, Puerto Rico, and the Philip-
pines, where 200,000 Filipinos were killed with U.S. rifles and bayo-
nets.) Rather, the point is to see how post–Civil War assumptions of
global redemption and millennial-utopian virtue, which alone were
taken to justify mass violence, underwrote the new American enterprise. Here is how Senator Albert J. Beveridge explained the doctrine
to his colleagues in the U.S. Senate in 1900:

> God has not been preparing the English-speaking and Teutonic peo-
> ples for a thousand years for nothing but vain and idle self-contem-
> plation and self-admiration. No! He has made us master organizers of
> the world to establish system where chaos reigned. He has given us the
> spirit of progress to overwhelm the forces of reaction throughout the
> earth. He has made us adept in government that we may administer
> government among savage and senile peoples. Were it not for such a

force as this the world would relapse into barbarism and night. And of all our race, He has marked the American people as His chosen nation to finally lead in the redemption of the world.[95]

And the distinguishing "mark" of that chosenness was no longer the unspoiled bounty of a Promised Land, as it had been for the Puritans, but the monumental blood sacrifice that had made America the suffering and redeeming Christ among nations.

One man in particular was born and raised in the very heart of this millennialist ethos. It stamped him, and through him it crystallized the American mind, setting a course that would be followed right into the twenty-first century. He was born in Virginia four years before the outbreak of civil war, the son of an evangelical Presbyterian minister who had moved south from Ohio in 1851 to support the cause of slavery, buying slaves himself. The minister served as a chaplain in the Confederate army, and then as a professor at the Columbia Seminary in South Carolina. The son grew up steeped in the deadly mix of both lost-cause sacrificialism and victoriously anointed apocalypticism. He was Presbyterian to the core, and his sense of divine predestination fueled an evangelical nationalism, and it followed naturally that he grew to maturity with the firm conviction that God had chosen him for greatness. He was Woodrow Wilson.

In 1902, he became the first nonminister to hold the presidency of Princeton University, but he could not have been more fervent in his support of the progressive Christian liberalism that was to remake the world. "I believe that God planted in us the vision of liberty," he said. "I cannot be deprived of the hope that we are chosen, and prominently chosen, to show the way to the nations of the world how they shall walk in the paths of liberty."[96]

This was a matter of Christian missionary activity, which, in the late nineteenth and early twentieth centuries, was the initiating American expression of an expansionist foreign policy. Princeton, before, during, and after Wilson's presidency, would be one of its main engines.[97] When he eventually became president of the United States, Wilson trumped the "dollar diplomacy" of his predecessor, William Howard Taft, with "missionary diplomacy," sending Bible-bearing proselytizers abroad as, in a phrase of one noted preacher, "God's right arm in His battle with the world's ignorance and oppression and sin."[98] Not surprisingly, God's left arm, swinging in close behind the missionaries, would regularly show itself to be the U.S. Marines, whom, for example, Wilson dispatched to Haiti and Nicaragua. Virtue and muscle would be permanent pillars of American foreign policy.

Early on, when the nations of Europe entered into their mutual suicide pact of 1914, Wilson clearly saw how to show them the better way to walk. To him, the bitter conflict of the Great War was more than a last gasp of the old imperialisms of greed, territory, and conquest; slaughter on that scale could be nothing less than Armageddon, and the two sides shared a moral equivalence — apocalyptic immorality. America's place was to rise above such wickedness, hoping to tame it only by naming it. In 1916, Wilson ran for reelection on the slogan "He kept us out of war." By January 1917, as he began his second term, millions of corpses had decorated the gnarly scar of the trench lines that bisected the northern half of Europe. Wilson chose that moment to preach his finest sermon, "Peace Without Victory," a resounding denunciation of the immoral ways of warmaking. "Never before," Georges Clemenceau of France declared, had the world "heard so fine a sermon on what human beings might be capable of accomplishing if only they weren't human."[99]

"Humans being what they are" — the mantra we have from Thucydides. From the mists of prehistory, humans had been finding the solution to the problem of violence in yet more violence, always under the illusion that the "yet more" would be the last. The way to peace is war. That something more ferocious than ever took hold of the human psyche in modernity, when violence became both impersonal and industrial, is suggested by the work Sigmund Freud did on what he called the death wish, a social outbreak of nihilism, cloaked as ever in virtuous talk. The reduction to the absurd of this phenomenon was "the war to end all wars," a cockeyed formulation that Wilson at first had seen through. But it was as if his roots in the culture of total war into which he had been born and bred — he and Freud were born in the same year — went deeper into his psyche than he knew. His glorious speech for peace-without-victory was in January, but by April (after an upsurge of German U-boat attacks on American shipping and British exposure of a German offer of military aid to Mexico) President Wilson was leading his nation in its own declaration of war.

The United States threw in with suicidal nihilism, and it did so with enthusiasm, promptly raising an army, almost from scratch, of four million men. "This took religion," a character in an F. Scott Fitzgerald novel would observe about the battle America joined, "and tremendous sureties . . . You had to have a whole-souled sentimental equipment going back further than you could remember."[100] But Wilson's memory was long. After the armistice, he would claim the American partnership in the lunacy of the trenches as a further credential for moral instruction. The doughboys have been seen, he said, "as crusaders, and their transcendent achievement has made all the world believe in America as it believes in no other nation organized in the modern world." America, he said, invoking the old image of the holy hill, was "marching at the fore of a great procession [to] those heights upon which there rests nothing but the pure light of the justice of God."[101] Alas, for all of Wilson's postwar good intentions, his procession at home and abroad turned out to be a procession of one. His only lasting legacy, in fact, was in having led his nation in exact imitation of those who bowed down before what Rainer Maria Rilke would call the "War God."[102] The worship goes on.

As was true in the Civil War, death had, by the third year of the Great War, taken on a mythical meaning and a mystical power that was as irrational as it was irresistible. The measure of that power is found in America's jubilant reversal of course to embrace the collective effervescence of a charnel house in which ten million men died. All the sacred Jerusalem themes were on parade: Sacrifice. Martyrdom. Atonement. Substitution. Divine sanction. Altar as national focal point. Redemption through destruction. What Wilfred Owen called "the old lie."[103] The measure of its nihilism is found in what came afterward: no new world order, no League of Nations, no heights of justice, no city on a hill, but an unimagined catastrophe that began with the frenzied rage of one young Austrian "front fighter" who set out in Europe to convert the daylight horror of the trenches into the nightmare of crematoria.

7. Apostolic Succession

But in the United States, Wilson's political-religious ethos generated a particular apostolic succession that carried the Civil War spirit of God-sanctioned total-war-joined-to-sacrifice directly into the nuclear age. One of Wilson's own Princeton boys, for example, was John Foster Dulles, class of 1908, a zealous Presbyterian who would become the paradigmatic Cold Warrior–statesman. Wilson left the presidency of Princeton in 1910, only two years ahead of the arrival of Allen Dulles, who decades later gave the Central Intelligence Agency its rogue character, and James Forrestal, who would become the first secretary of defense. The Dulles brothers and Forrestal, along with his protégé George Kennan (Princeton, class of 1925), did more to shape the post–World War II American mind than any other figures. And though they came from different denominational backgrounds, they were all stamped with a like evangelical fervor matched to the self-anointing mysticism of a new weapon, the first test of which was code-named "Trinity."

Forrestal was the linchpin, the single most influential figure in shaping America's Cold War policies. A captain of finance (he had been chief of the investment house Dillon, Read), Forrestal had the face and ferocity of a boxer. If he carried forward the prevailing moralism that divided the world between forces of good and evil, he did so not as an heir to the Puritans but as an Irish Catholic, the scrappy son of immigrants who had settled in upstate New York. Forrestal's worldview was stamped with an equally Manichaean Jansenism.[104] But such ideological bipolarity, whether Puritan or Jansenist, had unexpected consequences when joined to decision making about the new atomic weapon.

A mind disposed to the apocalyptic could perversely welcome the capability to inflict an apocalyptic level of destruction. If the atomic bomb carried unusual risks — well, so be it. The values for which one fought and died were supreme, and if they were worth an individual life, perhaps they were worth life itself — regrets to be sorted out, and healed, in the world-without-end hereafter. But such complacency assumed a prior religiosity that included a horror-trumping acceptance of a coming Armageddon. The end of *this* world ("this vale of tears") was never far from the Irish Catholic — or Puritan — imagination, and the epoch-closing return of the Messiah, even if in a destructive battle of good angels against bad, could be contemplated as somehow fulfilling a divine plan.

As the nation's first secretary of defense, in office from 1947 to 1949, Forrestal presided over a Pentagon that was a center of belligerent hysteria. For an apocalyptic analysis of the evil represented by Stalinist Marxism, he depended on Kennan, whose "Long Telegram" (1946) and "Mister X" article in *Foreign Affairs* (1947)[105] interpreted Soviet totalitarianism in expressly religious terms. Kennan had a certitude of

America's predestined salvation worthy of any City-on-a-Hill Calvinist. Probably the most influential political analysis ever published in America, the "Mister X" article was called by one historian a "Puritan Jeremiad."[106] Soviet Communism, Kennan declared, is "a mystical, Messianic movement." He likened it to a Church, even to the Catholic Church, with its doctrine of infallibility. No mere competing imperial power, Moscow was ontologically the enemy of the West. Normal diplomatic negotiations with the Soviets were pointless, Kennan wrote, "until the internal nature of Soviet power is changed." The implications of Kennan's analysis of the transnational, even transhistoric, threat posed by the Soviet Union were soon elevated to a quasi-religious American creed — officially designated as the Truman *Doctrine*, no less — the idea that Soviet Communism was a cosmic enemy that had to be "contained" diplomatically, economically, and militarily wherever it showed itself.[107] This doctrine would lead to U.S. interventions large and small in more than a dozen civil wars around the globe, and it would lead to an overreliance on the nuclear arsenal as the doctrine's main backup.[108]

Truman's trusted adviser Bernard Baruch, perhaps recognizing that such bipolar moralizing had long been turned against his own Jewish people, criticized the doctrine as "tantamount to a declaration of . . . an ideological or religious war."[109] Indeed, Truman's war against an evil enemy outside, just like Pope Urban's Crusade in 1096, soon unleashed a scapegoating campaign against a wicked enemy inside — and as before, that internal enemy was the Jew. Truman's anti-Communist demonizing set off America's domestic Red Scare, a decade-long witchhunt that disproportionally targeted Jews as subversives.

Though Truman was a Baptist, he and the Catholic Forrestal were singing from the same hymnal, to the music of what the historian Richard Hofstadter famously called "the paranoid style in American politics."[110] Religious bipolarity, the Crusades, anti-Semitism, Islamophobia, imperialism, Calvinism, Jansenism, Puritanism, exceptionalism, revivalism, restorationism, Wilsonianism, Manichaeism, messianism, apocalypticism, Armageddon — the disparate elements of this long history came together in a kind of critical mass that linked politics, religion, and military power in ways never seen before. The moral absolutism of the Truman Doctrine took the form of a radical spirit of no compromise; a readiness for total war; a preference, on the nuclear precipice, for the sacrifice of the very earth rather than capitulation to, or accommodation with, Communist power anywhere. This morbid patriotism was captured in a chilling slogan of the time, "Better dead than Red," a motto chosen not by a few nut-case extremists, as it is usually remembered, but one imposed by the leaders of the free world upon human civilization. The way to redeem the world was to destroy it.

It was at this time that the story of the actual Jerusalem resurfaced: Truman was presented with the decision of whether to recognize the newly independent state of Israel. In 1948, as we will see, interlocking shadows cast by Auschwitz and Hiroshima affected all of Truman's choices, even if neither could be referred to as shaping policy. A broad amnesia was setting in: as the culture-wide responsibility for the Nazi genocide was downplayed, so the initial conviction of Manhattan Project scientists that a moral threshold had been crossed was forgotten. The lost past put the future in peril. But whether remembered or not, the Holocaust and the nuclear age underlay the new human condition.

On the surface, the Baptist president's roots in restorationist Christian Zionism inclined him to quickly affirm the Jewish state, but in a flip, Truman's strongest opponent on Israel was Secretary of Defense Forrestal, for whom the higher stakes involved the death struggle with the Soviet Union. Israel would be a pawn in the superpower standoff between Washington and Moscow for the entire forty years of the Cold War. But regarding Israel, Forrestal's instinctive motives were as potently negative as the Baptist president's were positive. As a Roman Catholic, the secretary of defense was imbued, however unknowingly, with the ancient theological need to keep Jews away from their homeland. He based his arguments on concerns about Middle Eastern oil and the danger of Russian intrusions into the Arab realm. But in his denigrations of Israel, echoes of gutter anti-Semitism could be heard, and Forrestal was denounced for it in the press. He was already suffering from the stress of his responsibility for the atomic bomb, and his political paranoia became personal. Convinced of a coming Soviet attack and of a Russian plot to kill him, he began to come unglued. "The Reds" obsessed him, but not only that. In classic fashion, Forrestal's psychotic paranoia fixed on the traditional Christian hate object, and he told intimates that "the Jews" and "Zionist agents" were out to get him, too. In May 1949, after being forced by Truman to resign his cabinet post and after being found in the street in his pajamas crying "The Russians are coming!" Forrestal killed himself by jumping from his room on the fourteenth floor of the Bethesda Naval Hospital in Washington.

The Messiah had not come, but, in a way, the Russians did. Only months after Forrestal's death leap, Moscow successfully detonated its own atomic bomb. Truman announced the news that the Soviets had the bomb in September 1949. Within days, a heretofore obscure evangelical preacher pitched his revival tent in Los Angeles.

Over a few previous years, the itinerant minister had stoked Christian fervor in standard fundamentalist style along the sawdust trail, drawing modest crowds in rural and small-town America. It was coincidental that he found himself in a big city that week in September, and it soon became apparent, as pastors from around Southern California informed him, that his usual tent was not going to be big enough. Thousands flocked to hear him at his expanded revival camp. Over subsequent days, hundreds of thousands came, perhaps the largest spontaneous religious display in American history. The evangelist's name was Billy Graham. The anguish of a people panicked at the news of the Communist A-bomb launched him on his career as the most famous revivalist in U.S. history. He became the personification of all-American virtue, the White House pastor, a guarantor of the nation's divine election.

Graham had a pitch-perfect ear for the message his throngs wanted to hear, an ingenious mixture of religion and politics, of apocalyptic dread and sacrificial purification. "God is giving us a desperate choice," Graham preached at that Los Angeles assembly, "a choice of either revival or judgment. There is no alternative . . . The world is divided into two camps. On one side we see Communism . . . [which] has declared war against God, against Christ, against the Bible, and against all religion . . . Unless the Western world has an old-fashioned revival, we cannot last."[111] Graham's genius was to sanctify the approach of Armageddon through nuclear war, even while sounding alarms, and to make such doom-laden fervor a staple of his preaching. More than any single spiritual figure, Graham made the threat of nuclear annihilation religiously relevant. As preached by Graham, only religious categories, especially those drawn from the Book of the Apocalypse, could give people a way to live with nuclear dread.[112]

Graham's Los Angeles campaign marked the arrival of what would be called the religious right, a potent brew of God and hard-conservative politics, of end-of-the-world terror tied to a coming nuclear holocaust, of fevered suspicion of Communist enemies at home and abroad (and of Jews, whom Graham referred to as the "Synagogue of Satan" in conversation with Richard Nixon[113]) — all countered by the act of coming to Jesus, whose new kingdom is the United States. First the Republican Party would rebuild itself around these ideas, and then so would America's "vital center."[114] It is far from incidental to this long history that Billy Graham, then and after, throughout the Cold War, called his mission a "crusade." Jerusalem fever American style had come fully into its own.

CHAPTER EIGHT

Jerusalem Builded Here

1. The Last Crusader

IN THE SUMMER OF 1917, David Lloyd George, the British prime minister, proposed to give the disheartened people of England a Christmas gift. After three years of savage war, the only hope of defeating Germany still lay on the Western Front, though the trench lines had not moved for more than a year. With the United States having entered the war in April, there was some hope that the stalemate could be broken. But the arrow point continued to be in the mud fields of France and Belgium. For that reason, one could wonder why Lloyd George, looking for a morale booster, tapped one of the strongest Western Front commanders to lead a campaign far away.

Field Marshal Edmund Allenby, a cavalryman known as "Bull," was named head of a new Egyptian Expeditionary Force, purportedly to launch a thrust against the soft underbelly of the Central Powers, through the Middle East front of the Ottoman Empire. But the Entente allies had tried such an indirect offensive earlier in the war, through the second half of 1915, with the assault at Gallipoli, resulting in nearly half a million casualties. The Turks had successfully repelled the attack, inflicting such catastrophic losses, on New Zealanders and Australians especially, that Gallipoli is memorialized Down Under to this day. But the battle was an Ottoman trauma, too — twice as many Turks died as French and British. That sparked the rebellion of Mustafa Kemal Atatürk, a heroic Gallipoli commander, whose bloody revolt would eventually bring down the Istanbul caliph, usher in a "modern" Turkey, and — in a backlash against Atatürk's methods — stir up widespread Muslim hatred of forced secularization by modernizing rulers.

Arabs, from Mecca north, likewise revolted against Ottoman domination, with support from the mythic Colonel T. E. Lawrence, "Lawrence of Arabia." The Allenby thrust up from Egypt was meant to capitalize on that. But in truth, the Middle East theater was a distraction, and Lloyd George's main purpose was not strategic. "Compared with the Western Front, Palestine was unimportant," one historian writes, "yet [Lloyd George] told Allenby that the matter was so important that he could have whatever men and materials he needed to achieve the conquest."[1]

Why? The prime minister had been a Baptist lay preacher, and his imagination was braced by the British version of evangelical restorationism that had so fired the American religious imagination, kindling even Abraham Lincoln's. St. Paul's "salvation will come from Zion" had mobilized English Bible readers as much as American.[2] Lloyd George was acting out of faith, not martial prowess, and the gift he had in mind had far more religious than military meaning, but in the boomeranging mechanisms of morale enforcement, that could have the largest military consequence of all. If home-front upper lips could not be kept stiff, the war was lost. That is why the prime minister told Allenby that he wanted him to take "Jerusalem before Christmas as a Christmas present for the British people."[3] As the Christ child had been summoned from Egypt, and the Hebrews were rescued from Egypt, so the shaken Allied war effort would be saved from Egypt now. Nothing would lift the spirits of the bereaved British nation like the ultimate gift — not from but of the holy place where Christmas itself began.

Despite being far removed from, and irrelevant to, the make-or-break gash of no man's land that sliced across the European continent, Jerusalem was key to the way English leaders and the English people had only recently come to think about their war.

It had begun the year before. In the lush valley of the River Somme in the far north of France, beginning on July 1, 1916, the British people had been undergoing the greatest trial since the Battle of Hastings. The French were already being tested at Verdun, where casualties would approach a million. Then came London's turn. On the first day of the Battle of the Somme, 57,000 British soldiers fell. It was the bloodiest day in the nation's history. Over the subsequent weeks and months, a seemingly infinite succession of Tommies, Jocks, and Micks had hurled themselves over the top, out of trenches against the fortified positions of German defenders. Eventually the Somme would outstrip even Verdun in lives lost and wounds inflicted. An endless "supply of heroes," in the words of the British leader David Carson.[4]

This carnage was the next step in the industrialization of killing that had begun in the United States sixty years earlier, when a new technological capacity matched the spirit of total war. As in the American Civil War, the violence quickly became its own justification. Why did men keep going over the top? To redeem the loss of those who'd preceded them. The bloodied soil became an altar. The British commanders imagined that their soldiers would eventually overwhelm the defenders, or that the defenders' weapons would fail. The commanders did not comprehend that the machine gun was a *machine*. It was no more likely to fail than a factory lathe was.

The machine gun had made the offensive charge obsolete, but the British high command did not see that. Instead they launched one assault after another, defining the futility and absurdity of the war. That the pointless British Somme offensive went on for five months — British losses alone surpassed 500,000 — with no appreciable gain in territory and with the final exhaustion of the volunteer army, embodied a moral defeat of such proportions that even the lowliest soldier grasped it. The catastrophe was a blow to the communal psyche from which Britain never recovered, and the nation knew it at once. Here at last was an epiphany of total war, a conflict that had ceased being purposeful and had become mythic. And the operative myth was the ancient one, the collective effervescence of sacrifice, with which this book began.

The great literature that came out of World War I repeatedly struck the theme of redemptive sacrifice. Indeed, it was anticipated on the eve of war with the Paris performance of *Le Sacre du Printemps,* the Stravinsky dance of death that had first been titled *The Victim.* Its second part was called "The Great Sacrifice." The work was instantly notorious because the choreography caricatured ballet and the score mocked musical convention, but what made it modernism's masterpiece was its forecast of the twentieth century's main dynamic: the orgiastic sacrifice of the young to the sacred assumptions of the old. Out of violence, apocalyptic radicalism, atonality, jerks, and percussive noise, art was made. A figurative moment later, and for nothing — with the masses joyfully crying "It's on!" — Europe went to suicidal war.[5]

All categories of meaning would be cut down in rows, like the men.

But at first the continent was gripped by the communal enthusiasm that had defined the primitive hunters' ecstasy of the kill. The kill — we had forgotten this — was what had made us human. On September 19, 1914, Lloyd George, then chancellor of the exchequer, addressed his nation: "We have been living in a sheltered valley for generations. We have been too comfortable and too indulgent . . . and the stern hand of Fate has scourged us to an elevation where we can see the great everlasting things that matter for a nation — the great peaks we had forgotten, of Honour, Duty, Patriotism, and, clad in glittering white, the great pinnacle of Sacrifice pointing like a rugged finger to Heaven."[6]

Soon enough, the glittering white was gone, and the scene looked different when viewed from the low-down point of those for whom such pretty words were only that much more load in the backpacks that weighed them down like crosses.[7] Siegfried Sassoon, in his poem "The Redeemer," wrote of his fellow Tommie: "He faced me, reeling in his weariness . . . I say that He was Christ." The less celebrated Great War writer Leonard Green, in the short story "In Hospital," described a dying soldier: "His blood poured out in sacrifice made possible the hazardous success of the more fortunate. He was the pattern of all suffering. He was Christ . . . He was my God and I worshipped him."[8] The worship extended, in fact, to war itself, which took on an absolute ethical value of its own. War becomes total war when patriotic self-denial is trumped by willing self-destruction, at which point death, instead of the hoped-for peace, becomes the source of meaning. When that happens, all previous moral assumptions are reversed.

The poet laureate of the war's absurdity was Wilfred Owen, who recognized in the mad stubbornness of the commanders and in the dumb willingness of their subjects the most elemental reversal of all — Jerusalem's. Here is "The Parable of the Young Man and the Old":

> So Abram rose, and clave the wood, and went,
> And took the fire with him, and a knife.
> And as they sojourned, both of them together,
> Isaac the first-born spake, and said, My Father,
> Behold the preparations, fire and iron,
> But where the lamb for this burnt-offering?
> Then Abram bound the youth with belts and straps,
> And builded parapets the trenches there,
> And stretched forth the knife to slay his son,
> When lo! An angel called him out of heaven,

Saying, Lay not thy hand upon the lad,
Neither do anything to him. Behold,
A ram, caught in a thicket by its horns;
Offer the Ram of Pride instead of him.
But the old man would not so, but slew his son,
And half the seed of Europe, one by one.[9]

On November 4, 1918, one week before the war's end, Owen was killed on the Western Front, one of the last of nearly ten million men to die.[10] The bitterness of his poem does not defuse the dynamic it exposes, how a biblical tale (anchored to the rock on the Temple Mount) of God's rejection of the sacrifice of the son morphed over time (we saw this in the Hebrew books of Daniel and Maccabees, in St. Paul's Letter to the Romans, in the medieval treatise of St. Anselm, and in the modern theology of Søren Kierkegaard) into a parable that praises Abraham for his faith-inspired willingness to kill his son. Abraham was "justified by faith," in Paul's phrase, and by the readiness to kill. Clearly, the carnage of World War I went on as it did, unchecked for years, because the European imagination shifted its frame of reference from the pragmatic and rational to the mystical and apocalyptic. The God who deplores killing yielded to a God who relishes it. The more deadly the experience, the more spiritualized it became. And why else, during the Great War, should nearly twenty thousand church bells *not* have been melted down into guns and bullets?[11]

In the British case, this transformation was dramatized by the anthem the army and the nation embraced as rivers of blood were transforming the fertile farmland of the Somme into reddish mud. The young men whose beloved elder brothers and admired senior classmates had already been condemned by the betraying fathers were dismayed, and afraid of what awaited them, but public disillusionment with the patriarchal ideals of the empire was general. The fathers were not to be trusted. Looking for a rousing hymn that would "brace the spirit of the nation [to] accept with cheerfulness all the sacrifices necessary,"[12] the poet laureate of England, Robert Bridges, commissioned the composer Hubert Parry to set to music the text of a William Blake poem. Though dating to the early nineteenth century, the poem seemed apt to Bridges because it took off from an ancient legend according to which the risen Jesus had come to England. Jerusalem with its surrounds, the archbishop of York had declared in 1865, "belongs to you and me; it is essentially ours. It is the land from which news came of our Redemption. It is the land we turn to as the foundation of all our hopes. It is the land to which we look with as true a patriotism as we do this dear old England."[13] Indeed, England, in the myth that inspired Blake, was the first place to have a foretaste of the "city of my God," referred to in Revelation, "which is new Jerusalem."[14] Blake seemed to have in mind as counterpoint to his millennial vision the brutalities of the Industrial Revolution, but the counterpoint in 1916 was the industrial war.

Blake's poem had been a neglected preface to a much longer masterwork, *Milton,* but set to Parry's melody, the verses became instantly celebrated in England as "Jerusalem."[15] King George V, on hearing it, no doubt felt the unconscious reinforcement of the ideals upholding his own position, and he declared his wish that the hymn be sung as an anthem. From the year of the Somme forward, it was. Today English soccer and rugby games begin with fans' rousing renditions of "Jerusalem," and at the other end of the social scale, dozens of English public schools — and Anglophilic American prep schools — have it as an alma mater. (Of the Eton class of 1908, to take one establishment school, nearly half were killed in the war. Of the roughly 5,000 Eton graduates who served in the war, nearly 1,200 were killed.[16] "Jerusalem" is beloved at Eton to this day.)

But the song's importance to our story lies in the way it first invited a war-exhausted British public — and their shell-shocked sons — to keep fighting "till we have built Jerusalem in England's green and pleasant land." War fighting was the precondition of the rescue of establishment values. Jerusalem embodied the culture of divine election, hierarchy, and ordained social class that defined the Victorian empire, but the war had given it irresistible resonance as the holy city of sacrifice, atonement, and redemption through killing. Abraham, Jerusalem's progenitor, was a father to be trusted, even as the killing continued. The young men would keep dying. The heavenly city come to earth was the emblem of the war's hypnotic ineffability.

What "The Battle Hymn of the Republic" was for the Union forces during the American Civil War, "Jerusalem" was to Britain and its armies. Because the English people had taken the anthem to heart, and in doing so had reclaimed their bond with the imagined holy city, what could have been a more heartening Christmas gift the year after the Somme than the delivery into British control of the actual city that had inspired such longing in the first place? Hence Lloyd George's order to Allenby. Once again a fevered idea of Jerusalem was about to curve back onto the real city with massive consequences for the men and women — Jew, Muslim, Christian — who, against the currents of history, had continued to make their home there.

The nineteenth century had been pivotal for Jerusalem, with liberalization and prosperity sparked by the reforms of the modernizing Egyptians we have already noted. Even when the Turks reasserted controls in the 1840s, equal rights for non-Muslims were continued, with, for example, foreigners allowed to buy property and establish those consulates and colonies (the "American Colony," the "German Colony"). The opening of the Suez Canal in 1869 had led to a regional boom, and Jerusalem was connected to it through the port city of Jaffa (a railroad connecting the cities opened in 1892). Communication and transportation systems flourished, kerosene streetlamps were introduced, and a vigorous tourist industry (souvenirs, weaving, banks) thrived. Across the century, Jerusalem's population had increased by a factor of eight, with the largest growth occurring among Jews, whose population increased twentyfold. (At the outbreak of World War I, there were about 12,000 Muslims, 13,000 Christians, and 45,000 Jews.[17]) While European Christians built churches and archeological institutes mainly inside the walls of the Old City, around the Holy Sepulcher and the Via Dolorosa, Jews spread to the west (Mishkenot Sha'ananim with its windmill) and north (Mea Shearim with its synagogues). Jewish residents crowded into the newly constructed apartment blocks of the New City, built with the distinctive white stone. While Arabs and Muslims remained concentrated in the Old City, they, too, built new neighborhoods just outside the walls, like Sheikh Jarrah, where notable families constructed impressive villas in a distinctive Oriental style.[18]

As Muslims were dominated by the Constantinople-based Turkish rulers, European powers stamped the lives of both Christians (the German emperor Wilhelm II personally dedicated the imposing Church of the Redeemer in 1898) and Jews (philanthropists like Moses Montefiore and the Rothschilds built hospitals, yeshivas, and synagogues). With the outbreak of war in 1914, however, the Turks were immediately thrown on the defensive. Jerusalem's ties with Europe were broken, and the non-Turkish population — Christian, Jewish, and Muslim — suffered new restrictions.

It was to that complicated and now insecure city that the British looked for mystic rescue. Having set out from Egypt with a combined French, Italian, and British force, and with Arab irregulars led by Colonel Lawrence,[19] Allenby crossed into Palestine, making for Jerusalem. The Ottoman defenders of the city, with a contingent of Germans, saw them coming and, not wanting to see the city destroyed, abandoned it.[20] On December 11, 1917, in time for Christmas, and on the second day of Hanukkah (which celebrates the memory of Maccabean martyrdom and resistance in Jerusalem[21]), Allenby entered Jerusalem through a gate in Suleiman the Magnificent's wall. The field marshal had the dramatic flair of a cavalryman, but he did not cross through Jaffa Gate on horseback. Jesus had entered the city mounted on a donkey, and so Allenby, displaying due humility, entered on foot. But whether consciously or not, Allenby's act referred not so much to Jesus as to Umar ibn al-Khattab, the first Muslim conqueror of the city. In 637, as we saw, Umar expressed his respect for its Jewish and Christian sacred soil by dismounting and crossing into Jerusalem on foot. In fact, what Allenby dismounted was not a horse but his Rolls-Royce,[22] and if he had an Islamic conqueror in mind, it would more likely have been Saladin, whose 1187 conquest Allenby was finally reversing.

To the chagrin of his French, Italian, and Arab allies, Allenby ordered only one flag raised on the pole above the Tower of David. That flag was the Union Jack. Jerusalem, and Palestine, were being claimed for the British Empire, pure and simple. In London, "bells were rung and Te Deums sung in the cathedrals; Allenby was hailed as 'the last Crusader.'"[23] An English magazine imagined Richard the Lionheart declaring, "At last my dream has come true." According to Arabic sources, when Allenby entered the Temple Mount, he announced, "Today, the Crusades have ended."[24] He may not have uttered those precise words, but there is no doubt that across Europe, the recapture of Jerusalem, stoked by British "Christmas present" propaganda, resulted in a frenzy of Crusader references. That history was used to justify manifold claims for a share in the control of the holy city. The Italians cited the pope as the originator of the Crusades, and the French reminded the world that, over the centuries, most of the actual Crusaders were Frenchmen. Subdued Germans of Jerusalem emphasized their Knights Templar roots to cling to their colony. Arabs, for their part, sensed a coming betrayal in the English domination of Jerusalem, for they had been promised there "an independent Sovereign Muslim State," a commitment on which Lawrence had staked his honor, in return for support against the Ottomans.[25]

Allenby's stake in the center of Palestine was a stake in the heart of Arab identity, just when it had begun to coalesce as an expressly Palestinian identity — and explicitly around Jerusalem.[26] Allenby's betrayal was the pivot around which Palestinian Arab culture would spiral down into the corruptions and oppressions of colonialism, which would themselves spark fierce reactions that continue to this day, with Palestinians perceived, if at all, "only as refugees, or as extremists, or as terrorists."[27]

Jews, too, could sense a double game. Their steady return to Jerusalem throughout the nineteenth century amounted to a check on the simultaneous Christian missionary (restorationist) moves on Jews, as well as the European powers' incursions through consulates and national churches. Late-nineteenth-century pogroms in Russia, Ukraine, and Poland increased the pressures on Jewish flight to Palestine.[28] That Jews, for the first time in nearly two millennia, were a growing majority in Jerusalem marked the beginning of the end of Jewish exile. And this occurred before Zionism took off as a formal movement. (The First Zionist Congress took place in Switzerland in 1897.) The Balfour Declaration, promising London's support for a "national home for the Jewish people" in Palestine and named for the British foreign minister who made it, was issued on November 2, 1917, only five weeks before Allenby's raising of the Union Jack. The Jewish homeland was to be, if anything, a mere canton within the larger empire.[29]

Allenby moved on from Jerusalem into northern Palestine to engage Ottoman forces in a decisive battle at Megiddo. After their defeat in that place, the Turks soon surrendered altogether, the first of the Central Powers to sign an armistice. Such an outcome was no surprise to millennialist Christians, since Megiddo is, in fact, Har Megiddo, or Armageddon, the site of the fifteenth-century-BCE battle between the pharaoh's forces and the Canaanites, the first battle in recorded history. Of course, according to Revelation, Armageddon is the place to which all the world's armies will be summoned for the final conflagration that will establish the messianic age.[30] And why should the world-historic defeat of the Muslim empire not have occurred right there?

If the 1917 conquest of Jerusalem, as one historian put it, was indeed "the last Crusade, Christianity recovering its own city from the benighted infidel,"[31] then Jews and Arabs alike had reason to feel misused, and alarmed about what was coming. Allenby's claim for England was affirmed by the League of Nations in 1920, which gave Great Britain the mandate for Palestine. In hindsight this could be seen as the death knell of colonialism, but at the time European powers had laid claim to 85 percent of the globe — "imperialism the theory, colonialism the practice"[32] — a world order they were determined to preserve. That determination was symbolized now by the retaking of Jerusalem. Soon enough, however, as if biblically ordained, disorder followed — and massively.

The regal progress of the British Empire, which ruled by means of exploiting ethnic and religious divisions wherever the Union Jack was planted, left an endless tumult of internecine conflict in its wake (Irish Catholic versus Protestant in Northern Ireland; Hindu versus Muslim in India, Pakistan, Kashmir, and later Bangladesh; Muslims in northern Sudan versus Christians and animists in southern Sudan; Sinhalese versus Tamil ethnic groups in Ceylon, now Sri Lanka; and so on), and it could seem that the Israeli-versus-Arab conflict in Palestine draws its heat from that imperial furnace.[33] But Allenby embodied something more — a European (and American) visionary radicalism, centered on contested Jerusalem and rooted in the bifurcated religious imagination that condemned both Jews and Muslims. Jews first: The ancient Christian tradition of anti-Judaism had already led to the first anti-Jewish pogrom in the Arab world, sparked in Damascus, not by Muslims but by Franciscan friars. European anti-Semitism is the soil out of which Arab hatred of Jews has grown. If Jews had long been Christendom's enemy inside, Islam had become the enemy outside — a twin-set "negative other" against which Europe continued to find its positive identity. An "imaginative geography," focused on the mystical and suspect "East," made it real.[34] Allenby was that legacy in jodhpurs, and he planted it as a permanent — if often unnamed — party to the wars that rack Palestine and Israel to this day.

2. Diaspora's End

Zionism takes its name from Jerusalem, centered on Mount Zion. Though early Zionists, with no particular interest in the city itself,[35] seemed not to have been infected by Jerusalem fever, the movement from its origins envisioned a return of Jews to the ancient homeland. The most religiously conservative Jews regarded any thought of political restoration as a preemption of the Messiah and an offense against God's plan, but other Jews, including those whose belief included a sense of responsibility for history, were influenced by the fervor of large numbers of Christians for whom the "restoration" of Jews was the urgent prelude to the messianic age. These Christians, with their missions, consulates, hospices, hospitals, convents, compounds, gardens, schools, and archeological digs, were reshaping Jerusalem even as thousands of eastern European and Russian Jews arrived in Palestine seeking refuge under Turkish rule. The temperature of Jewish Zionism, centered in Jerusalem, would steadily rise, until it, too, was feverish.

Theodor Herzl, the founder of the Zionist Organization in 1897, was a secular person, not given to the mysticism that had led many Christians to regard the holy city with a hyperreligiosity. For Herzl, there were two questions of geography, and the first, more urgent one had to do with emigration, not immigration. In proposing a mass exodus of Jews from threatening Europe, he was reacting to the rampant anti-Semitism in his native Vienna and in the pogrom-ridden Ukraine, Poland, and Russia — and, according to his own later account, in France, where he covered the Dreyfus Affair for a Vienna newspaper.

The resettlement of Jews in Palestine was, as noted, already under way, usually dated to the pogrom-instigated First Aliyah of 1882 (as we saw, *aliyah* means "going up," as in going up the mountain to Zion, the city on a hill). Something like thirty thousand Jews, including Jews from Iran, Algeria, and Morocco, had come to Palestine by the time of Herzl's initiative.[36] They worked as hired laborers on farms and in towns, establishing rural settlements on thousands of purchased acres; they congregated in small cities like Jaffa and in traditional Jewish areas like the old center of mysticism in Safed, in Galilee. Though Jews had tipped the majority in Jerusalem, the city was far from their only destination.

Such a Jewish influx to the region, when joined to simultaneous Christian missionary and European consular activities in Jerusalem, had stoked fears in Istanbul, which had reacted by tightening its control over the region north of Gaza and south of Beirut. Removing it from the authority of Damascus, the Turkish caliphate established Jerusalem as a provincial capital, which was a first designation of the area as a governing district distinct from Lebanon, Transjordan, and Syria — the true origin of a separate Palestinian identity. Muslim Arab leaders of the Jerusalem municipality were already alarmed by Christian and European incursions, and Herzl's launching of an organized movement of Jews to Palestine prompted them to protest, writing, for example, a letter to the chief rabbi of France, an ally of Herzl's, with the plea "to leave Palestine in peace."[37] The Jerusalem "notables" protested to Istanbul as well, but as Arabs they were also resentful of an increased local Turkification as the distant regime tightened its control.[38] Despite the religious bond of a Muslim devotion to the Istanbul caliph as head of the House of Islam, a first Arab nationalism was stirring.

In the beginning, Herzl took for granted that Palestine would be the place of Jewish resettlement, but firm objections from the sultan in Istanbul, pressed by the anti-Zionist organizing of Arab notables, made that prospect seem unlikely, at least in the short term. Unlike some of the Zionist leaders who followed him, Herzl was not unattuned to the claim of those already living in Palestine. The Ottoman Empire was shaky, but one of the places the Sublime Porte was determined to reinforce was Jerusalem. No tipping its delicate balance with a further influx of Jews! Thus, when, at the turn of the century, the British government responded to Herzl's concern about European anti-Semitism with indications of support for a semiautonomous settlement of Jews in Uganda, in British East Africa, Herzl put the idea before the Zionist Congress. Jewish escape, more than any Jewish reclaiming of Palestine or Jerusalem, was the goal for those who favored what was called the Uganda Project, and some Zionists warmed to the British proposal.

But what about nearly two millennia's worth of Passover rituals, including the hopeful declaration "Next year in Jerusalem"? What about all those prayers offered in the shtetls and ghettos of Europe for rain in the Galilee, Samaria, and Judea, an unbroken tie to particular hills and valleys that had transformed memory into longing? What about the endlessly imagined city and the unforgotten pledge from God tying the covenant to Eretz Yisrael? As we saw, religious Jews were convinced that the physical city of Jerusalem had been superseded in God's plan by the spiritual city, with the Temple religion forever defined not by priestly sacrifice of animals but by the daily acts of every Jew: Torah observance and the performance of good deeds and acts of loving-kindness. The actual Jerusalem would be restored to the Jews, but only by the Messiah at the end of time. For now, the homeland could be anywhere Torah was studied, Shabbat observed, the ancient story of God's saving deeds recounted. It deserves repeating that in this theology, the point of remembering Jerusalem lies in being absent from it, since God's absence was the mode of his presence to the people now.

But this apophatic reading of holiness and Holy Land had been yielding, at least since 1882, to actual numbers of Jews finding refuge in Palestine. As Christian Zionists from America and Britain had discovered Jerusalem with all its resonances, so European Jews, including secular Jews, were doing so, too. When, for example, the religiously detached Jewish writer A. S. Hirschberg arrived in Jerusalem in 1901, he expected a city of bazaars and rat-infested alleys. What stunned him was the Western Wall, the Temple remnant that had been made sacrosanct for Jews by Suleiman the Magnificent and by the numberless Jews who'd filled its crevices with their prayers. Yes, it was a token of ruin and defeat, but it was also a relic of survival. "All my private troubles mingled with our nation's misfortunes," Hirschberg wrote of his sudden flood of tears at the wall, "to form a torrent." Such a reaction was not unusual among European Jews who found themselves there. The wall reemerged as a token of Jewish identity.[39] In 1905, the Zionist Congress rejected the British offer of resettlement in Uganda and formally determined to create the Jewish homeland in Eretz Yisrael. The question had been unresolved when Herzl died in 1904, but his expectation was made explicit in the instructions he left: "I wish to be buried in the vault beside my father and to lie there till the Jewish people take my remains to Palestine."[40]

3. Waiting to Baptize You

Arab and Islamic opposition to Zionism was one thing, but there was a greater obstacle to the project of Jewish return embedded in the consciousness—or perhaps by now the unconscious—of Western civilization. Herzl had made one valiant effort to overcome it. The first-century Jews who followed Jesus had interpreted the destruction of the Temple, and then of Jerusalem, in typical Jewish fashion—as acts of God, teaching the people lessons, purifying them. We saw some of this earlier—how "Christians" understood the Roman savagery enacted between 70 and 135 as God's punishment for the broad rejection of Jesus. If this interpretation had occurred only in a prophetic mode, the note would have been self-critical, since according to the Church's own texts, Jesus was rejected in the end as much by his closest disciples — all abandoned him, and Peter denied him three times — as by the Jewish authorities.

But the interpretation of the Roman destruction of Jerusalem as God's mighty act was offered not in a prophetic but an apocalyptic mode (recall that the Book of the Apocalypse, or Revelation, was written in the midst of the Roman destruction and in response to it), with the judgment cast solely on someone else — the forces of Satan, ultimately "the Jews." Yes, the disciples forsook Jesus in his hour of need, but that was amply forgiven by the risen Jesus, who embraced Peter. What was not forgiven, and what was used to vindicate the Christians, was the Jewish rejection. That was punished by what happened to Jerusalem, which the increasingly Gentile Jesus movement remembered as a Jewish city in which an increasingly non-Jewish Jesus was alien. Jerusalem's tragic fate began to take on theological meaning — a theology of revenge. Thus, in Luke, Jesus is quoted as saying, "When you see Jerusalem surrounded by armies, you must realize that she will soon be laid desolate . . . For this is the time of vengeance when all that scripture says must be fulfilled. Alas for those with child, or with babies at the breast, when those days come."[41]

In the time of Constantine, in the early fourth century, after two hundred years of its being a pagan city known as Aelia Capitolina,[42] Jerusalem was reconstituted as a Christian holy place — a symbol of the Church's having replaced Israel. Where the True Cross was "discovered" by Constantine's mother, the Church of the Holy Sepulcher was constructed, giving the city its new Temple. Replacement theology had a geographical context: since the sign of God's covenant was "the land that I will give you," the land was forfeited when the covenant was broken. By the fourth century's end, St. Augustine was understood as tying the Jewish absence from Jerusalem — he cited a Psalm to decree "Scatter them!" — to the proof of Christian claims. Here began "the wandering Jew." Ever since, as we saw, when Christians ruled the city, Jews had been forbidden from living there.[43] The Roman Catholic Church and Eastern Orthodoxy were the primary custodians of this tradition, and it was not altered in the slightest by the nineteenth-century restorationist beliefs among Protestant evangelicals in Britain and the United States. For Catholics and other mainstream Christians, No Jews in Jerusalem, period.

No wonder Theodor Herzl, by his own account, was agitated when he arrived at the Vatican, on January 25, 1904, for a private audience with Pope Pius X. Herzl had successfully recruited monarchs and government figures to his cause, and now he hoped to enlist the Vatican's support. In fact, he was launching what one historian calls "a revolt against Jewish destiny"[44]—against the Jerusalem fever that had long infected the most sacred niche of the Western imagination. His Vatican initiative had been arranged by a papal count of his acquaintance, and the count had carefully instructed him to kiss the pope's ring. But Herzl could not bring himself to do it. When Pius offered his bejeweled hand, Herzl merely shook it. "I believe this spoiled my chances with him," he confided to his diary the next day, but given Herzl's agenda, the chances had been spoiled 1,800 years before.

"I briefly laid my request before him," Herzl noted. "But annoyed perhaps by my refusal to kiss his hand, he answered in a stern categorical manner.

"Pope: 'We are unable to favor this movement [Zionism]. We cannot prevent the Jews from going to Jerusalem—but we could never sanction it. The ground of Jerusalem, if it were not always sacred, has been sanctified by the life of Jesus Christ. As the head of the Church, I cannot answer you otherwise. The Jews have not recognized our Lord, therefore we cannot recognize the Jewish people.'"

As if to pick the scab of Christendom's thousand-year-old wound, Herzl replied, "And its present status, Holy Father?"

To which Pius answered, "I know, it is disagreeable to see the Turks in possession of our Holy Places. We simply have to put up with it. But to sanction the Jewish wish to occupy these sites, that we cannot do." For all of Christendom's long conflict, even hatred, of the Islamic enemy, there was no theological affront from Muslims to compare with the eternal insult the Church took from Jews. As if explaining why, the pope continued, "The Jewish faith was the foundation of our own faith, but it has been superseded by the teachings of Christ, and we cannot admit that it still enjoys any validity. The Jews who should have been the first to acknowledge Jesus Christ have not done so to this day."

The encounter between the pope and the Zionist had taken on the character of a medieval disputation. Herzl fired back, "Terror and persecution [are] not precisely the best means for converting the Jews."

Pius parried, with a blade sheathed in a rare papal appreciation of historical origins, "Our Lord came without power. He came in peace.

He persecuted no one. He was abandoned even by his apostles. It was only later that he attained stature. It took three centuries for the Church to evolve. The Jews therefore had plenty of time in which to accept his divinity without duress or pressure. But they chose not to do so, and they have not done it yet."

And then each man in his own way came to the nub of the issue. Herzl said, "But, Holy Father, the Jews are in a terrible plight. I do not know if Your Holiness is aware of the full extent of their tragedy. We need a land for these harried people."

And the pope, reiterating the core tradition, asked, "Must it be Jerusalem?"

Herzl's answer is fraught with the implication that Zionism was not yet infected with the fever of religious restoration: "We are not asking for Jerusalem, but for Palestine — for only the secular land."

"We cannot be in favor of it," Pius declared. And he threatened the ultimate in Catholic doom: "And so if you come to Palestine and settle your people there, we will be ready with churches and priests to baptize all of you." After that, Herzl reports, the pope "took a pinch of snuff and sneezed into a big red cotton handkerchief . . . The audience lasted about twenty-five minutes." After leaving Pius's presence, Herzl passed the Vatican art gallery. "I saw a picture of an Emperor kneeling before a seated Pope and receiving the crown from his hands. That's how Rome wants it."[45]

In 1897, the official Jesuit publication *Civiltà Cattolica* had taken aim at Herzl's World Zionist Congress with the Church's theological crossbow:

> One thousand eight hundred and twenty-seven years have passed since the prediction of Jesus of Nazareth was fulfilled, namely that Jerusalem would be destroyed . . . that the Jews would be led away to be slaves among all the nations, and that they would remain in the dispersion until the end of the world . . . According to the Sacred Scriptures, the Jewish people must always live dispersed and *vagabondo* (vagrant) among the other nations so that they may render witness to Christ not only by the Scriptures . . . but by their very existence.
>
> As for a rebuilt Jerusalem which might become the center of a reconstructed State of Israel, we must add that this is contrary to the prediction of Christ himself who foretold that "Jerusalem would be downtrodden by the Gentiles until the time of the Gentiles is fulfilled" (Luke 21:24), that is . . . until the end of the world.[46]

This ancient Roman Catholic and Eastern Orthodox conviction that God forbids the return of Jews to Jerusalem could not contrast more sharply with the modern evangelical Protestant certainty that God wants the restoration of Jews to Jerusalem — yet at bottom both of these Christian visions put the Jewish relationship to Jerusalem at the center of End Time theology. Catholics see Jews returning to Jerusalem only at the end of the world, while Protestants see it happening *before* the end, as a causal instrument of that climax. But both foresee the destruction of the earthly Jerusalem as a prelude to the establishment of the heavenly Jerusalem.

Here is the common doom-laden creed as articulated even by a leading Catholic figure of Jewish-Christian reconciliation at the historic Second Vatican Council in the 1960s, Cardinal Augustin Bea: "The fate of Jerusalem constitutes a sort of final reckoning at the end of a thousand years of infidelities and opposition to God. Here, too, it is not the fact of belonging to the people of Israel which determines the judgment, but the act of opposing God and his prophets and messengers, above all Jesus." It should be emphasized that, in coming from the liberal Catholic prelate Bea in the midst of the Church's liberal heyday, this statement shows how important the apocalyptic vision is to mainstream Christian thought. "The judgment of Jerusalem and its destruction form part of God's revelation to man whereby he makes manifest in a particular episode something of the terrible reality of the judgment with which the story of mankind will end."[47]

So what happened in 70 CE — the city centered on the Temple Mount, ringed round with thousands of resisters hung on crosses — is a foretaste of what will happen at the end of time, with Catholics casting Jews in leading roles as permanent antagonists, and Protestants casting them, after being restored to Jerusalem and given a last opportunity to convert, as the decisive agents of the messianic climax. These two eschatologies, however different, combined to underwrite savage programs of apocalyptic violence. One began in the late nineteenth century, through the instrument of racist imperialism: the local conflict between Jews and Arabs in Palestine, with Arab victimhood expressed as the ongoing rage over Palestinian dispossession. The other began slightly later and was on a vastly larger scale, escalated by Nazi neopaganism: the world-historic assault against the Jewish people, which eventually swung back to Jerusalem. Note that the mythic Catholic cities of Rome and Constantinople have never been a magnet of apocalyptic fervor. Nor have the mythic Protestant cities of Geneva, Canterbury, Leipzig, Stockholm, and Plymouth. No, only Jerusalem, the eternally Jewish city, has sparked the fury of the Christian imagination, and that, of course, is yet another aspect of Christian contempt for Jews.

4. Grand Mufti

The year of the First Aliyah, 1882, was also the year in which the British took control of Egypt. Cotton rich, canal rich, the crossroads of the Middle East and Africa. This seizure was the midpoint of the great last phase of the European imperial land grab, a third of a century during which fully one-fourth of the world's surface was claimed as colonies.[48] British lust for Middle East sway would be redoubled when the new-fangled combustion engine created a need for petroleum, which was just then discovered beneath the region's parched soil,[49] much as the automobile's need for rubber tires would accelerate Belgium's interest in the rubber trees of Congo. Thus old religious assumptions were joined to new "scientific" theories of racial ranking, nation-state prerogatives, capitalist expansion, and industrial technologies made lethal to quicken an ideology of "English-speaking and Teutonic" dominance for the sake of "civilization."[50] The Arabs would be as much at the mercy of this virtuous subjugation as the Apaches or the Aboriginal peoples of Australia.

For the Arabs of Palestine, a decisive intermingling of the British imperial impulse and the Jewish intrusion could seem to be embodied in the fact that, once the mandate was established after World War I, its first high commissioner, Sir Herbert Samuel, appointed in 1920, was a British Jew.[51] Perhaps, given its consequence, his most notable act of governance was his appointment as mufti of Jerusalem (a mufti is an expounder of Islamic law[52]) the scion of a leading family, Muhammad al-Hajj Amin al-Husayni. The Husaynis regarded themselves as descendants of the Prophet and had long served as Ottoman functionaries in the province.[53] Amin's brother, father, and grandfather had served as muftis of Jerusalem, with offices on the Haram al-Sharif, and though the position was not hereditary, Amin may have expected to succeed them. But the British claimed the authority to make the appointment, and they enhanced the mufti's position, giving him greater authority over other Islamic officials, although only in the religious and communal spheres. (Arab politics in other colonial centers, like Baghdad, Amman, and Beirut, would evolve more robustly than in Palestine because the designated local authorities were not restricted in their identities in this way.)

Sir Herbert was openly a Zionist, and Husayni had been an outspoken opponent of Jewish immigration. Husayni had also participated in the nationalist Arab revolt against the Turks, and had then led demonstrations in Jerusalem against the Zionists and the Balfour Declaration. He had honed his leadership skills as an artillery officer in the Turkish army, but he was not well educated and lacked the qualities of a strategic thinker, which would put him at a disadvantage in a long-term geopolitical chess match where he faced not one but two savvy opponents. Yet, with a feel for the mood of his people and a capacity to manipulate it, he was a formidable agitator. That some of the demonstrations he led at Al Aqsa had turned violent (and are remembered by Arabs as a revolt) should have eliminated Husayni from consideration for appointment as mufti. But it seems that Sir Herbert, in best British fashion, thought he could co-opt the young Arab, and through him channel the "native" restlessness.[54]

No sooner had Mufti al-Husayni established himself as leader of the Arab population than he sponsored an Islamic revival, with schools, clinics, mosques, and a restoration of the shrines on the Haram. He also embraced an extreme rejectionist position, criticizing the British overlords and their Balfour plan (which, after all, never mentioned "Palestinians" or "Arabs" but only "non-Jewish communities") and demonizing the Jews, whom he regarded as the real threat. Totally mischaracterizing the attitude of the majority of Zionists, whose main interest in Palestine continued to be in the new rural settlements and the coastal cities (Tel Aviv was founded as a Jewish city in 1909), Husayni raised alarms about Jewish intentions to destroy the Muslim holy sites at the Haram al-Sharif in order to rebuild the Temple. Eventually, as messianic Jews adopted an apocalyptic vision for Israel, those alarms would not seem quite so irrational. Once more, fear of destruction, and longing for it, would enter the story as engines of religious and political desire. To this day, the multigenerational rage of Jerusalem's several hundred thousand Arab Muslims, centered on hyperdefensiveness around Al Aqsa Mosque and the Dome of the Rock, drives the Palestinian side of the Israeli-Palestinian conflict.

The larger point is that when Husayni fully sponsored a positive Palestinian (as opposed to pan-Arab) identity, he did so by casting a threatening Judaism as its negative foil. In doing that, he was reproducing the dynamic that had informed early Christianity's coming into a sense of itself in opposition to Judaism, and medieval Christendom's coming into a sense of itself in opposition to Islam. Such self-affirmation depends on the denigration of the "other." Focused on Jerusalem's Noble Sanctuary as a sacred Islamic precinct, the Palestinians in effect created a homeland movement that was the mirror image of a perceived Zionism, what the Palestinian scholar Edward Said calls "a dogmatic, almost theological brand of Arabism."[55] The one reflected the other, which reflected back, multiplying the effect until each became a kind of infinite reflection of the other. From then on, like sibling antagonists in an epic tragedy, the dual movements were bound to clash.

Lost in this bipolarity was a fault line within the Arab community that divided local Arab Christians from Muslims—a distinction that would take on ever more significance as Arab aspirations were defined in almost exclusively Muslim terms. Eventually, Christian Palestinian alienation from Arab Muslims would be expressed in high rates of Christian expatriation—and in a mostly suppressed Muslim hostility.[56] That division only reinforces the larger conundrum. That the Israeli-Palestinian conflict remains unresolved nearly a century after it was launched is ample testimony to the fact that, conceived in the deadly European mix of imperialism and Christian apocalypticism, it began as an unthreadable needle. In any consideration of contemporary politics, the conflict is an unavoidable subject, yet as the denouement of this long story of ignited Jerusalem, it is equally unavoidable, having been burning beneath the surface of this narrative from the start.

How to disarm this dispute? Perhaps the only way is to unpack the elements that made it absolute in the first place, naming the Western mind as the usually ignored and only apparently innocent third party. Yes, the Israelis are right to demand the recognition of the Jewish state's legitimacy, and yes, Palestinians must insist on a Jewish reckoning with the cost *to them* of that state's coming into being, but even larger matters must be dealt with. We saw this image earlier, but now its full poignancy is apparent: the Palestinians and Israelis may have painted themselves into a deadly corner from which only one may yet emerge alive, but they did not create the corner. One of its walls is colonialism; the other is anti-Semitism.[57] The witnessing Western mind, meanwhile, is always full of wide-eyed astonishment at the beastly behavior of antagonists caught within confines it has no memory of having created.

Husayni also set the long-continuing pattern of internal Palestinian polity, for by staking out an extreme rejectionist position, he empowered more moderate Arabs (including some rival notable families) who, while resisting both Zionism and British rule, sought ways to ameliorate conditions by cooperating where possible with both Jewish and British leaders. The municipal officeholders — mayors and council members — would, in contrast to the religious authority of the mufti, seek ways to make Jewish and British power work for Palestinians. This political bipolarity can be seen today in the tensions between the Palestinian Authority, rooted in the secular Fatah movement, and Hamas, which defines itself religiously.

As time went on, Husayni became more extreme. In 1928, he promoted the inflammatory proposition that the Western Wall was sacred to Islam, exclusively so. Since Jews, with "their unlimited greedy aspirations," were using it as a foothold from which to take over the entire Noble Sanctuary, they should no longer be permitted to worship there.[58] That some Jews had designs on the Temple Mount is clear — to repeat the important point — but in that early phase of Zionism, with its mainly socialist ethos, they were a distinct minority. Most of those who envisioned any kind of restoration of the Temple did so mystically, looking toward an undefined messianic age. But these distinctions were lost on most Palestinians, who instinctively rallied to a threatened Haram al-Sharif.

In attacking Jews at the Western Wall, the mufti was undoing a respectful Muslim tradition that went back further than Suleiman's formal establishment of the Temple remnant as a place of Jewish worship, all the way back to Umar ibn al-Khattab, who in the seventh century, before Al Aqsa or the Dome of the Rock were built, had invited Jews to revere that remnant. There was a new existential insecurity embedded in the mufti's position here, since what was at issue was the prior Jewish claim to the sacred precinct. It was as if the Muslim leader could not stand the truth of historical Jewish precedence, which meant he was at the mercy of the same dread that prompted Christians to denigrate Jews because their position as the first custodians of messianic hope gave the Jewish rejection of Christian claims for that hope's fulfillment

in Jesus a savage bite. What Muslim Arabs were feeling about and doing to Jews in 1929, that is, repeated what followers of Jesus felt and did
in the first century.

Tensions around the Western Wall and on the Noble Sanctuary
mounted, breaking into full-blown Jewish-Arab violence in August
1929. Dozens were killed on both sides. The British intervened, ruthlessly suppressing what was called a Palestinian rebellion. Among Zionists, and in the Western press, the mufti was seen as an instigator;
among Palestinians, his leadership was as confirmed as it was defined
by his hatred of Jews. *We know who we are by whom we hate.*

Meanwhile, Jewish immigration to Palestine continued. In the early
1930s, as anti-Semitic pressure grew in Germany, the number of Jewish arrivals picked up considerably, from about 4,000 in 1931, to more
than 40,000 in 1934, to more than 60,000 in 1935.[59] By the late 1930s,
350,000 Jews had fled from Nazi-controlled territory, causing a huge
refugee crisis, and even such countries as Britain and the United States
refused to lift immigration quotas to accept them.

Palestine was one safe haven. By 1939, almost 500,000 Jews lived
there, two-thirds of whom had come in that decade. Meanwhile, Arabs
in Jerusalem and elsewhere in Palestine were either ignorant of or indifferent to what was driving this extraordinary phenomenon, as wave
after wave of European Jews showed up, burdened with strapped suit-
cases and bundles that held what was left of their possessions. "Hitler
Zionists," they were labeled by their ambivalent Jewish predecessors,[60]
who disliked the idea of the aliyah out of desperation rather than desire. Yet most of these refugee Jews, their own experience notwithstanding, arrived with the ingrained bias of Europeans, and took Arab
"racial" inferiority for granted.[61] What could only seem to Arabs as
rank colonial condescension further exacerbated the conflict, and further blinded Palestinians to the primal identity with the land of Israel
that every Jew could retrieve. But in context, empathy was not a Palestinian option, as the position of the Jewish rival strengthened with each
new immigrant. A nearly automatic Palestinian hostility reinforced the
Jews' readiness to think badly of the Arabs.

The mufti, meanwhile, was playing a delicate game, trying to placate
an increasingly threatened and angry Arab population while encour-
aging the evident British uneasiness with a more energized Zionism.
What the mufti failed to appreciate at first was the simultaneous uneasiness of the British elite with Arab ambitions and British readiness

to use Zionism to thwart those ambitions. Overriding both of these factors was the gap that opened between the Jewish and Arab experience in Palestine "in a variety of economic, social and organizational realms." Palestinian society could not match the Zionist community's "truly exceptional levels of capital investments per capita and human capital inflow, which were among the highest in the world at that time."[62] The tinder was set for an explosion.

It came in April 1936 when self-anointed Arab resisters attacked a bus, murdering two Jews. By then Jews had formed their own militia, the Hagana, and it retaliated, killing a pair of Arab farmers. The British high commissioner declared a state of emergency, but more reprisals, strikes, and riots followed, with Arabs attacking both Jews and British. The mufti's hand was forced, and he assumed leadership of a movement that demanded, in a manifesto to the "Arab Nation," an end to all Jewish immigration, the prohibition of Jewish acquisition of Arab land, and the creation of a Palestinian national government. An Arab general strike was called, demonstrations grew violent. Jews were killed, including nine children when their school was bombed.[63]

Zionist leaders condemned what they called "the forces of the desert" against "the forces of civilization." They defiantly declared, "We will not be stopped."[64] Jews recognized an Arab determination to fight to the death, and from then on had reason to see Arab statehood in Palestine as a lethal prospect. Jewish armed resistance groups, notably the Irgun and the Stern Gang, came into their own, and with them an ethos of military force that became central to Israeli identity. In rebellion against the ancient role of the supplicant Jew forced to cower, the Zionist "new man" would forever be armed.

The British, with reinforcements from Egypt and Malta surpassing in Palestine the number of troops that Britain had on the entire subcontinent of India, ruthlessly cracked down on the Arab rebels.[65] A British commission saw a solution to the Jewish-Arab tension in the idea of partition, a sharing of the land of Palestine, which the Arabs rejected outright.[66] The disturbance grew into a full-bore anticolonial Arab uprising that would last into 1939, leaving more than five thousand Palestinians dead (along with hundreds of Jews and British fighters).[67] Whole Arab neighborhoods and villages were leveled, the Palestinian social fabric was ripped apart, never fully to be restitched, with political and economic institutions similarly damaged.

Arab Palestine, in effect, was crippled in its crib. Its advocates, while always responsible for actions and omissions, would never have the unity of purpose needed to assert a coherent national will, and it was perhaps inevitable after this that Zionists would find no locals on the other side with whom to deal. Hence the phenomenon of Palestinian "invisibility." A fractured Jerusalem would emerge as the permanent symbol of the cult of lost-cause martyrdom that defined the peculiar form of Jerusalem fever that infected Palestinians from then on.

The mufti's precise roles in these events is in dispute, with some seeing him as the leading anti-British rebel, and others as a man caught in the middle of forces he could not control. But his attitude toward Zionism and Jews was never in doubt, and grew ever more extreme. Crucially, he rejected a British white paper in 1939 that may well have given Palestinians much of what they were demanding, including restrictions on Jewish immigration and land acquisition, and the promise of an independent Palestine with Arabs in the majority. This rejection, in the words of Rashid Khalidi, was "the last important decision the Palestinians took by themselves for several decades."[68]

Husayni's no-compromise defiance played well with fellow notables and an angry and powerless people. Across the Middle East he was seen as a leader of the pan-Arab cause, which only heightened the British need to corral his influence. When the British declared him stripped of his authority and liable to arrest, he fled, descending the walls of the Haram under cover of darkness, making his way to the coast, and escaping by boat to Lebanon. From then on, he was as much the self-declared enemy of Britain as of the Zionists. Winston Churchill, exercising authority as a member of the War Cabinet, ordered him assassinated, and dispatched a group of Irgun commandos to do the job in Iraq. They failed.[69]

In a calculation that would permanently haunt the Palestinian cause, the mufti, on the principle of "the enemy of my enemy is my friend," threw in with Hitler—which perhaps did more than anything else to delegitimize Palestinian claims, and therefore was an essential factor in the ongoing dispossession of his people. Especially once the crimes of the Nazi regime against the Jewish people became known, Israelis would find it almost impossible, remembering Husayni's pro-Axis pact, not to regard the anticolonial resentment of Palestinians as a virulent strain of Nazi anti-Semitism. That Arabs at the mercy of French and British colonial intrusions were broadly pro-German would also serve as permanent fuel for an intense Israeli hatred, for what Edward Said labeled "the implacability of the Israeli refusal to acknowledge, deal with, or come to any sort of understanding with Palestinian nationalism."[70] Arab friendliness toward Hitler would also foster both American and Soviet pro-Israel attitudes once the State of Israel came into being.[71] Because of the infection of Nazism, normal geopolitics took on a diabolical aspect, pivoting around the unforgivable.

Hitler, for his part, regarded Husayni as a lever with which to move Arab sympathies into the German orbit. Making his way through Iraq, Iran, Turkey, and Rome, the mufti arrived in Berlin in 1941 and would remain there through most of the war. He became an agent of Nazi anti-Semitic propaganda. He met with Hitler, who, on the basis of Husayni's blue eyes and fair hair, promoted the Arabs from near the bottom of the racial ranks closer, as Hitler himself put it, to "the best Roman stock."[72] The mufti offered to order and organize a pan-Arab revolt against the British in the Middle East and to generate Muslim support for Axis forces fighting in the Balkans, in return for a German guarantee of Arab, including Palestinian, independence. Hitler agreed, and the text of their accord included a German commitment "to the abolition of the Jewish National Homeland in Palestine."[73] The date of this agreement was April 28, 1942, three months after the Wannsee Conference at which leaders of the Thousand-Year Reich, implementing the millennial apocalypse after all, adopted a plan for the "Final Solution to the Jewish Question."

The extent of the mufti's knowledge of and cooperation with the Final Solution is in dispute. Accusations were made (including the charge that he planned the extermination of Jews in the Middle East[74]), yet the mufti was never indicted by any court. But in 1961, one of those with whom he was associated in Germany and with whom he worked to prevent Jewish emigration to Palestine,[75] a man who had served as recording secretary of the Wannsee Conference, was brought to trial in Jerusalem.

5. Eichmann in Jerusalem

Is it presumptuous to write, not about political conflict, but about the states of mind undergirding it? The trial of Adolf Eichmann in 1961 represented nothing if not a revolution in states of mind as the people of Europe and America—"the West"—began to confront the facts and significance of the Holocaust for the first time. That trial, in combination with related and nearly simultaneous events, like the movie version of Anne Frank's *Diary of a Young Girl*, the publication of *Night* by Elie Wiesel, and stage productions of *The Deputy* by Rolf Hochhuth, marked the beginning of the end of widespread avoidance, if not outright denial, of the meaning of what the Nazis had done in systematically murdering six million Jews.[76]

To take one obvious instance, the state of mind of institutional Christianity, especially the Roman Catholic Church, was profoundly changed by its having to reckon with what was laid bare in the Eichmann trial—and in the Hochhuth play, which criticized the behavior of the wartime pope, Pius XII. The historic shift in the Church's self-understanding, articulated in numerous declarations of the Second Vatican Council, was a direct result of that reckoning.

Adolf Eichmann was in charge of the bureaucracy that managed the transfer to "the East" of millions of Jews, where they were starved and murdered in Nazi death camps. His oversight of the deportations grew to include everything from the scheduling of trains to the construction of track to the assignment of guards and camp supervisors to the recordkeeping of the killing process (including meticulous inventories of confiscated property) to the selection of inmates who worked and those who were gassed to the disposal of mountains of ash to, in the end, attempts to destroy the evidence of what he and his underlings had done. After the war, with the help of Catholics who facilitated the escape of various Nazis, he obtained credentials in support of a new identity, including a visa to Argentina, where he lived until Israeli agents captured him in 1960.

Eichmann's trial in Jerusalem lasted for more than three months. He was charged with crimes against the Jewish people and crimes against humanity, defined in fifteen counts. He did not dispute the charges, although he insisted throughout that he had no blood directly on his hands. The proceedings were covered by hundreds of journalists from all over the world, including Hannah Arendt, whose dispatches appeared in *The New Yorker* and later in a controversial book, *Eichmann in Jerusalem: A Report on the Banality of Evil*. The trial was the first ever to be televised, with videotapes shipped overnight to cities throughout Europe and America. In New York, a thirty-minute summary of highlights was televised every night. In Israel, where few households had televisions, the sessions were broadcast live on radio,[77] and you could walk in any Jewish neighborhood and follow the court proceedings as you went by the open windows.

The trial was the first international event of the television age. The nondescript, bald, bespectacled bureaucrat, sitting passively in his bulletproof glass booth, flipping through reams of documents, was the "banal"[78] face of a horror that could finally be perceived. The prosecution called more than a hundred Holocaust survivors to testify, and their accounts filled the hours, days, and weeks. An outpouring of rage, grief, and bewilderment accompanied this testimony and followed it, with, for example, many thousands of letters pouring into the offices of the Israeli prosecutors—most of them from survivors who were at last crying out with what they had seen, lost, and been made to suffer. The trial amounted to the breaking of a worldwide silence about the fate of Jews in Europe, a silence that, oddly, had been observed almost as much in Israel as anywhere.[79]

The Holocaust is the most referred-to public event in modern times and a universal point of reference, even for those who deny that it occurred. Yet this familiarity makes it nearly impossible to enter into the facts of what happened with anything more than received, or manufactured, feeling or understanding. One knows how one is to respond, and one does. But what actually was the Holocaust?

Start with Hitler. His project of murdering every living Jew was rank madness, an evil that stands in a category apart. But it was not merely that. We have already seen how the fate of the Jews had long lodged in a certain kind of Christian imagination as the key to bringing about the millennial age. Here, too, the assumption was that the Jewish people needed to be eliminated, albeit by conversion. And if, at the dawn of the End Time, Jews still refused to convert, then Jesus himself would usher them into, if not gas chambers and crematoria, an eternal lake of fire. Hitler was no Christian, but he was a millennialist, influenced by strains traceable to the Book of Revelation, where such a vision is sketched out in graphic detail. The "thousand-year reign" of Christ[80] gave Hitler his temporal motif, which is why he conceived of himself as the founder of the Thousand-Year Reich. Jewish disappearance, in each case, was the millennial precondition.

The insistence on Hitler's uniquely evil character, and on the genocide as the work of a relatively small cabal of Nazi perpetrators, can let the broader culture—with *its* apocalyptic strains and anti-Semitism, and within which the Nazi evil unfolded and nearly succeeded—off the hook. Indeed, one recognizes in Hitler's program a classic, if highly industrialized, instance of the scapegoat mechanism identified by René Girard as basic to the human condition. So all people, surely including all members of Western civilization and all Christians, have something of their own at stake in a moral reckoning with the Holocaust. Yes, the Nazis did it, but they could not have done it alone. Yes, Christian anti-Judaism spawned lethal anti-Semitism, but in-groups have been pouring blame on out-groups since before recorded history. The crime was particular, but the impulses behind it were universal. That is what made the Eichmann trial momentous.

But Jews and Israelis also had a reckoning to accomplish. As the systematic murder of Jews unfolded in Europe, Zionists were as powerless to help as anyone. An immediate terror of the Nazi onslaught gripped Jews in Palestine early in the war, when it seemed as though Field Marshal Erwin Rommel's invincible Afrika Korps would sweep from its victories in North Africa up the Levant. Ahead of Rommel, Jews fled into Palestine from Egypt and other conquered territories. The "Desert Fox" was coming! Jews from all over Palestine, hearing that the Old City would be a demilitarized zone under the protection of the Red Cross and the Vatican, fled to Jerusalem. Zionists who had been indifferent to the city before then had a new reason to cherish it. The "new man" pioneers rediscovered the most ancient dynamic of Jewish history — that war and the threat of war could give precious significance to the city of David. For a time in 1941, the walled enclave seemed like the refuge of old, and Jews turned toward it with more heat than they could consciously understand, igniting their version of the Jerusalem fire that had been burning in Christian hearts for a century. Field Marshal Bernard Montgomery's defeat of the Germans at El Alamein in 1942 relieved the Jewish fear of overrunning Nazis, but the idea of Jerusalem as refuge and sanctuary had taken hold, the beginning of a dramatic shift in the city's meaning.[81]

The "new man" of Zionism had not prevented Jews in Palestine from an outbreak of Hitler panic, and Zionist leaders began to learn in detail what was befalling their fellow Jews in Europe. At first there was a "less than compassionate response of the Jewish community in Palestine to the destruction of the European Jews." Those who had successfully fled from German-controlled territory in the 1930s could feel contemptuous of the naiveté — or assimilation — that had prompted others to remain behind. As the horrors of the death camps came to be known to Jews in Palestine, it was not unusual when the "victims were censured for having let the Nazis murder them without fighting for their lives." Here began what might be called the "lambs to the slaughter" syndrome, a contempt for the murdered population by Jews who were not themselves ever tested by the Nazi death machine. How could they not have resisted? Why did they go so passively into railroad cars and gas chambers? Why did they obey? Where was their rebellion? A vast shame accompanied the news from Europe, a collapse of Jewish pride. "This attitude," the Israeli scholar Tom Segev observes, "in time became a sort of psychological and political ghost that haunted the State of Israel."[82]

Jewish anguish in Palestine over the Holocaust was real, but it was necessarily experienced in the abstract, with a stronger focus on the increasingly implication-laden Jerusalem. The memory of exile from and destruction of the city surfaced with new force. This was nothing more than a reentry into the past experience that had repeatedly made the Jewish people a *people*. For Christians, Jerusalem may have come to stand for heaven, but for Jews its only "restoration" was to grief — and wasn't grief once more the central act of peoplehood? "Cry, Jerusalem, for the fallen of your exile," as Segev reports, was the way one Israeli newspaper related news of the death camps. "Shout, Zion: save your sons and daughters, be refuge to my children and little ones." It was a potent, if subliminally powered, impulse to take in the news of the mass slaughter by cloaking it in references to the cultic center of ancient Jewish sacrifice. Sacrifice once more emerged as a theme, along with the primal mystery of Israel's Lord, whose will it was. The word "Holocaust" had been applied to what was happening as early as Kristallnacht in 1938, a word that in Greek means "burnt offering" and refers to the gift offered to God, by God's own requirement.[83]

And then the war ended. Two things happened in Palestine, and they should have been impossibly contradictory. One was that the gaze of Zionism turned away from what had just happened in Europe. Since the anti-Jewish crime of the Nazis was unspeakable, it would not be spoken of. This silence had its global equivalent in the habit of discussing "refugees," "displaced persons," and "concentration camp inmates" without reference to their Jewishness. In the *New York Times* account of the 1945 liberation of Auschwitz, the victims and survivors were defined solely by nationality: Hungarian, Dutch, Italian, French, Polish. In an extensive news story that offers details down to the name of the manufacturer of the ovens in which human remains were incinerated, the word "Jew" never appears. The story's author was C. L. Sulzberger, nephew of the paper's publisher and soon to be its most eminent columnist.[84]

Such avoidance was general. The war crimes trials at Nuremberg would bring charges of the various Nazi atrocities without pointing to the "Final Solution to the Jewish Problem" as such. Israelis, of course, knew very well what had happened, and to whom. The trauma drove them on to the last great push for independence, energizing their wars against the vestigial British Mandate, the Palestinians, and four Arab nations. But that push toward the historic Jewish victory was what was emphasized, not the catastrophic Jewish defeat that made it irresistible.

The other postwar event that should have made such deflection impossible was the beginning of a monumental influx of Jewish refugees, waves of survivors that—despite the last-ditch efforts of the Arab-protecting British, who forced tens of thousands of Europe-fleeing Jews into internment camps in Cyprus—broke on the shores of Palestine again and again. Before 1945 was out, nearly 100,000 emaciated and gaunt-eyed survivors arrived fresh from the camps. "As the pogroms in Russia in the 1880s had launched modern Zionism," Benny Morris observes, "so the largest pogrom of them all propelled the movement, almost instantly, into statehood."[85] When Israel became an independent nation in 1948 and no other power could stop the immigration, another 200,000 Holocaust survivors arrived in short order. By the end of the decade, the number of "brands plucked from the fire of Europe"[86] approached 350,000, "almost one of every three Israelis."[87]

Imagine what this meant for individuals and for the new nation. Every third person a camp survivor! The bronzed pioneer Zionists; the prewar boulevardiers from Vienna and Berlin; the Sephardic transplants from Cairo, Tunis, and Baghdad; the anti-Zionist Orthodox Jews from Ottoman days; the warrior sabras—each of the self-satisfied segments of Israel's multifaceted society was all at once overwhelmed by a cohort of Jewish dispossession. The survivors were by every measure the largest single subgroup of Israelis. But even those who, by an earlier escape, were themselves physically untouched by wartime events in Europe were hardly spared, since a majority of Jews who had come to Palestine in the decade before the war—and we saw that their numbers accounted for two out of three Jews living in Palestine by 1939—had lost family members to the crematoria. "They, too, were in mourning;

many tortured themselves with the same guilt feelings that plagued the survivors."[88]

The dispossession of most of the refugees, though, was total: a vacancy of meaning, nakedness of dignity, stripped of any reason to believe in their fellow man. And their dispossession was literal. There were far too many to house or properly care for — something like 100,000 people who, after months or years of torture chambers and killing fields, followed by ad hoc shelter and food lines, still had the barest acquaintance with what could be called healthy nourishment or minimal security. Once again, even in the Jewish homeland, the new arrivals found themselves in provisional shelters, transit camps, and "agency beds." Their tents and shanty dwellings in village outskirts, on urban rooftops, and in alleys made their presence dramatic, yet by the young nation's ever averted eyes, they were also unseen for what they were. If the individual survivors were clear victims of what a later generation would diagnose as post-traumatic stress disorder, so was the nation that took them in.

Israel was a refuge for victims, but not only that. As if the trauma of its wars for independence was not enough, including the unaddressed shock of what those wars did to Palestinians, Israel can itself be understood as Hitler's last victim, for the as yet unhealed wound he inflicted on the Jewish people was Israel's wound. Hitler had annihilated nearly six of every nine Jews living in the most advanced civilization in history.[89] That alone was enough to sear every Jewish imagination, certainly in Israel, with, as one Israeli scholar-statesman put it, an "ever present, almost apocalyptic fear of annihilation."[90] That fear, of course, did not begin with Hitler but with the original "apocalypse" two thousand years earlier. Across those millennia, something like one of every three Jews — Hitler's total ratio[91] — were murdered, almost always in the name of Christ. Jewish survival within an anti-Jewish culture is one of history's astonishing sagas, the contradiction of any impulse to tell the story as one of mere victimhood. But that survival came at a cost.

As events in the decades after 1948 would show, not even unparalleled military supremacy would untie the knot of existential anxiety that binds the soul of Israel. As Americans are incapable of imagining the world without their nation riding high, so Israelis, by their own account, regard the deletion of their nation from history not only as possible but, all too often, as imminent. And why shouldn't every conflict — there have been nine wars involving Israel since 1948 — be taken as kill-or-be-killed? It has been said since 1948 that the State of Israel came successfully into existence because of Europe's guilty conscience, as if the loss of the six million were Israel's gain, but as a measure of the impact of the Holocaust on Israel, that is perverse distortion — and not the half of it, either.

6. Nakba

The war of 1948, for Palestinians, was the *Nakba*, simply "the catastrophe."[92] But the normal outlines of the brute story of colonial oppression, however much it satisfies the Palestinian need to understand their victimization, would never approach the full truth of what had happened. It was as if a vat of acid had been spilled on one people and it splashed over on another. The Palestinians became, in a phrase of Edward Said's, "the victims of the victims."[93]

A narrative pitting those peoples against each other ignores the filling of that vat and the tipping of it. The Palestinian response to their own lethal, almost accidental, inundation was given eloquent expression, ironically, by David Ben-Gurion: "Why should the Arabs make peace? If I was an Arab leader I would never make terms with Israel. That is natural. We have taken their country. Sure, God promised it to us, but what does that matter to them? Our God is not theirs. We come from Israel, it's true, but two thousand years ago, and what is that to them? There has been anti-Semitism, the Nazis, Hitler, Auschwitz, but was that their fault? They only see one thing: We have come here and stolen their country. Why should they accept that?"[94]

In February 1947 the British washed their hands of the mandate responsibility, an aspect of imperial collapse that was echoed just then in India's declaration of independence (and Pakistan's, Burma's, and Ceylon's) and the Republic of Ireland's rejection of membership in the Commonwealth. The United Nations proposed, the following November, a partition of Palestine, offering statehood to Palestinians and Jews alike, with Jerusalem reserved as a *corpus separatum* under international control. The Palestinians, still influenced by Mufti Husayni's rejectionism — he was by now ensconced in Cairo, recognized by the Arab League as the Palestinian leader[95] — said no and engaged in a series of violent protests. Arab mobs burst out of old Jerusalem, for example, to attack Jewish businesses, buses, and random pedestrians in the west-

ern area of the city. But they had already lost the war a decade earlier
when the "Arab revolt" — and the order of Palestinian cohesion — was
utterly smashed by the British. Palestinians were no match for the Israeli fighters, and within weeks, tens of thousands of Arabs — the first
of what would be hundreds of thousands — had been forced or frightened from their homes. They fled, driven toward lines controlled by
the Hashemite kingdom of Transjordan. Units of Arab armies invaded
Palestine, the first of the forces that would eventually come from four
Arab nations. The Arab Legion from Transjordan successfully solidified control of the Old City. Israel's war for independence was under
way — and Palestine's *Nakba*.

Israeli savagery is emphasized in the Palestinian narrative of these
events: a notorious Irgun massacre of dozens, perhaps hundreds, of
civilians at the village of Deir Yassin, near Jerusalem[96]; grotesque instances of what would later be called "ethnic cleansing," which, until
the recent work of Israel's so-called new historians,[97] was denied by
Jews. "Israel as a society," writes Shlomo Ben-Ami, the minister of foreign affairs in the government of Ehud Barak, "suppressed the memory
of its war against the local Palestinians because it could not really come
to terms with the fact that its finest Sabras, the heroes of its war for
independence, and the role models of the new nation, expelled Arabs,
committed atrocities against them and dispossessed them. This was
like admitting that the noble Jewish dream of statehood was stained
forever by a major injustice committed against the Palestinians, and
that the Jewish state was born in sin."[98] The Israeli-American writer
Bernard Avishai comments that "to be born in tragedy is not the same
as to be born in sin," a complexity acknowledged, too, by the Pales-
tinian-American writer Edward Said, who observed that "the Jewish
national liberation took place upon the ruins of *another* national existence, not in the abstract."[99]

The harsh fact is that Israel came into being after a conflict that
included what today would inevitably be designated as war crimes.
"Record! I am an Arab," the Palestinian poet Mahmoud Darwish de-
mands, wanting the details of Palestinian suffering put on record.[100]
But the recording has hardly happened. Underlying the post-1948 denial of the brutal Jewish assault against a local enemy was a denial
of what preceded it: a staggering confrontation with the transcendent
enemy. More than in sin, or tragedy, the Jewish state was born in a
brute determination not to be obliterated. However strong the Israeli

fighters were—and they were strong—Jewish annihilation was felt as beckoning in that struggle, the apocalypse after all. And why should it not have been?

The Jews were up against ferocious local resentment—three days after the Deir Yassin massacre, Arabs attacked a medical convoy, killing forty medical personnel.[101] But they were also up against history and fate, as is shown by three distinct factors, instances of the broad Jerusalem fixation that is our subject, and that shaped the events of 1948. The post–World War II British determination to hold on to Palestine (100,000 British troops were deployed there after the war, one for every twenty people, Arab and Jew alike[102]) and keep the Zionists from establishing their state is usually understood in terms of London's shifting strategic priorities: the need to solidify relations with Arab states that controlled oil, the Suez Canal, and communication lines to the Far East. True enough. Throw in an element of a resurgent British anti-Semitism, sparked by decades of tensions with the uncooperative Zionist establishment in Palestine. But below the surface of both strategic logic and Anglo-Saxon condescension was the prior and deeper attachment to the old Crusader ideal, Jerusalem as England's true preserve, Allenby's Christmas present to the British people, the spine of patriarchal election, the island nation's innermost selfhood. Unacknowledged in all ways, by the late 1940s, except for Parry's melody and Blake's lyric, which were more popular than ever, the grip of that attachment surpassed even the colonial impulses that were then being thwarted throughout the empire. India, Ireland, Africa. Not Jerusalem, too! was the feeling. Not Palestine—that's ours![103]

On a separate front, the United Nations' affirmation of the right of Jews and Palestinians to their independent states, including that idea of a *corpus separatum* for Jerusalem, had a particular bite. "Internationalization" of Jerusalem was rejected by Arabs, but it was aimed more at the Jews, who in fact were prepared to accept it. Recall that the early Zionists, David Ben-Gurion among them, were not fixated on Jerusalem, which they perhaps considered a city too far when it came to establishing the homeland. The pragmatic Zionists would take what they could get, when they could get it, and that defined the attitude in 1947. But the hidden dynamic identified by René Girard as mimetic desire was powerfully at play. Arabs, both Christian and Muslim, wanted control of the sacred centers, but they were not alone in being unable to abide the thought of Jewish control. Yes, the city was the most disputed real estate in Palestine, but mere political turf was not really the issue. The clue to the significance of the *corpus separatum* proposal for the city lay in its being offered in a Latin phrase — the language of Rome, which had initiated Jerusalem's condition as an apocalyptic nerve center (see the Arch of Titus, near the Colosseum, with its bas-relief celebration of the first-century destruction), and of Catholicism, which had kept the condition current. Greeks, too, were part of this, as Byzantium had carried forward assumptions of Jewish expulsion from the land that Constantine and his mother, Helena, had made holy. But by now the Vatican was the chief custodian of exile theology, and it was universally expected to be a party to any internationalizing arrangement. Rome's unfulfilled desire for Jerusalem was the very genesis of the mimesis — the mimetic rivalry.

Again, the stated justification for the proposed policy appealed to reason and fairness: internationalization would respect the religious needs of the three monotheisms that had shrines in the heart of the Old City. But also at work was the theological dogma that Pius X had so frankly expounded to Theodor Herzl, which required Jewish absence from Jerusalem as a proof of Christian claims for Jesus, who predicted it. As would be shown by the lack of Vatican objections to Jordanian control of the Old City, which lasted from 1948 to 1967, it was expressly *Jewish* sovereignty that posed the problem. No demand for a *corpus separatum* when Arabs were in control. Rejection of Jewish power over Jerusalem was embedded in the DNA of Christendom, and therefore, by 1948, of Western civilization. For the Catholic Church that rejection had the status of dogma. Indeed, because of its divinely commanded obligation to oppose the return of Jews to the Jewish homeland, the Vatican would refuse diplomatic recognition to Israel for almost half a century.[104]

But even an opposite impulse could glow with the heat of history and destiny. When President Harry Truman extended recognition to the Jewish state immediately upon its declaration of independence on May 14, 1948 — the first world leader to do so — more was at work than the reasons usually offered. Truman needed to shore up support among Jewish American voters ahead of a contested election, and he felt sympathy for the plight of Jews after the Holocaust. But would these motives have been enough for him to overrule the vigorous and unanimous opposition of his State and Defense departments, both of which foresaw a crippling Arab oil boycott and a geopolitical coup for the Soviet Union?

Truman was no philo-Semite,[105] but crucial to his pro-Israel decision was his lifelong association, as a Baptist (and member of the American Christian Palestine Committee), with the Christian Zionist agenda, as we have seen, of supporting the restoration of Jews to the land of Israel as a precondition of the Second Coming of Jesus. There can be no doubt that, in recognizing their state, Truman wished Hitler's victims well, but, perhaps unconsciously, he also took for granted, in advancing their return to Zion, that the Jews were to be instruments of their own final defeat.

All these currents generated energy in the flood of 1948, tides of meaning flowing across arid landscapes, as well as streams of fleeing people — and, ultimately, rivers of blood and tears, more from one side than the other. The problem of the dispossession of tens of thousands of Jewish refugees from Hitler's horror (and of the two thousand or so Jews who were driven out of the Jewish Quarter of the Old City by the Arab Legion) was readily solved when tens of thousands of Palestinian homes were suddenly unoccupied.[106] The deracinated Jewish death-camp survivors found themselves ensconced in fully outfitted abodes, with kitchen utensils, bedding, lamps, and lush gardens. As quickly as they took occupation of such places, just as quickly they forgot, or rather sublimated and denied, what had put them in a place of such desperate need, and whose loss had seen to its being filled. The Palestinians "didn't exist," Golda Meir famously declared. Ben-Gurion's assessment was equally direct: "There are no refugees — there are fighters who sought to destroy us, root and branch."[107]

The flight of refugees is not unusual during wartime. What made the condition of Palestinian refugees forever different — a flashpoint well into the twenty-first century[108] — was that Israel never considered allowing the Palestinians to return. The formerly Arab homes were occupied. Period. This applied particularly to West Jerusalem, where 30,000 Arabs lost their homes. All told, the war created about 750,000 displaced Palestinians.[109] Related anti-Jewish repression in Arab regimes throughout the Middle East and North Africa, meanwhile, resulted with near simultaneity in the expulsion or firmly encouraged emigration of nearly 600,000 Jews, most of whom fled to Israel, an "exchange of population" that was seen as establishing a kind of moral balance.

In the Jewish imagination, the dispossessed Palestinians not only ceased to exist; they never existed in the first place. If they were herded into foul transit camps on the other side of the barbed wire, where they would remain for decades, they would be permanently invisible. To Israelis, the abrupt supply of urgently needed housing was "the Arab miracle," completing the miracles of British collapse, American affirmation, and the sudden irrelevance of ancient Catholic opposition. "Accordingly," in an area approximately the size of Massachusetts, they did "hereby declare the establishment of a Jewish state in Eretz-Israel, to be known as the State of Israel."[110]

7. Soap

If the dispossessed Palestinians were unseen by the Israeli eye, the same was not quite true of Holocaust survivors, but the Israeli eye squinted at them. The survivors were living reminders of what the pioneer Zionists and their sabra descendants experienced as the great shame of the Jewish failure to resist—something, as we noted, to be avoided. "The young state of Israel," as the Israeli writer David Grossman put it, "believed that its strength depended partly on its ability to forget so that it could cobble together a new identity for itself."[111]

A memorial culture was born in the aftermath of the Holocaust, but it was heroic. Its primary emphasis was the harsh truth that while the Nazis were the ones to attempt the genocide, the rest of the world had done almost nothing to oppose it. Jews stood alone. Stories of the Warsaw Ghetto Uprising and of the small contingents of Irgun paratroopers who'd dropped into battle zones to fight the Nazis gained prominence. One symbol of this esprit in the early days of Israeli statehood was the elevation of the myth of Masada. The mountaintop plateau rising more than a thousand feet above the Jordan Valley was the site where Jewish fighters had battled to the last man against the Roman legions that had just destroyed Jerusalem in 70 CE. We saw earlier how that violence marked an interruption in history—the end of the Temple religion of Jews and the beginning of Christianity, of rabbinic Judaism, and of Jewish exile. Because of the spirit of resistance embodied at Masada, Jews had found ways of escaping annihilation, but they had always stood alone; their bravery was always epic. Beginning in the 1950s, young Israeli military recruits climbed the harshest face of the Masada mountain to be presented with their weapons and take their commissioning oaths.

Against this martial heroism, the "sheep to the slaughter" motif of the Holocaust was cloaked in a deafening silence. Indeed, to the extent that the presence of so many survivors could hardly be ignored, native-born Israelis generally regarded survivors with condescension, even contempt. This is a delicate matter, and only the witness of Israelis themselves draws our attention to it. In Tom Segev's report, survivors were described as "human debris," *avak adam* in Hebrew.[112] But in fact, for many, they became debris only after arriving in their Promised Land. Resettlement was hard enough, but there was contempt in the air they had to breathe. *Who died so that you could live?* The inevitable guilt of survivors was reinforced by the implicit accusation that they had somehow behaved badly, betraying the murdered ones. "Everywhere I turned," one survivor recalled of his early time in Israel, "the question was fired at me: why did the Jews not rebel?" Then he added something worse. "Suddenly I realized that we were ashamed of those who were tortured, shot, burned. There is a kind of general agreement that the Holocaust dead were worthless people. Unconsciously, we have accepted the Nazi view that the Jews were subhuman." A common Israeli nickname for the survivors came into vogue in the 1950s: *sabon*, which means "soap." It is a callous reference to the rumor about the foul use to which Nazis put the flesh of the crematoria victims.[113]

All of this changed with the Eichmann trial, the breaking of Israel's silence, and the world's, about what had happened. Of chief significance for our purposes is that the trial took place in Jerusalem, defined in its ancient origins by blood sacrifice, both before King David on prehistoric Mount Moriah and, with the construction of Solomon's Temple, after him. "They will be like the sheep for sacrifices," the prophet Ezekiel had decreed, "like the sheep in Jerusalem during the appointed feasts."[114]

Eichmann was in no way a sacrificial victim, yet his trial, too, came to seem like one of those appointments. In fact, the war criminal might not have been brought to justice in Jerusalem. After the international sensation of his capture by Israeli agents, influential Jews like Martin Buber, and leaders of groups like the World Zionist Organization and the American Jewish Committee, urged that Israel extradite Eichmann for trial by an international court, or by West Germany. Such calls were based partly on regard for established norms of international law (Buber argued that the victim cannot be the judge) and partly on the opinion of Jews in America and elsewhere that Israel did not speak for all Jews. Ben-Gurion, Israel's prime minister, would not hear of it. Bringing the Nazi leader to trial in Israel amounted to a claim by Israel and Israel alone as having standing to represent the six million dead, who, while alive, had been shut out of every other nation, America included. West Germany was already honoring Israel's claim to represent the six million by making reparations payments not to "world Jewry" but to the State of Israel. The trial would, in a phrase of Shlomo Ben-Ami's, nationalize the Holocaust, making it the ground of the Israeli-Jewish identity.[115] The Israeli prosecutor, in his opening statement, made the assertion explicit: "As I stand before you, judges of Israel, to lead the prosecution of Adolf Eichmann, I am not standing alone. With me are six million accusers . . . Their blood cries out, but their voices cannot be heard. I, therefore, will be their spokesman."[116]

More than that, bringing Eichmann to trial in West Jerusalem, the part of the city under Israeli control (recall that the 1948 armistice line had kept the walled Old City to the east, under Jordanian sovereignty), amounted to a Jewish declaration before the world of Jewish return. That alone could serve as the antidote to the exile that was the spine of anti-Semitism. Ben-Gurion, the pioneer Zionist whose early interest was in the coastal cities of Palestine and the kibbutzim of Galilee, and who, like most Israeli leaders, had regarded Jerusalem as "a remote little village," had become a Jerusalem Zionist, seeing it as "the very soul of our people . . . the heart of hearts of the State of Israel."[117]

And why? Most obviously because the logic of Jewish history, and the determination to reverse Jewish destiny, required the return to Jerusalem. As we have noted repeatedly — and it cannot be emphasized enough — it was the Roman destruction of Jerusalem in 70 CE, and the Roman banishment of Jews from Jerusalem forever, that established the rivalry between two groups claiming the mantle of Israel. When one of those groups, Christianity, picked up on the Roman act to prove its claims by theologizing the Jewish exile from Jerusalem, the central mandate of Jewish identity, tracing back to the Babylonian exile in the sixth century BCE and its breakthrough insight into the Oneness of God, was carried forward into the indefinite future, and that mandate was to return to the city of David. After the Holocaust, nothing could both symbolize and realize that return more powerfully than bringing its chief living perpetrator to trial in Jerusalem. It had to happen there, period.

But this Jerusalem was not the golden city of Christian fantasy. In no way heavenly, the Jerusalem of 1961 was still the cockpit of violence, even if a truce enforced by a barbed-wire divide had stilled the guns for the moment. For Jews then and after, the return was to the messily contested city. But, except for those periods when Crusader uniformity had been imposed upon it by the sword, that was what Jerusalem had always been in reality. Jerusalem, after all, had begun as the city of sacrifice, built around a sacred mountain from which primitive offerings were made to deities. Violence in the name of God. In that action is found the city's beginning as a pulsing epicenter of crushing physical force. That current, too, was operative in the "return" represented, if unconsciously, by the determination to bring Eichmann to trial there.

That putting Eichmann on trial in Jerusalem immediately sparked contention, in other words, was nothing new. And even the objection, made by Hannah Arendt and others,[118] that Eichmann, as a mere functionary, a banal bureaucrat, could not be made responsible for the entire crime of the Holocaust had its answer precisely in that ancient character of Jerusalem as the site of sacrifice — the projection onto the accused of the broader sins of the world. Eichmann was indicted for his own actions, which were criminal in the extreme, but he was also in the dock representing Hitler, Göring, Himmler, and all the others. Eichmann, the perpetrator absolute, belonged in the city absolute.

Thus the principle of the necessity of Jewish return to Jerusalem was established by events of the distant past and by events within living memory. That principle drove far more deeply into group identity than any otherwise comparable claim by ethnic or national groups aiming to recover home territory from which they were driven by conquerors or colonists, including Palestinian claims. I write this as a Christian, aware of Christian responsibility for the tragedy implied in this conclusion for the indigenous people of modern Palestine, but there should be no doubt of the urgent moral legitimacy of a reversal of the primordial banishment of Jews *as Jews* from their ancestral home. This is not to assert a divine sanction for Israeli claims to acreage, such as are made by an Israeli ultra-Orthodox minority, for the conflicts here are as old as humankind. If there is a will of God to be acknowledged, it has to do with the recognition of the tragic nature of equally valid and contradictory assertions. If there is a will of God to be discerned, it is in the human invention of a just resolution to these irreconcilable claims.

Religious meaning continues to be part of the story, however. The early Zionists may or may not have been God-fearing, but the Jewish return to Jerusalem necessarily involved a spiritual reckoning, for it was the city in which God's absence was discovered to be the most important form of God's presence — the central religious insight of Judaism, as this Christian sees it. That insight, symbolized first by the strict prohibition of idolatry, then by the vacancy of the Holy of Holies in the Temple, and then by the experience of exile from the Temple and its city as a mode of God's nearness, opened eventually into forms of identity that seemed not to be religious at all.

Indeed, this depth of history in the complications of Jewish notions of the sacred came more sharply into relief when modernity separated religion from culture, as if the faith of Israel could be divided so. Today's atheism can be a purification of yesterday's religious anthropomorphism, while an entirely secular devotion to the Jewish state can, for all intents and purposes, serve transcendent purposes every bit as much as religious dogma, cult, or creed do. The old distinctions, that is, are modern distinctions. Jerusalem continues, willy-nilly, to contain within itself all such subliminal currents, from those that located their wellsprings in the prehistory of Fertile Crescent manifestations to those that, after Auschwitz, transformed belief into, at most, undisbelief. Jerusalem, for all its divisions, knows nothing of the too easy division between secular and sacred. It never did.

By bringing Eichmann to trial in Jerusalem, the myth of sacrifice as applied to the Jewish people (from "lambs to the slaughter" to "eternal victims") could be confronted and dismantled. Indeed, beginning around the time of the Eichmann trial, the liturgical word "Holocaust," which in Greek, as we saw, means "burnt offering" and which carries a clear implication that the Lord somehow wills or even welcomes the sacrifice, began to yield to the Hebrew word *Shoah*, which can be translated simply as "catastrophe," as the preferred term for what had happened. No implication of a sanctioned sacrifice or redemptive act of suffering. No assumption that sacrifice is somehow foundational to Judaism — or, for that matter, to the religions that spring from it. Enlightenment categories were broken open, and exposed as such.

The more than one hundred witnesses told their stories before the court. Allowed by special procedure to "deviate from the rules of evidence," they were granted "the right to be irrelevant," describing horrors that far transcended the puny Eichmann.[119] Jewish businesses were shuttered and classes in Israeli schools were canceled so that the Jewish nation, old and young, could hear. For the first time, large numbers of Sephardic Jews, refugees of less catastrophic persecutions, identified with the suffering of Ashkenazic Jews; what the Jews of Europe had been through now was felt as weighing on Jews who'd been forced from Arab realms.

As the trial proceeded, thousands of other survivors came forward to speak publicly of their experiences — an outpouring that would mark many of them for the rest of their lives. "The urge to tell," the Israeli prosecutor later wrote, "began to overwhelm the need to be silent." And the telling changed history, as the breaking of Israel's silence and the ending of Israel's denial laid the groundwork for the broad cultural reckoning with the Holocaust that followed everywhere. The murder of six million Jews simply for being Jews was both an interruption in history and a fulfillment of it, and only now did that scale of meaning dawn on the West. The prosecutor who elicited this historic testimony, and justified it, spoke of the Jewish state as spreading "its protection, through its judicial arm, over the entire Jewish people."[120] Like the wings of an angel, the angel that had spared Isaac from his fate on the altar of Mount Moriah, the Temple Mount. *Sacrifice of the chosen ones no more.* All at once, Israel realized what it had denied, and in effect it repented of the insult it had been unconsciously dealing the survivors. They stopped being victims, and became heroes.

But there was a new danger. In cementing a national ethos around the *Shoah,* Israel made the inner logic of Hitler's crime a permanent part of the Jewish memory — and of state policy. The apocalyptic defined one pillar of the Israeli imagination, and a readiness to expect the worst (since it had already happened once before) defined another. "Look, this feeling of restlessness has a history," the Israeli writer and concentration camp survivor Aharon Appelfeld explains. "I don't open windows without thinking that perhaps someone might jump in. Somebody once noticed that I always walk near the wall, not in the center of the room . . . This is wired into the collective now."[121]

More than that, by locating its national meaning in the uniqueness of the Nazi crime and the existential threat it would forever represent, Israel implicitly understood itself as unique among nations. That seemed to obliterate the essential aim of Zionism, which was to create a Jewish state distinguished only by its normalcy, a nation like any other. After Eichmann in Jerusalem, and the realizations that accompanied the trial, that dream of normalcy would disappear. Just as the Jews stood alone, Israel stands alone. After listening to the Eichmann trial as a boy of seven, for example, David Grossman writes that "my generation lost its appetite, but there was another loss, too . . . We lost our faith in the possibility that we, the Jews, would ever live a complete, secure life, like all other nations. And perhaps, above all, we felt the loss of the natural, childlike faith — faith in man, in his kindness, in his compassion."[122]

In nothing is this Israeli exceptionalism more evident than in the way military power continually trumps other forms of statecraft. Not to say that Israel is unique in building its economy and power structure on the military: the United States has done precisely that since World War II, and continues to, with negative consequences at home and abroad.[123] But this similarity to the United States opens into the ironic recognition that Israel, in understanding itself as exceptional, turned out to be normal after all, for every state has its version of exceptionalism, perhaps especially those states that share in the legacy of biblical election. Wasn't that the point of the self-sanctification of the City on a Hill?

But Israel's is a sense of state election recovered, and the circumstances of that recovery matter. In fashioning itself as a garrison state, Israel's permanent temptation is to regard every adversary as Hitler brought back to life, both threatening annihilation and deserving to be killed without political restraint, or, at times, ethical restraint.[124] From its reckoning with the Holocaust forward, Israel simply knew better than ever to allow itself to be dependent for its security, therefore for its existence, on any other nation or alliance. Not even the United States. Israel would have to maintain the ability not only to defend itself from attack but to deter attacks from occurring in the first place. Israel would accumulate overwhelming force, and would use it, if only to make sure that its transcendent might was perceived as such.

That such a frame of mind was almost certainly an inevitable consequence of the *Shoah* does not mitigate its tragic character — tragic for Palestinians as much as for Israelis. "There is not and never will be a cure for this open wound in our souls," the Israeli writer Amos Oz said during the Lebanon War of 1982. "Tens of thousands of dead Arabs will not heal that wound . . . This urge to revive and obliterate Hitler over and over again is the result of a melancholy that poets must express, but among statesmen, it is a hazard that is liable to lead them along a path of mortal danger."[125]

The chief symptom of the wound of which Oz wrote is the fever of our diagnosis, and for the State of Israel, military force became a salve and a means of salvation. Military force assumed a kind of religious meaning, even for the sector of Israeli society that remained resolutely secular, and once more Jerusalem was the telling emblem. After Israel captured the Old City in the Six Day War of 1967, extending Jewish control to the entire city and its suburbs for the first time since the Roman war at the start of the first millennium, the long-absent Jews felt the actual Jerusalem heat from which, through two thousand years of history, they had been more or less shielded. "Jerusalem is all ours," a headline in the liberal Israeli daily *Haaretz* proclaimed. "Rejoice and celebrate, O dweller in Zion." An unprecedented pious zealotry gripped large segments of the Israeli population, leading to, among other things, a fiercely messianic settler movement that would claim occupied territories as the God-given Eretz Yisrael, generating a whole new impasse between Israelis and Palestinians, and *among* Israelis, many of whom oppose the building of settlements, despite the fact that successive Israeli governments have facilitated it.[126] The settlement impasse continues to this day. But the central fetish of this new land obsession would be Jerusalem, and some Jewish extremists now plan to destroy the Islamic shrines of the Noble Sanctuary, to make way for a restored Temple. Restored for what? Not even the zealots seem to envision a return to a cult of animal sacrifice with a reestablished priestly caste — the essence of Temple-based religion. But such reckoning with the actual meaning of the extremist impulse presumes a rational content it simply does not have.

Extremism and religious zealotry, though, are relative categories, and as we have seen, when sharply distinguished from supposedly more rational secular impulses, they are categories that reflect modern preoccupations more than ancient ones. Often the discrediting of zealotry serves to reinforce moderation, which can have its own fetishes. After 1967, with the reconquest of the entire city of Jerusalem, a shift occurred in Israeli society. New recruits to the Israel Defense Forces left behind Masada with its epic resonance and began to take their oaths and receive their weapons in commissioning ceremonies at the Western Wall. Uniformed soldiers are ubiquitous at the *Kotel*. Now Jerusalem, as the locus of Jewish memory, which gave the nation its ethic and ethos, defined what Israel meant and what every Israeli soldier was sworn to protect. Or as Yitzhak Rabin, then the IDF chief of staff, put it in 1967, "The countless generations of Jews murdered, martyred, and massacred for the sake of Jerusalem say to you, 'Comfort ye our people.'"[127]

8. Twins in Trauma

There was no comfort for Palestinians. If Israelis and other Jews use a word that translates as "catastrophe" to define their trauma, so do the people who were displaced by the longed-for Jewish return. *Shoah* and *Nakba:* the synchrony of language expresses the mirroring of loss and grief. The Palestinian refusal to acknowledge the Jewish state's legitimacy matches Israel's refusal to reckon with its role in Palestinian suffering, whether through premeditated ethnic cleansing or war-caused ad hoc expulsions, never undone. Until these twin grievances are resolved, there will be no peace between these peoples or in the place of their dispute.[128]

There is no equivalence, moral or physical, between the two foundational disasters. The *Shoah* remains historically unique. But that does not mean the *Nakba* lacks gravity as a uniquely Palestinian trauma, or that Palestinians did not feel the dispossession, impoverishment, and ongoing humiliation of Israeli occupation that followed the 1967 war as a kind of annihilation. Oddly, a post-1967 preoccupation with Israel's "occupied territories" led to a de facto Palestinian recognition of Israel's 1948 legitimacy. But just as ironically, as the 1967 war set loose a messianic drive in the Israeli breast, it similarly put "the exiled and dispersed Palestinians in touch with their *place.*"[129] Even without a remembered promise from God, the land became as holy to Palestinians from Ramallah, Amman, Cairo, and New York as it was to the most fervent of ultra-Orthodox Jewish settlers. Refugee rights, equality for Arab citizens of Israel, the terrible abuses of generalized retribution, extrajudicial killings, the clamp on movements, water deprivation, house demolition, and economic lockdown—such would be the permanent obstacles to a mutuality that might cool the Palestinian fever, but the land itself was now what mattered most. And the land embodied a far deeper reality than mere territory or borders, or fights over water sources and building permits. The conflict "is and always has been about religion, history, and identity, and the main difficulty in solving it derives from its irrational nature."[130]

Religion, history, and identity. That is why Jerusalem remained the epicenter of Palestinian suffering and unhappiness. When the city was reunited under Israeli sovereignty in 1967, its population consisted of about 200,000 Jews and 70,000 Arabs.[131] Its boundaries were expanded to nearly fifty square miles, in a "de facto annexation"[132] unrecognized by any other nation, to accommodate a massive assertion of Israeli control. By 1987, Israeli authorities had built 26,000 new Jerusalem housing units for Jews, compared to 450 for Arabs—an inequity that provided one of the sparks for the First Intifada, or uprising (1987–1993). Yet building disparities of that proportion continued through the first decade of the twenty-first century. Arabs in Israel and the occupied territories are nevertheless continually drawn to the city because it is one of the few places they can find employment. Jerusalem's population is now pushing 800,000 people, with fully one-third of them Arabs, most of whom find good reason to expect a replay of the *Nakba*.

After the Eichmann trial, Israeli cohesion, combined with a renewed contempt for the sympathy Arabs had displayed for Hitler's genocide, effectively undercut whatever possibility there might have been of Zionist empathy for, or Israeli self-criticism concerning, the indigenous population of Arabs. For their part, Palestinians reacted with a total refusal, in the words of the Palestinian scholar Rashid Khalidi, "to come to terms with the idea that what they saw as their country, Palestine, might also be considered as a national home for what they saw as another people."[133] Events of 1947–1949 were remembered by Palestinians as the defining trauma, and in the way that the *Shoah* had been transformed by Jewish memory into the ground of Israeli national identity, so the *Nakba* did the same for Palestinians. Jews *as Jews* were commonly cast as the villains, though the prior British crushing of Palestinians had had more devastating consequences—so much so that a committed Palestinian nationalist like Khalidi can call the *Nakba* "no more than a postlude, a tragic epilogue to the shattering defeat of 1936–39."[134] But Khalidi's view is unusual. Mainly, the brutal manipulations of the imperial British are unreckoned with, and once again an eternal hatred is lethally focused on Jews.

In 1964, the Palestine Liberation Organization had its first meeting, and it took place in Jerusalem. Islam was not mentioned in the PLO national charter, but religion was the inevitable basis on which claims stood.[135] In an astounding act of moral obtuseness and historical blindness, these Palestinians denied that there was any prior Jewish link to Jerusalem or Palestine, a patently absurd position that would define the movement for decades. Motivated by an otherwise admirable love for the Al Aqsa Mosque and the Dome of the Rock, defensive Palestinians would baldly assert that there had been no Jewish Temple on the plateau of the Noble Sanctuary. Alas, this embrace of ahistorical irrationality would permanently undercut authentic claims to national legitimacy and also make Palestinian perceptions all too vulnerable to a stereotypical bigotry about Jews, which had been mostly foreign to Arab and Islamic culture. Palestinians bear responsibility for such a reduction of their national hope to the latest iteration of anti-Semitism, but more was at work here than Arab recalcitrance. The third party to the conflict, the domineering one — Western civilization with its Jew hatred and imperialist racism — remained the unindicted coconspirator, an invisible hand operating from behind the curtain of history.

So when Palestinians adopted a strategy of forceful resistance, they were not perceived as heroic anticolonial rebels, but as terrorists. When they vowed in their charter to replace the intrusive Jewish state with a Palestinian state, they were the post-Hitler eliminationist anti-Semites. They were trapped in their own trauma, but it was not a trauma of their making. What embodied that complexity was the saga of Jerusalem, both the idea and the place. The cockpit of violence lived up to its history, for the fundamental PLO mistake was to invest a kind of mystical power in armed struggle, as if violence stripped of political maneuvering could achieve the longed-for liberation.[136]

In 1968, the PLO exploded its first car bombs in civilian population centers, in Tel Aviv and in the heart of Jewish Jerusalem.[137] That year an El Al plane was hijacked en route from Rome to Tel Aviv, the beginning of a long siege against civilian airliners. And in 1972, the organization carried out its infamous raid on Israeli athletes at the Munich Olympics, which led to the deaths of nine Israelis and five hostage takers. The pattern was set, and it would be as destructive of Palestinian purposes as it was inevitably reinforcing of Israeli intransigence.[138]

For Palestinian resistance leaders, strategic violence would evolve into violence for its own sake, cloaked in a sacred aura. The Second Intifada, or Al Aqsa Intifada, the far more violent uprising that was launched in 2000, took its name from the mosque. God-intoxicated suicide bombers reduced the idea of sacrifice to the demonic, killing more than 830 Israelis, wounding and maiming more than 4,600.[139] Soon both Palestinians and Israelis, even as their leaders arrived at a mutual understanding that there was no conceivable military solution for their double siege, would be taken hostage by anachronistic figures, marginal characters caught in the ancient spell of bloody sacrifice, for whom violence and religion, as if the son-saving revelation of Abraham never occurred, had once again become the same thing.

CHAPTER NINE

Millennium

1. The Temple Weapons

JERUSALEM IS AN ANCIENT locus of apocalypse, but no longer its source. A new condition of the human imagination transforms the primordial meanings. One generating engine of this new condition is the Holocaust. The other is Hiroshima. Both are tied to the question of sacrificial violence, which began our consideration at the start of this book. The question is broadly human and has been building since before written history. Every age declares its own ultimacy, yet the times *have* changed, and a place of denouement presents itself.

The climax of the old question is occurring now, as these ancient currents meet and reinforce one another in the transformed cult of sacrifice that has subliminally taken hold more in the New Jerusalem, America, than anywhere. This is why, earlier, we considered the question of the Puritan vision, when Jerusalem was first invoked as the founding image of the City on a Hill, and appeals to God were used to justify violence against the heathen and the unorthodox. We noted what that Puritan vision of divine election spawned, not only in religion but in the national ethos, even in a nation eventually defined by the separation of church and state. Violence knows no divide between the sacred and the secular. Total war, however justified, coarsened the American soul. Ultimately, as we saw, the tragic figure of James Forrestal embodied the final transformation when self-assured servants of God found themselves with an infinite capacity for destruction, which heretofore had belonged to God alone. But the multifaceted examination of this book argues that the newly foreseeable apocalypse—a true millennium—can in no way be considered an act of God. The apocalypse, that is, looms as a real and human-created possibility. That marks the difference in the nuclear age.

Here is where the idea of Jerusalem, as it took hold in the Western imagination, and ultimately in the American mind, comes full circle to the actual city of Jerusalem, where the existential threat is not local (Jews versus Arabs) but transcendent, a theological conception of violence as a mode of redemption. The unlimited destructiveness of nuclear weapons has changed the meaning of total war from massive hurt inflicted on an enemy to the final obliteration of human culture—as a mode of affirmation! The Book of the Apocalypse has come into its own with the nuclear age and the doctrine of mutual assured destruction.

The iron rule of this era is known as deterrence theory: there is no possessing the absolute weapon without the absolute readiness to use it. Preparing to destroy the world to save it has defined America's national purpose since 1945, but how can an ethical distinction be drawn between preparing for a deed of such magnitude and enacting it? "Better dead than Red," to repeat, was more than a crackpot slogan. It was a creed that applied to a race of individuals and was forced on the whole human species. The Soviet Union engaged in its half of this dance of death, but America prevailed in the Cold War with its arsenal intact and with the era's necrophilic nuclear ideology unchallenged. The point is not to engage in judgmental criticism of U.S. military orthodoxy—as if one could have managed events differently after the Holocaust, Hiroshima, or even after the fall of the Berlin Wall—but only to ask how this ongoing, subliminal fact of our moral condition changed us.

Ironically, one of the two most dangerous test cases of this new condition took place in Jerusalem (the other in Cuba), when the ancient city fell under a shadow—a cloud—that would change its meaning more drastically than any of the momentous events we have tracked in this book. That the change is rarely discussed does not remove its significance. Here is the story of Jerusalem fever today, how it threatens to blister the very planet. The story starts with the Yom Kippur War of 1973.

That began with a double-barreled surprise attack by the Arabs, designed to take advantage of Jewish religious scruples tied to the most solemn day of the Jewish year. The Arab sneaks, the friends of Israel complained. But what was war if not one sneak attack after another? So on October 6 Egypt invaded Israel across the Sinai, while Syria stormed the Golan Heights. Israeli soldiers, caught at prayer, were thrown back—"a stunning rout."[1] Five hundred Israeli tanks were destroyed in the first engagements. Nearly fifty Israeli warplanes were shot down, including fourteen prized F-4 Phantom jets, a staggering defeat for the proud air force. Two huge Egyptian armies readily crossed the Suez Canal, killing Israeli fighters where they stood. Within days, the Syrians, rolling in 1,400 tanks, were in the Galilee, headed for Haifa, the third-largest city in the country and Israel's main seaport. Not even in 1948 had the Jewish state been so vulnerable. Israeli defense minister Moshe Dayan said on the third day of the war, "This is the end of the Third Temple." The first Temple was destroyed by the Babylonians in the seventh century BCE, the second by the Romans in the first century CE. Now the Arabs—all but victorious.

It was then that Prime Minister Golda Meir gave the order for the arming of what were secretly referred to as "the Temple weapons," Israel's nuclear warheads. Only later would this come out. At the time, Jews and non-Jews alike understood that the very existence of Israel was at stake. What was not widely understood was that with this war, the future of human civilization was put at risk—a prospect of obliteration sparked in the place where civilization began. Even today, Israel does not acknowledge possessing a nuclear arsenal, yet historians agree that at the time of the Yom Kippur War, it had at least thirteen 20-kiloton atomic bombs (the Hiroshima bomb was 15 kilotons). Israel went on nuclear alert, mobilizing Jericho missiles and F-4 bombers, with preprogrammed targets in Egypt and Syria, notably the city centers of Damascus and Cairo.[2]

Given the widespread devastation caused by any such bomb and the hair-trigger nature of the broader nuclear context, the Israelis were preparing for nothing less than what the writer Norman Podhoretz subsequently called "the Samson Option," a reference to the biblical figure "whose suicide brought about the destruction of his enemies."[3] As one senior Israeli official later recalled, "There were a few days there when it seemed that the end of the world was near. For those of us who'd lived through the Holocaust, we knew one thing—it will never happen again." If Syria had succeeded in taking Haifa, there was a possibility, perhaps a likelihood, that Israel's nuclear warheads would have obliterated Damascus, a city of a million and a half people.[4]

During the frightening days of the Yom Kippur War, many Americans were less worried about Jerusalem than about Washington, where

Richard Nixon was in the throes of the Watergate crisis. While the Arab-Israeli conflict unfolded, the infamous "Saturday Night Massacre" occurred: the U.S. attorney general and his deputy resigned rather than carry out Nixon's order to fire the special prosecutor who was closing in on him. Most nights, it would later be learned, the president of the United States was drunk, and he had in effect stopped governing. Talk of impeachment swirled through the capital. Before Nixon's eventual resignation, James Schlesinger, the secretary of defense, quietly issued orders in the Pentagon that no one was to carry out instructions from the White House without consulting him first—a clear sign that the military establishment no longer trusted the commander in chief to exercise his authority over the nation's nuclear arsenal.[5] That the United States was on the verge of a constitutional crisis gave dispatches from the Arab-Israeli war a surreal character, especially as the prospect of a defeated Jewish nation sank in. The Final Solution at last, Hitler's posthumous victory.

It was inevitable that the white heat of the Arab-Israeli proxy fight would ignite the Moscow-Washington conflict, but no one imagined it would happen so soon, or so dangerously. The October war drew into its brutal maw the two sponsoring superpowers, bringing the world closer to disaster than at any time since the Cuban Missile Crisis exactly eleven years before. Henry Kissinger, serving as both U.S. secretary of state and national security adviser, was informed of Jerusalem's move to the nuclear brink by the Israeli ambassador in Washington. Appalled at the prospect of Armageddon, Kissinger demanded of Israel an immediate nuclear stand-down. He did not get it until he made concessions of his own—an instance of nuclear blackmail.[6] Meir called off the Temple weapons only when Kissinger agreed to an emergency resupply of Israeli equipment, including the addition of previously embargoed high-tech weapons, like the latest antitank missiles. A massive airlift occurred within hours, and much of the American arsenal based in Europe was moved to Israel. Among other things, Israel's new antitank capability enabled a rollback of the Syrian offensive, sparing Haifa. Secretly, Kissinger informed Egyptian leader Anwar Sadat that if he, Kissinger, did not give Israel what it was demanding, Jerusalem would be "going nuclear."[7]

Ironically, it was Kissinger who, in an era-defining (and career-shaping) article in a 1955 issue of *Foreign Affairs,* "Nuclear Weapons and Foreign Policy," had shown that the real strength of nuclear weapons is not their use but the *threat* of their use. The mere possession of nukes translates into dominating power. Kissinger's theorizing, perhaps more than any other single factor, underwrote the massive expansion of the American nuclear arsenal that occurred from 1955 on. The accumulation of nukes far in excess of any conceivable strategic need (the U.S. arsenal grew from about 300 bombs in 1950 to almost 19,000 bombs and warheads in 1960[8]) simply served the purpose of superpower swagger. Moscow and Washington both bought the notion: the more nukes one possessed, the more weight one could throw in the global arena. The arms race had nothing to do with war-fighting strategy and everything to do with the psychology of threat. The two superpowers between them would eventually produce more than 100,000 nuclear bombs and warheads—Hiroshima raised to infinity.[9]

As a theorist, Kissinger displayed such astounding complacency about nuclear war as merely a tool in the kit of national power that, though his influence was acknowledged, he was ridiculed as a figure of the absurd, Dr. Strangelove.[10] Yet he made the unthinkable thinkable, and the American national security establishment organized itself around his dogma. Far from lost on others, however, was the key Kissinger lesson: any nation that has even the smallest nuclear arsenal was guaranteed transcendent power.

It was a lesson the Israelis took to heart, and beginning around the time of Kissinger's article, they moved to acquire a nuclear capability.[11] The arithmetic was irresistibly simple: possession of the absolute weapon, combined with the readiness to use it, added up to power no one could resist. It was probably inevitable, after the Holocaust, that Israel would make such a move. Yet when confronted with an instance of his own logic in 1973, Kissinger was no longer a mere theorist but a statesman responsible for the real-world consequences of his theory—and he was frightened. Israel was not only prepared to obliterate the two largest cities in the Arab world, killing millions of innocents, but had set in motion the means to do so. Kissinger moved first, ordering the immediate resupply of Israeli forces that Meir demanded.

Moscow was not going to sit still while America intervened on Israel's side. The Soviet ambassador Anatoly Dobrynin made an urgent phone call to the White House on the evening of October 24. Kissinger took the call. Dobrynin declared that the Soviets intended to send in its paratroopers, an act of "peacekeeping" that would separate the combatants—and protect Egyptian gains. It is known now that the Soviets rushed nuclear submarines to the area, and that Moscow had provided nuclear warheads for the Soviet Scud missile brigades stationed in Egypt. In one of his memoirs, Kissinger states that he had to interrupt Dobrynin's phone call to take a call from his "drunken friend" President Nixon, who was, Kissinger writes, "as agitated and emotional as I had ever heard him." Agitated not about the crisis in the Middle East but about his possible impeachment. Nixon chose that moment to whine of his political enemies, "They are doing it because of their desire to kill the President. And they may succeed. I may physically die."[12]

Kissinger interrupted Nixon to tell him of Dobrynin's call, and in his memoir Kissinger makes no pretense that he involved the president in shaping a response to "the gravest foreign policy crisis of the Nixon presidency." He simply informed the president of the Soviet move, and then "I said curtly that we would veto it." Nixon went on drinking while Kissinger assembled the National Security Council in the White House Situation Room and began giving commands. Kissinger, "playing chicken," as he put it,[13] and acting on his own authority, ordered America's worldwide military force to full nuclear alert, the so-called DEFCON 3 status.

It was as if Kissinger had taken cues from Golda Meir in this extraordinary (and probably unconstitutional) action — only the third time, including the Cuban Missile Crisis, that the U.S. strategic force was brought to that level of readiness. The message? If the Soviets carried out their plan to intervene in Egypt, they were risking all-out nuclear war with the United States. When the British prime minister, Edward Heath, learned of the American nuclear brinksmanship, he immediately called the White House to protest. Kissinger refused to put Heath through to Nixon because Nixon was by then completely drunk.[14] When the Israelis learned of the U.S. alert, the Temple weapons were rearmed and made ready to fire. Around the globe, fail-safe settings were removed from thousands of nuclear missiles and B-52 bombers. It was the Soviets who, in calling off the paratrooper intervention, and thereby "blinking" (as they had in Cuba), walked the world back from this precipice.

When the reinforced Israelis had stabilized the preinvasion lines, Golda Meir accepted a cease-fire. "We can forgive the Arabs for killing our children," she said. "We cannot forgive them for forcing us to kill their children."[15] The Israeli leader never publicly addressed what it meant to her that, in the post-Holocaust name of Jewish survival, she was prepared to bring down the pillars of the earth — on the earth. Even without knowing that the Soviets had actually deployed nuclear weapons with its "adviser" units in Egypt, or that Nixon had come unhinged, with Kissinger "playing chicken," Meir was savvy enough to understand that, in the world of mutual assured destruction, there was no introducing nuclear use into the Middle East conflict without igniting an all-out nuclear exchange between Moscow and Washington. That Jerusalem nearly triggered the doomsday catastrophe is a fact of such magnitude that it must eventually be reckoned with. This paradox — the ultimate in child sacrifice — defines the moral conundrum that lies at the heart of the tragedy of Israel, but only because Israel, too, joined in making the nuclear devil's bargain. Zionism's purpose was to make Israel a normal state like other states, and that is exactly what it did, in what passes for normalcy in the nuclear age.

In the years since the Yom Kippur War, a post-traumatic Israel has conducted its affairs with an unrelenting belligerence that many outsiders criticize and few understand. The word "survival" became synonymous with "security," in the name of which almost nothing was excessive. Perhaps only Israelis can understand the double vision that a constant state of public anguish had imposed. "To our great misfortune," David Grossman wrote in 2008, "we in Israel have been living for almost a century in a state of violent conflict, which has an enormous influence on all realms of life, including, of course, on language. When a country or a society finds itself — no matter for what reasons — in a prolonged state of incongruity between its founding values and its political circumstances, a rift can emerge between the society and its identity, between the society and its 'inner voice.' The more complex and contradictory the situation becomes and the more the society has to compromise in order to contain all its disparities, the more it creates a different system for itself, an ad hoc system of norms, of 'emergency values,' keeping double books of its identity."[16]

That double vision has emerged as a symptom of Israel's version of the fever we have been diagnosing, showing itself more blatantly in Jerusalem than anywhere else. In recent decades, Jewish Jerusalem has imprisoned itself with the "facts" of settlements that ring the holy city just as cruelly as the concrete barrier that went up against Islamic suicide bombers early in the twenty-first century. Of all the various pushes and pulls of the Israeli-Palestinian conflict, none were as savage as the suicide bombings by jihadists, but none made an ultimate resolution more difficult to imagine than the endless expansion of Jewish settlements across the Palestinian landscape. As much as that expansion destroyed Palestinian hopes, it effectively undercut Israeli security, the supposed absolute value. Settlements require the occupation, which itself is the source of Israel's moral and existential dislocation.

Jerusalem was born in insecurity, and despite the ways its true history is regularly deleted from memory, war, as Grossman rightly points out, has constantly defined the city and its surroundings. "Life is largely conducted," as Grossman says, "within the fear of fear."[17] But war is not what war was: nuclear weapons have transformed war's meaning. Only yesterday, Saddam Hussein was the great menace, and there is good reason to believe, as Israeli military officials do, that only Israel's nuclear arsenal prevented the Iraqi dictator from loading chemical and biological weapons into the Scud missiles that fell in and around Israeli cities during the first Gulf War (although the suspected existence of Israel's nuclear weapons did not deter Egypt and Syria from their 1973 attacks). Today, a Taliban-threatened Pakistan is braced for Israel's attack (perhaps in coordination with India) on its nuclear installations.[18] Tomorrow, a Jew-hating Iran may well be ready with its nukes, the "Islamic bomb" ticking away. And Al Qaeda, not subject to the constraints of such nation-states and therefore undeterrable, is resolutely working to acquire a nuclear weapon. Israel is poised on the knife's edge of all that. But Israel, too, has put its chisel to the edge, making it sharper.

Meanwhile, top-secret Dimona, Israel's Los Alamos, remains active only a few miles into the Negev Desert from Jerusalem—the chisel at work.[19] Israel's nuclear arsenal is a taboo subject among the Jewish state's friends, but to nations in the region it ignites impatience and rage at the "nonproliferation" double standard. When Egypt and others call for a nuclear-free zone in the Middle East,[20] many of Israel's supporters dismiss the idea as anti-Israel, yet in the long run, keeping nuclear weapons out of range of Israel is the only possible meaning of the state's security. From being the center of the anti-Semitic structure of the Western imagination, Jerusalem has become the pivot of the bifurcated mindset, a nuclear-armed demonizing of the "other" that now threatens the human future. Indeed, nuclear dread is the unaddressed contemporary malady, and it has found one very hospitable host in the Third Temple. In effect, Dimona and Los Alamos are the Holy of Holies. The more a nuclear nation does in the name of security, the more insecure it becomes. Israel is the test case of that paradox, nothing more. The fate of Jerusalem is the fate of the earth.[21] What the terrifying nuclear standoff of 1973 suggests is that the Jews, once again, are at the avant-garde of catastrophe.

2. Sacrifice Operatives

Billy Graham, as we saw, was the avatar of the new American mindset. As he was publishing his most apocalyptic texts—*Till Armageddon* in 1981 and *Approaching Hoofbeats: The Four Horsemen of the Apocalypse* in 1983—the Cold War was approaching one of its most dangerous climaxes. Ronald Reagan had come into office as the most openly belligerent president of the modern era, labeling the Soviet Union as the "focus of evil," threatening Moscow with a massive arms buildup, and making jokes about his authority to launch a nuclear war.[22] Among Reagan's first acts was to arrange a top-secret National Security Council briefing on the Middle East and the Soviet Union for Reverend Jerry Falwell, the fundamentalist founder of the Moral Majority. Falwell, with whom Reagan met more than any other religious leader, revitalized the Christian Zionist vision of a restored Jewish nation as the prelude to the Messiah's return, and laid the groundwork for the rock-solid alliance between right-wing Christians and the government of Israel. But Israel is of interest to such Christians only for its role as a launch pad of the final Christian triumph. Israeli leaders, welcoming the support of millennial Christians, willingly ignore their culminating assumption of Jewish conversion to Jesus.

Reagan simultaneously courted what might be called neo-Catholics, right-wing Roman Catholic figures like his CIA head William J. Casey, his secretary of state Alexander Haig, and key aides like Patrick Buchanan and speechwriter Peggy Noonan, who made the Puritan vision of the City on a Hill Reagan's most resonant theme. Reagan was the first president to establish diplomatic relations with the Vatican, and his alliance with conservative Catholics would complete the recasting of the Republican Party as the vanguard of American Christian nationalism. Such Catholics[23] were less openly apocalyptic than evangelicals, but their dedication to the Manichaean fight against Communism was just as fierce, and they were no less ready for all-out war against the evil Soviet Union. All of this indicated a maturing of a nuclearized eschatology, with America's character as a Christian nation raised to a level of such absolute value that its protection was worth global destruction. Reagan's references to a coming "end of the world" through war were common enough that the *Washington Post* ran an article in 1984 titled, "Does Ronald Reagan Expect Armageddon?"[24] Soviet analysts, for their part, regarded Reagan as unstable. When Kremlin chief Leonid Brezhnev died, he was replaced with a man who was more than a match for Reagan: Yuri Andropov, who, as the longest-serving head of the brutal KGB, had crushed the Hungarian Revolution, the Prague Spring, and the Soviet dissident movement. Nothing "neo" about Soviet "cons," but they, too, had their hard core.

In America, Europe, and even in the Warsaw Pact nations, people became so concerned about the instability of the balance of terror under such leadership that the Cold War's only truly effective mass movement against nuclear weapons was launched—on both sides of the Iron Curtain.[25] When a nuclear reactor went into meltdown at Chernobyl, Ukraine, in 1986, Soviet leaders lied about the danger of radioactivity, were caught in their lie, and the tyrannical house of cards began to fall. The ever credulous Reagan, meanwhile, saw an apocalyptic omen when he was told that the word "Chernobyl" is Ukrainian for "wormwood," which the Book of Revelation identifies as one of the signs of the End Time.[26] Reagan's supreme self-confidence, as he danced along the edge of nuclear abyss, was rooted in a shallow religiosity that carried an assurance that nuclear war, as part of God's plan as foretold in scripture, would not be a catastrophe but a source of "rapturous" redemption.[27]

At the height of that delicate period between the Soviets and the Americans, a dangerous plot unfolded in Jerusalem. Shortly after the Yom Kippur War, a far-right religious-political movement named Gush Emunim (Bloc of the Faithful) was begun in Israel. Its members had aggressively moved to solidify Israel's claim to the occupied territories in the West Bank and Gaza by expanding settlements, in the conviction that the full restoration of Eretz Yisrael, the biblical land, would hasten the return of the Messiah. This was to be no mere land grab, but a closing down of history. The ultra-Orthodox settlers were Jewish Jerry Falwells, imbued with the apocalyptic spirit of the time.

Two Gush members, Yehuda Etzion and Menachem Livni, founded a secret movement whose object was the one action that was guaranteed to overthrow the hated status quo between Israelis and Palestinians, Jews and Arabs: the demolition of the Dome of the Rock. That act, they believed, would spark the Messiah's return and the final redemption of Israel. It would more likely have sparked the ultimate confrontation between the two sponsoring superpowers, who were already as close to open war as they'd been in decades. Just as Ronald Reagan was discussing Armageddon with Jerry Falwell, Etzion and Livni were accumulating explosives and surveilling the Temple Mount, a religious ground zero.

A mentally unbalanced Australian Christian had lit a near-disastrous fire inside the mosque in 1969, hoping to spark Christ's return, but the Jewish plot was far more serious. These conspirators prepared carefully, over nearly two years, drawing on demolition expertise and military discipline. But because most of the conspirators were ultra-Orthodox, they felt the need of a rabbi's sanction. When they were at last ready to carry out their attack on the Muslim shrine in 1982, however, every rabbi they approached refused to give his blessing to such an act. For that reason, the plot was called off. The secrets of the Etzion-Livni plan came to light in 1984, its seriousness and near accomplishment made clear. After these revelations, Muslims were less likely than ever to believe Israeli assurances that Jews had no interest in replacing the Islamic holy place with a Third Temple, and mainstream Jews would stop regarding their religious fringe as a joke.

Purim is a holiday of playing jokes, a favorite of Jewish children. But its roots are tragic. In the fourth century BCE, all but one of the people of Israel bowed before an Amalekite prince named Haman, the Persian overlord who had imposed his rule on Jerusalem. The one faithful Jew who refused to honor the blasphemer with an act of deference was Mordechai. Because of him, the vengeful Haman decreed that all the Jews in the kingdom were to be massacred, and he cast lots to decide on which day the slaughter would be carried out. (*Purim* is the Hebrew word for "lots.") Haman's scheme was foiled by a member of the king's harem, a secret Jew named Esther, Mordechai's cousin. The Jewish people were spared.[28] Purim is the happy festival that commemorates that deliverance.

In 1994, Purim fell on February 25. On that day, a thirty-eight-year-old American-born doctor named Baruch Goldstein entered the Cave of the Patriarchs in Hebron, south of Jerusalem. The cave is regarded as the grave of Abraham, the endpoint of his trekking. For the Bloc of the Faithful, that makes it the last stake in Israel's God-promised real estate claim. Therefore, fiercely messianic Jewish settlers had staked their claims in recent years to Hebron and the surrounding area. But as we saw, Abraham is revered by Muslims as well as Jews, and the Cave of the Patriarchs was serving as a mosque, which Goldstein regarded as a blasphemous expropriation, a violation of God's will. Using an automatic weapon, on the day that celebrates Jewish deliverance from a Persian oppressor, he massacred 29 praying Muslims and wounded 150 more. Goldstein was beaten to death on the spot.

A book was soon published in his honor, *Baruch the Man*. A twenty-five-year-old Orthodox student named Yigal Amir read the book and was inspired by its portrayal of Goldstein as a martyr, a defender of Israel's responsibility to maintain its claim to all of the land that came from God as a sign of the covenant. Goldstein was described as not only maintaining the claim but avenging every violation of it. Amir read that revenge "is like a law of nature. He who takes revenge joins the 'ecological currents of reality' . . . Revenge is the return of the individual and the nation to belief."[29]

So it was that on November 4, 1995, Amir went to Kings of Israel Square in Tel Aviv and took revenge against Yitzhak Rabin, the nation's prime minister. In 1993, Rabin had signed the Oslo Accords, which offered "land for peace," promising an ultimate withdrawal of Israeli forces from occupied Palestinian territories. Thus Rabin had violated God's solemn designation of Eretz Yisrael. Worse, this withdrawal would impede the Messiah's return and the accomplishment of God's End Time redemption of Israel. Amir shot Rabin twice at close range, killing him instantly. Immediately arrested, Amir said that he was satisfied. He is serving a life sentence in an Israeli prison. He has never expressed remorse.[30]

Nearly seven years later, in the spring of 2002, a teenage girl walked the four miles to Jerusalem from her native village, Bethlehem. Ayat al-Akhras was eighteen years old. She was raised and still lived in the Dheisheh refugee camp in Bethlehem, created in 1949 to temporarily house more than three thousand Palestinians who had fled and been forced from their homes in West Jerusalem during the 1948 Arab-Israeli war. Not only Ayat but her father, too, had been born in the camp. Her grandparents were the terrified fugitives who'd settled in Dheisheh, imagining a stay of weeks, not decades. By Ayat's time, concrete huts had replaced the tin shacks, which had replaced UNRRA tents, but water was still scarce, and the camp was home to more than ten thousand

Palestinians, squeezed into an area less than a mile square. Yet like many of her kind, Ayat had grown up happy. She was known for her buoyant personality. She had been a good student in school and was recently engaged to be married. But she changed. Before setting out for Jerusalem, she stood in front of a poster showing New York's World Trade Center, the disappearance of which only months before had so seared the human imagination. She stood before the towers posing for a photograph, her legacy. She had become what was referred to by jihadists as a "sacrifice operative."[31]

Arriving at a Jerusalem food market, Ayat crossed paths with seventeen-year-old Rachel Levy, another happy girl. Rachel had been raised in California, but was pleased to have recently made aliyah with her family. After the events of the previous September, her return to the Jewish homeland filled her with a sense of purpose. On this day, she had been sent by her mother to buy groceries for the Shabbat meal. Rachel and Ayat entered the store together. Around Ayat's waist was a belt of explosives, which she detonated, killing herself, Rachel, and a nearby security guard.[32]

We saw that Igor Stravinsky's *Rite of Spring*, performed so controversially in 1912, initiated the modern era, forecasting the slaughter and mayhem of the twentieth century. Its second part, "The Great Sacrifice," tells how "wise old men" preside over the selection of a virgin for sacrifice and then honor her with a marital dance. The "wise old men" who posed Ayat al-Akhras in front of the poster of the World Trade Center, having recruited her to the cause and prepared her to be one of its icons, were leaders of the Al Aqsa Martyrs Brigade, a coalition of Palestinian militias at war with Israel. Once, as we saw, the Al Aqsa Mosque had housed the Latin king of Jerusalem and then the Knights Templar. Farther back in time, on the same ground, Jesus of Nazareth had carried out the offense for which the Romans killed him. Within minutes of Ayat's self-detonation, a spokesperson for the Martyrs Brigade telephoned the Associated Press to identify her, and to claim responsibility for the bombing, which the spokesperson defined as God's will. The next day, in the Dheisheh camp, the old men enacted a marital dance in honor of Ayat, now the bride of Allah.[33]

The twenty-first-century epidemic of suicide bombing—or, better, suicide murder—by aggrieved Palestinians and, more broadly, the Islamic jihadists who wage war against infidels and against corruption within the House of Islam, may be the most malevolent mutation yet of the virus of violence in the name of God. In 2007, there were nearly seven hundred acts of suicide bombing globally, the vast majority in Iraq and Afghanistan.[34] Militarily, the suicide bomber is as deadly as any cruise missile, any piece of heavy artillery. In less than a decade, thousands have transformed themselves into ordnance.

Among Islamic sects, Shiites were especially energized by a revitalized mythology of the self-sacrifice of Husayn ibn Ali, Muhammad's grandson. As the leader of one side of a violent succession dispute after the Prophet's death, he mortally exposed himself to the violence of the opposition in a field at Karbala in the late seventh century. His death was the climax of the conflict that split Islam into Sunni and Shiite factions. To this day, on the annual commemoration of Karbala, called Ashura, penitents enact rituals of lamentation and atonement, with Shiites understanding Husayn's martyrdom as the final and full establishment of Islamic religion — bloody self-sacrifice as an essential note of the faith.

Karbala is like Golgotha and Masada, and like Golgotha and Masada it ignites contemporary imaginations, and not only on the fringe. Shiite Iran's bloody war against the Sunni regime of Iraq's Saddam Hussein was explicitly defined as revenge for the martyrdom of Husayn at Karbala.[35] The war raged from 1980 to 1988, costing more than a million lives. Most of the deaths occurred in a mindless replay of the trench warfare of World War I, with waves of men throwing themselves against impregnable redoubts across no man's land. With that, on the very terrain between the Tigris and Euphrates where this long history began, a ferocious passion for self-sacrifice against each and every enemy had been rekindled. In the way that World War I condemned the European imagination to a fetishism of death, so the Iraq-Iran War, which was proportionally even more brutal, did something similar in the arc bending from the Fertile Crescent to the Arabian Peninsula.

The most extreme opponents of Shiism were Wahhabist fanatics, descended from that Arabian desert zealot of the eighteenth century Abd al-Wahhab, whose purpose, recall, was to restore Islam to its primal Arabian purity. Wahhabists periodically attacked Shiites in a conscious replay of Karbala over the centuries — and that blood feud, too, came freshly into the modern era.[36] When Saudi Arabian totalitarianism jelled in the twentieth century, it was as a Wahhabist state, the most fundamentalist form of Islam. But Saudi Arabia's oil-enriched ties with the West brought what strict Wahhabists could only perceive as blasphemous corruption, sparking a reactionary puritanism that eventually resulted in a martyrdom cult called Al Qaeda.[37] Islam's fiercest argument is with itself, but these distinctions — and threats — are lost on the terrorized West, which forgets that it, too, has versions of these impulses embedded in its own traditions.

Extremism, terrorism, Islamofascism, the language falls short of expressing the depth of nihilism represented by the growing readiness of many Muslims to turn their physical selves into indiscriminate homicidal weapons — the body as an "improvised explosive device." Not all such actors are consciously motivated by religion, although most are.[38] But all are at the mercy of inhuman notions of sacrifice and martyrdom that have moved through this entire history — Jewish and Christian and Muslim, even if Muslims are most at the mercy of the nihilistic impulse of today. *God wills death.* "Infidels" in New York, London, Mumbai, and Madrid are targets. "Crusaders and Jews" are targets in Israel, Afghanistan, and Iraq. But so are Muslims in the Middle East, South Asia, and Arabia. Indeed, most victims of suicide terror are Muslims, as the battle rages within Islam between the minority of death-enthralled zealots and the vast majority of moderates for whom Islam is a religion of peace, not war; of life, not death.

3. Crusade

Millennial thinking is one note of the religious disorder that we have tracked in this book — a mystification of the number 1,000, with roots in the Book of the Apocalypse. At the recent turn of the millennium, the world was braced for terrible things — a replay of the irrational fears that gripped Europe in the year 1000. In the late 1990s, the computer phenomenon known as Y2K was a worry that seized the rational mind, but the turn in the calendar came and went, and that fear passed. Then, a year late, came 9/11. That trauma amounted to a drastic surfacing of the repressed anguish of the Cold War, when dread had been fixed upon nothing so much as nuclear war. With lower Manhattan all at once the site of an American ground zero — a designation that strictly belongs only to Hiroshima and Nagasaki — fears attached to what began as the Manhattan Project could seem to have been fulfilled. The millennial terror had been made real.

And sure enough, the assault that led to the living nightmare of the endlessly retelevised collapse of the Twin Towers was soon understood as having had an essentially religious meaning — *Allahu akbar!* If 9/11 was not nearly the apocalypse — it did not last, and its victims, however much individually mourned, were not legion — it was surely the first shot in an apocalyptic war. In truth, Americans had been subliminally bracing for some kind of 9/11 since John Winthrop defined the nation in terms of the End Time city, as Christians had been bracing for it since John of Patmos foresaw a New Jerusalem. Cities on hills are sitting ducks.

A few days after the September 2001 Al Qaeda assault, George W. Bush, as presidents are meant to do for the nation, defined what the experience meant and what action it called for. Speaking off the cuff, he explained with elegant simplicity the urgent American project: "This crusade," he said, "this war on terrorism . . ."[39] There is no need to rehash here a political analysis of the Bush years or of the failed policies he set in motion. Enough to note that for President Bush, "crusade" was a natural point of reference. That it was inadvertent — to Bush, only a hackneyed synonym for "struggle" — shows how deeply rooted in the Western imagination are the conflicts between irreconcilable cultures. Christendom came into a sense of itself only through the centuries-long war with Islam. From that first millennial trauma, Christendom's legacy cultures, including America, had unknowingly not recovered.

The Crusades are the pivot of this book because they were the hinge around which our entire civilization turned, around which culture spirals still. It was practically inevitable that a U.S. president would think as Bush did. Holy war and jihad call to each other, and at the summons fighters engage without a first thought, much less a second. That is why, in the beginning of "this crusade" against terrorism, Americans could receive their apocalyptic, millennial president's prescriptions so blithely, even as he then presided over a set of national reactions to 9/11 that unfolded over the remaining seven years of his administration.

Bush was widely criticized by American liberals[40] and many European leaders for the overtly religious nature of his responses, his demonizing of Islam, his division of the world into spheres of good and evil, and his swearing to eradicate the latter.[41] Bush displayed a transcendent ambition that signaled his readiness to match Osama bin Laden strike for strike. During the Bush tenure, it is true, the U.S.

military fell under the sway of conservative evangelical Christianity in unprecedented ways, with commanders ordering their juniors to attend Bible study; with proselytizing chaplains seeking to bring troops to Jesus; and with many U.S. soldiers encouraged to think of themselves as modern-day Crusaders. Pentagon intelligence briefing books, including those supplied daily to Secretary of Defense Donald Rumsfeld, bore covers with daily scripture quotes. The gun sights of army rifles carried by American soldiers in Iraq and Afghanistan were inscribed by their manufacturers with coded references to New Testament passages about Jesus.[42] There were many such examples of Christian incursions into formerly off-limits areas of government and military practice.

But despite the eccentric pieties that made President Bush seem unusual, his reactions came right out of core traditions of American ideology, and his post-9/11 rush to war — as opposed, say, to strategies based on court-supervised law enforcement — was an inevitable consequence of the militarization of American society and the economy over the previous century and a half. Bush's responses, that is, owed as much to Abraham Lincoln, Woodrow Wilson, and Harry Truman as they did to the much-maligned Dick Cheney, Donald Rumsfeld, and Colin Powell. And that Bush's deeds, his secular-minded advisers notwithstanding, were justified in explicitly religious language — "And we know that God is not neutral," he told a joint session of Congress[43] — put him solidly in the American mainstream.

Unfortunately, Bush's responses were so thoroughly rooted in the national ethos that they were entirely predictable, and he pursued exactly the policies at home and abroad that Osama bin Laden hoped he would. And, equally, those responses were so thoroughly American that, during the stressful years after 9/11, most politicians and citizens found little reason to dissent. Indeed, knowing full well how the contours of his imagination ran on matters military and religious, the voters reelected President Bush in 2004.

When Bush was replaced in 2009 by the very different Barack Obama, all crusader references were discarded. Fevers of every kind subsided under the supremely cool Obama. The wall of separation between church and state was promptly reconstructed. Yet the war policies pursued by the Obama administration were continuous with what had gone before. Evangelical zeal still animated the U.S. military and especially the private contractors who made up an ever larger part of the U.S. fighting force. In fact, under President Obama, Bush's crusade was escalated.[44] Bin Laden outlasted his nemesis, but by then it had become clear that the cosmic conflict transcended personalities and politics. The religious war that America insisted was not religious beat on. The unseen but always felt pulse of that beating remained Jerusalem.

CHAPTER TEN

Conclusion: Good Religion

1. Neither Secular Nor Sacred

CENTERED ON THE holy city, we have been tracking the history not of religious violence but of an endemic human bipolarity that has often been pushed further into enmity, more savagely into war, by appeals to God. The pattern predates recordkeeping. One group affirms its positive identity by asserting the equal and opposite negative identity of another, and that assertion takes on transcendent power when reinforced by the sanction of a deity. Religion is joined to power. Religion *is* power.

That this long consideration of history — a study of politics and war — should end by once more narrowing the focus to religion as such may seem anticlimactic. Religion again? And as the last note struck? But if the recent history of Jerusalem, its politics and wars, teaches anything, isn't it that keeping religion out of statecraft, through secular efforts of diplomacy and realpolitik, does nothing to bring about peace? The contemporary bias against open explorations of questions of religion has left the God-intoxicated Middle East at the mercy of its toxic fevers, while allowing the more implicit religious currents, like the American crusade, to run on elsewhere, as unchecked as they are uncriticized.

In fact, Israel-Palestine is the supreme present instance of the problem that follows from the imposition of a sacred-secular dichotomy, and is that problem's master symbol. Yes, the devastating Islamic turn to suicide bombing was taken in the 1990s by Allah-invoking zealots who repudiated the idea of a secular democratic state championed by the PLO,[1] but that religious madness was not unrelated to the wholly political despair of Palestinians whose half century of exile, secular or not, seemed only marked "No Exit." It is also true that the expansive God-given claim to Eretz Yisrael by a Jewish hard core of Messiah-expecting armed settlers has been nurtured, whether deliberately or not, by successive Israeli government occupation policies. But those policies, however worthy of criticism, have in turn caused new outbreaks of anti-Semitism from South Asia to Europe, with Israel taken to be the source of the war of cultures that terrorizes the globe. "Israel is the only state in the world whose legitimacy is widely denied," the British historian Anthony Julius observes, "and whose destruction is publicly advocated and threatened."[2] The resistance of embattled Palestinians is one thing, but the demonizing use to which a much broader population of Israel's "voluntary enemies," in Julius's phrase, have put the Palestinian cause is another. In a glibly condemned Israel, the old anti-Semitic thinking has found a new gyre around which to swirl. Meanwhile, in both Israeli-Jewish and Palestinian-Muslim cases, deeply buried apocalyptic streams have surfaced, with the End Time conditioned by both on the destruction of the other.[3] Israel-Palestine thus has its local war zone and its global one. A fight over territory has been made into a self-hypnotizing struggle for the cosmos, which can never be resolved. In this way, Jerusalem's ancient themes live on.

Our subject, therefore, is more than religion, and also less. Politics is the exercise of power within and by communities, and what modern secularity calls religion, imagining it as a realm apart, is one aspect of the community's life. More than a thread in the grand tapestry, religion is the whole work seen from a certain angle. The idea that politics and religion are distinct tapestries, hung on different walls, or even in different rooms, is a contemporary illusion. It goes hand in glove with the related fantasy that the solution to irrational violence is the separation of politics from religion, the separation of church and state, as if the state, on its own, were immune to the temptation of irrational violence. We saw how this fantasy took hold in America and Europe and played itself out into the nineteenth and twentieth centuries, with an imagined Jerusalem as a fixed point in the swirling but otherwise secular landscape of battlefields from Gettysburg to the Somme.

Ironically, the modern construct of church and state, or of the religious and the secular, considered as opposites, simply reiterates this ancient human tendency to dichotomize — what in the past has made enemies of the civilized and the savage, whites and blacks,

Christians and Jews, Europe and Islam, the East and the West, and, for that matter, in the American context, the North and the South. God against Satan, Christ against the Antichrist, the spirit against the flesh, good against evil, ultimately the sacred against the profane. Killing for God, martyrdom, redemption through violence, apocalypse, atonement theology, sacrifice — all such ideas have been understood as undergirding the religious element that so often led to war. The dream of enlightenment was that by getting rid of religious elements, war, too, would be disposed of. The profane would be rescued, renamed the secular, and allowed to live in peace. The end of history. But culture can no more separate itself from religion than the ocean can separate itself from the thermal currents that keep it alive. Sometimes those currents bubble to the surface at temperatures that make the water boil — hot springs can be thought of as wars — but always they infiltrate the entire mass of the sea. Violence, in other words, comes not from religion but from life.

That is why, in the enlightened secular age, war may have been purified, but it was not disposed of. Instead, it was somehow intensified and, with industrial technology, made total. The U.S. Civil War and World Wars I and II were not irrational but reasonable, according to this logic, mainly because they were not religious. In fact, as we saw, those wars were imbued with religion, while claiming not to be. Therefore they were not denigrated as the wars of religion were. The Enlightenment wars were "good" wars. As if ideas of sacrifice, atonement, martyrdom, and apocalypse played no role in the high grass of Virginia, the mud of Flanders, or the paper cities of Japan. We have seen, though, how the perpetrators and victims even of those secular events turned finally, in flight from absurdity, to a justifying God as war's creator, sanctifier, and redeemer.

Jerusalem today is defined by the hopeless, mutually self-destructive war between Palestinians and Israelis. The conflict is easily, and inaccurately, reduced to its being seen as a war between Arabs (read Muslims) and Jews, a slide toward a denominational definition. If the holy city is still in the grip of such fever — so the diagnosis goes — isn't that because Jerusalem, unlike so many other cities, remains hostage to the ferocious irrationalities of religion? An especially brutal Muslim religion, which is roundly indicted for its blatant refusal to separate politics and religion, confronts the irredentist ultra-Orthodoxy of fanatical

Jewish settlers, who have fallen back into a fundamentalism that has no other purpose but to reject the Enlightenment. Jihad against holy war.

Yes, Jerusalem fever is an illness, but what if its viral niche is not the new outbreak of zealotry on the margin—Hamas, Gush Emunim, or, for that matter, the Christian Zionism of the American religious right—but the long mainstream history of Western civilization? The history, after all, that generated both anti-Semitism and racist colonialism. In that case, our obligation is to reevaluate the most hallowed assumptions of that civilization and, where necessary, to transcend them. Such a task amounts to the reinterpretation of what has already been interpreted. That is the work this last chapter aims to do—reinterpret the themes, events, revelations, and mysteries this book has already taken up.

The Bible is the record of human self-transcendence achieved through endless reinterpretation, and that is why it is so odd that, in the Bible's name, fundamentalism rejects interpretation.[4] While condemning a secular will to separate religion from the rest of life, fundamentalism does the same thing by walling off "fundamentals" from the realm of critical study. Fundamentalism declares that religion is all of life, while simultaneously consigning religion to its own ahistorical enclave, where its origins, myths, dogmas, and rituals are not to be scrutinized. The consequences of that absolutism—suspicion of the intellect; rejection of material culture even while exploiting it; condemnation of modernity while expertly using modern methods and tools; investment of all hope in a messianic age to come or a post-apocalyptic afterlife; and always, male supremacy, since the father-god mandates patriarchy—are remarkably alike whether the assertion is made by Christian, Jew, or Muslim.

What if fundamentalism is not the crime, but the evidence? Fundamentalism, mirroring the dichotomy between the religious and the secular, if to oppose rather than to sponsor, shows what's wrong not with a part of our culture (or theirs), but with the cramped inner life of a morally paralyzed world, the bifurcated world in which we all live. If that doubleness is a symptom of what we have called Jerusalem fever, fed by the heat of the city's ancient conflicts, it is also true that the idea of that city, embedded in Oneness, has been the fever's constant antidote. Jerusalem differs from comparably layered cities of the contemporary world (we know that Athens and Rome have histories as cult centers, but are at peace) because in Jerusalem, more than any other place, the line between the secular and the sacred, as between politics and religion, regularly shows itself as drawn in sand, always ready to be blown away.

Islam, to the extent that a world religion can be spoken of univocally, does not even imagine such a marked distinction between sacred and profane. But, paradoxically, something similar is true also of contemporary Judaism, which, while profoundly influenced by the Enlightenment that Jewish thinkers helped inspire, knows little of the Enlightenment's secular-sacred divide. Judaism, as this Christian sees it, remains a confluence of religious expression, norms for political culture, and, above all, a vessel of memory. Not doctrine and not creed but history itself provides the cohesion of Judaism. The nature of that history, which begins in tension with the divine — the God of Abraham, Isaac, and Jacob (not to mention Sarah, Rebecca, and Rachel) — necessarily makes Judaism religious. But because peoplehood outlasted changes in the meaning of the divine — atheism, too, can be a form of spiritual insight — Judaism is *not only* religious. In the same way, it is partly secular, but *not only* secular. This peculiar mixture is nowhere more evident than in Jerusalem, which, while holy, is also profane.

"My thoughts are not your thoughts," the Lord is remembered as having told Isaiah. "My ways are not your ways."[5] And so with the Lord's own city, with, in a phrase of the Jesuit scholar John O'Malley, "its insistence on the incomprehensibility, the transcendence, the utter otherness of God." Jerusalem was defined at the start by the primordial dichotomy between the creature and the wholly other who is the Creator, which, despite the Hebrew insistence on the unity of spirit and flesh, not to mention on the Creator's Oneness, does indeed make Jerusalem the seat of bipolar thinking. That is why Jerusalem has always been the north star of the Martyr and the Inquisitor and the Crusader and the Reformer and the Colonizer and the Puritan and the Fundamentalist and the Fanatic — and now the Jihadist. "This is the culture," O'Malley says of Jerusalem, "that makes the greatest purity claims and that unmasks as abominations what others welcome as the normal give-and-take of life. It cannot compromise. Rallies and protests, yes. The negotiating table, never!"[6] So today Israelis declare they have no partner with whom to make peace, while Palestinians denounce the Jewish state as a product of racism, pure and simple.[7] Jerusalem is the seat of such contention — an unsettling vision of Jerusalem and its meaning, but one that our investigation has stead-ily borne out. Something irreducibly true about the human condition shows itself in this place again and again.

2. Not God's Way, But Man's

So instead of talking about the virtuous secular realm and the wicked realm of religion, or vice versa, let's talk about good religion and bad religion. In other words, consider religion as part of the human condi-tion, not above it. An object of critical scrutiny, not an exception to it. A double-edged reflection of what Erich Fromm calls the "genius for good and genius for evil" that reside, like an inseparable pair of ven-tricle chambers, in the human heart.[8] Such a complicated view might give our story a different slant, for Jerusalem is a place where, since the dawn of history, good religion has sought to push out bad. Jerusalem, that is, has been a center of religion's self-scrutiny, the method of which is interpretation and interpretation again, ad infinitum. Self-scrutiny is the mode of self-transcendence. Jerusalem is home to both, and that is why we are concerned with it.

Hence the city-establishing story in Genesis of Abraham's trek up Mount Moriah, where human sacrifice was called off by the God who does not will it. This mythology, as we saw, locates the very origin of Jerusalem — the sacrificial rock of the Temple Mount, the Dome of the Rock — in the humane repudiation of the scapegoat mechanism, or, rather, since the mechanism seems eternal, in the humane substitution of the ram for the son. Humans *at* the altar, yes. *On* the altar, no. Good religion pushing out bad. But human beings are constitutionally drawn to bad religion, which is forever in the throes of a comeback, with an unending supply of human scapegoats ready to be sacrificed. This long story shows that.

Genesis is the record of how the Hebrews conceived God as outside of nature, and therefore as its Creator — that bipolarity. But this vision had a profoundly humane consequence. Because the God of Genesis is seen as creating the very cosmos, which is the precondition of uni-versality, it marked the start of a truly ethical religion, the beginning of the end of tribalism and of tribal wars understood as holy. The Bible is the record of the human effort to leave the violence of the tribal gods behind. The language for this intuition of broad commonality among all people, showing itself in compassionate love and extending to all that exists, is Oneness.

What protects this revelation from a bland universality is its being rooted in the particularity of chosenness — the One God choosing the one people — much the way the intimate commitment of loving partners, while exclusive, is also the opening to love itself, and therefore to neighbors and strangers. Through exclusivity to inclusiveness. One people opening to all people — "a light unto the nations."[9] Here we touch upon the particular genius of the religion of election, involving not the oneness of total union in which individuality is lost — uniformity — but the oneness of *communion,* of a relationship in which separate beings, while remaining separate, come together. The inevitability of fear is replaced by the possibility of friendship. That this *E pluribus unum* is a fundamental principle is expressed in the breakthrough religious affirmation "God is One."

When Enlightenment thinkers, much later, find things to criticize in the religion that begins with Genesis, what they don't realize is that their criticism of narrow particularity in the name of universal hope (typified, say, in the 1948 U.N. Universal Declaration of Human Rights) *begins* with Genesis.[10] That the idea of God's Oneness was reduced, in modernity's devaluing of religion, to an excluding monotheism (and, as we saw, that peculiarly modern suffix "ism" is the tipoff), as if God's Oneness means the One God is at war with other gods, as if union assumes the destruction of difference, provides just another instance of bad religion striking back. The total becomes totalitarian.

Jerusalem is the place in which Hebrews came to the recognition of these things — or, rather, the place *in relationship to which* they did so, because it was only when they had been kidnapped away to Babylon, recall, that they understood how their God differed from all the gods whose altars punctuated the place of exile. It was in Babylon that the editors, redactors, and authors of Israel began their monumental task of reinterpretation. They rearranged the varied creation myths, bodies of law, collections of sayings, oral traditions, songs, and etiological tales that had defined their communal memory. They reorganized this multifaceted set of sources, going back to Moses, David, and Abraham to the prehistory of Adam and Eve, around the new idea of the God whose main attribute was Oneness — the oneness that unites rather than destroys. Inconsistency, repetition, and self-contradiction inevitably marked the texts they assembled from the itinerant past, but an irreducible principle of reconciliation among humans was at their core, and it was put first — the proclamation "In the beginning, God!" And "In the beginning, God created the heavens and the earth."

Thus the genius of Genesis, and of the religions that follow from it, is the insight that all that exists was and is created by the same God. More: all that exists was and is created in that God's image. Oneness, not cosmic war, is the ground of existence. God is One, and each of God's creatures participates in that Oneness, with humans as the creatures who know it, even if, having genius for evil as well as for good, they tend to imagine otherwise. It was in looking back on Jerusalem, where this God's presence was so concentrated as to be palpable, that this people came to these realizations — the presence of God discovered in being absent from it. That paradox — presence in absence, like the paradox of universality through particularity — would define the religion of the Hebrews, a religion of distance from the divine, not possession of it. That distance is what makes human friendship with God, and love *of* God, the appropriate categories within which to understand the relationship of creature to Creator.

When, leaving Babylon, God's people returned to their Temple city, their Temple was vacant ever after. Following the Babylonian destruction, the sacred Ark of the Covenant was missing, and so from then on the Holy of Holies pointed to the Holy One by being empty. From then on, each time yet another sanctuary was destroyed, Jews would find in the immensity of absence their most eloquent manifestation of God's presence.[11] Jerusalem defined this imaginative spiritual breakthrough. "Here, perhaps for the first time," as Amos Elon writes, "God was conceived as righteous and transcendent, completely outside nature, unbounded by any form of physical existence, the sole creator of the universe. Religion, until then best defined as a form of extreme fear, was made moral."[12]

If only it were so simple. Or at least lasting. In reclaimed Jerusalem, a wound remained unhealed. "By the streams of Babylon we sat and wept," the returned people sang, "at the memory of Zion." The root meaning of "Zion," in Hebrew, is "parched desert," and moral aridity, too, defines the story of the place.[13] They sang, "Jerusalem, if I forget you, may my right hand wither." But in remembering Jerusalem, where

God's Oneness showed itself, they remembered also how their captors had destroyed it: "how they said, 'Down with her! Raze her to the ground!'" That remembering of the destruction of Jerusalem set loose bad religion to push back against the good they had just discovered, as if Babylonians were not children of the One God, too. And so in recalling their exile, the Hebrews, giving us our permanent warning of how the religious imagination operates, wailed, "Destructive daughter of Babel, a blessing on the man who treats you as you have treated us; a blessing on him who takes and dashes your babies against the rock!"[14]

Babies against the rock. If anything defines the violence of Jerusalem, that sacred verse from Psalms does. The author of that verse is of the community that has just recognized the elegant and hopeful vision of God's Oneness, and yet look: we are back to the slaughter of children. Such is the curve of history that humans can never will the slaughter of someone else's children without finding their own babies dead at their feet. The text that some call the Old Testament and others the Torah begins with Genesis and culminates, in the chronology of composition, with 1 and 2 Maccabees and the Book of Daniel,[15] records of religious struggle that span a thousand years. The Oneness of God that opens to all becomes monotheism, according to which my God is better than your God, and that superiority gives me license to kill. There is only one truth, and I have it. Bad religion pushing out good religion, the permanent underside of monotheism.

Once again Jerusalem winds up as the cockpit of violence. However divine its religion, Jerusalem's religion is also human. That is not an accusation brought *against* the Bible, but a reckoning that occurs repeatedly *within* the Bible. Thus the Maccabean Jews are at war with the Hellenizing Seleucids, who aim to quash Jewish resistance by smashing public observance of the Jewish cult.[16] The Seleucids order the young Jews to eat pork, but the young Jews' parents would rather see them die. And so it was that, as these texts show, the story of Abraham was reinterpreted. What began in Genesis as a celebration of the end of child sacrifice was reversed, with the founding father glorified not for obeying the divine command to spare his son, but for his readiness to plunge the knife into the boy's heart. In the Book of Daniel, that mother celebrates her sons for offering themselves to the fire rather than commit the dietary abomination. Why was the story retold this way? Because in their warmaking, the Maccabees found it useful, in their conscription of heroes, to return to the celebration of the sacrifice of sons. "Hear, O Israel, in those days in this time, Maccabee is the savior and redeemer," Jews sing at Hanukkah. "In every generation he will rise, the hero rescuer of the people."[17]

And in that succession — bad religion pushing out good — would come Wilfred Owen and all who died on the Western Front to the music of Jerusalem, the Abrahamic fathers "slaying all the sons of Europe one by one." But well before that, as a sacrificed beloved son, came Jesus of Nazareth, in whose story these same themes are reiterated, and once more reinterpreted. In fact, it was in terms of these preexisting themes in the Jewish milieu of which he was so firmly a part that his story was told and understood. The contingencies of history shape meaning. Reinterpretation, it becomes clear, works for ill as well as for good. By Jesus' time, the brutal Romans had replaced the Seleucids as rulers of Jerusalem, but the spirit of apocalyptic resistance was still a defining part of the Jewish response to an oppressive foreign occupation, and the holy city was itself defined by the renewed cult of human sacrifice, conceived now as self-sacrifice.

This is the context that supplies, for example, the Gospel of Luke with its entire narrative structure, for that telling of the Jesus story is as a fateful, and lethal, journey that begins in Bethlehem and ends in Jerusalem, now taken to be the city of death. When, in Luke, Jesus was warned that the Roman procurator Pontius Pilate was putting to death troublemaking Galileans — "whose blood Pilate had mingled with that of their sacrifices" — and that the Roman puppet Herod meant to kill Jesus, as he had killed John the Baptist, Jesus refuses to do the expected thing and head away from danger. Instead he steers into it, toward the seat of oppressive power, into the teeth of Pilate and Herod both, the place that was also God's home. "I must go on," he declares, "since it would not be right for a prophet to die outside of Jerusalem."[18]

The other Gospels construct the drama less drastically than Luke, but the essential story, rooted in what actually happened, remains the same. In the Gospel of Matthew, Peter is alert to what awaits Jesus in Jerusalem and attempts to block him from going. "Heaven preserve you, Lord," Peter says. "This must not happen to you!" To which Jesus replies, "Get behind me, Satan! You are an obstacle in my path."[19]

There are many hints in the Gospels that the Jesus of history was no apocalypticist — that for him the Kingdom of God was no hereafter but was here and now; that the transspatial and transtemporal dimensions of reality did not add up, by his calculation, to a devaluing of earth in favor of heaven. Jesus' intuition of the permanence of existence ("eternal life") was based on the experience of instances of such present intensity that they were "out of time" or even timeless, but this was more a fluency of consciousness than a pointer to another world. Everlastingness, for him, assumed not the immortality of the soul but a depth of knowing the face of God. And for Jesus that face was fully turned away from destruction ("Never again," God swore to Noah after the Flood). For Jesus there was no regarding destruction as a path to salvation. It is one of the historically most certain things about him that he rejected violence, which is the prime reason for separating Jesus from the idea that came to animate so many of his followers — that God redeems the world by destroying it; that the earth can be sacrificed to heaven; that God shows love for children by seeing their heads smashed against the rock in God's name. That God wills the death of God's beloved Son.

But political and religious events in the cockpit of violence over a hundred years led precisely to those interpretations, devaluing the present in favor of a coming age, giving sanctified primacy to suffering, reveling in a bloody climax between forces of good arrayed against forces of evil, whether on Calvary or at Armageddon. The Book of Revelation, with its ocean of blood and lake of fire, outdoes the Book of Daniel. The undisputed fact of history that Jesus was murdered in Jerusalem had generated, by the time of the written texts, a theology that drew upon the apocalyptic milieu into which Jesus was born, and that only grew more apocalyptic through the century that took its number from his birth. The message boiled down to: *God wants Jesus in Jerusalem. God wants Jesus dead.* That is how God shows favor to God's beloved Son. Instead of coming to *reveal* that God's love for God's creatures (like the father's love for the prodigal son) is boundless and unconditional, Jesus was understood as coming to *save* God's creatures from God's own punitive judgment.

"The way you think," the Jesus of Matthew tells Peter, "is not God's way, but man's."[20] God's way of thinking, or so it seemed to the survivors of the savage Roman war against the Jews who, in the thick of that war, told the story this way, is Jerusalem fever. Bad religion pushing out good. The boiling thermal stream below the ocean of our entire civilization. And why should Arabs and Jews of Jerusalem not have been scalded, and remain so to this day?

3. Learning from History

The Bible is so full of violence because it came into being to resist violence. Jerusalem is the cockpit of violence, and within its precincts, for three thousand years, humans have pushed and pulled to the point of blood against their own inbred tendency to push and pull: the solution to violence was more violence. Yet humans are distinguished by the capacity to learn from history. We saw how the invention of writing about five thousand years ago, in farm settlements not far from the hill from which golden Jerusalem would shine, led to the capacity to carry experience through time. Written texts and their interpretations were the precondition of tremendous breakthroughs in individual intellect and communal imagination, learning that led to massive mutations in culture and social organization. Texts and their interpretations gave us religions of the Book—religions of *this* book. Most importantly, texts and their interpretations transformed past experience into lessons for the future. If now one eye is cast back upon the long pilgrimage through sacred violence, the other is fixed upon the new capacity of the human race to bring about its own extinction. Does the pilgrimage that is history lead to a dead end? If, instead, the pilgrimage through history leads to a new possibility, it is that so-called sacred violence must be tamed, and can be. Holiness must be removed entirely from the realm of war, and can be. In that case, this pilgrimage has been toward human survival. If there is a God, what other meaning can there be to God's will?

Today, political and social conflict is broadly defined as between tradition and modernity, with each of the three monotheistic religions engaging the tension in a unique way. Is religion rational? Does reason fulfill itself by openly acknowledging the leap of faith that it, too, must make in a world still defined more by ignorance than by knowledge? Islam is rushing through its Reformation and its Enlightenment all at once, while all too many Muslims regard accommodation with universal ideals of human rights that originated in the West as anathema (equality for women, say) *because* they originated in the West. Christians, for their part, divide between those whose reckoning with modernity has undercut certitude, with mainline, moderate belief in drastic decline across denominations, and those whose rejection of modernity has led into the cul de sac of fundamentalism — a dead end crowded, nevertheless, with more and more members. Among Jews, though, the challenges of secularity have been taken on more directly than by any others, with many Jews acknowledging no God, while affirming the peoplehood that springs from God's covenant. Against secular Jews stand the Haredim and others, hurling anathemas like artillery. A partial Jewish retreat into a fundamentalism of land, defended by the artillery of settler violence, is an ongoing source of discord. And spreading a sponsoring canopy over all of this heat is the ever exceptional America, the center of armed Christian nationalism that is the more dangerous for being denied.

Yet the oceanic tradition through which all these currents flow carries a deeper and wider stream, which is the principle of the tradition's own self-criticism. There is the key to biblical hope. That the story begins with mythic Abraham, who was required by God, in Jerusalem, to put down his knife, remains defining. But Abraham is surpassed by the figure of David, the historical founder of Jerusalem, precisely because, for all his victories, his greatness was unattached to special virtue. That was made dramatic when the prophet Nathan — "That man is you!" — rebuked him for murderous lust. Yes, David ordered the building of God's Temple, but because of his too ready recourse to violence, God disqualified him as the Temple's builder.

The king by definition abuses kingship, yet the prophet Samuel had warned of that, even while establishing kingship as necessary to the commonwealth. The religion of the Temple was a religion of bloody sacrifice, yet the prophet Jeremiah declared on God's behalf, "I desire mercy, not sacrifice, acknowledgment of God, not burnt offerings." And Jesus, speaking out of the Jewish tradition, described his Father's love, in the parable of the prodigal son, as dependent on nothing but itself. No sacrifice needed; no religion, even; not good behavior either. God loves because God loves, period. When the followers of Jesus got that wrong, fencing in God's love with conditions of orthodoxy, obedience, and a new cult of sacrifice, they were only showing the strength of their connection to the thickly human biblical tradition. This tradition defined itself in the beginning by its need of self-correction, and, obviously, it still does.

What does that mean today, in light of epiphanies attached to the diagnosis of Jerusalem fever? Now, to speak of the hope of peace for Jerusalem is to acknowledge the enormous varieties of religious experience, to use the great phrase of William James, which in the twenty-first century face each other in the intimacy of the global village. Jerusalem is that village writ small, a living image of how all believers and nonbelievers inevitably encounter — or confront — one another as near neighbors, unable to avoid each other's differences, and therefore unable *not* to be influenced by them. Jerusalem has long been the most absolute of cities, yet it is the capital today of encounters in which absolutisms are shown to be mutually interdependent, and therefore not absolute. Neither values nor revelations exist outside of history, and if Jerusalem does not show that, nothing does. Yet Jerusalem also shows how each religion that finds a home there, including "the religion of no religion,"[21] understands itself as offering a comprehensive vision of the whole of reality, even if it does so from the necessarily partial perspective of its contingent tradition. The religions, while emphasizing the whole to which their revelation points, have tended to forget the inevitable partiality that arises from the basic fact of the human condition, that truth is always perceived from one point of view or another — never in itself.

That is what Rabbi Abraham Joshua Heschel meant when he declared that "God is greater than religion."[22] Every religion. That might seem a modern insight, yet it encapsulates the breakthrough vision that the captive Jews were given in Babylon nearly three millennia ago, the vision that made Judaism the first of the three monotheisms. Those religions, like every religion, came into being with an inbuilt tendency to confuse themselves with the object of their devotion, as if the worshiped deity were the religion. Religious orthodoxies of every kind tend to forget that at their center is an unknown mystery — unknown because unknowable. "So what are we to say about God?" Augustine asked. "If you have fully grasped what you want to say, it isn't God. If you have been able to comprehend it, you have comprehended something else instead of God."[23] Humans are restless in the face of what they cannot know, which is why the essential unknowability of God has prompted humans to make gods out of what we can and do know. Our selves, tribes, nations — and doctrinal beliefs. When religions substitute themselves for God, as they have done from the time of Jeremiah to the time of Crusading popes to the time of *fatwa*-issuing ayatollahs, they become igniters of sacred violence, which, with its transcendent claims, can be more enflaming than any other fire, any fever.

The connection between religion and violence has been powerfully laid bare in the twenty-first century. How will its exposure shape the next generation of believers? Do the full accommodations of post-Enlightenment intellect with faith undercut faith, condemning religion to zealotry? Can the religious meaning of particular revelations (for a Christian, for example, the "Christ of faith") be separated from scientific historical criticism (the Jesus of history)? Is there a defensible continuity between the earliest elements of a tradition (to use another Christian example, Jesus of Nazareth) and later complexities emerging from text and interpretation (the "high Christologies" of the Gospel of John, the Church fathers, and medieval theologians)? What if the interpretations (emphasizing, say, the hyperviolence of Christ's Passion as God's mode of redemption) contradict what historical criticism illustrates (the radical nonviolence of Jesus)? And how have such foundational religious assumptions (God's sanctioning of violence) shaped the inner core of culture? Can a strategic vision of secular politics, say, include the normally unseen religious influences that generate political energy — and secular wars? How important is this line of inquiry if most institutionally committed religionists care not a fig for it? If they even knew of the conceit, wouldn't most believers mock the "second naiveté in and through criticism"[24] with which a few postmodern thinkers, attempting to purge belief of violence, carry on the forms of religious tradition while declining to understand them traditionally? Or, to ask, having learned from history, the most basic question of this long inquiry: Given the depth of religion's complicity in violence, what would good religion look like, anyway?

First, good religion would celebrate life, not death. The deepest pitfall of the apocalyptic imagination consists of its affirmation of earthly annihilation as God's purposeful plan. On the contrary, humans weren't put here to die; we were put here to live. Religion is precious for offering consolations to the inbuilt sufferings of the human condition, the two main facts of which are mortality and the knowledge of mortality. Religion invented a language of "afterlife" in which to define its hope that mortality, the end of the story, is not the whole story. Yet that afterlife language — consisting mostly of an apocalyptic expectation of, or even a lust for, the End Time — has brought grave problems. Any glorification of the afterlife that denigrates the value of the present life is itself inhuman. The devaluing of the here and now in the name of the by-and-by is a mortal offense against the temporality that defines consciousness, but it also can lead to terrible impassivity in the face of injustice, an invitation to accept the given unacceptability instead of working to change it. The present is elusive, but humans were created as creatures of time for the sake of the present alone. What religion refers to as "beyond" is often conceived as outside of time and space (the supernature beyond nature), but the beyond that matters is in the depth of present life.

Time, therefore, is an invention. The past and the future are present realities because they are imagined constructs, aspects of consciousness but not its brackets. As memory is indulged for the sake of the present, not the past, thereby avoiding the dead end of nostalgia, so hope intends to strengthen the present, not flee to the fantasy of tomorrowland. *Belief in God means to deepen present experience, without any particular regard for its consequences hereafter.* Good religion, in other words, is not magic. It tells of the end of the story, yet also of the story's unboundedness. Good religion reckons with a natural order that may go on without an End Time, without humanity as its necessary pinnacle, with its only sure purpose as what humans bring to it. There is no other life, and religion is how one penetrates to the deepest level of that mystery, a level to which religion gives a name. The only life that lasts forever, that is, is the life of God. Humans, by virtue of God's creation as creatures with awareness, have been brought into that life, the eternal life that is only the present moment. To be fully alive is to be aware of being held now in what does not die, and in what does not drop what it holds. Religion calls that God.

Second, good religion recognizes in God's Oneness a principle of unity among all God's creatures, a unity that is also known as love. Religion, in its essence, is about love, and every great religion defines compassionate love for the neighbor as the surest sign of God's presence on the earth. This is true of the three monotheistic religions, despite the evidence that their monotheism itself has been what makes them so violent. Monotheism, properly understood, is not a numerical denomination, as if God's Oneness claims a primacy in which God's followers can participate: "We're number one. Watch out!" Alas, that seems to define the ways in which many, if not most, monotheists have understood God's self-explanation to Moses.[25]

Holy wars, waged by psalm-singing Hebrew armies, Christian Crusaders, and Islamic jihadists, have been fought in the name of the One

God across the millennia, and their equivalents are still at it. But does the One implied in monotheism have the numerical meaning — "one and not two and not three . . ." — that would explain, if not justify, such zero-sum violence? Or does One have a moral component, pointing to a principle of unity that includes diversity as of its essence instead of taking diversity as a contradiction and a threat? The Oneness of God is not the lonely singleness of a digit but the solidarity of a Creator in communion with all creatures. Religious Oneness, therefore, is inclusive, not exclusive, even as it affirms the many only through its embrace of the One. Paradox, not contradiction, is its method.

Religious Oneness assumes differences, and assumes respect for differences, which is also known as pluralism. Crucially, this means that religious claims, however absolute, are made in the full knowledge that there is more than one way to understand their meanings. And the plural there is operative, since the meaning of God-who-is-One adheres in meanings that are multiple. God is greater than religion, and greater than meaning, too.

Third, good religion is concerned with revelation, not salvation. Millions of believers have found consolation and liberation in the idea of salvation, especially those who have been oppressed or impoverished, with little hope of relief in this life. Such belief can provide meaning to an otherwise meaningless existence. The idea of salvation in that sense is humane and to be treasured, yet the question arises: Salvation from what, or whom? To be saved from an enemy is one thing, but when the enemy is identified with God — beware! Then salvation stands as the opposite pole of damnation, and the two depend on each other for the gravity, whether of awe or terror, with which they fall upon the human imagination. The threat of hell, with its assumption of a monstrous God, goes hand in glove with apocalyptic religion — the monstrous God who would destroy the earth to save it is the same God who would condemn an individual to an eternity of suffering for, well, having inflicted a lesser suffering on fellow humans. The violence of hell serves, in effect, as the aftershadow of the violence that this bad religion ultimately justifies, the violence of holy war, hell on earth. In this scheme, God's answer to violence is violence, too. What religions promise salvation *from*, therefore, are not merely the woes of life in the vale of tears, the heartsickness of the motherless child. No, religions, in return for acts of virtue or repentance or sacrificial offerings of one kind or another, promise salvation from the God who condemns. That heartsickness is deserved, and only a foretaste of what is coming, unless . . . unless . . .

Appeasement, atonement, satisfaction, such are the mechanisms with which to ward off the hatred of the divine enemy, changing the doom in the mind of a judging deity, through the paid ransom of sacrifice, into the love of an all-forgiving friend. An Old Testament God becomes a New Testament God (and that transformation, enabled by Christ, shows how this theology is slyly anti-Semitic). But good religion intends not to save but to reveal that God's mind is never in need of changing, since God's attitude is one of constant and overflowing love. Creation is itself that overflowing. There is no question of "needing to be saved" from God, even though the existential insecurity into which all humans are born inclines us to think otherwise. It is the human mind that needs to be changed, not God's.[26] Good religion offers revelation, not salvation, proclaiming that creation is God's self-expression, and that as creatures, humans are, simply by virtue of existing, already part of it: *saved by virtue of being*. Religion and its accoutrements, like sacrifice, are therefore of interest to God only to the extent that they open the human mind to this revelation. Religion at its best is only a way of knowing that religion is unnecessary.

Fourth, good religion knows nothing of coercion. That is because attention to the presence of God is an internal activity occurring in the realm of conscience. Conscience cannot be forced. Not even God forces the human conscience. Though God is both the depth and the horizon of each person's being, God and humans are forever separate. That means the purpose of religion is not identity, with the creature swallowed up in the extravagant Creator, but relationship, with the creature standing before God as one worthy of the encounter. God invites, welcomes, and bids one to come ever nearer. That humans are free to say no to God means humans are free to say yes, making religion a possible relationship of love. If God does not coerce, how blasphemous that any person or group should be coerced in God's name. Good religion, therefore, is never joined to force.

Christianity has had to recover from the Constantinian mistake when church and empire became the same thing and the cross of Jesus became a sword. One form this recovery takes is the American-style

separation of church and state, a theoretical removal of the magistrate from the realm of conscience altogether. Yet explicitly Christian
aspects of American nationalism (and the present-day U.S. military's
use of religion to build discipline and morale) threaten to breach the
wall of separation. Islam, meanwhile, is measured against its own foundational text, the Qur'an, which abjures coercion in religion. Muslim
nations work to accommodate the politics of individual rights, including freedom of religion, but outcomes are uneven. Many Islamic
regimes routinely coerce the consciences of non-Muslims, if only by
restricting the open practice of other religions. Islam's encounter with
those who believe differently will be to the benefit of Muslims, too,
for neither should Muslim consciences be coerced. Jews, for their part,
confront their own version of the Constantinian temptation, having
come into state power with Israel. The Jewish state is firmly committed to democratic liberalism, including the theoretical principle of minority rights. Yet only peace will vindicate that principle — for Muslims
and Christians, but also for the diversely believing Jews. That Israel is
both Jewish and democratic need not be a contradiction, which means
the state exists to protect the conscience of every citizen. Not all Jews,
meanwhile, define themselves in terms of Israel, and that, too, is a claim
to freedom of conscience. Diaspora, at last, can be a choice.

Fifth, in the new age, good religion may, paradoxically, have a secular character. This is so as more and more people find organized religion too tradition-bound and historically enmeshed with the intolerance that is complicit with violence. The rejection of bad religion may
require the rejection of religious forms, categories, and symbols that
prove incapable of self-criticism or renewal. A *conception* of the person
in relation to a *conception* of the divine — these are what contemporary
experience more and more disqualifies.

But one may ask, Whose conception? Atheism may consist of the rejection not of God but of patently irrational (even violent) conceptions
of God (Zeus, Yahweh, the Trinity, Allah) understood to be affirmed
by others, whether philosophers, popes, rabbis, or imams. There can
be a fundamentalism of atheism that entirely misses the subtleties, say,
of an apophatic faith that knows that it does not know God. But that
does not remove the question atheists ask. Good religion may indeed
presuppose a religion of no religion, which implies a capacity to recog-

nize the impulse toward transcendence outside traditionally conceived realms of the sacred. Other realms opening to the transcendent may include science and art and the psychoanalytic. The muse is holy, and so perhaps is the therapist. Good religion acknowledges that each of these paths of understanding is not necessarily more limited than its own. To understand is to stand under, where deep speaks to deep.

The shift from faith as certitude to faith as including both ignorance and doubt can mean that the worship of God is the worship of God beyond "God." And who is to say that so-called secular approaches lead to that reality less readily than the religious? Dietrich Bonhoeffer wrote searchingly of this question from a Nazi prison not long before he was hanged for having opposed Hitler. "How do we speak of God without religion? How do we speak in a secular fashion of God?" Bonhoeffer seems already to have anticipated the revolution in consciousness that cut the late twentieth century adrift, acknowledging what others would come to far more slowly than he, namely that "the linchpin is removed from the whole structure of our Christianity to date." And what was that linchpin if not the scapegoat mechanism that was then being so brutally exposed by the Holocaust?

Bonhoeffer could not have known how deeply into religion his instinctive critique was penetrating—the religion of bloody sacrifice that was complicit in the horrific violence against which he had set himself. He asked, "If we had finally to put down the western pattern of Christianity as a mere preliminary stage to doing without religion altogether, what situation would result for us, for the Church? How can Christ be the Lord even of those with no religion? If religion is no more than the garment of Christianity—and even that garment has had very different aspects at different periods—then what is a religionless Christianity?"[27]

And one might ask, What is a religionless belief? The question goes to every tradition. This is not a matter merely of the well-documented and undenied failings of religion, nor of an intellectual leap into an age of reason in which "primitive" structures of religion are left behind. No, this is a matter of learning, from an honest reckoning with religion's limits, something new about the One to whom religion aims to submit. "The God who is with us," Bonhoeffer wrote, "is the God who forsakes us. The God who makes us live in the world without using him as a working hypothesis is the God before whom we are ever standing. Before God and with God, we live without God."[28] Because this incomprehensibility is built into the faith as its core, believers can be grateful to those nonbelievers who have emphasized it with their critiques, especially their critiques of religious violence. But believers can respond to the skepticism of modernity with a skepticism of their own, certainly including skepticism about the ultimate truth claims (as about the putative nonviolence) of a wholly secular culture.

But skepticism is the revelation, and it is most valuable when applied to one's own cherished faith, measuring it against the standard of love that religion intends to uphold. To take a blatant example of what drives the rejection of religion, consider anti-female violence, on a continuum from intellectual assumptions of male supremacy to pornographic denigration to physical abuse to enslavement and murder. Misogynist sexism is a special symptom of religious disorder, and among the mainstream institutions, including Judaism, Christianity, and Islam, it is, to one or another degree, endemic. The opposite of male supremacy is not female supremacy, but equality. For many, there can be no God for whom such equality is not essential, which can lead many to conclude, from the evidence offered in the religions, that there is no God.[29]

Still, the rejection of religion that cozies up to injustice can amount, in biblical terms, to a repudiation of idolatry, for in regard to women, as to many others, the religions have betrayed themselves by accepting transient cultural forms, like patriarchy, as divinely mandated. In evaluating the "neo-atheisms" of the twenty-first century, it can be useful to recall that both Judaism and Christianity, in rejecting the prevailing religious categories, forms, and symbols of the Roman Empire, were denounced as atheist. Women who leave the church, synagogue, or mosque to protect their lives and self-respect are authentic pilgrims of transcendent value, however they describe themselves, or it. So are all the pilgrims of justice whose quest takes them away from "God." Thus the single most compelling test facing the three monotheistic religions today is how they define the place of women. Given the breakthrough understandings that have illuminated global culture in the twentieth and twenty-first centuries—how women fare is how the culture fares—the religions will disqualify themselves as agents of God's presence or work unless females can claim therein positions of complete equality.

Good religion understands, in sum, that bad religion is inevitable and that pure religion is impossible. Religions, too, are sinful. That is because they began with the tragic intuition that the solution to violence is violence — the sacrificial cult. Religion promulgates that idea (and so does politics), but if religion (and politics) does not change, then human civilization is finished. That is why the touchstone to which every consideration must circle back is the essential role of religious self-criticism, now made urgent by the new human vulnerability. Good religion is not perfect religion, and knows it. Renewal of religious practice, doctrine, cult, creed, tradition, and worship must be ongoing. This radical commitment to purification is built into the tension between the sacred text and its forever unfolding interpretation, a process by which belief is measured against its real-world consequences. In other words, experience takes precedence over doctrine.[30] Beliefs that lead to transgressions of the primal law of love must change. Religion that leads to violence must be reformed. Which is to say, every religion is forever in need of reformation.

Jerusalem is where humans first learned this, and where it remains to be learned. Jerusalem, Jerusalem.

Notes

1. Introduction: Two Jerusalems

1. Exodus 3:1–15. Except where noted, biblical citations are from the Revised Standard Version (RSV).
2. Acts 2:1–13.
3. Psalms 14:7. "Salvation" is used in *The Jerusalem Bible* (JB). The RSV has "deliverance."
4. Zechariah 12:2. "Intoxicating" in JB. RSV uses "reeling." When Peggy Lee sang "You give me fever," she was not complaining. "Fever in the morning, fever all through the night."
5. Ezrahi, "'To What Shall I Compare Thee?': Jerusalem as Ground Zero of the Hebrew Imagination," *Publications of the Modern Language Association* 122, no. 1, January 2007, 220–34.
6. Amos Elon, *Jerusalem*, 113.
7. Har Meggido means "Mountain of Meggido." It refers to a place not far from the Sea of Galilee, which was the site of numerous ancient military campaigns, and at least one during World War I.
8. "Jerusalem of Gold" by Naomi Shemer. http://www.jerusalemofgold.co.il /translations.html.
9. Elon, *Jerusalem*, 227.
10. See, for example, the *Christian Science Monitor Report* "Why 88 Arab Homes Received Eviction Notices," http://www.csmonitor.com/World/Middle-East /2009/0226/p04s01-wome.html.
11. The phrase is Bernard Avishai's. Essential reading for today's Israel is his *The Hebrew Republic: How Secular Democracy and Global Enterprise Will Bring Israel Peace at Last.* New York: Harcourt, 2008.
12. Isaiah 2:2. The term *aliyah* survives in Israel today as the official word for immigration. Its opposite, *yerida* (descent), derisively defines emigration.
13. Elon, *Jerusalem*, 214.
14. From the Sykes-Picot Agreement of 1916 to the "Clinton Parameters" of 2001

and the Annapolis Agreement of 2007. Berger and Idinopulos, *Jerusalem's Holy Places and the Peace Process,* xv.

15. Elon, *Jerusalem,* 173, 116.

16. Amos Oz, *In the Land of Israel,* 8.

17. Avishai, *Hebrew Republic,* 157.

18. Tzipi Livni, Israel's former foreign minister, told the Seventh Jerusalem Conference in 2010 that "the Jewish state has been taken hostage by the ultra-Orthodox parties." *Israel News Today,* February 19, 2010. The mayors of Jerusalem have included Haredi Orthodox like Uri Lupoliansky as well as secular businessmen like Nir Bakat. Although a minority in the city, Haredim made up a majority of the city council in 2009.

19. Bernard Avishai, "Keep the Heat On," Bernard Avishai Dot Com, March 15, 2010. Note the echo of our metaphor.

20. The arguments of Jerusalem are efficiently defined by Avishai, who sees the city as the hub of the "five tribes" of Israel — Ashkenazim, North African Jews, Russians, West Bank settlers, and Arabs who hold Israeli passports. "Tribe Three hates Four, condescends to Two, doubts One; Two hates One, resents Three and (for different reasons) Four; One is afraid of Two, patronizes Three and hates Four; Four hates One, proselytizes Two, and is afraid of Three. All four are afraid of Five." Avishai, *Hebrew Republic,* 118.

21. The chair of the board of the Jerusalem YMCA is Dorothy Harman, who came to Israel from New York in 1971. The CEO is Forsam Hussein, a Palestinian Israeli, appointed in 2010.

22. "Greater, unified Jerusalem is being torn apart. The Israeli — Jewish and Arab — capital is becoming the capital of the hallucinatory, dangerous fanatics," Avraham Burg wrote in 2010. "This is not the city of all its residents nor the capital of all its citizens. It is a sad city that belongs to its settlers, its ultra-Orthodox, its violent residents, and its messiahs . . . Jerusalem is emptying out faster than any city in the world. At first its wealthy residents left, then its moderates abandoned ship, followed by the secular, and the young adults. Very soon there will be no one left to leave and the city will be completely alone. The sources of light are being extinguished, occluded by rays of darkness." Avraham Burg, *Haaretz,* March 7, 2010. Burg is no fringe figure. In 1995, he was appointed chair of the Jewish Agency and of the World Zionist Agency. He was Speaker of the Knesset from 1999 to 2003.

23. Sari Nusseibeh, *Once Upon a Country,* 24.

24. In 2010, I wrote about evictions in Sheikh Jarrah, describing the plight of the fifty-member family of Fouad Ghawi, who had lived in the house since 1954, when he was eight. He and his family were Palestinian refugees from Jaffa during the 1948 war, and his father traded in his U.N. refugee card, which guaranteed him basic support, for the right to move into the house the U.N. Refugee Agency and Jordan were building on vacant land. In return for finishing the house, the Ghawi family would get the legal deed. Three generations of the Ghawi family lived there ever since — until the previous August, when an Israeli court ordered them out. They had no deed because, he told me,

"The Jordan government would not put it in our name until we had proper plumbing, and then the 1967 war broke out." Jordan's authority ended. The family was evicted by Jerusalem's municipal police, and their house was taken over by extremist Jewish settlers. Ultimately, thousands of protesters rallied to the Ghawi family, including members of the Knesset. James Carroll, "Stop the Palestinian Evictions," *International Herald Tribune,* February 24, 2010. See also Nir Hasson, "Thousands of Protesters Rally Against Jewish Presence in East Jerusalem," http://www.haaretz.com/hasen/spages/1154448.html.

25. "Today one quarter of Israeli first graders are Arab, and one quarter are ultra-Orthodox Jews . . . You don't have to be a prophet to see where the children of Israel are heading." Avishai, *Hebrew Republic,* 21.

26. Elon, *Jerusalem,* 177.

27. Psalms 150:3. JB says "lyre." RSV says "lute." Calatrava is the designated architect for the transportation hub at ground zero in New York. There, instead of lyre strings, his motif is wings.

28. Avishai, *Hebrew Republic,* 153.

29. Some argue that Israel, as a self-proclaimed liberal democracy, is properly held to a higher standard than the Palestinians, who do not make the claim. Others hold Israel to higher standards of accountability simply because, in its conflict with Palestine, it is the stronger party. Nevertheless, an age-old pattern of holding Jews to exceptional standards is evident, for example, in Western academic boycotts against Israel, when no such boycotts are mounted against China for its treatment of Tibet, or Russia for its oppression of Georgia — or Syria, for that matter, for its involvement in the murder of the prime minister of Lebanon.

30. Perhaps the most powerful argument over *hic* has to do with the Palestinian insistence on the right of return — an actual, physical return to specific places from which their grandparents were expelled — to *this* house *here,* no matter what has become of it across sixty years.

31. Genesis 22.

32. Psalms 137:1.

33. Not for nothing was the 2005 Ridley Scott film about the Crusades entitled *Kingdom of Heaven.*

34. "There was death in every shape and form . . . fathers who killed their sons . . . men dragged from temples, butchered on the very altars . . . the whole of the Hellenic world convulsed . . . in many calamities — as it happens and will always happen while human nature is what it is . . . But war is a stern teacher." *History of the Peloponnesian War* 3.82.2.

35. This line from Thomas Merton, for example, spoke powerfully to me: "What is the use of living for things that you cannot hold on to, values that crumble in your hands as soon as you possess them, pleasures that turn sour before you have begun to taste them, and a peace that is constantly turning into war?" *The Waters of Siloe.* Garden City, NY: Image Books, 1962, 72.

36. Fr. Pierre Benoit of L'École Biblique et Archéologique Française in Jerusalem.

37. I first wrote of this encounter in *An American Requiem: God, My Father, and*

the War that Came Between Us. I write of it here with a very different understanding of the experience.

38. Since 1997, I have been a participant in the annual Theological Conference at
the Shalom Hartman Institute, initially sponsored by the late Lutheran scholar
Krister Stendahl. Rabbi David Hartman is the founder of the conference, and
Rabbi Donniel Hartman has succeeded him as director.

39. My understanding of the Jewishness of Jesus and of his opposition to Rome
has been shaped, especially, by the work of Paula Fredriksen and John Dominic Crossan. I acknowledge the debt.

2. Deep Violence

1. I acknowledge that I continue here the tradition of relating myths that account
for basic human tendencies and that justify the creation of institutions that
control them. Ancient creation myths (Prometheus) and modern ones (Hobbes, Rousseau, Freud) address the question of aggression, with some asserting
that humans are "by nature" violent (Freud, Hobbes) and some asserting the
opposite (Rousseau). That origin myths are so varied suggests how it falls to
each person who considers the deep question of violence to reach conclusions
of his own. I present the question here, as much as any answer. That I draw
on scientific accounts, which are necessarily laden with speculation, does not
remove this activity from mythmaking, even if scientific myths belong to a
distinct realm.

2. The calculation assumes one second per number. It would take thirty years to
count to one billion. http://www.si.edu/exhibition/gal111/universe.

3. "The Expectancy of Faith," Kierkegaard discourse, quoted in Bellinger, *Genealogy of Violence,* 65. "The ability to be occupied with the future is, then, a sign
of the nobility of human beings; the struggle with the future is the most ennobling . . . He who battles with the future has a [more] dangerous enemy: he
cannot remain ignorant of himself, since he is battling with himself . . . There
is one enemy he cannot conquer by himself, and that is himself."

4. Here is Karl Barth's expression of this idea: "It is because man is not at one in
himself that we are not at one with each other. It is because inner consistency
and continuity are lacking in the life of the individual that there is not fellow-
ship among men." *Church Dogmatics.* Edinburgh: T. and T. Clark, 1957, 726–27.

5. Bronowski, *Ascent of Man,* 54.

6. Thurman, "First Impressions: What Does the World's Oldest Art Say About
Us?" *The New Yorker,* June 23, 2008, 62.

7. Anthropologists "note that in contemporary gatherer-hunter societies, wom-
en, not men, are typically in charge of processing food. It would thus have
been more likely that it was women who first dropped seeds on the ground of
their encampments." Eisler, *The Chalice and the Blade,* 69.

8. Kugel, *How to Read the Bible,* 55. "A knowledge of the physiology of paternity
is hardly an inborn trait, nor is it necessary for sexual reproduction to take
place; thus, it seems quite impossible that, at some point in the prehistory of
all societies, an ignorance of paternity did not exist in fact" (702).

9. "All at once" is an appropriate designation on the scale of time we are marking, even though developments like these may have unfolded over many generations. Scholars do not precisely define the time spans within which these biological and moral revolutions occurred.

10. Leakey, *Origins*, 122.

11. Agriculture was independently "invented" in other places. For example, rice cultivation in Thailand dates to about 6000 BCE. Corn was cultivated in Mexico beginning around 5000 BCE. The silk moth was domesticated in China around 4000 BCE. Eisler, *The Chalice and the Blade*, 252.

12. Humans "came to depend on a drastically reduced number of plant and animal species, which could be cultivated only in a biologically pauperized environment by repetitive labor." Humans are now "specialized to eat the seeds of four kinds of grass — wheat, rice, corn and millet. If these fail, from disease or climate change, we too shall fail." Wilson, *The Creation*, 139, 11.

13. In Anatolia, on the edge of Mesopotamia, around 800 BCE, silver and gold nuggets were used by merchants as supplemental values in trade. A mark designating the purity of the metal was pressed onto the nugget. This seal had the effect of crushing the nuggets, making them flat. This was the beginning of the coin. Jack Weatherford, "Prometheus Unbound," *Lapham's Quarterly* 1, no. 2, Spring 2008, 188.

14. The writing is called cuneiform because of the wedge-shaped grooves made in the clay by the pointed stylus.

15. At the time of the invention of agriculture, the human population was about ten million. It is approaching seven billion today. http://www.pbs.org/wgbh/nova/world balance/numbers.html.

16. Archeologists find evidence of this "pattern of disruption" in all the areas "where the first great agricultural civilizations spread out along the lakes and rivers in the fertile heartlands." Nomads invaded them all. Eisler, *The Chalice and the Blade*, 43.

17. I owe the insight about the connection of the domestication of the horse and war to Bronowski. He adds, "But war, organized war, is not a human instinct. It is a highly planned and cooperative form of theft. And that form of theft began ten thousand years ago when the harvesters of wheat accumulated a surplus, and the nomads rose out of the desert to rob them of what they themselves could not provide. The evidence for that is the walled city of Jericho and its prehistoric tower. That is the beginning of war." *Ascent of Man*, 88. As the earliest extant writing is Sumerian, so the oldest portrait of a horse at war is on the "Battle Standard of Ur," a panel showing the Sumerian army, discovered by early-twentieth-century archeologists south of present-day Baghdad and dating to about 2500 BCE. At about that time, the elephant was domesticated in the civilization that had grown up in the Indus Valley, and it, too, was harnessed to war. Eisler, *The Chalice and the Blade*, 253.

18. The primordial Babylonian mother dragon, for example, was slain by her son, Marduk, the warrior god. From the two halves of her corpse came the vault of heaven and the plain of earth. Brock and Parker, *Saving Paradise*, 11.

19. I owe this formulation to Drew Gilpin Faust, *The Republic of Suffering*, 83.

20. "Ideas do not produce ritual; rather, ritual itself produces and shapes ideas." Walter Burkert, "*Homo Necans:* The Anthropology of Ancient Greek Sacrificial Ritual and Myth," in Carter, *Understanding Religious Sacrifice,* 227.

21. "Man became man through the hunt, through the act of killing." Burkert, "*Homo Necans,*" 224.

22. Durkheim, *Elementary Forms of Religious Life,* 268.

23. The various Christian theories of atonement are an example of this.

24. Burkert, "*Homo Necans,*" 224.

25. J. Z. Smith, for example, argues that "animal sacrifice appears to be, universally, the ritual killing of a domesticated animal." It did not occur, that is, before the arrival of agriculture. Carter, *Understanding Religious Sacrifice,* 327. Adolf E. Jenson argues that hunters had no need to ritualize the kill, since it "was part of the natural order of things and needed no explanation." Carter, *Understanding Religious Sacrifice,* 177.

26. Carter, *Understanding Religious Sacrifice,* 211.

27. The great tragedies of high-culture Greece take human sacrifice for granted. For example, in Aeschylus' *Agamemnon,* the daughter of the king is sacrificed when animal victims prove insufficient. Bas-reliefs on the Parthenon, dating to the fifth century BCE, include three young women en route as victims to the sacrificial altar. Two thousand years later, when Spaniards arrived in Aztec Mexico in the fifteenth century CE, they found a thriving cult of human sacrifice. The Templo Mayor, excavated in Mexico City in the late twentieth century, was "a theater for large numbers of human sacrifices of warriors, children, women, and slaves." Corrasco, *City of Sacrifice,* 56.

28. Girard, *Violence and the Sacred,* 47.

29. Girard's reflections begin with primitive humans, but they apply to the twenty-first century, when exactly this irrational and spiritualized violence is embodied in nuclear deterrence theory and nuclear arsenals. Girard said, "Today ultimate violence — the truth of human history — circles over our heads more or less like satellites and could, if we wished, put an end to all human history in an instant. The specialists tell us without blinking that only this violence protects us. It will not be long before we understand why human beings could throw their own children into the furnaces of the idol Moloch in the belief that this could protect them from worse violence." Cited in Schwager, *Must There Be Scapegoats?,* 31.

30. Jeffrey Carter comments: "With such a sweeping theory, it is no wonder that [Girard] has attracted both devoted followers and highly vocal critics." *Understanding Religious Sacrifice,* 241.

31. I owe the image of people desiring what others want at the sale table to Gil Bailie. Bailie, *Violence Unveiled,* 116.

32. This calls to mind Thomas Hobbes's notion of the state of nature, prior to the social contract, as the "war of all against all." *Leviathan,* chapter 13.

33. Hammurabi (c. 1810 BCE–1750 BCE) was a king of Babylon. His code of laws was a detailed set of strictures designed to rein in envy and revenge. "If anyone is committing a robbery and is caught, then he shall be put to death."

34. The scapegoat appears in Leviticus 16.

35. Bailie, *Violence Unveiled*, 127.

36. "We know that animals possess individual braking mechanisms against violence; animals of the same species never fight to the death, but the victor spares the life of the vanquished. Mankind lacks this protection. Our substitution for the biological mechanism of the animals is the collective, cultural mechanism of the surrogate victim. There is no society without religion because without religion society cannot exist." Girard, *Violence and the Sacred*, 221.

37. The phrase is René Girard's, who explains it as "collective transfer of violence to a random victim." Schwager, *Must There Be Scapegoats?*, vii.

3. The Bible Resists

1. The theories of René Girard, in particular, have come in for criticism. See, for example, Klawans, *Purity, Sacrifice, and the Temple*, and Chilton, *The Temple of Jesus*.

2. Here are three texts detailing the covenant Yahweh made with Abraham:

> *Genesis 15:7–10, 17–19:*
> And he said to him, "I am Yahweh, who brought you from Ur of the Chaldaeans to give you this land to possess." But he said, "Lord God, how am I to know that I shall possess it?" He said to him, "Bring me a heifer three years old, a she-goat three years old, a ram three years old, a turtledove, and a young pigeon." And he brought him all these, cut them in two, and laid each half over against the other . . .
> When the sun had gone down and it was dark, behold, a smoking fire pot and a flaming torch passed between these pieces. On that day the Lord made a Covenant with Abram, saying: "To your descendants I give this land, from the river of Egypt to the Great River, the River Euphrates."

> *Deuteronomy 11:24–31:*
> The Lord will drive out all these nations before you, and you will dispossess nations greater and mightier than yourselves. Every place on which the sole of your foot treads shall be yours; your territory shall be from the wilderness to Lebanon, and from the River, the river Euphrates, to the Western Sea. No man shall be able to stand against you; the Lord your God will lay the fear of you and the dread of you upon all the land that you shall tread, as he promised you.
> Behold, I set before you this day a blessing and a curse . . . And when the Lord your God brings you into the land which you are entering to take possession of it, you shall set the blessing on Mount Gerizim and the curse on Mount Ebal. Are they not beyond the Jordan, west of the road, in the land of the Canaanites?

> *Joshua 1:3:*
> Every place that the soul of your foot will tread upon I have given to you, as I promised to Moses. From the wilderness and this Lebanon as far as the

great river, the river Euphrates, all the land of the Hittites, to the Great Sea toward the going down of the sun shall be your territory.

3. Schwager, *Must There Be Scapegoats?*, 55.
4. "The Battle Hymn of the Republic," which was the music of one of history's most violent wars, derives its grape-stomping, enraged image of God from Revelation's verse predicting that Christ "will tread the winepress of the fierceness and wrath of Almighty God." Revelation 19:15. We will see more of this song, and its war, later.
5. Joshua 10:40.
6. Crossan, *God and Empire*, 73.
7. Eisler, *The Chalice and the Blade*, 44.
8. Kugel, *How to Read the Bible*, 288.
9. James Kugel compares the small band of escaped Hebrews to the Pilgrims. Kugel, *How to Read the Bible*, 232.
10. The idea that the human aggressor innately feels regret seems belied by, say, the so-called realist tradition in international relations. The realist refuses to be morally troubled by violence, but rather embraces it as necessary (see the Melian Dialogue in Thucydides' *History of the Peloponnesian War*). But realist policy choices (for example, war for the sake of oil) are almost always cloaked in the nonrealist language of morality (just war) because publics will rarely fight or support fighting except for higher causes. I am grateful to Nir Eisikovits for this point.
11. "Faith is the state of being ultimately concerned." Tillich, *Dynamics of Faith*, 1.
12. *Homo sapiens sapiens* is an ad hoc construction, not correct Latin. The further elaboration, with a third *sapiens,* is equally ad hoc and used to make the point of "being known," since the verb *sapio* does not have a passive form.
13. Speaking to reporters on the eve of the first Gulf War, Joint Chiefs Chairman Colin Powell defined his purpose with these words. But not only military leaders concern themselves with war. In *The Prince,* Machiavelli argues that the prince must always concentrate on the preparation for and waging of war. That is the real business of political leadership. Contemporary leaders, even civilians like the American president, are mainly military commanders ("the commander in chief"). So biblical projections of such a characteristic onto God are not as primitive as imagined.
14. Kugel, *How to Read the Bible*, 475.
15. Kugel points out that this slaughter of an enemy, together with the destruction of all the enemy's property, was not mere divine ruthlessness. By eliminating booty, God was here putting an end to war as a profit-making enterprise. Total war, that is, could be an indirect way to mitigate violence. Kugel, *How to Read the Bible*, 448.
16. The oldest reference to Jerusalem is found engraved on pottery shards found in Luxor, Egypt, and dating to 1878–1842 BCE. The engraving lists nineteen cities in the land of Canaan, one of which is "Rushalimum," which, translated, means "Shalem has founded," a reference to the Syrian god Shalem, who was worshiped as the evening star or setting sun. Armstrong, *Jerusalem*, 6. This is

the first of a number of citations of Karen Armstrong, whose books have been especially helpful to me. I gratefully acknowledge my debt to her.

17. 1 Kings 8.

18. For example, during the Enlightenment, the myth of Atlantis, a lost primeval civilization, gained currency as an alternative to the tacky idea that Western civilization grew in substantial part out of biblical Israel.

19. Shakespeare, too, notes the human love of war in *Coriolanus*: "Let me have war, say I. It exceeds peace as far as day does night; it's spritely, waking, audible, and full of vent. Peace is very apoplexy, lethargy, mulled, deaf, sleepy, insensible, a getter of more bastard children than war's a destroyer of men" (act 4, scene 5).

20. Bailie, *Violence Unveiled*, 134.

21. "God repented of the evil that He had said that He would do to them." Jonah 3:10.

22. Scholars define the four main sources of the Pentateuch, the first five books of the Bible, as "J" (for Yahwist, because the name of God is given as YHWH); "E" (for Elohist, because the name of God is given as Elohim); "D" for Deuteronomist; and "P" for priestly. The first two are thought to have been written in about 900–700 BCE, the latter two in about 600, during and after the Babylonian exile.

23. Kugel, *How to Read the Bible*, 129.

24. Genesis 11:1–9.

25. Babylon was probably the first city in history to surpass 200,000 in population. In the seventeenth century BCE it achieved its status as the world's largest city, and then lost it — until Nebuchadnezzar's time.

26. Daniel 3:12.

27. Jeremiah 4:7.

28. Jeremiah 52:12–14.

29. Lamentations 1:1–2.

30. The removal of Jews from Jerusalem as a way of destroying their group identity had a modern echo in the 1990s when Serbian Orthodox Christians forced the removal of Bosnian Muslims from their ancestral home in Sarajevo. The point was not just to have an "ethnically cleansed" city, but to destroy the communal memory of the Bosnians.

31. Kugel, *How to Read the Bible*, 288. "The oldest surviving Mesopotamian remains of temples go back to the early 5th millennium BCE — long before there were written records of any kind — but it is quite likely that temples existed even before then" (285).

32. Kugel, *How to Read the Bible*, 421. It is impossible to say precisely when the Jewish religion became monotheistic. The texts suggest that the Oneness of God was a feature of Moses' faith (and so around 1200), but those texts were probably composed in the forms we read in the exilic period or shortly after, reflecting a developed monotheism of that time.

33. Genesis 4:10. Among authors who reflect on the Cain-Abel story in light of the Romulus-Remus story are Heim, *Saved from Sacrifice*, 72; Kugel, *How to Read the Bible*, 208; Girard, *The Girard Reader*, 249.

34. Genesis 8:21.

35. Isaiah 44:6; 45:18; 46:9. This text, the so-called Second Isaiah, was composed during the last years of the exile.

36. Christopher Hitchens, for example: "By its very nature, monotheism is totalitarian and dictatorial and hence it is anathema to me." http://www.deeshaa .org/2007/03/25/hitchens-on-free-speech-and-monotheism.

37. The *Oxford English Dictionary* dates the first use of the word to 1660.

38. *Credo* is Latin for "I believe," the first two words of the Nicene Creed: "I believe in One God." The first words of the *Shema* are *Shema Yisrael, Adonai Eloheinu, Adonai Echad,* meaning, "Hear, O Israel! The Lord is our God, the Lord is One" (Deuteronomy 6:4). The word *Shahada* is from the Arabic for "to testify," and refers to the basic Muslim affirmation "There is no god but God. Muhammad is the Messenger of God."

39. Moses Maimonides, *Guide for the Perplexed,* chapter LVII. http://www.sacred texts.com/jud/gfp/gfp003.htm.

40. Isaiah is the poet laureate of God's universalism, with Jerusalem at its root: "It shall come to pass in the latter days that the mountain of the house of the Lord shall be established as the highest of the mountains and shall be raised above the hills; and all nations shall flow to it, and many peoples shall come and say, 'Come let us go up to the mountain of the Lord, to the House of the God of Jacob, that He may teach us His ways, and that we may walk in His paths.' For out of Zion shall go forth the law and the word of the Lord from Jerusalem. He shall judge between the nations and shall decide for many peoples, and they shall beat their swords into plowshares and their spears into pruning hooks: nation shall not lift up sword against nation; neither shall they learn war any more." Isaiah 2:1–4. This vision is shared by the prophet Micah, 4:1–5.

41. Exodus 3:14. The translation of YHWH is sometimes given as "I am what I am" or "I am who I am," as if the Lord is refusing to answer with a name, which gives power over the named. Under the influence of Greek philosophy, the name is sometimes taken as expressing God's essence, being itself, *ipsum esse.* But scholars also take the answer, rendered as an archaic form of the verb "to be," as indicating God's unlimited, generative existence. The verb "to be," in the third-person form of "he is," translates as Yahweh.

42. John 10:30. While Jesus' followers recognized his oneness with God as a sign of his divinity, John's gospel shows Jesus' antagonists, "the Jews," as hearing that claim as blasphemy: "The Jews fetched stones to stone him."

43. Exodus 20:3: "You shall have no other gods before me . . . For I, the Lord your God, am a jealous god." Deuteronomy 5:6: "I am the Lord your God who brought you out of the land of Egypt, out of the house of bondage. You shall have no other gods before me . . . For I the Lord your God am a jealous god."

44. Genesis 17:6.

45. Whitehead, *Science and the Modern World,* 192. A necessary caveat should be added here. The "nobler form and with clearer expression" of religion emerging over time should not be taken as a kind of supersessionism, as if later forms of religious belief are inevitably superior to earlier ones. The evolutionist view of religion—Whitehead's "upward trend"—has often been used

in that denigrating way, Christians denigrating Jews, Protestants denigrating Catholics, post-Enlightenment secularists denigrating traditional belief. Still, the expansion of consciousness over time does define the human story.

46. See Armstrong, *The Great Transformation*, 3–48.

47. Heraclitus, fragment 50, quoted in Hippolytus, *Refutations*, trans. Richard Hooker. http://wsu.edu/~dee/GREECE/HERAC.HTM.

48. John's Gospel opens, "In the beginning was the Word, and the Word was with God, and the Word was God."

49. "Hebrews" and "Israelites" become known as "Jews" because, around the time of the return from Babylonian exile, the remnant of the tribe of Judah came to prominence. They began to refer to themselves as "Yehudin," in Aramaic—"resident of the colony the Persians called Yuhud (Judah, in Persian)." Shulevitz, *The Sabbath World*, 49.

50. "Second Isaiah" is the name given to chapters 40–55 of the Book of Isaiah, verses that were tacked onto the preexisting Isaiah scroll.

51. Isaiah 42:1–4; 49:1–6; 50:4–11; 52:13–53:12.

52. "I did not speak to your fathers, or commanded them concerning burnt offerings and sacrifices. But this command I gave them, 'Obey my voice.'" Jeremiah 7:21. (See also Jeremiah 6:20.) "For I desire steadfast love, not sacrifice; the knowledge of God rather than burnt offerings." Hosea 6:6. (See also Hosea 5:6, 9:11–13.) For other prophetic denunciations of sacrifice, see Isaiah 1:10–17; Amos 5:21–25; Micah 6:6–8.

53. Deuteronomy 12:1–32.

54. 2 Kings 17:10; 16:4.

55. Kugel, *How to Read the Bible*, 313.

56. Levenson, *Death and Resurrection*, 37.

57. Remains of ritually burnt children have been found at Knossos, suggesting that child sacrifice was a common phenomenon in the middle of the second millennium BCE. But it appears also in the golden age of Pericles a thousand years later. Greek drama itself grew out of rituals of human sacrifice, and the greatest tragedies, from Aeschylus' *Agamemnon* to Euripides' *Electra* to Sophocles' *Oedipus*, are built around the ritual slaughter of beloved children.

58. The god Baal, also called Moloch, against whom Hebrew prophets railed, required offerings of human children. References to Moloch are found throughout the ancient Middle East and North Africa. In Carthage, for example, "MLK" is engraved on stones found at a necropolis dating to between 400 and 200 BCE and containing the deliberately charred remains of thousands of infants, who probably were killed in religious rituals.

59. Human sacrifice is referred to in 2 Kings 16:3, 17:17, 21:6, 23:10; 2 Chronicles 28:3, 33:6; Psalms 106:37; Isaiah 57:7; Jeremiah 7:31, 19:4–5, 32:35; Exodus 16:20, 20:26, 23:37.

60. Micah 6:7–8.

61. Genesis 22.

62. Crossan, *God and Empire*, 64.

63. Crossan, *God and Empire*, 73.

64. Kugel, *How to Read the Bible*, 130. Child sacrifice is referred to in Deuter-

onomy 12:30–31, 18:10. In Judges 11:29–40, Jeptha, who is dated to about 1200 BCE, prays for safe passage home and vows to sacrifice whatever first comes to greet him on his return. It is his daughter, his "only child," and he burns her up.

65. In the Qur'an, Ibrahim says to his unnamed son, "My son, indeed I see in a vision that I sacrifice you. Look, what do you see?" He said, "My father, do what you are commanded to do." Ibrahim "pushed his son's forehead down," but Allah called out to him, "Ibrahim! You have already fulfilled the vision." The Qur'an comments, "This was an obvious trial." Al Saffat 37:84–111. Translated by Bruce Chilton, *Abraham's Curse*, 148–49.

66. Later in this book, we will examine themes of sacrifice and war in the twentieth century.

67. By the "Elohist" author, to whom we referred in note 22, so called because he referred to God as Elohim, in contrast to the "Yahwist" author, who referred to God as YHWH. Recall that these two sources, "E" and "J," of the first five books of the Bible (the Pentateuch) wrote in about the ninth century BCE. The other two sources, "D" for Deuteronomist and "P" for priestly, wrote in the sixth century, during and after the exile. "D" is thought to have written Joshua, Judges, 1 and 2 Samuel, and 1 and 2 Kings. The two books of Chronicles were written later, probably in the fourth century.

68. Exodus 22:28–30. "The firstborn of your sons you shall give to me; you must do likewise with your oxen and with your sheep: seven days it shall be with its mother; on the eighth day you shall give it to me."

69. Genesis 22:2.

70. Levenson, *Death and Resurrection*, x.

71. Armstrong, *Jerusalem*, 90. The claim made here for Judaism is not absolute. The issue is not whether Jews were the first humans in history to come to sophisticated religious interiority (Greeks, Hindus, Buddhists, Confucians, and Egyptians were all evolving systems of thought and belief around the same time), but to note the originating uniqueness of biblical faith.

72. 2 Chronicles, written in about the fourth century, declares, "Then Solomon began to build the house of the Lord in Jerusalem on Mount Moriah" (3:1).

73. Armstrong, *Jerusalem*, 71.

74. We will return to Kierkegaard in considering modernity. Enough to note here that *Fear and Trembling*, published in 1843, uses the story of the Binding of Isaac as a jumping-off point from which to consider questions about moral absolutes (How can readiness to slay the child be "good"? Can obedience to God contradict ethical norms?) and the absurd (Is faith beyond rationality?). Kierkegaard's reflection on the Abraham-Isaac story led to the introduction of the absurd as a philosophical category, one that became a pillar of twentieth-century thought.

75. Chilton, *Abraham's Curse*, 44.

76. 1 and 2 Maccabees are considered canonical books of the Bible by the Roman Catholic and Eastern Orthodox churches. Jews and Protestants regard them as historically reliable, but not biblically canonical.

77. Amos 3:9. "Proclaim to the strongholds in Assyria . . . and say, 'Assemble yourselves upon the mountains.'"

78. Amos 4:11–12.

79. Jeremiah 25:8.

80. "Daniel 7 presents us with one of the first instances of a Jewish 'apocalypse.' The term apocalypse refers to a kind of literature — a literary genre — that started becoming popular during the Maccabean period and continued to be popular for centuries afterward, among Jews and eventually among Christians." Ehrman, *God's Problem*, 197. The Book of Enoch, written around the same time, is another example of Jewish apocalypse.

81. "I saw in the night visions . . . one like a son of man . . . and to him was given dominion and glory and kingdom . . . an everlasting dominion which shall not pass away and his kingdom shall not be destroyed." Daniel 7:13–14. I owe the thought about a religion of space becoming a religion of time to Shulevitz, *The Sabbath World*, 4.

82. Ehrman, *God's Problem*, 201.

83. I owe this appreciation of the new significance of martyrdom, promising resurrection, to Bruce Chilton. See, for example, Daniel 12:1–3, 2 Maccabees 7:11.

84. Shulevitz, *The Sabbath World*, 80.

85. 2 Maccabees 7:41 (JB).

86. Genesis 15:6.

87. 1 Maccabees 2:52 (JB).

4. The Cross Against Itself

1. To name only two, there was the discovery of texts, including the Gospel of Thomas, at Nag Hammadi, Egypt, in 1945, and of the Qumran manuscripts near the Dead Sea in 1947. These writings demonstrated that Judaism and the Jesus movement within it were far more varied and sectarian than scholars had previously believed. For the first time, it has been possible to understand Jesus (and, for that matter, John the Baptist) in the context of their own lives — very much in line with how they may well have understood themselves.

2. The Dead Sea is more than 400 meters below sea level. By contrast, Death Valley, the lowest point in the Western Hemisphere, is less than 90 meters below sea level.

3. Luke 7:24–28.

4. Matthew 14:13. Adam Gopnik, in a review of Jesus literature in *The New Yorker*, captures the dilemma Jesus faced at that moment. "Jesus seems to have an intimation of the circumstance he has found himself in — leading a rebellion against Rome that is not really a rebellion, yet doesn't really leave any possibility of retreat — and some corner of his soul wants no part of it." Adam Gopnik, "What Did Jesus Do?," *The New Yorker*, May 24, 2010.

5. "Go and give that fox this message: Learn that today and tomorrow I cast out devils and on the third day attain my end. But for today and tomorrow and the next day, I must go on, since it would not be right for a prophet to die outside of Jerusalem." Luke 13:32–33.

6. For "Be not afraid," see, for example, John 6:17; Matthew 14:26, 17:7, 28:10. In this preaching Jesus was firmly Jewish. "Be not afraid" appears dozens of times

in the Hebrew scriptures. See, for example, Deuteronomy 1:21 and 31:8, Joshua 1:9, and Isaiah 7:4.

7. Crossan's phrase, as we saw.

8. Tacitus, *Annals* 15.44.

9. Tacitus puts the number of Jewish defenders of Jerusalem of both sexes and all ages at more than 600,000. It is impossible to draw definitive conclusions about such estimates. Scholars today accept that the Jewish population of Palestine in the first century may have reached 2.5 million. If so, somewhat more than half a million defenders in Jerusalem is plausible. Fredriksen, *Jesus of Nazareth*, 64. E. P. Sanders notes that the Sacred Mosque at Mecca, which is only somewhat larger than Herod's Temple was, accommodates 500,000 pilgrims at prayer. Herod's Temple, Sanders concludes, could readily accommodate 400,000 pilgrims. *Judaism*, 127.

10. Mark 13:1–2.

11. Luke 13:34.

12. One of the peculiarities of the Christian memory is the way in which the crucifixion of Jesus is memorialized as if it were unique and uniquely violent (even the two thieves are remembered as having been roped, not nailed, to the adjacent crosses), as if the redemption action required Jesus to undergo the most extreme suffering imaginable. In fact, the pain and humiliation inflicted on Jesus was mundane, even cliché, which was its point. More than a thousand rebels were crucified around Jerusalem shortly before Jesus was born, as tens of thousands were crucified while the story of his Passion was taking form. Crucifixion was ubiquitous wherever subject people resisted Rome.

13. Nero ruled until 69 CE, when, after being forced out of power, he committed suicide.

14. Josephus puts the number of dead during just the first Jewish War (66–70) at 1.1 million. *The Jewish War* 6.9.3.

15. That the Jewish Christian community of Jerusalem, whose head was James, the brother of Jesus, was deleted from the Gentile Christian memory is reflected in the fact that the New Testament mentions Peter 190 times, Paul 170 times, and James only 11 times. Küng, *Islam*, 38.

16. Matthew 5:45.

17. Acts 2:46, 3:1.

18. 1 Corinthians 16:1–3; 2 Corinthians 1:1–9:15; Romans 15:25. See Fredriksen, *Jesus of Nazareth*, 36–38.

19. Mark 15:6–15. The opposition between Jesus and Barabbas is embedded in the latter's name, for Jesus is *bar abbas* also — literally a son of the Father. *Abba,* "Daddy," is the name Jesus uses to address the Lord God. I owe this insight to Bailie, *Violence Unveiled*, 223.

20. Fredriksen, *Jesus of Nazareth*, 86.

21. John 15:25, which repeats "without a cause" from Psalms 69:4.

22. This uprising against Rome became literally suicidal in its denouement. A remnant group of Jewish resisters took to the redoubt of Masada, a natural rock fortress in the mountains of Judea. In 73, after a long Roman siege, the

defenders killed one another, until an ever smaller group was reduced to a bloodied sole survivor. At last, he fell upon his sword — depriving the Romans of any captives and searing in the Jewish mind an image of radical refusal.

23. Philostratus, *The Life of Apollonius of Tyana* 6.29, http://www.gnosis.org /library/grs-mead/apollonius/apollonius_mead_05.htm.

24. In Galatians 4:26, Paul contrasts "the Jerusalem above" and "the present Jerusalem." The image picks up on Isaiah 65:17–25, which reads in part, "Behold I create a new heaven and a new earth, and the former things shall not be remembered . . . But be glad and rejoice forever in that which I create; for behold, I create for Jerusalem a rejoicing and her people a joy. I will rejoice in Jerusalem and be glad in my people, no more shall be heard the sound of weeping and the cry of distress." Jewish apocalyptic hope, in contrast to Christian, tended to cling to a literal restoration of the earthly city of Jerusalem. Typical is the third-century-CE Palestinian rabbi Yohanan, who wrote, "The Holy One said, 'I will not enter the Jerusalem which is above until I enter the Jerusalem which is below.'" Cited by Wilken, "Early Christian Chiliasm," 304.

25. "The seventh day is like a palace in time with a kingdom for all. It is not a date, but an atmosphere." Heschel, *The Sabbath*, 21.

26. Jon D. Levenson, "The Temple and the World," 298.

27. Shulevitz, *The Sabbath World*, xxiii.

28. Shulevitz, *The Sabbath World*, xxiii.

29. Hosea 6:6–7.

30. Shulevitz, *The Sabbath World*, 27.

31. "Jesus answered them, 'Destroy this Temple and in three days, I will raise it up.' The Jews then said, 'It has taken forty-six years to build this Temple, and you will raise it up in three days?' But he spoke of the Temple of his body. When therefore he was raised from the dead, his disciples remembered that he had said this, and they believed the scripture and the word which Jesus had spoken." John 2:19. Note that this text, the Gospel of John, dates to about 100, thirty years after the Temple was destroyed.

32. The Gospel of Matthew, for example, puts that judgment in the mouth of Jesus, who is grief-stricken at the thought of a destroyed Jerusalem: "O Jerusalem, Jerusalem, killing the prophets and stoning those who are sent to you, how often would I have gathered your children together, as a hen gathers her brood under her wings, and you would not." Matthew 23:37.

33. The Gospel of Luke, for example, makes the charge explicit: "Behold your house is forsaken. I tell you, you will not see me until you say, 'Blessed is he who comes in the name of the Lord.'" Luke 13:35.

34. Mark 12:32–33. Jesus' opposition to Temple authorities can be seen in Mark 11:11, 11:15, 11:12–21. Jesus is seen drawing on the prophets of Israel to justify this opposition. Isaiah 56:7, Jeremiah 7:11.

35. In the Synoptic Gospels, the demonstration in the Temple occurs early in the Passion week and is the immediate cause of Jesus' murder. In John, the demonstration occurs at the start of his public ministry, well before his Passion.

36. Chilton, *The Temple of Jesus*, 121–27. This denigration of the Temple is also

seen in Acts of the Apostles, when the conflict with "the Jews" has shifted from Jesus to his surviving disciples. When the first Christian martyr, Stephen, is killed by "the Jews," it is also for his attack on the Temple, which he justifies by attributing to God the words found in the prophet Amos: "I despise your sacrifices." *God despises what Jews do in their worship.*

37. "Modern scholars, both Jews and Christians, are inclined to see the temple system as corrupt, or as detrimental to the people's welfare, I think, because both represent movements that replaced it. We all like moral reform, and it is nice to see our spiritual ancestors as moral reformers. The first-century predecessors of modern Jews and Christians (Pharisees, rabbis, Jesus and his followers) must have thought there was something wrong with common Judaism, the Judaism of the temple." Sanders, *Judaism,* 91.

38. Josephus, *The Jewish War* 1.148. Quoted in Sanders, *Judaism,* 92. Sanders adds, about the priests, "They did not grab the day's profits and run."

39. Kosher laws intend to ensure the purity, and therefore the hygiene, of animal slaughter. Here is Philip Roth, describing what the son of a kosher butcher witnessed: "I saw them kill hundreds of chickens according to kosher laws . . . He [the slaughterer] would bend the neck backward—not break it, just arc it back . . . For the chicken to be kosher, he had to cut the throat in one smooth, deadly stroke . . . To kosher an animal, you have to get the blood out. In a nonkosher slaughterhouse they can shoot the animal, they can knock it unconscious, they can kill it any way they want to kill it. But to be kosher, they've got to bleed it to death." *Indignation,* 158–59. By contrast, consider the phenomenon of mass slaughterhouses, which, in the words of the historian William Cronon, "distanced their customers most of all from the act of killing . . . In the packers' world, it was easy not to remember that eating was a moral act inextricably bound to killing. Such was the second nature that a corporate order had imposed on the American landscape. Forgetfulness was among the least noticed and most important of its by-products." *Nature's Metropolis,* 256.

40. At his baptism by John the Baptist, for example (Luke 3:21), and at his transfiguration (Matthew 17:9).

41. "The person, not the book, and the life, not the text, are decisive and constitutive for us." Crossan, *God and Empire,* 95.

42. Luke 22:42, Matthew 26:39, Mark 14:39.

43. Hebrews 10:1–18.

44. John 1:29.

45. I depend on Robert J. Daly for this summary of the interiorization of sacrifice. "The Origins of the Christian Doctrine of Sacrifice," in Carter, *Understanding Religious Sacrifice,* 349.

46. Psalms 51:16–17.

47. Daly, "Origins of the Christian Doctrine of Sacrifice," 346.

48. Thus, against the sacrificial understanding of Jesus, signaled by John the Baptist's designation of him as "Lamb of God," soon to be offered "for the sin of the world," Girard insists that "there is nothing in the Gospels to suggest that the death of Jesus is a sacrifice . . . The sacrificial interpretation of the Passion must be criticized and exposed as a most enormous and

paradoxical misunderstanding." Girard, *The Girard Reader,* 178.

49. Hebrews 10:22.

50. Words reported to have been spoken by third-century pagans observing Christians. Tertullian, *Apology* 39.6.

51. Bailie, *Violence Unveiled,* 19.

52. Quoted in Schwager, *Must There Be Scapegoats?*, 41.

53. Bailie, *Violence Unveiled,* 7.

54. The Bible—Old and New Testaments alike—is, Girard argues, "the only literature in the world that exposes the violence perpetrated by humans, sides with the victim, and thus calls humans to renounce violence in the name of the One who forged for us another way to live and die." In Swartley, *Violence Renounced,* 26.

55. One strain of Christian teaching—that Christ died as a result of the sins of all humanity—upholds the idea that all humans, not "the Jews," were responsible for the death of Jesus, but that is a minor countercurrent in an otherwise powerful torrent of a quite particular act of scapegoating embedded in the sacred texts themselves. That all sinners bear responsibility for the crucifixion was affirmed, for example, at the Council of Trent in the sixteenth century, but much more consequentially, that council continued the punishment of Jews for being Christ killers.

56. Matthew 27:25.

57. John 1:11.

58. Mark 1:23–26.

59. Luke 22:52.

60. John 8:44. The loaded phrase "the Jews" (in Greek, *hoi Ioudaioi*) appears a total of 16 times in the Gospels of Mark, Matthew, and Luke, while it appears 71 times in John. Pagels, *The Origin of Satan,* 104–5. See also Carroll, *Constantine's Sword,* 92.

61. Here is a succinct summary of Girard's argument by one of his most astute interpreters, Mark Heim: "Sacrifice is the disease we have. Christ's death is the test result we can't ignore, and at the same time an inoculation that sets loose a healing resistance. The cure is not more of the same." *Saved from Sacrifice,* xii.

62. John 11:50. "Jesus willingly and knowingly accepts to undergo the fate of the scapegoat to achieve the full revelation of scapegoating as the genesis of all false gods." René Girard, "Violence Renounced," in Swartley, *Violence Renounced,* 318.

63. Heim, *Saved from Sacrifice,* 210.

64. When, for example, the fathers of Vatican Council II, in the 1965 declaration *Nostra Aetate,* renounced the "Christ killer" charge against "the Jews," they did not explain how Christians were to read the Gospel texts that lodge exactly that complaint. Every Good Friday, when the Passion is read aloud in Christian churches around the world, Jews are once again indicted for the murder of Jesus.

65. "Blair Warns Taliban of Military Strikes," *Independent,* October 2, 2001.

66. Acts 21:27–32. "When the seven days were almost completed, the Jews from Asia, who had seen him in the temple, stirred up all the crowd and laid hands on him, crying out, 'Men of Israel, help! This is the man who is teaching men

everywhere against the people and the law and this place. Moreover, he also brought Greeks into the temple, and he has defiled this holy place.' For they had previously seen Trophimus the Ephesian with him in the city and they supposed that Paul had brought him into the Temple. Then all the city was aroused, and the people ran together. They seized Paul, and dragged him out of the temple, and at once the gates were shut. As they were trying to kill him, word came to the tribune of the Roman cohort that all Jerusalem was in an uproar. He at once took soldiers and centurions and ran down to them. When the rioters saw the tribune and his soldiers, they stopped beating Paul."

67. Matthew 23:27.

68. Armstrong, *Jerusalem*, 180.

69. Bailie, *Violence Unveiled*, 231.

70. Eusebius, Constantine's biographer, called him the new Abraham, an assertion tied to Eusebius's effort to downplay the significance of Jerusalem, since Eusebius was bishop of the rival Caesarea. Constantine was like Abraham, Eusebius argued, because the patriarch had worshiped God without a temple, without Jerusalem. *Ecclesiastical History* 1:4, cited by Armstrong, *Jerusalem*, 175.

71. Carroll, *Constantine's Sword*, 178–207.

72. Armstrong, *Jerusalem*, 183.

73. Stark, *One True God*, 61.

74. Stark, *One True God*, 117.

75. The Didache, a set of liturgical rubrics originating in first-century Syria, for example, does not refer to the crucifixion. Eucharistic emphasis is given to life, not death.

76. Daly, "Origins of the Christian Doctrine of Sacrifice," 350.

77. Chilton, *Abraham's Curse*, 135. Chilton points out that Christian iconography thereafter portrayed Abraham with a sword, not a knife, raised above Isaac's head. One of the most famous examples is Titian's *Sacrifice of Abraham*, which illustrates the cover of Chilton's book.

78. As the eighteenth-century Jewish philosopher Moses Mendelssohn put it, but for Augustine's "lovely brainwave, we would have been exterminated long ago." Saperstein, *Moments of Crisis*, 11. The most important explanation of Augustine's intervention is given by the Jewish scholar Paula Fredriksen in her *Augustine and the Jews*.

79. Said, *Orientalism*, 391.

80. One witness, the monk Antiochus Stratego, said the Persians slaughtered 65,555 Christians. Armstrong, *Jerusalem*, 214.

81. Pope Leo the Great. Armstrong, *Jerusalem*, 208.

82. The oldest detailed cartographic map, dating to 565, is a mosaic rendition of the known world in the floor of the Byzantine church in Madaba, Jordan. Jerusalem is at the center of the world. The first printed map — the Brandis map, dating to 1475, referred to earlier — is a world map centered on Jerusalem. The Bunting cloverleaf map, of 1581, shows the world's "three" continents — Europe, Africa, and Asia — joined by Jerusalem.

83. Crossan, *God and Empire*, 218.

84. The seven stars in the hand of Christ in Revelation are said to refer to the seven churches of Asia Minor—Ephesus, Laodicea, Smyrna, Sardis, Thyatira, Pergamum, and Philadelphia. Ehrman, *God's Problem*, 234.

85. Revelation 1:1, 4:9, 22:8. By the early second century, "John" was commonly identified with the apostle John, who was also identified as the author of the Gospel of John.

86. Gilbert, *Atlas of Jewish History*, 15.

87. I say "mainly." Some scholars, like John Dominic Crossan, deny that Jesus was an apocalypticist.

88. Matthew 11:5, Luke 7:22.

89. Matthew 13:16, Luke 10:23.

90. Dunn, *Unity and Diversity*, 321.

91. Revelation 6:15–17.

92. Revelation 14:1, 17:14.

93. Revelation 6:9–10.

94. Revelation 13:18. Nero's name in Hebrew equals the numerical value of 666.

95. Jesus says, "You are of your father the devil, and your will is to do as your father desires. He was a murderer from the beginning." John 8:44.

96. Revelation 5:1.

97. Revelation 6:2–8.

98. Revelation 18:2.

99. Revelation 19:15. The image of grapes appears in Jeremiah, but not as a figure of bloody mayhem aimed at the world. Jeremiah cites the Lord as saying, "There shall be no grapes on the vine," a deprivation aimed not at destruction or redemption through violence, but at the chastening of faithless Israel. Jeremiah 8:13.

100. John Dominic Crossan regards Revelation as a slander against Jesus, a blasphemy against Christ. *God and Empire*, 224. Other Christian commentators have sought to absolve Revelation by insisting it does not mean what it says. One example: "Nowhere [in Revelation] do God's people 'wage war.' What they do is 'conquer' or 'become victors' (the same word in Greek)—and they do that by the Lamb's own blood and by their courageous testimony, not through Armageddon or war." Rossing, *The Rapture Exposed*, 121–22. Another: That "the heaven Warrior kills all his enemies" is not an act of violence, "for his conquest is by means of a sword that comes from his mouth, not by the power of his arm." Barr, "Toward an Ethical Reading of the Apocalypse," 361.

101. "Put your sword up, for all who live by the sword die by the sword." Matthew 26:52.

102. Hebrews 4:2.

103. Revelation 19:11.

104. Isaiah 25:6–8.

105. Revelation 19:21. Crossan drew my attention to the contrast between the banquet image of Isaiah and the apocalyptic meal in which vultures feed on the slain. Crossan, *God and Empire*, 227.

106. Revelation 21:2, 22.

5. The Rock of Islam

1. Aslan, "Islam's Long War Within," 40.
2. Rauf, *What's Right with Islam,* xviii.
3. Aslan, *No god but God,* 81.
4. "Show me just what Muhammad brought that was new and there you will find things only evil and inhuman, such as his command to spread by the sword the faith that he preached." From the 1391 "Dialogue with a Certain Persian, the Worthy Monterizes in Anakara of Galatia," representing the thought of the Byzantine emperor Manuel II Paleologus. This slander was repeated, to much controversy, by Pope Benedict XVI at the University of Regensburg in 2006, on the occasion of the fifth anniversary of the 9/11 terrorist attacks. Western ignorance of the seventh-century Qur'an is indicated by the fact that there was no Latin translation of the book until halfway through the twelfth century. There was no "approximately objective account of Islam and the Prophet" until the eighteenth century—a book that was promptly put on the Roman Index of Prohibited Books. Küng, *Islam,* 9, 11.
5. The Qur'an, surah 2, includes the verse "There is to be no compulsion in religion."
6. Mahatma Gandhi, *Young India,* 1924. http://www.cyberistan.org/islamic/quote1 .html#gandhi.
7. Orthopraxis, not orthodoxy—in the argot.
8. Makiya, *The Rock,* 291.
9. His supposed illiteracy is crucial to the miraculousness of the highly literate revelation that was given him, enshrined in the Qur'an. But some observe that his success as a merchant would have presupposed basic skills of reading and writing.
10. Monophysites held that Christ had only one nature, a human nature that evolved into a divine nature. Nestorians affirmed the extreme opposite position that he had two radically distinct natures, one human and one divine. The orthodox doctrine, defined at the Council of Chalcedon in 451, was that the two distinct natures of Christ are joined in the "hypostatic union" of his one person.
11. To cite one example of the subtle and careful Christian use of philosophical categories to sketch an understanding of God, see St. Augustine's *On the Trinity,* an analysis of the triune nature of human experience (time divided into past, present, and future; knowing divided into memory, sensation, and anticipation) as a great analogue of the otherwise unknowable Transcendent. Such, in Augustine's scheme, are the "traces" of God.
12. Armstrong, *Islam,* 10.
13. The call to prayer is "God is greater! I bear witness that there is no god but God. I bear witness that Muhammad is God's messenger. To prayer! To salvation! God is greater! There is no god but God." As a rebuttal to this affirmation, Christopher Hitchens called his 2007 book *God Is Not Great.* But the title is a misunderstanding based on a mistranslation.

14. Aslan, *No god but God,* 150.

15. Genesis 25:18.

16. The succession to Muhammad was disputed, with some followers preferring the Prophet's son-in-law, the husband of Fatima, Ali ibn Abi Talib. He would become the fourth caliph, in 656, but not before his supporters had become known as Shiah-i Ali, "Ali's party," which is the origin of Shiite Islam. Shiites would be a minority movement, centered in Iraq, while Sunni Islam (from *sunnah,* for "words," as in the words of the Prophet) would dominate elsewhere.

17. "Caliph" is from *khalifah,* the Arabic for "successor" (to Muhammad).

18. Though accounts of Umar's nonviolent arrival in Jerusalem are numerous and ancient, they may also be apocryphal. The more important point is that Muslim and Christian sources alike believed them and repeated them. Peters, *Jerusalem and Mecca,* 90.

19. There is no doubt that Christians had denigrated the site of Herod's Temple, but it is also true that the rubble Umar saw would have been added to by Persian assaults against Jerusalem in 628.

20. The "rock" may have been a natural outcropping uncovered in the centuries since the Roman destruction. It seems from the detailed first-century descriptions of Josephus, for example, that no such rock formed any part of Herod's Temple. One apparent consequence of Umar's order to build a mosque at some remove from it was a significant expansion of the Temple Mount area. Peters, *Jerusalem and Mecca,* 82, 84.

21. Judges 1:21, Joshua 15:63.

22. Küng, *Islam,* 100.

23. Surah 17:1 of the Qur'an reads: "Glory to Allah who did take His Servant for a Journey by night from the Sacred Mosque to the farthest Mosque, whose precincts We did bless — in order that We might show him some of Our signs: for He is the One who heareth and seeth all things."

24. An elaborated version of Muhammad's night journey, including his ascension to the divine throne from the Noble Sanctuary in Jerusalem, is given in the *sirah* (or life) of Muhammad written a generation after the Dome of the Rock's construction by Muhammad ibn Ishaq. In each of seven heavens the Prophet met one of the other prophets of the biblical tradition, from Moses to Jesus — a kind of initiation into the religion of the Book.

25. Makiya, *The Rock,* 15. One is tempted to add "Hard Rock Café."

26. Elon, *Jerusalem,* 214.

27. "Oh, you people of the Book! Do not exaggerate in your religion, utter nothing concerning God save the truth. The messiah, Jesus, son of Mary, was only a messenger of God, and his Word which he conveyed unto Mary, and a spirit proceeding from him. So believe in God and His messengers, and say not 'Three.' Cease! It will be better for you. God is only one God. Far be it removed from his transcendental majesty that he should have a son. He is all that is in the heavens and all that is in the earth. And God is sufficient . . . the Almighty, the Wise. Lo! Religion with God is Islam. Those who formerly received the Book differed only after knowledge came unto them, through transgression

among themselves. Who so disbelieves the revelations of God will find that, Lo! God is swift at reckoning!" The inscription is on the inner octagonal arcade of the Dome of the Rock, dating to 692 CE.

28. Qur'an 3:64.

29. Qur'an 9:29–31 indicates the severity of the Islamic military assault against "unbelievers": "Fight against those who — despite having been vouchsafed revelation — do not believe either in God or the Last Day . . . And the Jews say 'Ezra,' while the Christians say, 'Christ is God's Son.' . . . May God destroy them! How perverted are their minds! They have taken their rabbis and their monks — as well as the Christ, son of Mary — for their lords beside God, although they have been bidden to worship none but the One God, save whom there is no deity."

30. Armstrong, "The Holiness of Jerusalem," 17.

31. Küng, *Islam*, 241.

32. This battle is remembered by British historians as having occurred at Tours, but that is to give place-name primacy to the British triumph over the French in the Hundred Years' War at "the Battle of Poitiers" in 1356.

33. "Perhaps the interpretation of the Koran would now be taught in the schools of Oxford, and her pulpits might demonstrate to a circumcised people the sanctity and truth of the revelation of Mahomet." Edward Gibbon, *History of the Decline and Fall of the Roman Empire,* http://www.ccel.org/g/gibbon/decline/volume2/chap52.htm. Against Gibbon, some scholars suggest that if Muslim forces had dominated the north of Europe in the eighth century, the result would have been a far more rapid end of the Dark Ages, the early arrival of science, arithmetic, and the Greek classics, and freedom from the deadening hand of clerical religion. See Lewis, *God's Crucible,* 173–75.

34. Al Azhar University began in 970 as a madrasa. On June 4, 2009, President Barack Obama made reference to the provenance of the Cairo university: "For over a thousand years, Al Azhar has been a beacon of Islamic learning."

35. Küng, *Islam*, 8. St. John of Damascus (675–749), a leading Syrian Christian, "first provided European Christianity with the theological and (usually scurrilous) doctrinal materials with which to attack Islam and Mohammed . . . Most of the common stereotypes about Mohammed as a whoremonger, as a false prophet, as a hypocritical sensualist, come from the Syrian Christians who, because they knew Arabic and one or another ecclesiastical language, were able to give nasty myths much currency . . . It is out of this long-forgotten background that many of the grudges felt by Christians and Muslims in Lebanon today spring. And to this unedifying legacy, many Zionists have made themselves subscribers." Said, *The Question of Palestine,* 147.

36. Stark, *One True God,* 149.

37. Küng, *Islam*, 219.

38. Because evangelization of most of Europe was by the sword, imposed by victorious rulers on vanquished subjects, in contrast to the grassroots spread of the faith before Constantine, the Christian religion was never fully authentic in much of northern Europe — nor was it purged of superstition or magic. Some see in this sources of later ills, from the divisiveness of the Reformation to

the neopaganism of the Nazis to the final collapse of European belief in the twenty-first century.

39. At a Church council at Nicaea in 787, for example, it was ordered that all new churches were to be consecrated with relics of a dead saint, turning each altar into a kind of tomb—a rule that holds to this day. In this way, Christianity, whose primal symbol was the "empty tomb," became another tomb cult, like so many in the ancient world, from pyramidal Egypt to Olympian Greece.

40. Harpur, *Revelations,* 76.

41. Voltaire famously quipped that if the pieces of the True Cross were reassembled from churches across Europe, there would be enough wood to build a hundred-gun ship.

42. These themes are taken up in René Girard's *Violence and the Sacred* and *Things Hidden Since the Foundations of the World.*

43. "Through Abel, Joseph, Job, Jonah, the Suffering Servant, and of course Jesus, and along many other stories exposing oppressive violence, the biblical text undergoes a progressive travail that announces the culture of murder, and rehabilitates its victims. This Hebrew and Christian revelation is at the heart of the Western history of concern for the victim." Bartlett, *Cross Purposes,* 37.

44. "Then I saw an angel coming down from heaven, holding in his hand the key of the bottomless pit and a great chain. And he seized the dragon, that ancient serpent, who is the Devil and Satan, and bound him for a thousand years, and threw him onto the pit, and shut it and sealed it over him, that he should deceive the nations no more, till the thousand years were ended. After that he must be loosed for a little while . . . And when the thousand years are ended, Satan will be loosed from his prison and come out to deceive the nations which are at the four corners of the earth, that is Gog and Magog, to gather them for battle; their number is like the sand of the sea. And they marched up over the broad earth and surrounded the camp of the saints and the beloved city; but fire came down from heaven and consumed them, and the devil who had deceived them was thrown into the lake of fire and brimstone where the beast and the false prophet were, and they will be tormented day and night for ever and ever." Revelation 20:1–10.

45. The Córdoba caliphate was named for its founders, the Umayyads. The Baghdad founders were Abbassids; the founders in Damascus and Cairo were Fatimids. These identities marked the caliphates.

46. Islamic universities often began as madrasas, centers of religious learning, and evolved differently from European, doctorate-granting universities like Oxford, but these, too, began as centers of religious learning.

47. When a puritanical sect of Muslims, the Almohads, reflecting their own militancy but mirroring the Crusading fervor sweeping the north of Europe, crossed over to Iberia from North Africa in the mid-twelfth century, *convivencia* would begin to shatter. Maimonides, for one, would flee to Egypt in 1159, where the caliphate remained tolerant.

48. Stark, *One True God,* 151. The *reconquista* would not be seriously launched until the mid-twelfth century. The Spanish epic poem *El Cid,* for example, dates to c. 1140. The decisive defeat of the Almohad Muslims by Christian armies

would not occur until 1212, and Islamic forces retreated to the enclave around Granada, from which they would not be expelled until 1492.

49. Armstrong, *Islam*, 95.

50. "The bastard Turks . . . hold sway over our brothers. Your own blood brothers, your companions . . . are flogged and exiled as slaves or slain in their own land. Christian blood, redeemed by the blood of Christ, has been shed, and Christian flesh, akin to the flesh of Christ, has been subjected to unspeakable degradation and servitude . . . The Turks shed blood like a river that runs around Jerusalem. Upon whom does the task fall to avenge this, upon whom does it fall to relieve this, if not upon you? . . . Whoever goes on the journey to free the church of God in Jerusalem can substitute the journey for all penance for sin." Pope Urban II in Clermont France, in 1095. Mastnak, *Crusading Peace*, 52–53.

51. "The Chronicle of Solomon bar Simson," in Eidelberg, *The Jews and the Crusaders*, 21. Medieval chroniclers put the number of first-wave Crusaders as high as 600,000. John France, "Patronage and the Appeal of the First Crusade," in Phillips, *The First Crusade*, 6.

52. Blake, E. O., and C. Morris, "A Hermit Goes to War: Peter and the Origins of the First Crusade," in W. J. Sheils, ed., *Monks, Hermits and the Ascetic Tradition: Papers Read at the 1984 Summer Meetings and the 1985 Winter Meetings of the Ecclesiastical History Society.* London: Basil Blackwell, 1985, 85.

53. Blake and Morris, "A Hermit Goes to War," 87. That Jerusalem's Christian sites or Christians themselves were under Muslim assault in 1095 was a fantasy, although a "mad caliph," al Hakim, had attacked both eighty years before. But al Hakim, substituting his own name for Allah's at Friday prayers, had been overthrown by his own people. Decrees against Christians were promptly revoked, and Christian shrines, including the Holy Sepulcher, were restored. When the 1096 "rescue" was launched, tolerance of Christians had been the rule in Jerusalem for fifty years. Armstrong, *Jerusalem*, 273.

54. Bartlett, *Cross Purposes*, 105. Also, Mastnak, *Crusading Peace*, 53. As suggested by Urban's reference to "the road to the Holy Sepulcher," Crusading built on the idea of pilgrimage. The Crusade was first referred to as *peregrinatio* (pilgrimage), then as *opus Domini* (the Lord's work), then as *praelium Dei* (God's battle) and *bella Domini* (the war of the Lord). Mastnak, 57. As Mastnak points out, the "crusade idea came after the crusade itself."

55. Quoted in Flannery, *Anguish of the Jews*, 92.

56. I recount this history in *Constantine's Sword*, 236–300.

57. Bartlett, *Cross Purposes*, 107.

58. Mastnak, *Crusading Peace*, 46.

59. Mastnak, *Crusading Peace*, 57.

60. Hidd, Rosalind, ed., *Gesta Francorum: The Deeds of the Franks and Other Pilgrims to Jerusalem.* London: Thomas Nelson, 1962, 91.

61. Quoted in Hillenbrand, *Crusades: Islamic Perspectives*, 64–65.

62. "Non-eyewitness Latin chroniclers, writing several years later, gave the number of Muslims killed in the mosque as 10,000, while much later Muslim chroniclers gave the figure as 70,000 or even 100,000." Benjamin Z. Kedar and Denis Kringle, "1099–1187: The Lord's Temple (Templum Domini) and Solo-

mon's Palace (Palladium Salmons)," in Grabar and Kedar, eds., *Where Heaven and Earth Meet*, 133.

63. Mastnak, *Crusading Peace*, 93.

64. Girard, *Things Hidden*, 225.

65. Bartlett, *Cross Purposes*, 136–38. Christianity "stands historically under judgment from its own central motif and message" (138).

66. Baldwin actually succeeded his brother Godfrey as Latin ruler of Jerusalem, but Godfrey, ruling only briefly, had declined the title of king. In accepting it, Baldwin was preempting the authority of the patriarch, the religious leader who had intended to govern the city, as his predecessors had before the Muslim conquest.

67. Idinopulos, *Jerusalem*, 170.

68. Nicholson, *Love, War, and the Grail*, 50.

69. Read, *The Templars*, 131. An irreverent but pointed portrait of the Templars is given by a character in Umberto Eco's *Foucault's Pendulum:* the original knights "were probably idealists caught up in the mystique of the Crusade. But later recruits were most likely younger sons seeking adventure. Remember, the new kingdom of Jerusalem was sort of the California of its days, the place you went to make your fortune" (80).

70. The cross, of course, had been used as a martial symbol as early as Constantine, and it had become a ubiquitous Crusader symbol, but the Knights Templar cross took the stylized form of a sweepingly curved, equal-armed bisection familiar today in its vestige, the Maltese Cross. Warrior saints were commonly pictured with versions of the Templar cross, like the mythic St. George.

71. Read, *The Templars*, 106.

72. Chartres Cathedral, on the site of an earlier structure, was begun in 1145 and formally dedicated in 1260. Legend had it that the Knights Templar helped pay for the church, to secretly house the Ark of the Covenant that they had discovered hidden in their Jerusalem temple. At the north portal there is an engraving of the Ark being moved on a cart, as if in transit to France.

73. In 1131, for example, only a few years after the Templars' establishment, King Alfonso of Aragon, having no heirs, left his "whole kingdom" to the order. The Templars were not able to claim the legacy from Alfonso's rivals. Read, *The Templars*, 110.

74. The London temple is a case in point. Established in the late twelfth century in what is now the City of London, around the still standing round Temple Church, the temple was the city's first treasury.

75. Kedar and Kringle, "1099–1187: The Lord's Temple," 141.

76. "In Praise of the New Knighthood," quoted in Nicholson, *Love, War, and the Grail*, 5.

77. The feminization of Jerusalem is an old story. "How is the faithful city become a harlot!" complained the prophet Isaiah. "Be glad for her, all you who love her," he declares elsewhere, ". . . that you may be suckled, filled from her consoling breast, that you may savor with delight her glorious breasts" (1:21, 66:11). The Christian equivalent of this feminizing occurs in Revelation, where Jerusalem is envisioned as "a bride coming down from Heaven . . . a beautiful bride

all dressed for her husband" (21:2). A feminized Jerusalem, as lover, wife, and daughter, all needing to be rescued, has been history's great casus belli. When Jerusalem becomes feminized, its eroticization as an object of male love follows. Mystics and warriors alike, among Jews, Christians, and Muslims, have found the allure of the longed-for female Jerusalem irresistible. That Jerusalem was for so long unattainable for exiled Jews and stymied Christians only heightened the erotic desire. When such lovers — whether Crusaders, Zionists, or jihadists seeking *reconquest* — were able to take possession of her at last, as the scholar Sidra DeKoven Ezrahi asserts, the holy places, ancestral graves, and ruined shrines were as if fondled, having become "the erogenous zones of the city-woman." Ezrahi, "'To What Shall I Compare Thee?,'" 220.

78. The knights of female spirituality were figures like Hildegard of Bingen in the twelfth century, Julian of Norwich in the fourteenth century, and Theresa of Ávila in the sixteenth century. It would be nineteenth-century women like Jane Austen and George Eliot who would mock and reverse this image of courtly and spiritual femininity. Lest one think that the religious life as the one realm of female action is a medieval restriction long left behind, it survives to this day as professional women overcome the stereotype that female initiative belongs in the home or, at most, in philanthropy. See Conway, *When Memory Speaks,* 40–59.

79. The post-Enlightenment Western mind prefers to imagine the Knights of the Round Table as a secular fraternity, but that is because modernity — including the modern Church — stumbles at the notion of a truly religious military order. The Arthurian romances were first collected and published by Thomas Mallory in 1485, in *Le Morte d'Arthur.* Mallory was the principal source for T. H. White's *The Once and Future King,* published in 1958. White's book was the source of the 1960 Broadway musical *Camelot.* That John F. Kennedy is associated with the Camelot myth suggests how his covert promiscuity was fueled by this tradition. The Knights Templar had their most overt reincarnation in the mid-twentieth-century American cult of the western, with cowboys like the Lone Ranger and actors like Gary Cooper embodying the type. There, too, Kennedy picked up the thread with his "New Frontier." The Templar reference was made explicit in the hit television show of the 1950s and 1960s *Have Gun, Will Travel,* the hero of which was named, simply, Paladin — a word originating in the medieval *Song of Roland,* referring to a knight, ultimately applied to the knights of King Arthur's Round Table. Templar myths and legends continue to inspire popular culture, most notably in recent years in the books of Dan Brown, the spectacularly successful author of *The Da Vinci Code, Angels and Demons,* and *The Lost Symbol.*

80. Beha ed-Din ibn Shaddad, *Saladin, or What Befell Sultan Yusuf.* Whitefish, MT: Kessinger Publishing, 2004, 115.

81. Supreme, but confused. As Christians began to imitate the Islamic practice of enslaving captives (especially once warfare went to sea, where galleys needed endless supplies of oarsmen), the urge to proselytize was tempered by the fact that if Muslims were baptized, they could not be enslaved, since no Christian could hold any other Christian as a slave. Read, *The Templars,* 210.

82. Read, *The Templars*, 159.

83. Armstrong, *Jerusalem*, 294.

84. To Muslims, the reconquered Jerusalem's "political significance was negligible. Her religious importance, on the other hand, was inestimable. Pilgrims and religious scholars from all over the Muslim world arrived to worship and study there, particularly around the Noble Sanctuary." Kedar and Kringle, "1099–1187: The Lord's Temple," 194.

85. In addition to institutionalizing what would be a permanent divisiveness among Christians over Jerusalem — not only between Greeks and Latins, but among Latins themselves — this rejection of compromise by the Knights Templar reified the division among the military orders, with the German Teutonic Knights and the Hospitallers of St. John increasing their distance from the Templars, each to survive with its own legacy.

86. That the Inquisition would be the undoing of the Templars is ironic because its theological grounding — the "two-sword theory of church-state power" — had been laid by St. Bernard of Clairvaux, whose sponsoring theological justification of the Knights Templar, "In Praise of the New Knighthood," had given them their start. Küng, *Christianity*, 394.

87. Ultimately, both Louis XIV and Marie-Antoinette would be held there.

88. Mastnak, *Crusading Peace*, 340, 344.

89. In the 1950s, when I wanted to join my neighborhood chums in the youth group of their fathers' fraternity, a group called Demolay, my parents forbade it. I remember asking my friends why the club was called Demolay, and they had no idea.

90. "One has only to think of the Christian validation of warrior heroism in the West to get a sense of what is at stake here . . . The Victoria Cross, the George Cross, the Croix de Guerre are a continued inversion of the figure of the Crucified in the culture of violence." Bartlett, *Cross Purposes*, 139. Surely Bartlett could have included in that list the Iron Cross.

91. The Military Order of Christ lost its religious standing in the sixteenth century. (In 1492, Pope Alexander VI reduced the vow of celibacy to a vow of "conjugal chastity," and in 1501, Pope Julius II reduced the vow of poverty to a straightforward tax, payable to the pope.) But the king of Portugal continued to carry the title of grand master of the Order of Our Lord Jesus Christ until the elimination of the monarchy and the establishment of the republic in 1910.

92. Küng, *Islam*, 312. The victorious push of the Ottoman Turks would continue almost unabated: in 1522, the Knights Hospitallers lost Rhodes; in 1571, Cyprus fell; in 1669, Crete fell; in 1683, the Turks laid siege to Vienna — the deepest penetration ever into Europe.

93. Morison, *Admiral of the Ocean Sea*, 5. Morison is not alone in downplaying Columbus's religiousness. For example, a 1991 Spanish history derides him as a "socially ambitious . . . embittered escapee . . . [an] adventurer" in pursuit of wealth and fame. Delaney, "Columbus's Ultimate Goal," 10. I acknowledge Carol Delaney for first showing me the place of Jerusalem in Columbus's ambition.

94. "The Edict of Expulsion of the Jews," http://www.sephardicstudies.org/decree

.html. Certainly, the Spanish crown's expulsion of Jews and Muslims led to the opposite of regeneration. Spanish culture had reached its high point as a result of the mingling of the three traditions, and, though New World riches funded the empire and its military, Spanish culture went into intellectual, spiritual, and artistic decline, never to fully recover. The univocal Hapsburg Empire, rooted in Spain, would drive one side of the civilizationally suicidal religious wars of the sixteenth century. Ironically, as the Ottoman Turks drove intellectuals, Greeks, Italians, and other Westerners out of Constantinople after its fifteenth-century conquest, something similar happened with Islamic culture — a profound missing out on the arrival of Renaissance humanism, despite the clinging military and imperial sway of the Ottomans. "In the house of Islam," Hans Küng observed, "from Anatolia to India, people were above all interested in new European weapons rather than in the new European picture of human beings and the world." Thus, expulsion and the embrace of univocal thinking led to long, slow decline. Neither Spain nor its colonies, neither the Ottoman Empire nor its subsidiary emirates, benefited from the threefold invigoration of Renaissance, Reformation, and Enlightenment. Ultimately, antimodern Wahhabism would seize the Arab Muslim imagination, and fascism would seize the Spanish. Küng, *Islam*, 383.

95. Hamdani, "Columbus and the Recovery of Jerusalem," 39.

96. Hamdani, "Columbus and the Recovery of Jerusalem," 43–44.

97. In a letter of March 1493, as he returned to Spain from his first voyage, he wrote of "the war and conquest of Jerusalem for which purpose this enterprise was undertaken." Nine years later, in a letter addressed to the pope, he wrote, "This enterprise was undertaken with the purpose of expending what was invested in aiding the holy Temple and the holy Church." Delaney, "Columbus's Ultimate Goal," 5.

98. Delaney, "Columbus's Ultimate Goal," 4.

99. LeBeau, "Christopher Columbus and the Matter of Religion."

100. Delaney, "Columbus's Ultimate Goal," 5.

101. Here is Alexis de Tocqueville on Plymouth Rock, in 1835: "This Rock has become an object of veneration in the United States. I have seen bits of it carefully preserved in several towns in the Union . . . Here is a stone which the feet of a few outcasts pressed for an instant, and the stone became famous; it is treasured by a great nation; its very dust is shared as a relic." The step onto the rock in Plymouth Colony, of course, was not "foundational." The *Mayflower* Pilgrims had first gone ashore weeks earlier, in 1620, in what they dubbed Provincetown. The tradition of venerating Plymouth Rock would not begin until more than a century later. The point is that veneration of the rock, continuing to this day, satisfies a subliminal need.

6. City on a Hill

1. This summary of European transformation draws especially on Landes, *The Wealth and Poverty of Nations*, 29–45.

2. Whatever happened in the history of religion elsewhere, and there were cer-

tainly variations on these themes, the fact is that Jerusalem did indeed take on transcendent meaning.

3. Daniell, *The Bible in English*, 11.

4. The English people hungrily consumed Tyndale's outlawed verses, both as readers and as hearers, transforming not only the faith but the nascent language. The majesty of Tyndale's work in English stands as a cultural milestone. When the King James Version of the Bible was published most of a century later, in 1611, 85 percent of its New Testament was taken directly from Tyndale. The English of William Shakespeare was Tyndale's English. Daniell, *The Bible in English*, 152.

5. Daniell, *The Bible in English*, 129.

6. Landes, *The Wealth and Poverty of Nations*, 52. Landes points out that in Ottoman Istanbul, Jews and Christians had printing presses, but not Muslims.

7. On July 13, 2009, President Barack Obama, with his wife and daughters, visited Elmina Castle, now a museum and memorial to the millions of Africans who were held there before being shipped away. It was reported that, inside the dungeons where the Africans were held, the president wept. http://article.wn.com/view/2009/07/14/How_Obama_Wept_in_Ghana.

8. The phrase originates with Alfred W. Crosby Jr.'s 1972 book *The Columbian Exchange*.

9. In the three centuries after Columbus, the population of Europe increased by between 400 and 500 percent, while "the original population of America . . . fell by 90 or 95 percent." Lindqvist, *"Exterminate All the Brutes,"* 111, 112. Landes points out that it is unclear why Europeans in America encountered so few pathogens to which they were vulnerable. Africa proved to be a different story, with mosquito-borne diseases like malaria making the European occupation of all but coastal cities impossible.

10. The English and Dutch would advance slavery, but as traders, not as masters. The Dutch took control of Elmina away from the Portuguese in 1637, which was when its function as a slave depot really took off.

11. The milestone analysis of the economic consequences of Calvinism is *The Protestant Ethic and the Spirit of Capitalism* by Max Weber, published in 1904.

12. Quoted in Marius, *Martin Luther*, 378.

13. "When I said that the possessors of state power have rights over everything, and that all rights are dependent on their decrees, I did not merely mean temporal rights, but also spiritual rights." Spinoza quoted in Cavanaugh, *The Myth of Religious Violence*, 250.

14. Scruton, *Spinoza*, 112, 12. For my own treatment of Spinoza, see *Constantine's Sword*, 406–14.

15. Armstrong, *The Battle for God*, 22.

16. For more on how Protestant and Catholic groups fought intramurally as well as between each other, see Cavanaugh, *The Myth of Religious Violence*, 142–50. I am particularly indebted to Cavanaugh for his critique of the way religious violence is remembered.

17. Martin Luther panicked at the violence that followed his protest, and he turned against the peasants who thought they were rallying to him. He called his trea-

tise on the matter "Against the Robbing and Murdering Hordes of Peasants."
"Let everyone who can," he wrote, "smite, slay, and stab, secretly or openly,
remembering that nothing can be more poisonous, hurtful, or devilish than a
rebel. It is just as when one must kill a mad dog." Bellinger, *The Genealogy of
Violence*, 102.

18. The St. Bartholomew's Day massacre occurred over several days in 1572, the
worst Catholic violence during the French Catholic-Protestant war. Many of
those killed were the Huguenot movement's aristocratic leaders, which effectively undercut French Protestantism as a force. Rodney Stark puts the figure
slain at five thousand. *For the Glory of God*, 248.

19. Cavanaugh, *The Myth of Religious Violence*, 11.

20. These casualty figures come from the Twentieth Century Atlas: Historical Body Count. http://users.erols.com/mwhite28/warstato.htm#european.
For witches, other scholars find a much higher number. Some say millions
of women were killed as witches — a wild overestimate. Rodney Stark accepts
sixty thousand. Stark, *For the Glory of God*, 203.

21. Butler, *Awash in a Sea of Faith*, 15.

22. Revelation 20:1.

23. http://www.lutherdansk.dk/Web-Babylonian%20Captivitate/Martin%20
Luther.htm.

24. Bellinger, *Genealogy of Violence*, 102.

25. In 1516, Calvin gave a series of lectures on the Book of Daniel, which were
widely reprinted. Gordon, *Calvin*, 318–19. Here is Harold Bloom on the point:
"Sixteenth-century Protestants, throughout Europe, believed that all of human history had been prophesied obscurely but definitively in the Book of
Daniel and in Revelation. In the early seventeenth century, Protestant scholars returned to the faith held by the first Christians, which was that Christ
would come again not just to end time, but initially to bring about the millennium, a golden age here, in this world, that would precede the apocalypse,
or final judgment. As the European Enlightenment spread, this Protestant
expectation began to be identified with the idea of progress." *The American
Religion*, 267.

26. Ephesians 1:4.

27. Schlesinger, *Cycles of American History*, 14. "Exterminating havoc" is a phrase
of Thomas Jefferson's (21).

28. Perry Miller, *The American Puritans*, 29–30.

29. "The Lord will be our God and delight to dwell among us as His own people, and will command a blessing upon us in all our ways, so that we shall
see much more of His wisdom, power, goodness, and truth than formerly we
have been acquainted with. We shall find that the God of Israel is among us,
when ten of us shall be able to resist a thousand of our enemies; when He shall
make a praise and glory and men shall say of succeeding plantations, 'May the
Lord make it like that of New England.' For we must consider that we shall be
as a city upon a hill. The eyes of all people are upon us . . . Therefore let us
choose life, that we and our seed may live, by obeying His voice and cleaving

to Him, for He is our life and our prosperity." John Winthrop, from "A Model of Christian Charity," sermon preached on the *Arbella* in 1630. It may be that Winthrop delivered the sermon earlier in the voyage, but it is memorialized as if preached on the shore of New England. The sermon was cited by John F. Kennedy before his inauguration in 1960, by Ronald Reagan in farewell in 1989, and by Sarah Palin in accepting the Republican vice presidential nomination in 2008. The entire text of the sermon was read by Justice Sandra Day O'Connor at Reagan's funeral.

30. Matthew 5:14. "You are the light of the world. A city that is set on a hill cannot be hidden."

31. It is also true that Arab nations did not establish political capitals in holy cities: Iraq's capital has long been Baghdad, but its Shiite holy cities are Karbala and Najaf. Most significantly, the Saudi kingdom has its capital in Riyadh, not in Mecca. Nevertheless, Jerusalem has always been a "sanctified" city. According to Sari Nusseibeh, the president of Al-Quds University, "Jerusalem has always occupied a 'semi-divine' status in Islam, which explains its so-called non-centricity in the political context . . . From the Muslim point of view, therefore, Jerusalem was never regarded as a political capital or center, not because Arabs thought little of it, but, on the contrary—because they believed its status was sanctified." Emmett, "The Capital Cities," 236.

32. So the *loss* of Jerusalem is the key to its cult status, and something like that began to happen to Arabs and Muslims once *they* lost the city to the British in 1917. In the early twentieth century, Palestinians resided primarily around Jaffa and Haifa, while most Jewish Zionists were focused on Tel Aviv—but in a classic instance of Girard's "mimetic desire," all groups began to want Jerusalem to the extent that others did. It was the British seizure of the city that set this new dynamic in motion. "Only as competing nationalist claims became more volatile in the 1930s did Jerusalem become more important to both groups." Emmett, "The Capital Cities," 237.

33. Tuveson, *Redeemer Nation,* x. Robert Bellah sums up the point this way: "The Roman Church was identified with the Whore of Babylon and the Protestant Church with the New Jerusalem as they are described in Revelation. In this perspective, the Reformation could be interpreted as an event presaging the end of times and the birth of a New Heaven and a New Earth." That would be America. Bellah, *The Broken Covenant,* 10.

34. American democracy would be, in a phrase of the nineteenth-century writer John O'Sullivan, "Christianity in its earthly aspect—Christianity made effective among the political relations of men." He wrote that in the newspaper the *Morning Star,* December 27, 1845. Schlesinger, *Cycles of American History,* 40, 42.

35. Stephanson, *Manifest Destiny,* 4. We saw that something like this happened in ancient Israel, when a national myth grew up around the experience of what was probably a very small band of Hebrews who escaped from Egypt. A whole people identified with them later as a way of drawing a distinction with the Baal-worshiping Canaanites, from which, in all likelihood, Israel itself grew. The Exodus band was to Israel what the Pilgrims are to America.

36. Stephanson, *Manifest Destiny*, 5. In the version that was adopted, the seal draws on classical not biblical themes — with the eye over the pyramid above a Latin line from Virgil: *Annuit coeptis, novus ordo seclorum* (God has blessed this undertaking, a new order for the ages). But even that reference strikes a messianic note, which would repeatedly be picked up by American leaders proclaiming a "new world order."

37. Herman Melville, *White Jacket*, chapter 36, quoted in Schlesinger, *Cycles of American History*, 15.

38. Quoted in Tuveson, *Redeemer Nation*, 25.

39. "The whole earth is the Lord's garden and he has given it to the sons of men, with a general condition, Genesis 1:28: Increase and multiply, replenish the earth and subdue it . . . Why then should we stand here striving for places of habitation . . . and in the meantime suffer a whole continent, as fruitful and convenient for the use of man, to lie waste without any improvements?" John Winthrop, "Conclusions for the Plantation in New England," 1629, explaining that the American continent, unoccupied and unimproved, was free for the taking.

40. Howard Zinn, *A People's History of the United States*. New York: Harper and Row, 1980, 15.

41. Miller, *Nature's Nation*, 6.

42. Gordis, *Opening Scripture*, 179. In recounting these displays of Puritan intolerance, it is important to note that the story is more complex than mere dogmatism or what a later age would call fundamentalism. In addition to being rigid about their orthodoxies, the Puritans were classic humanists, dedicated to critical learning. The classics made up the core of their education. They and their direct descendants were the founders of Harvard University, after all — and of Yale, Princeton, Brown, and Dartmouth. Similarly, it is anachronistic to regard dissenters like Hutchinson as forerunners of secular liberalism, as if she and, as we note below, Roger Williams, were not fiercely attached to their own notions of right belief.

43. Feldman, *Divided by God*, 24. See also Jon Meacham, *American Gospel*, 53. Note that Williams's phrase "wall of separation," applied somewhat differently, would be used by Jefferson in his supportive letter of 1802 to the Danbury Baptists who were complaining about Connecticut's established Congregational Church.

44. Meacham, *American Gospel*, 54.

45. Gaustad, *Roger Williams*, 13.

46. "The Bloody Tenent of Persecution," http://www.reformedreader.org/rbb/williams/btp.htm.

47. The Hutchinson River and the Hutchinson River Parkway are named for her.

48. http://www.rootsweb.ancestry.com/~rigenweb/history.htm.

49. A common characterization of Fox's charisma as a preacher. Ingle, *First Among Friends*, 54.

50. Walt Whitman wrote, "George Fox stands for something too — a thought — the thought that wakes in silent hours — perhaps the deepest, most eternal thought latent in the human soul. This is the thought of God, merged in the

thoughts of moral right and the immortality of identity. Great, great is this thought—aye, greater than all else." *November Boughs,* http://www.bartleby .com/229/5022.html.

51. "A Declaration from the Harmless and Innocent People of God, called Quakers," http://hrs.harvard.edu/urn-3hul.ebookbatchEEBON_batch:ocm15353517e.

52. LaPlante, *American Jezebel,* 2004.

53. Soderland, *William Penn,* 5. Penn wrote of a threefold purpose in his project: "The service of God, the honor and advantage of the King, with our own profit, shall I hope be [the result of] all our endeavors" (5). The classic treatment of the difference between New England and Pennsylvania is E. Digby Baltzell's *Puritan Boston and Quaker Pennsylvania.* Baltzell, observing that while Philadelphia has produced much wealth and a social upper class, Boston has produced far more political, artistic, and intellectual leaders, emphasizes the consequence of Puritan hierarchy and Quaker egalitarianism: "The people in Boston all want to be chiefs, while in Philly they are all content to be Indians" (6).

54. Schultz and Tougias, *King Philip's War.* Three thousand out of a population of about 20,000 Wampanoag, Narragansett, Algonquian, and other native peoples were killed by the English settlers, who lost about 800 out of 52,000. King Philip was the name by which the English knew the Indian leader Metacom, whose father, Massasoit, first welcomed the *Mayflower* settlers.

55. In 1682, Penn concluded "the Great Treaty" with Delaware chiefs, establishing what the Indians called "a chain of friendship." Penn's benign legacy outlasted him, even as successive leaders of the colony abandoned his methods to steal from and lie to Indians. When violence broke out between Indians and colonists most of a hundred years after the Great Treaty, during the Seven Years' War (1755–1762), the Indians refrained from attacking Quakers.

56. Schlesinger, *Cycles of American History,* 22.

57. It is not clear why Penn chose the name. He might have been thinking of Philadelphians, a Quaker-like dissenting sect in England, or he might have had the ancient city in Asia Minor in mind, since it is named as one of the seven churches (and a faithful one at that) in the Book of Revelation.

58. Abolition began at the Philadelphia Yearly Meeting in 1754, and only later spread to New England churches. Stark, *For the Glory of God,* 340.

59. Jacoby, *Freethinkers,* 16.

60. That is in the First Amendment. The only reference to religion as such in the Constitution itself is in Article 6, providing that "no religious Test shall ever be required as a Qualification to any Office or public Trust under the United States."

61. The significance of the U.S. separation of church and state, in the context of Europe's thousand-year war against Islam, is made plain by the Treaty of Tripoli, which the U.S. Senate ratified in 1797. "As the Government of the United States of America is not, in any sense, founded on the Christian religion; as it has in itself no character of enmity against the laws, religion, or tranquility, of Mussulmen; and, as the said States never entered into any war, or act of hostility against any Mahometan nation, it is declared by the parties, that no pretext arising from religious opinions, shall ever produce an interrup-

tion of the harmony existing between the two countries." http://www.stephen jaygould.org/ctrl/treaty_tripoli.html.

62. John Locke, "A Letter Concerning Toleration" (1689), http://www.constitution .org/jl/tolerati.htm.

63. Genesis 14:18. "And Melchizedek, king of Salem, brought forth bread and wine. He was the priest of the most high God."

64. Butler, *Awash in a Sea of Faith,* 61. This fact of nonaffiliation is a reminder that, even in New England, the Americans were never *only* Puritans.

65. His most famous sermon was called "Sinners in the Hands of an Angry God," and it included such lines as "Natural men are held in the hand of God, over the pit of hell . . . The devil is waiting for them, hell is gaping for them, and the flames gather and flash about them . . . The fire pent up in their own hearts is struggling to break out . . . You have nothing to stand upon nor anything to take hold of; there is nothing between you and hell but air." Quoted in Schlesinger, *Cycles of American History,* 4.

66. Aaron, *America in Crisis,* 3.

67. Bellah, *The Broken Covenant,* 52.

68. "Between 1740 and 1800, the clergy of Massachusetts and Connecticut alone published over 1800 sermons, in addition to other kinds of books and treatises." Hatch, *The Sacred Cause of Liberty,* 176, 172.

69. "This amalgam of traditional Puritan apocalyptic rhetoric and eighteenth-century political discourse I have chosen to call 'civil millennialism.'" Hatch, *The Sacred Cause of Liberty,* 22.

70. Geographic Encyclopedia: http://www.placesnamed.com/s/a/salem.asp and http://www.placesnamed.com/j/e/jerusalem.asp. Wikipedia says that Clinton, recurring 27 times (perhaps because DeWitt Clinton, as the father of the Erie Canal, was identified with the early-nineteenth-century opening up of the West), is the most common place name, and that Salem is the fifth most common, recurring 22 times. But the Geographic Encyclopedia provides the latitude and longitude for each of the 127 Salems it records.

71. Michael B. Oren says that "over a thousand towns and cities in North America" are named for Salem, Shiloh, and Zion. *Power, Faith, and Fantasy,* 84.

72. Jacoby, *Freethinkers,* 13.

73. "In extracting the pure principles which he [Jesus] taught, we should have to strip off the artificial vestments in which they have been muffled by priests." Jefferson to John Adams, October 13, 1813.

74. Butler, *Awash in a Sea of Faith,* 256.

75. Jacoby, *Freethinkers,* 35. "Thomas Paine's arrogantly titled *Common Sense* called for independence based on a belief in a *non*supernatural inevitability." As such, it was the ultimate rebuttal to John Winthrop. Butler, *Awash in a Sea of Faith,* 215.

76. Pope Benedict XVI, when he was head of the Congregation for the Doctrine of the Faith, reiterated the Church's condemnation of the Freemasons in 1983, calling the organization "irreconcilable" with Catholic belief. The reasons for this are not clear.

77. In Dan Brown's *The Da Vinci Code,* Robert Langdon is a "Harvard symbologist," an academic discipline that does not exist. Brown's more recent novel, *The Lost Symbol,* concerns the Freemasons.

78. An alternative explanation for the name defines "free masons" as the specially skilled craftsmen who worked with "freestone," the softer material used in fine decorations on cathedrals and castles, as opposed to "rough masons," who worked in the rougher stone of building blocks.

79. Butler, *Awash in a Sea of Faith,* 235.

80. That I say "the core intellectual history" is centered in Christian theology, philosophy, and iconography does not give short shrift to the non-Christian classical heritage, the great cultures of Greece and Rome. Whether it was Thomas Aquinas thinking about Aristotle or Dante following Virgil, the classics of course informed Christian culture and therefore defined Europe through Christian mediation.

81. The word is Ronald Knox's. For such believers, "grace has destroyed nature, and replaced it." *Enthusiasm: A Chapter in the History of Religion, with Special Reference to XVII and XVIII Centuries.* New York: Oxford University Press, 1950, 2.

82. Schlesinger, *Cycles of American History,* 30.

83. Bloom, *American Religion,* 195.

84. Bloom, *American Religion,* 37. Bloom comments, "When they speak, sing, pray about walking with Jesus, they mean neither the man on the road to eventual crucifixion, nor the ascended God, but rather the Jesus who walked and lived with his Disciples again for forty days and forty nights . . . The American walks alone with Jesus in a perpetually expanded interval founded upon the forty days' sojourn of the risen Son of Man" (40).

85. Bloom, *American Religion,* 64. In 1783, there were more than 100,000 Indians between the Atlantic and the Mississippi. Over the next fifty years, they were forcibly moved beyond the Mississippi, or killed. This was done in accordance not only with biblical injunctions to defeat heathens, but with the law of God by which farming white people were given dominion over hunter-gatherer lower races. Schlesinger, *Cycles of American History,* 25.

86. "But you have there the myth of the essential white America. All the other stuff, the love, the democracy . . . is a sort of by-play. The essential American soul is hard, isolate, stoic, and a killer. It has never yet melted." D. H. Lawrence, *Studies in Classic American Literature.* Cambridge: Cambridge University Press, 2003, 65.

87. In fact, the separation of church and state has been a long work in progress. Though the First Amendment banned the establishment of religion by the federal government, state governments "disestablished" their religions on their own schedules — with several doing so at the Revolution in 1776, while others did so gradually. Connecticut disestablished the Congregational Church in 1818. Some states continued to require membership in Christian churches as a requirement to hold office. For example, until 1877 members of the New Hampshire legislature could only be Protestants. As for religion in public schools, that did not become a lively issue until the mid-twentieth century, with reli-

gious instruction banned by the Supreme Court in 1948, and prayers and Bible reading banned in 1963. In 1987, the court upheld the Creation Act, requiring instruction in biblical creationism to counterbalance the teaching of evolution.

88. This illiteracy would be highlighted in the twentieth-century controversy over evolution, epitomized when, at the 1925 Scopes "Monkey Trial," Clarence Darrow forced William Jennings Bryan's admission, "I don't think about what I don't think about." Bloom, *American Religion*, 56.

89. The congregational growth represents a twentyfold increase, while the national population went from 4 million to 31 million in the same period—a sevenfold increase. Baptists went from 400 congregations to 12,500; Methodists from 50 to 20,000. Less "enthused" congregations did not grow nearly so rapidly: Lutherans went from 225 to 2,100; Catholics from 50 to 2,500. Butler, *Awash in a Sea of Faith*, 270.

90. The moral conflict among Protestant denominations like Methodists and Baptists would lead to denominational splitting (with Southern Baptists and Southern Methodists going with Southern morality). But the divide could also be seen among Catholics, with popes having condemned slavery as evil as early as 1435 (Eugene IV's bull *Sicut Dudum*) and as recently as 1839 (Gregory XVI's *In Supremo*), yet Jesuits and other religious orders owned slaves in America right up to the Civil War. Catholics in the South were no different from their Protestant neighbors in defending slavery, while in the North, Catholics were almost entirely absent from the abolition movement.

91. Vincent Harding, "Symptoms of Liberty and Blackhead Signposts: David Walker and Nat Turner," in Greenberg, *Nat Turner*, 82. Kenneth Greenberg, my colleague at Suffolk University, editor of the most important study of the Turner history, and producer and writer of a documentary film on the subject, was the first to draw my attention to the importance of the Nat Turner episode for this book. Reliable sources identify Turner as a Methodist exhorter. Various accounts also note his Baptist background.

92. "Nat Turner was obviously living within the popular 19th-century Euro-American millenarian religious tradition, marked by a belief in the imminent return of Christ to rule on earth." Harding, "Symptoms of Liberty," 79.

93. Harding, "Symptoms of Liberty," 79.

94. Thomas C. Parramore, "Covenant in Jerusalem," in Greenberg, *Nat Turner*, 59.

95. Harding, "Symptoms of Liberty," 83.

96. Harding, "Symptoms of Liberty," 83.

97. Jerusalem had been established in 1791. In 1888, the name of the town was changed to Courtland. The lawyer, Thomas Ruffin Gray, compiled Nat Turner's *Confessions* with his own interpolations, leading historians to debate the document's validity as a reflection of Turner's experience and attitudes. But *The Confessions of Nat Turner*, and the story of his rebellion, had tremendous impact. In 1967, that impact was revived with the publication of William Styron's novel of the same name. It was a huge bestseller, but also a source of controversy, criticized by many for its unintended reiteration of racist attitudes. See Clarke, *William Styron's Nat Turner*.

98. Harding, "Symptoms of Liberty," 102.

7. Messiah Nation

1. Ezrahi, *Booking Passage,* 9.
2. Recall that the population of Jerusalem grew enormously during holy days. On Passover in 70, as the Roman siege began, Tacitus says 600,000 people were in Jerusalem, and Josephus puts the number at 1,200,000. Jeremias, *Jerusalem in the Time of Jesus,* 75.
3. Ibn Ali Ibn Arabi lived from 1165 to 1240. Makiya, *The Rock,* 291.
4. The scholar Neil Asher Silberman writes, "Rising from the haze and fog of Upper Galilee's deepest ravines and valleys, Safed has no biblical pedigree, no deep roots in the scriptural or prophetic history of Israel . . . Yet after 1492, with the horror and uncertainty of the Spanish Expulsion and the increasing flow of Jewish immigrants toward the Ottoman Empire, Safed was one of the several towns in the Holy Land that received a significant number of refugees . . . a massive influx of sages back into the Land of Israel." *Heavenly Powers,* 169.
5. Here are the realms from which Jews were expelled, and dates: Provence, 1490; Sardinia, 1492; Sicily, 1492; Lithuania, 1495; Portugal, 1497. In the fourteenth and early fifteenth centuries, Jews had been expelled from England, Paris, Austria, and Hungary. Gilbert, *Atlas of Jewish History,* 46–47.
6. Kenneth R. Stow, "Sanctity and the Construction of Space: The Roman Ghetto as Sacred Space," in Menachem Mor, ed., *Jewish Assimilation, Acculturation, and Accommodation: Past Traditions, Current Issues, and Future Prospects.* Lanham, MD: University Press of America, 1992, 54. Here are cities in which Jewish ghettos were enforced, with the initiating years: Fez, 1450; Frankfurt, 1460; Prague, 1473; Turin, 1490; Kraków, 1494; Venice, 1517; Rome, 1556; Vienna, 1570; Florence, 1571; Mainz, 1662. Gilbert, *Atlas of Jewish History,* 44.
7. The earliest book to be printed in Hebrew was a commentary on the Pentateuch, in the 1470s, not long after Gutenberg's Bible. Early Hebrew printed books were among the finest in Europe. Papal ambivalence about printing became yet another source of tension between the Church and the Jews. With the printing press, the period of the early commentators was regarded as closed. A new era of the Jews' relationship with texts was begun. http://www.jewishvirtuallibrary.org/jsource/Adret.html.
8. Harold Bloom, *Kabbalah and Criticism.* New York: Continuum, 1983, 41.
9. For an introduction to the figure of Isaac Luria, see Armstrong, *A History of God,* 266–71.
10. George Steiner, "Our Homeland, the Text," *Salmagundi,* no. 66, Winter–Spring 1985, 5, 24–25.
11. Steiner, "Our Homeland, the Text," 19. I am grateful to Sidra DeKoven Ezrahi for drawing my attention to Steiner's work here.
12. Today, ultra-Orthodox Jews in Israel justify their exemption from military service by arguing that their study of Torah is what keeps Israel safe and in God's favor. Not only that, it involves the essential act of patriotic sacrifice. The telling Talmudic phrase with which they make this point is "to die in the tent of the Torah."

13. Ezrahi, *Booking Passage,* 13.

14. I acknowledge, again, that I offer this summary of Jewish vision from outside it, as a Christian. I emphasize, therefore, that this is my *understanding* of the vision, however limited.

15. Johannes Gutenberg (1398–1468) perfected his mechanical printing press, with movable type, in about 1440. His edition of the Bible (180 copies) came off his press in 1455.

16. Daniell, *The Bible in English,* 11.

17. After the traumas of the Reformation, especially as they had involved Protestant claims of Catholic disregard of scripture, the Inquisition pounced, in 1615, on Galileo's assertion that the earth revolved around the sun. It was not only, or perhaps even mainly, that Ptolemy's geocentric schema of the universe had been the scientific paradigm since the year 150, but that Ptolemy was backed up by biblical texts, which Church authorities of the Counter-Reformation felt bound to take literally. "The world is firmly established and it cannot move," reads Psalm 93. "The Lord set the Earth on its foundations, and it cannot be moved," reads Psalm 104. The Book of Joshua assumes a moving sun when it describes that motion stopped: "And the sun stood still, and the moon stayed, until the nation took vengeance on their enemies . . . So the sun stood still in the midst of heaven, and hastened not to go down about a whole day" (10:13). Galileo was charged by the Inquisition with claiming "that the language of the Holy Scripture does not mean what it seems to mean." Galileo replied, "There are in Scripture words which taken in their strict literal meaning, look as if they differ from the truth." The point was not to take them literally. Some Church authorities, perhaps aware of the precedents of Augustine and Aquinas, agreed with Galileo that if what would later be called "hard data" contradicted scripture, then the sacred texts must be reinterpreted. But even such enlightened prelates were forced by pressures of the age to go along with the inquisitors who required Galileo's recantation. "To affirm that the Sun, in its very truth, is at the center of the universe . . . is a very dangerous attitude," Cardinal Robert Bellarmine, a chief investigator, declared, "and one calculated not only to arouse all Scholastic philosophers and theologians, but also to injure our faith by contradicting the Scriptures." At his climactic heresy trial in 1633, Galileo renounced his intellectual conviction that the earth moves around the sun, but then, according to a well-known legend, he followed that renunciation with a muttered *"E Pur si Muove."* And yet it moves. Santillana, *The Crime of Galileo,* 45, 99.

18. Landes, *The Wealth and Poverty of Nations,* 393.

19. The Abbassids in Baghdad; the Fatimids and the Mamluks in Cairo; the Umayyads in Córdoba; the Ghaznavids in Iran, Afghanistan, and northern India; and the Saljuqs, who controlled the rest of India. Aslan, *No god but God,* 137.

20. Once the Ottoman Empire fell, the caliphate fell, too. There has been no single Islamic spiritual authority since 1924. Osama bin Laden's goal has been to restore the caliphate, and with it the political, spiritual, and military unity of the *ummah,* the House of Islam.

21. Idinopulos, *Jerusalem*, 264. The term "Middle East" was coined in 1902 by an American naval officer, Alfred Mahan. Oren, *Power, Faith, and Fantasy,* 42.

22. The Ottoman navy, opposed by the Holy Alliance of European powers, would be decisively beaten in the sea battle at Lepanto in 1571. Turkish forces would lay siege to Vienna as late as 1683, to be turned back again. Asali, *Jerusalem in History,* 208. See also Barber, *Lords of the Golden Horn.*

23. The name Istanbul would supersede Constantinople, but it derived from the Greek and had been used by the Byzantines, meaning simply "the City."

24. Landes, *The Wealth and Poverty of Nations,* 398. Such suzerainty meant that local elites arose to manage the systems of taxation. In Jerusalem, a handful of families became relatively rich and powerful through shares of the taxes they collected for the sultan. Their descendants dominate Jerusalem society to this day. Asali, *Jerusalem in History,* 214, 239. "Notable Jerusalem families — the Khalides, Nusseibis, Alamis, Husseinis, and Dajanis — grew rich and powerful by dominating the money producing areas of the society: tax collecting, farming, commerce, and trade, and by monopolizing appointments to the lucrative religious positions of cadi, imam, and Koran reader." Idinopulos, *Jerusalem,* 265.

25. The ruthlessness of that rule is indicated by the way in which the problem of royal succession was solved. When the sultan had more than one son — and given the concubinage of the harem, he nearly always did — the rivals to the elected heir were simply killed off in childhood. Landes, *The Wealth and Poverty of Nations,* 399.

26. Amnon Cohen, "1516–1917: Haram-I-Serif — The Temple Mount Under Ottoman Rule," in Grabar and Kedar, *Where Heaven and Earth Meet,* 212.

27. Rashid Khalidi, Introduction to Asali, *Jerusalem in History,* xx.

28. Meticulous Ottoman census records show the steady growth of Jerusalem after Suleiman. The population figures for the city, peaking above 13,000 in the sixteenth century, declined as the Ottoman Empire began to fail. By 1896, Jerusalem's population had fallen below 8,000. http://www.jerusalemites.org /jerusalem/ottoman/24.htm. The early fate of Jerusalem differed from greater Palestine, because there was no religious motive to bring such improvements except to the holy city. Cohen, "The Temple Mount Under Ottoman Rule," 216.

29. Rauf, *What's Right with Islam,* 4.

30. Even today, converts to Islam must learn sufficient Arabic to recite the sacred text, even if not understanding it. Translations obviously exist, but they are regarded as interpretations, not as the Qur'an itself. Aslan, *No god but God,* 159.

31. Aslan, *No god but God,* 159. The Ottoman sultan did not allow the printing of secular works until the early to mid-eighteenth century, and only then did the technology of Arabic typesetting develop. The printing of the Qur'an was prohibited until the nineteenth century. In the twenty-first century, illiteracy remains more a mark of the Arab world than the non-Arab world, with, for example, Mexico (at 91 percent literate) surpassing the most literate Arab nation, Bahrain (86 percent). Turkey, which switched to a modified Latin-based alphabet only in the twentieth century, has a literacy rate of 85 percent. The

Muslim world was slower to value literacy in part because Muhammad himself was remembered as illiterate, which emphasized the miraculousness of his revelation. Reza Aslan argues that Muhammad's illiteracy is mythical, since, as a successful merchant, he would have needed at least rudimentary reading skill. *No god but God,* 35.

32. Landes, *The Wealth and Poverty of Nations,* 402. Take one example: We saw that Jews had a Hebrew printing press in Safed, Palestine, by the early sixteenth century. There would not be a Muslim printing press in Palestine until the late nineteenth century. Idinopulos, *Jerusalem,* 272.

33. Armstrong, *The Battle for God,* 60.

34. http://www.turizm.net/turkey/history/ottoman3.html.

35. The 1800 population figures are in dispute, as Jewish and Muslim sources advance estimates that have contemporary political implications. Muslim sources put the 1800 figure at 12,000. A prominent Jewish source puts it at 8,750. Asali, *Jerusalem in History,* 220, 231.

36. Greek Orthodox, Armenian, and Roman Catholic clerics share custodianship of the Anastasis, the Holy Sepulcher, and the Calvary site, strictly alternating periods when they pray in the rotunda that surrounds the tomb and in the chapel marking Golgotha. Each church, together with Coptic, Ethiopian, and Syrian Christians, has primary responsibility for other, lesser shrines in the ancient basilica.

37. Asali, *Jerusalem in History,* 221.

38. Asali, *Jerusalem in History,* 223.

39. Muhammad ibn Abd al-Wahhab (1703–1766) was a radical preacher whose attacks on Shiites and Sufis in the desert towns of Arabia, and on the Istanbul-credentialed sharif (governor) of Mecca, concealed a larger alienation from the Turkish caliph. Wahhabism flourished among the freelancing tribal nomads for whom loyalty to the far distant authorities was unthinkable. Wahhabism in one form or another would maintain its grip on the Saudi religious imagination into the twenty-first century. Aslan, *No god but God,* 241.

40. Armstrong, *Battle for God,* 114, 115.

41. Egyptian cotton exports brought in $7 million in 1861; in 1865, as Confederacy exports collapsed, the Egyptian figure had grown to $77 million. Oren, *Power, Faith, and Fantasy,* 190.

42. Dodwell, *Founder of Modern Egypt,* 44.

43. Asali, *Jerusalem in History,* 238. This was partly a function of the new telegraph, which would link Jerusalem directly to Cairo and Istanbul, bypassing Damascus (237).

44. The British consulate was established in Jerusalem in 1838, as a protector of Jews; the French in 1843, as a protector of Catholics; the Russian in 1857, as a protector of Greek Orthodox. The Americans opened a consulate in 1856, to protect Protestants, the newly arriving missionaries. Asali, *Jerusalem in History,* 229.

45. Asali, *Jerusalem in History,* 230. The first prominent American missionary to Palestine, the evangelist Harriet Livermore, set out in 1837. She was followed by the restorationist Warder Cresson in 1844. Oren, *Power, Faith, and Fantasy,* 1.

46. Armstrong, *Battle for God,* 123.

47. Oren, *Power, Faith, and Fantasy*, 13. We will see more of this later in this book. Suffice to emphasize here that these two effects — modernity as an intrusive source of Arab-Muslim alienation and the God-sponsored return of Jews to sovereignty in Jerusalem for the sake of Christ's final triumph — make colonizing and missionizing Christians key shapers of the present conflict between Israelis and Palestinians.

48. Oren, *Power, Faith, and Fantasy*, 80.

49. The idea that Jews had to be "restored" to Palestine as a precondition of the messianic age was sparked by a passage in St. Paul's Letter to the Romans: "A hardening has come upon a part of Israel until the full number of Gentiles come in, and so all Israel will be saved. As it is written, 'The deliverer will come from Zion'" (11:25–26).

50. Oren, *Power, Faith, and Fantasy*, 90–92. Michael Oren, an Israeli with American roots, is Israel's ambassador to the United States. I acknowledge him as a main source of my understanding of the American Protestant restorationist movement and its influence on Jerusalem. Because of his diplomatic position, some distrust his work as a historian, but I find him reliable on nineteenth-century American trends.

51. Butler, *Awash in a Sea of Faith*, 234.

52. The denominations that fell under the sway of evangelical fervor were most restorationist: Methodist, Baptist, Congregationalist, and Presbyterian. The coolly rational Unitarians were indifferent to the idea, and so were the more "Catholic" Episcopalians. Curiously, a leading restorationist was a New York University professor of Hebrew named George Bush, whose 1844 book, *The Valley of Vision, or The Dry Bones of Israel Revived*, was influential. He was the ancestor of two presidents. Oren, *Power, Faith, and Fantasy*, 141, 142.

53. This ignorance was reflected in the slogan "A land without a people for a people without a land," which many critics, like Edward Said and Yasir Arafat, associated with twentieth-century Zionism. In fact, the slogan originated in 1843 with the British Christian restorationist Lord Shaftesburg. Oren, *Power, Faith, and Fantasy*, 141. The idea was picked up by Zionists, however. In 1917, David Ben-Gurion declared that in "a historical and moral sense," Palestine was a place "without inhabitants." Armstrong, *Jerusalem*, 369. The idea that Palestine was unpopulated, of course, paralleled the Catholic idea, reflected in various papal bulls during the Age of Exploration, that "discovered" territories were *terra nullius* — areas that could be claimed by Christian kings because they were empty.

54. The journalist John O'Sullivan, in 1845, in reference to the U.S. appropriation of Texas and Oregon, decreed "the right to our manifest destiny to overspread and to possess the whole continent, which providence has given us for the development of the great experiment of liberty and federated self-government." This was religious for Sullivan. We saw earlier his statement that American democracy is "Christianity in its earthly aspect — Christianity made effective among the political relations of men." He wrote that in the newspaper the *Morning Star*, December 27, 1845. Schlesinger, *Cycles of American History*, 40, 42. See also Stephanson, *Manifest Destiny*, 42, 40.

55. This was the practice of the Chicago-born Spofford family and their collective, the "American Colony," in East Jerusalem. Their compound stands today as the American Colony Hotel, a haunt of Western journalists who have no idea of the place's origins. Oren, *Power, Faith, and Fantasy*, 281.

56. Faust, *Republic of Suffering*, 172.

57. Oren, *Power, Faith, and Fantasy*, 223. Mark Twain recounted his experience of Jerusalem in *The Innocents Abroad, or The New Pilgrim's Progress* (New York: New American Library, 1980). For all his vaunted skepticism, Twain, too, fell under the old spell: "I am sitting where a god has stood, and looking upon the brook and the mountains which that god looked upon, and am surrounded by dusky men and women whose ancestors saw him, and even talked with him, face to face. I cannot comprehend this. The gods of my understanding have always been hidden in the clouds. Palestine is no more of this workaday world. It is dreamland" (332).

58. Peter Grose, *Israel in the Mind of America*. New York: Knopf, 1983, 26. Grose dismisses Lincoln's remark as "genial noncommitment," but the point is that Jewish return to Palestine was an idea that reached even to the White House.

59. Stephanson, *Manifest Destiny*, 65.

60. The statement is from a letter Lincoln wrote in 1864. He adds, "I cannot remember when I did not so think and feel." http://showcase.netins.net/web/creative/lincoln/speeches/hodges.htm.

61. The war began with the firing on Fort Sumter on April 12, 1861. The resolution was approved on July 25, 1861, declaring that the war's purpose was not "overthrowing or interfering with the rights or established institutions of those [seceding] States." Instead it was to "defend and maintain the supremacy of the Constitution and to preserve the Union." Lincoln's motive in keeping the abolition of slavery out of the equation is clear: it was urgently important to keep in the Union the four border slave states (especially Maryland, which would have choked off Washington, and Kentucky, which would have stopped navigation on the vital Ohio River).

62. Donald, *Lincoln Reconsidered*, 137.

63. By comparison, the number of soldiers in the Continental Army of the American Revolution was never more than 30,000. Faust, *Republic of Suffering*, 3.

64. "Antietam implicitly rewrote the rules for acceptable losses in war, and no one protested." Stout, *Upon the Altar*, 153. Union forces at Antietam forced Lee to retreat south, keeping the violence away from Maryland — and Washington. The battle marked the end of any chance that European powers would recognize the Confederacy. Antietam was also the first battle at which photographs of the dead were taken (156). The Emancipation Proclamation shows, in fact, that Lincoln, even then, was no moral absolutist on the question of slavery. The proclamation was hardly "abolition," declaring the freedom of slaves only in those states that had left the Union — immediately outlawing slavery in the Confederacy but not in the United States. The proclamation proposes only the most gradual implementation of "freedom" within states loyal to the Union — allowing the holding of slaves to continue until 1900. That Lincoln was pro-Negro is belied by the proclamation's recom-

mendation of the "voluntary colonization of the freedman" back to Africa.

65. "Were" is subjunctive here, but its implication of the plural is the point, since the United States was not taken to be a singular term until the Union was reified — deified? — by the sacrifices of those who died.

66. Stout, *Upon the Altar*, 167. The term "total war" came into being in the early nineteenth century, as the modern nation-state came into its own, with the ability to mobilize all the resources and population of a society to warfare. This capacity was joined to the Enlightenment idea that certain abstractions (universal peace) are worth such a scale of suffering. Total wars require graver, holier levels of justifying sacrifice than limited wars. See Bell, *The First Total War*.

67. The most evangelically minded denomination, the Methodist, grew from one "conference" in 1783 to thirty-two conferences in 1843. Butler, *Awash in a Sea of Faith*, 268, 270.

68. Goen, *Broken Churches*.

69. Donald, *Lincoln Reconsidered*, 29. Donald identifies as abolitionist denominations the Congregationalist, Presbyterian, Quaker, Methodist, and Baptist.

70. Aamodt, *Righteous Armies*, 81.

71. Butler, *Awash in a Sea of Faith*, 294.

72. "The new team of Lincoln, Grant and Sherman was evolving a new kind of war." Donald, *Lincoln Reconsidered*, 94. Here is Stout's comment: "When forced to choose between a principled war and victory, Lincoln chose victory. He removed McClellan from command." *Upon the Altar*, 138.

73. Stout, *Upon the Altar*, 183. Here is what Lincoln said in his 1862 State of the Union address: "Fellow citizens, we cannot escape history. We of this Congress and this administration will be remembered in spite of ourselves. No personal significance or insignificance can spare one or another of us. The fiery trial through which we pass will light us down in honor or dishonor to the latest generation. We say we are for the Union. The world will not forget that we say this. We know how to save the Union. The world knows we do know how to save it. We even here hold the power and bear the responsibility. In giving freedom to the slave we assure freedom to the free — honorable alike in what we give and what we preserve. We shall nobly save or meanly lose the last best hope of earth. Other means may succeed: this could not fail. The way is plain, peaceful, generous, just — a way which if followed the world will forever applaud and God must forever bless." http://www.infoplease.com/t/hist/state-of-the-union/74.html.

74. www.nationalcenter.org/lincolnsecondinaugural.html.

75. Charles Sumner, *The Works of Charles Sumner*, vol. 7, 235–36.

76. Faust, *Republic of Suffering*, xi.

77. Faust, *Republic of Suffering*, xiv.

78. Faust, *Republic of Suffering*, xiii.

79. http://showcase.netins.net/web/creative/lincoln/speeches/gettysburg.htm.

80. http://www.infoplease.com/t/hist/state-of-the-union/74.html.

81. "The Battle Hymn of the Republic" is "the most popular hymn of wars and moral crusades of the English-speaking peoples." Tuveson, *Redeemer Nation*, 198. The irony is that Julia Ward Howe was a rationalist, not an evangelical

millennialist. Yet, as Tuveson observes, "When urgent and baffling questions about the right course for the nation have arisen, the apocalyptic view of its history has come to the front" (199).

82. Tuveson, *Redeemer Nation*, 191.

83. Butler, *Awash in a Sea of Faith*, 292.

84. See Douglas A. Blackmon's *Slavery by Another Name: The Re-enslavement of Black Americans from the Civil War to World War II*. New York: Doubleday, 2008.

85. Stout, *Upon the Altar*, 448.

86. Stout, *Upon the Altar*, 455. "The Lincoln cult is almost an American religion." Donald, *Lincoln Reconsidered*, 144. If the sacrifice of Lincoln centered that religion in the North, it was the equally sacrificial religion of the Lost Cause that braced the South, with the region's martyrdom itself taking on a deeply ironic character as a source of meaning, and piety in Southern evangelical religion. God was with the South, pure and simple, and the proof of its status as the chosen people was its crucifixion. See Charles Reagan Wilson, *Baptized in Blood*, 37–57.

87. Military service is normally a requirement for burial in Arlington National Cemetery. The spouses and dependent children of veterans are the routine exceptions. High national officeholders are another.

88. Here are the numbers of those killed in America's wars: Revolutionary War, 25,324; War of 1812, 19,465; Mexican War, 13,283; Civil War, 622,000; Spanish-American War, 2,446; World War I, 116,516; World War II, 403,339; Korean War, 54,246; Vietnam War, 58,220; Persian Gulf War, 383; Afghanistan War, 1,076, and Iraq War, 4,401 (both as of May 31, 2010). *New York Times*, May 31, 2010.

89. Mrs. Lincoln reported her husband's words to the Springfield pastor who presided at his burial. There is no reason to think his words, even spoken at such a moment of mortality, were meant mystically. The earthly Jerusalem was on Lincoln's mind, perhaps his last thought. But the unconscious implications stand. Hill, *Abraham Lincoln, Man of God*, 373.

90. Stephanson, *Manifest Destiny*, 53.

91. Stout, *Upon the Altar*, 460.

92. It came to Mr. Kurtz "like a flash of lightning in a serene sky—exterminate all the brutes!"—the solution to the white man's troubles in Africa. Conrad, *Heart of Darkness*, 65.

93. "About five million of the indigenous American population lived in what is now the United States. At the beginning of the nineteenth century, half a million still remained. In 1891 . . . a quarter of a million [remained], or 5 percent of the original number of Indians." Lindqvist, *"Exterminate All the Brutes,"* 114.

94. Tuveson, *Redeemer Nation*, 129.

95. Tuveson, *Redeemer Nation*, vii.

96. McDougall, *Promised Land, Crusader State*, 136.

97. Oberlin College, in Ohio, can be regarded as the birthplace of the American missionary movement, beginning with expeditions sent to China in the 1880s. But Princeton caught the fever. The Princeton Foreign Mission Society spawned the Student Volunteer Movement for Foreign Missions, which,

between 1900 and 1930, sent more than twenty thousand volunteers abroad under the banner "The evangelization of the world in this generation."

98. The phrase is Reverend Josiah Strong's. Stephanson, *Manifest Destiny*, 80.

99. McDougall, *Promised Land, Crusader State*, 135.

100. Dick Diver touring the Somme battlefield in Fitzgerald's 1934 novel *Tender Is the Night*: "This Western Front business couldn't be done again, not for a long time. The young men think they could do it, but they couldn't. They could fight the first Marne again, but not this. This took religion . . . and tremendous sureties . . . You had to have a whole-souled sentimental equipment going back further than you could remember."

101. Tuveson, *Redeemer Nation*, 212, 210.

102. Eksteins, *Rites of Spring*, 193.

103. "The old Lie: *Dulce et Decorum est / Pro patri mori.*" Wilfred Owen, "Dulce et Decorum Est." ("How sweet and fitting it is to die for one's country" is from an ode by Horace, a line that decorates the entrance of the Arlington Cemetery amphitheater.) The most eloquent expression of the old lie was given in an 1895 Memorial Day speech by Oliver Wendell Holmes Jr., looking back on his experience at Antietam: "I do not know the meaning of the universe. But in the midst of doubt, in the collapse of creeds . . . that faith is true and adorable which leads a soldier to throw away his life in obedience to a blindly accepted duty, in a cause which he little understands, in a plan of campaign of which he has no notion, under tactics of which he does not see the use . . . War, when you are at it, is horrible and dull. It is only when time has passed that you see its message was divine." Faust, *Republic of Suffering*, 270.

104. Forrestal carried the wound of the impoverished Irish Catholicism that marked his immigrant parents. In flight from that past, he did not regularly practice his faith, but he was intimate with Catholic figures, and at the end of his life he was tormented by the feeling that he had been a "bad Catholic." Townsend Hoopes and Douglas Brinkley, *Driven Patriot: The Life and Times of James Forrestal*. New York: Knopf, 1992, 454.

105. Kennan, "Sources of Soviet Conduct," 25.

106. Widmer, *Ark of the Liberties*, 234.

107. The Russian word for "containment" means "strangulation." Once Kennan saw where his theorizing was headed, especially after his notion of a broad "containment" was narrowly militarized, he distanced himself from the policies he had himself inspired. He became a lifelong critic of mainstream American anti-Soviet Cold War foreign policy.

108. Daniel Yergin comments, "American leaders might have seen themselves confronted by a cruel, clumsy, bureaucratized fear-ridden despotism, preoccupied with reconstruction of a vast war-torn land. Instead, the Americans were convinced they faced a cunning, sure-footed enemy, engaged in a never-ending drive for world hegemony." *Shattered Peace*, 245.

109. Freeland, *The Truman Doctrine*, 101.

110. Hofstadter, *The Paranoid Style*, 1965.

111. Whitfield, *The Culture of the Cold War*, 77.

112. See, for example, Graham's 1981 book *Till Armageddon*, or his 1983 book *Ap-*

proaching Hoofbeats: The Four Horsemen of the Apocalypse. We will take note of both again.

113. June 20, 2009. newsweek.washingtonpost.com/nixons_tapes_billy_graham_and.html. When the Nixon tapes revealed Graham using anti-Semitic language, he was humiliated and apologized. Graham's son and successor, Franklin, more shameless, is a leading and unapologetic denigrator of Muslims, having told NBC News on November 16, 2001, for example, that Islam "is a wicked and very evil religion." www.bpnews.net/bpnews.asp?ID=12201.

114. The phrase "vital center" was coined by Arthur Schlesinger Jr. and served as the title of his 1949 book.

8. Jerusalem Builded Here

1. Grainger, *Battle for Palestine*, 84.
2. Romans 11:26. While American groups like the Spofford family were establishing missionary outposts in Jerusalem, the London Society for Promoting Christianity Among the Jews ("The London Jews Society") was sending its proselytizers to Jerusalem. Armstrong, *Jerusalem*, 351.
3. Grainger, *Battle for Palestine*, 83.
4. Carson, who represented Ulster in Parliament, supported the unprecedented conscription law in Parliament by saying, "The necessary supply of heroes must be maintained at all cost." The phrase gave me the title of a novel. James Carroll, *Supply of Heroes*, New York: E. P. Dutton, 1985.
5. Eksteins, *Rites of Spring*, 56.
6. Eksteins, *Rites of Spring*, 132.
7. "The backpack thus became a symbol of the social and cultural baggage each soldier carried with him into battle." Eksteins, *Rites of Spring*, 188.
8. Fussell, *The Great War*, 119–20.
9. http://www.rjgeib.com/heroes/owen/owen-poetry.html.
10. Nine million dead, 21 million wounded. Here is the breakdown of the dead: 3.5 million German/Austrian, 1.7 million Russians, 1.7 million French, 1 million British, .7 million Turks, .5 million Italian. One-third of the European males between the ages of nineteen and twenty-two in 1914 were killed — "the lost generation." Keegan, *The First World War*, 422–23.
11. Eksteins, *Rites of Spring*, 202.
12. A definition of the aim of the 1916 "Fight for Right" campaign. *Guardian*, December 8, 2000.
13. Armstrong, *Jerusalem*, 361.
14. Revelation 3:12.
15. http://www.progressiveliving.org/william_blake_poetry_jerusalem.htm.

> And did those feet in ancient time
> Walk upon England's mountain green?
> And was the holy Lamb of God
> On England's pleasant pastures seen?

And did the Countenance Divine
Shine forth upon our clouded hills?
And was Jerusalem builded here
Among these dark Satanic mills?

Bring me my Bow of burning gold;
Bring me my arrows of desire;
Bring me my Spear: O clouds unfold!
Bring me my Chariot of fire.

I will not cease from Mental Fight
Nor shall my Sword sleep in my hand
Till we have built Jerusalem
In England's green and pleasant land.

16. Martin Green, *Children of the Sun: A Narrative of "Decadence" after 1918*. New York: Basic Books, 1976, 42.

17. In 1800, as we saw, the population of Jerusalem had been about 9,000, with Jews decidedly in the minority. http://www.shalomjerusalem.com/jerusalem/jerusalem3.htm. By 1900, Jews made up well over 60 percent of the 55,000 people resident in Jerusalem (with Muslims and Christians each at about 20 percent). Armstrong, *Jerusalem*, 352.

18. Dan Bahat, *The Illustrated Atlas of Jerusalem*. Jerusalem: Carta, 1996, 118–21.

19. Lawrence's collaborator and patron was the Arab nationalist Emir Feisal, whom the British would sponsor as the king of Iraq.

20. Grainger, *Battle for Palestine*, 210. Of the British conquest of Jerusalem Lawrence commented, "It has never fallen so tamely before." Elon, *Jerusalem*, 168.

21. Hanukkah was a minor holiday at the time. As a celebration of an ancient "reclaiming of land, expanding of boundaries, the expelling of foreign invaders" it would become "the symbol of Zionist revival. During World War II, Hanukkah also became the holiday of American Jewry." Burg, *The Holocaust Is Over*, 38.

22. Grainger, *Battle for Palestine*, 213.

23. Purcell, *Lloyd George*, 68.

24. Wessels, *Biography of Muhammad*, 160.

25. All Muslim holy places, which included the Dome of the Rock and the Al Aqsa Mosque, were to be under Arab control, according to the 1915 McMahon pledge. But as Britain was giving this pledge, it was also secretly negotiating the Sykes-Picot Agreement of 1916, a French-British-Russian accord that saw to the post-Ottoman partition of the Middle East, with Arab territories north of the Arabian Peninsula divided between France and Britain. Armstrong, *Jerusalem*, 373.

26. By the late nineteenth century, Jerusalem had replaced Acre as the main Palestinian city, and its governor reported directly to Istanbul instead of through Damascus. So as Christians and Jews put new emphasis on the centrality of Jerusalem, so did Muslims. How this defines an essentially Palestinian history is not clear, however, because the record is not self-evident. "One of the features of a small non-European people," as Edward Said has observed, "is that

it is not wealthy in documents, nor in histories, autobiographies, chronicles and the like. This is true of the Palestinians, and it accounts for the lack of a major authoritative text on Palestinian history." Said, *The Question of Palestine*, xxxviii.

27. Said, *The Question of Palestine*, xi.

28. In the United States, nineteenth-century Jews felt no need for escape comparable to that felt in Russia, so that when, for example, the poet Emma Lazarus tried to start an American Zionist movement in 1881, she found no support. The American movement to reclaim the Holy Land for Jews continued to be mainly Protestant, with figures like John D. Rockefeller strongly supporting it. Oren, *Power, Faith, and Fantasy*, 279.

29. The Balfour Declaration of November 1917 says in part, "His majesty's government views with favor the establishment in Palestine of a national home for the Jewish people." But the double game adheres in what it goes on to say: ". . . it being clearly understood that nothing shall be done which may prejudice the civil and religious rights of existing non-Jewish communities in Palestine." The declaration served British purposes by playing well with Jews in America, which had just entered the war, and with Jews in Russia, which was aflame with the Bolshevik revolution and in the process of abandoning the war. Purcell, *Lloyd George*, 69–70. But the British support for the Jews' return to their traditional homeland was also influenced by a British version of the restorationist Christian belief that such return was a necessary prelude to the Messiah's coming, and the fulfillment of history. In any case, it can be assumed that whatever others took from the Balfour Declaration, or the Sykes-Picot Agreement for that matter, in the British mind it would always have been assumed that local Palestinian entities, whether Arab or Jewish, would have been subordinate to the larger sovereignty of the British Empire. The Arabs and Jews, for their part, shaped their responses, whether consciously or not, in terms of the broader current of nineteenth-century nationalism that was already running against such imperial manipulations.

30. Revelation 16:16. Keegan, *The First World War*, 415.

31. Grainger, *Battle for Palestine*, 217.

32. Said, *The Question of Palestine*, 3, 78.

33. "Of course official Britain . . . was always pleased to be invisible in these sordid matters, or as close to invisible as was possible. The preferred posture of the greatest power of the age was to pose as the impartial external actor, doing its levelheaded, rational, civilized best to restrain the savage passions of the wild and brutish locals." Khalidi, *The Iron Cage*, 51.

34. This positive-negative identity, originating, as we saw, in the Middle Ages, comes into the modern era as the essence of what Edward Said defines as Orientalism: "the age-old conflict between the West and the Orient, whose main surrogate was Islam. This was not only a colonial matter, but a civilizational one as well." Said, *The Question of Palestine*, 29. See also Said, *Orientalism*, 49–72.

35. Khalidi, *The Iron Cage*, 97.

36. Gilbert, *The Atlas of Jewish History*, 85.

37. Asali, *Jerusalem in History*, 241.

38. Asali, *Jerusalem in History*, 244–45. Gilbert, *The Atlas of Jewish History*, 86.

39. Armstrong, *Jerusalem*, 367. Yet of the approximately 55,000 Jews residing in Palestine in 1905 (out of a total population of 700,000), only about 550 "could be identified as Zionist pioneers." Ben-Ami, *Scars of War*, 2.

40. In 1949, after the founding of the State of Israel, Herzl's remains were brought from Vienna to Jerusalem. His burial place is named for him, Mount Herzl, a cemetery for heroes of the Jewish state.

41. Luke 21:20–23.

42. After the destruction of Jerusalem in 135, Emperor Hadrian rebuilt the city around a shrine to Jupiter on the Temple Mount.

43. See Carroll, *Constantine's Sword*, 208–20.

44. Ben-Ami, *Scars of War*, 4.

45. Herzl diary entry, "Rome. January 26, 1904." Marvin Rosenthal, ed., *The Diaries of Theodor Herzl*. New York: Grosset and Dunlap, 1962, 427–30.

46. Kenny, *Catholics, Jews, and the State of Israel*, 24. *Civiltà Cattolica* attributes to "sacred scriptures" the "vagabondo" theology that actually originates after St. Augustine. It associates Jesus' "prediction" of the destruction of Jerusalem with "the end of the world," when, as we saw, that description of the city's fate refers to the Roman destruction that occurred in 70 CE, before the Gospel was written, and that was incorporated after the fact into the text as a prophecy of Jesus.

47. Bea, *The Church and the Jewish People*, 67.

48. Stephanson, *Manifest Destiny*, 72.

49. British interest in Arabia began with the simple ambition to control the navigation routes in the Persian Gulf, but oil trumped that. Hence the British alliance with the Arab tribal leader Ibn Saud, who, with British money and weapons, conquered the peninsula after World War I, including Mecca and Medina. He publicly executed forty thousand men and imposed the most severe form of Islam, Wahhabism, on what would then be known as the Kingdom of Saudi Arabia. Aslan, *No god but God*, 245.

50. Tuveson, *Redeemer Nation*, vii.

51. Armstrong, *Jerusalem*, 375. That Zionism inevitably drew energy from European colonialism is reflected in this assessment by Shlomo Ben-Ami, the former foreign minister of Israel: "Zionism was also a movement of conquest, colonisation, and settlement in the service of a just and righteous but also self-indulgent national cause. An enterprise of national liberation and human emancipation that was forced to use the tools of colonial penetration, it was a schizophrenic movement, which suffered from an irreconcilable incongruity between its liberating message and the offensive practices it used to advance it. The cultivation of a righteous self-image and the ethos of the few against the many, the heroic David facing the brutal, bestial Arab Goliath, was one way Zionism pretended to reconcile its contradictions." *Scars of War*, 3.

52. Samuel's was an "invented tradition," since there had been no "grand mufti" of Jerusalem. This religious enhancement was intended to deflect national aspiration. Khalidi, *The Iron Cage*, 57. The English word "mufti" refers to a military

person wearing civilian clothes. This derives from the Ottoman tradition of military commanders' using local civilian leaders — "muftis" — as adjuncts to their governance. For uniformed Ottoman viceroys, the mufti's usefulness depended on his civilian status.

53. "The al-Husaynis were one of the richest and most powerful families in Jerusalem, and their members had held the position of Hanafi mufti of Jerusalem for most of the preceding two centuries." Khalidi, *The Iron Cage,* 56. Mattar, *The Mufti of Jerusalem,* 6. It might also be noted that the al-Husaynis enriched themselves through the early twentieth century by selling large tracts of land to Zionists, even while loudly protesting the expansion of Jewish land holdings. Pappe, *The Ethnic Cleansing of Palestine,* 12. (Equivalent complaints have recently been lodged against leaders of the Palestinian Authority who sold cement to Israel for use in the detested "security barrier.")

54. Armstrong, *Jerusalem,* 377.

55. Said, *The Question of Palestine,* 88. Edward Said, the late Columbia University professor, was a leading voice among Palestinian exiles. His views were controversial. "Hackles are raised at the mere mention of Palestine," as the Jerusalem-based poet Peter Cole put it, "let alone The Question of —" The last phrase, Cole explains in a note to his poem "Palestine: A Sestina," refers to the title of Said's book. Cole, *Things on Which I've Stumbled,* 48.

56. One Muslim slogan that surfaced periodically over the years was "After Saturday, Sunday." That is, after finishing with the Jews, they would finish with the Christians. Morris, *1948,* 13.

57. Edward Said described Orientalism, the colonialist contempt of Europeans for the East, especially the Arab East, as a "secret sharer of Western anti-Semitism. That anti-Semitism and . . . Orientalism resemble each other very closely is a historical, cultural, and political truth that needs only to be mentioned to an Arab Palestinian for its irony to be perfectly understood." *Orientalism,* 27–28.

58. Mattar, *The Mufti of Jerusalem,* 39.

59. Figures for the Jewish population of Palestine are regularly in dispute, but even the mufti's biographer acknowledges the leap it made, growing from something like 50,000 in 1917 to nearly 385,000 in 1936. Mattar, *The Mufti of Jerusalem,* 149.

60. Segev, *The Seventh Million,* 77, 34. In 1933, there were 700,000 Jews in Germany and Austria. One-third of them were murdered. Of the two-thirds who escaped, a decided minority went to Palestine, a total of 50,000 to 60,000 people. In 1938 and 1939, they accounted for one half of the immigrants to Israel (35). Edward Said offers these figures: In 1931, the Jewish population of Palestine was 174,606 out of a total of 1,033,314. In 1936, there were 384,078 Jews out of 1,366,692. In 1946, there were 608,225 Jews out of 1,912,112. *The Question of Palestine,* 11.

61. Arab "inferiority" could seem confirmed by educational experience. "According to the 1931 census . . . only about 22% of Palestinian Arabs were literate, as against 86% of the country's Jewish population." The disparity only grew. Khalidi, *The Iron Cage,* 14.

62. Khalidi, *The Iron Cage,* 29.

63. Armstrong, *Jerusalem*, 383.

64. Chaim Weizmann, speaking in 1936. Ben-Ami, *Scars of War*, 1.

65. Pappe, *The Ethnic Cleansing of Palestine*, 14. Mattar, *The Mufti of Jerusalem*, 70–73. Arabs complained that the British crackdown was uneven, with Jewish groups allowed to arm themselves with impunity. The Irgun and the Stern Gang evolved into what today would be labeled terrorist groups, but they drew support from no more than 10 to 15 percent of Zionists. Asali, *Jerusalem in History*, 256, 257. Another Jewish fighting force, the Hagana, was relatively moderate in its methods and evolved into the Israel Defense Forces.

66. The Peel Commission of 1937. Though unhappy with the proposed borders, Zionists accepted the partition plan, establishing a pattern according to which Jews would pragmatically accept what they could get, while Palestinians would hold out for the impossible. The commission, not incidentally, introduced the language of "transfer" into the dispute. About 300,000 Arabs in territory to be set aside for Jews would be moved into Arab territory. The "balance" for this was the removal of about 1,250 Jews from Arab lands. This prospect was enough to guarantee Arab rejection. Morris, *1948*, 18.

67. The number is imprecise. Morris puts the figure at "between three thousand and six thousand." *1948*, 21.

68. In defense of this rejectionism, Rashid Khalidi points out that notes of British cabinet discussions of such concessions to Palestinians make clear that London never intended to carry them out. "These offers were far less tantalizing to the Arabs than they might have appeared . . . hedged around with conditions . . . [and] many hidden traps." *The Iron Cage*, 118, 36, 114.

69. Mattar, *The Mufti of Jerusalem*, 80–85, 148. Churchill was appointed First Lord of the Admiralty in September 1939 and prime minister in May 1940.

70. Said, *The Question of Palestine*, xii.

71. A poll in 1941 put the level of Palestinian Arab support for Germany at 88 percent, with 9 percent supporting Great Britain. Morris, *1948*, 21.

72. Mattar, *The Mufti of Jerusalem*, 100.

73. Mattar, *The Mufti of Jerusalem*, 103.

74. The mufti died in Lebanon in 1974 without ever being brought to trial. He had longed to be buried in Jerusalem, near the Haram al-Sharif. Authorities of the State of Israel did not allow it. In 1991, the Simon Wiesenthal Center cited evidence from uncovered archival material to bolster this charge, but other investigators find it "inconclusive." Mattar, *The Mufti of Jerusalem*, 139, 176.

75. When Jews could still have escaped in large numbers from German-controlled territory, up to and after Kristallnacht in 1938—when the Nazi policy was "Jews out!"—the British government, both by its refusal to raise immigration quotas in the United Kingdom and by its prevention of Jewish emigration to Palestine, was complicit. The harsh fact of this history is that until the outbreak of the war, Hitler would willingly have allowed Jews to leave—a grotesque ethnic cleansing that would seem benign only by comparison to what followed. The same charge of complicity can be brought against the United States, which discouraged the immigration of Jews throughout the war. Wylie, *The Abandonment of the Jews*, 157–59.

76. *The Diary of a Young Girl* was published in 1952, produced as a play on Broadway in 1955, and released as a movie in 1959. *Night,* having appeared in France in 1958, was published in English in 1960. *The Deputy* was produced in Berlin and England in 1963, and on Broadway in 1964.

77. "Sixty percent of Israelis aged fourteen and over listened to the live radio broadcast of the trial's opening session . . . Many of those children who were listening are today's leaders." Burg, *The Holocaust Is Over,* 122.

78. Hannah Arendt's word. Her summary formulation, "a report on the banality of evil," was based on her perception of Eichmann's ordinariness. "The trouble with Eichmann was precisely that so many were like him, and that the many were neither perverted nor sadistic, that they were, and still are, terribly and terrifyingly normal . . . This normality was much more terrifying than all the atrocities put together." That monstrous acts could be committed by someone who was not a monster seemed the real horror. Arendt, *Eichmann in Jerusalem,* 276. The thesis was widely disputed. See, for example, Cesarani, *Becoming Eichmann.*

79. Although some see the Eichmann trial as an overdue Israeli reckoning with the *Shoah,* others see it as having been the beginning of an overemphasis on the Holocaust, "of the Shoah chapter in Israeli identity," as Avraham Burg put it. *The Holocaust Is Over,* 142.

80. Revelation 20:4.

81. Segev, *The Seventh Million,* 69–72. I acknowledge a particular debt to Tom Segev for my understanding of the significance of the Holocaust for Israelis.

82. Segev, *The Seventh Million,* 109, 110. "Lambs to the slaughter" refers to a phrase in Isaiah 53:7.

83. Segev, *The Seventh Million,* 104, 105.

84. Carroll, "Shoah in the News."

85. Morris, *1948,* 22.

86. The phrase was used by Abraham Joshua Heschel to describe his own prewar escape. Heschel, *Moral Grandeur,* viii.

87. Segev, *The Seventh Million,* 154.

88. Segev, *The Seventh Million,* 160.

89. Between nine and ten million Jews lived in the European countries from which Hitler's approximately six million Jewish victims came. http://history 1900s.about.com/library/holocaust/bldied.htm.

90. Ben-Ami, *Scars of War,* 47.

91. While the ratio of Jews killed was two of three living in Europe, the ratio for all Jews in the world was one in three.

92. For a catalogue of destruction, the villages and neighborhoods lost, see Walid Khalidi, *All That Remains: The Palestinian Villages Occupied and Depopulated by Israel in 1948.* Washington and Beirut: Institute for Palestine Studies, 2006. The essential fact is that somewhere between 600,000 and 750,000 Palestinian Arabs fled or were forced to flee from their homes.

93. Said, *The Question of Palestine,* xxi.

94. Morris, *1948,* 393. It may seem odd to put the Palestinian experience in a Jewish voice here, but that a Jewish partisan like Ben-Gurion could see the Pal-

estinian point of view validates it. His empathetic understanding of Arab resistance was most influentially expressed in Zeev Jabotinsky's 1923 essay "The Iron Wall (We and the Arabs)." http://www.marxists.de/middleast/ironwall/ironwall.htm.

95. Morris, *1948*, 27.

96. Israel's authorities at the time did not deny that atrocities had taken place at Deir Yassin. On the contrary, they were condemned by the Jewish Agency, the chief rabbis of Jerusalem, and the senior military command. Morris, *1948*, 127. The number of civilians killed at Deir Yassin is disputed. Arab sources put the number as high as 250 (for example, Asali, *Jerusalem in History*, 258), while even controversial "new historians" see a figure as low as 93 (for example, Pappe, *The Ethnic Cleansing of Palestine*, 91). Karen Armstrong accepts the figure of 250 (*Jerusalem*, 386).

97. Revisions to the historical record of Israel's origins were prompted by the release in the 1980s of previously classified documents. Among the "new historians" are respected writers like Benny Morris and Tom Segev. Avi Shlaim is author of *The Iron Wall: Israel and the Arab World*, a book Tom Segev calls "the best comprehensive history of the Arab-Israeli conflict." But Shlaim's more recent book, *Israel and Palestine: Reappraisals, Revision, Refutations*, is regarded by Segev and others as "unbalanced." A more controversial figure is Ilan Pappe, whose work, depicting the dispossession of Palestinians as a result of long-planned criminal deliberation rather than as a consequence of the ad hoc dislocation typical of war, even the "new historians" find unreliable.

98. Ben-Ami, *Scars of War*, 48. "In truth," Benny Morris writes, "the Jews committed far more atrocities than the Arabs and killed far more civilians and POWs in deliberate acts of brutality during the course of 1948." *1948*, 405. When "new historians" use the phrase "born in sin," many Israeli hackles rise because the charge seems intended to delegitimize the State of Israel. The concept "born in sin" is foreign to traditional Jewish thinking, and is associated more with Christian, especially Catholic, notions of original sin. A standard Jewish reading of the Adam and Eve story emphasizes the choice to eat of the forbidden fruit as a kind of coming into moral responsibility, an initiating act of free will more than a condemning act of disobedience. See, for example, Erich Fromm, http://www.philosophyprofessor.com/philosophers/erich-fromm.php. For Catholics, the phrase "born in sin" does not delegitimize or stigmatize, since the doctrine of original sin holds that, except for Jesus and Mary, every human being (and by extension every human institution) comes into existence in a state of fallenness. Israel was born in sin, but so was Rome, with the fratricide of Remus by Romulus; Britain with the war of aggression known as the Norman Conquest; the colonies of America with their crimes against indigenous populations. To say that Israel is born in sin, in such a context, is not delegitimizing, but normal.

99. Avishai, *The Hebrew Republic*, 80. Said, *The Question of Palestine*, 52.

100. http://www.ipoet.com/archive/original/darwish/IdentityCard.html. The line is from Darwish's poem "Identity Card," which Said calls the Palestinian national poem. *The Question of Palestine*, 155.

101. Armstrong, *Jerusalem*, 386.

102. Pappe, *The Ethnic Cleansing of Palestine*, 25.

103. Jonathan Schneer finds evidence that the British were prepared in 1917 to allow the Ottomans to maintain control over Palestine, including Jerusalem, but that reveals how British Middle East policy always involved tension between realists and Jerusalem's visionaries. Schneer, *The Balfour Declaration*, 263–70.

104. Under Pope John Paul II, for whom reconciliation with the Jewish people was a priority, and after the Second Vatican Council of the 1960s had dismantled the "exile theology," the Vatican extended diplomatic recognition to Israel in 1994. Even then, the Vatican's inner circle was opposed.

105. Truman told his cabinet in 1946 that he "had no use for them [the Jews] and didn't care what happened to them." He openly resented the "pushiness" of Jewish pressures. Morris, *1948*, 25.

106. "Eight Palestinian neighborhoods and thirty-nine villages were ethnically cleansed in the Greater Jerusalem area." Pappe, *The Ethnic Cleansing of Palestine*, 99.

107. Armstrong, *Jerusalem*, 395. Segev, *1949*, 35. Meir liked to think of Palestinians as "South Syrians." Said, *The Question of Palestine*, 138. In 1969, Meir told an interviewer, "There is no such thing as a Palestinian people . . . It's not as if we came and threw them out and took their country. They didn't exist." *New York Times*, June 15, 1969. http://www.monabaker.com/quotes.htm.

108. About "5 million survivors or descendants of the 750,000 Arabs who fled (or were chased out) of Israel during the 1948 war, as well as the 500,000 who were displaced in 1967, remain refugees." Of those outside Palestine, two-thirds are in Jordan, with one-third in Syria and Lebanon. About 40 percent of refugees still live in camps. Avishai, *The Hebrew Republic*, 247.

109. The idea of "transfer," as we saw in note 66, had been introduced by the Peel Commission in 1939. But it was also an idea Palestinians took for granted in their aim of removing the Jewish population. Some Zionist leaders, including Ben-Gurion, had spoken of transfer, but Zionists equally had expected to share the Jewish state with Arabs. The extent of ethnic cleansing that occurred during 1948 was the result less of planned policy than of ad hoc actions taken during the war. See Morris, *1948*, 406–7.

110. Morris, *1948*, 412, 415. The phrase "Arab miracle" originates with Shaul Avigur. Segev, *The Seventh Million*, 161. The comparison with Massachusetts is Bernard Avishai's, *The Hebrew Republic*, 24.

111. Grossman, *Writing in the Dark*, 6.

112. Segev, *1949*, 116.

113. Segev, *The Seventh Million*, 183. The rumor about Jews being turned into soap, Segev suggests, began with a confusion over the letters stamped into German-manufactured bars of soap. "RIF," short for "pure industrial fat," was read as "RJF," for "pure Jewish fat."

114. Ezekiel 36:38.

115. Ben-Ami, *Scars of War*, 90.

116. Segev, *The Seventh Million*, 347.

117. Segev, *1949*, 42. Ben-Gurion declared, "Jewish Jerusalem is an organic and in-

separable part of the history of Israel and the faith of Israel and of the very soul of our people. Jerusalem is the heart of hearts of the State of Israel." Armstrong, *Jerusalem*, 391.

118. Arendt observes that "the bulk of the witnesses" came from death camps over which Eichmann's "authority had been almost nil." *Eichmann in Jerusalem*, 225.

119. This was another complaint Arendt lodged against the proceedings. *Eichmann in Jerusalem*, 225.

120. Segev, *The Seventh Million*, 339, 356.

121. Avishai, *The Hebrew Republic*, 161.

122. Grossman, *Writing in the Dark*, 71–72.

123. See Carroll, *House of War*, 491–512.

124. The Israel Defense Forces prides itself on upholding the highest ethical standards in its conduct of war, but its ability to do so has at times been challenged. During the Gaza war of 2009, for example, the IDF's openly stated policy of "disproportionate force" was held to be a source of war crimes by a U.N. commission led by the South African jurist Richard Goldstone. For a positive evaluation of the Goldstone report, see David Schulman, "Israel Without Illusions: What Goldstone Got Right," *New York Review of Books*, November 17, 2009. http://www.nybooks.com/blogs/nyrblog/2009/nov/17/israel-without-illusions-what-goldstone-got-right/. For a critical assessment, see Moshe Halbertal, "The Goldstone Illusion," *New Republic*, November 6, 2009. http://www.tnr.com/article/world/the-goldstone-illusion. In July 2010, Israel itself brought charges against eight soldiers for war crimes during the Gaza war. http://www.worldtribune.com/worldtribune/WTARC/2010/me_israel0624_07_07.asp.

125. Segev, *The Seventh Million*, 400. Amos Oz elaborates on "the incurable" in *How to Cure a Fanatic*. Princeton, NJ: Princeton University Press, 2006.

126. The settlement movement, in addition to the Eretz Yisrael impulse behind it, was given a huge boost when, as the Soviet Union was breaking up in the late 1980s, about a million Soviet Jews arrived in Israel, needing to be housed. Many of them were "settled" in the occupied territories.

127. Ben-Ami, *Scars of War*, 120, 121.

128. That irrational grievances are the obstacle to peace is suggested by the fact that at least since the so-called Clinton Parameters defined the broad outline of compromises acceptable to majorities on both sides, the "peace process" has gone nowhere. For years, everyone knew what the end agreement of the two-state solution would look like, but progress toward it (Oslo, Madrid, Camp David, Geneva, "road map," Annapolis, Mitchell "proximity" talks, and the Obama-sponsored direct talks begun in 2010) proved elusive. The Palestinian future may as likely rest with an "enlarged Jordan" as with a new independent state on the West Bank and Gaza, where Israeli settlements have made viable sovereignty for a Palestinian entity practically impossible. But all such "solutions" presuppose some kind of accommodation between the opposing understandings of history and identity. Tom Segev, "Israel and Palestine: Eternal Enmity?," *New York Review of Books*, January 14, 2010, 48.

129. Said, *The Question of Palestine*, 124.

130. Segev, "Israel and Palestine," 48.

131. Asali, *Jerusalem in History*, 269, 270. The Arab percentage of the Jerusalem population went like this: 73 percent in 1873, 46 percent in 1922, 40 percent in 1944, 28 percent in 1987 (249).

132. Khalidi, *The Iron Cage*, 200.

133. Khalidi, *The Iron Cage*, 119.

134. Khalidi, *The Iron Cage*, 123.

135. Susser, *The Rise of Hamas*, 42.

136. It is important to note, as Edward Said does, that the PLO came into being as a revolutionary people's movement in the same era as other liberation movements, like the African National Congress, the South West Africa People's Organization, the Sandinistas in Nicaragua, and the anti-shah movement in Iran—which Said describes as "the twentieth-century struggle against various forms of tyranny and injustice." *The Question of Palestine*, x. Said does not mention, but could have, the Provisional IRA in Northern Ireland and the Black Panthers in the United States.

137. Ben-Ami, *Scars of War*, 137.

138. The PLO competed with other Palestinian terror groups, like that led by Abul Abbas which, in 1985, hijacked the cruise ship *Achille Lauro* and murdered a passenger, Leon Klinghoffer. Eventually, such acts of terror were disowned by leading Palestinians—"an indication," as Edward Said put it, "of how far beyond them a justifiably anxious community has traveled in political maturity and morality." *The Question of Palestine*, xx.

139. Avishai, *The Hebrew Republic*, 157. Not all suicide bombers were "God-intoxicated," as we note below.

9. Millennium

1. Hersh, *The Samson Option*, 222.

2. Farr, *The Third Temple's Holy of Holies*, 12. Prime Minister Levi Eshkol (1963–1969) had committed Israel to a policy of no first use of nuclear weapons in the Middle East, but no one doubted in 1973 or, later, in 1991 that Israel would have used its nuclear arsenal before suffering a complete defeat by its Arab neighbors. Opacity about the existence of Israel's nuclear arsenal and ambiguity about its intentions to use it define the Israeli strategy. See Cohen, *The Worst-Kept Secret*.

3. In *Commentary* in 1976, Podhoretz wrote, "It used to be said that the Israelis had a Masada complex . . . but if the Israelis are to be understood in terms of a 'complex' involving suicide rather than surrender and rooted in a relevant precedent of Jewish history, the example of Samson . . . would be more appropriate than Masada, where in committing suicide the Zealots killed only themselves and took no Romans with them." Quoted in Hersh, *The Samson Option*, 137.

4. Hersh, *The Samson Option*, 225–26, 239.

5. Perry, *Four Stars*, 258. Nolan, *Guardians of the Arsenal*, 123.

6. "Israel called its first nuclear alert, and began arming its nuclear arsenal. And it used that alert to blackmail Washington into a major policy change." Hersh, *The Samson Option*, 223. When put on the spot by Golda Meir about his Jewish loyalty some months after the war, Kissinger replied, "First, I am American. Second, I am the Secretary of State of the United States of America. Third, I am a Jew." To which the prime minister replied, "That's all right, sonny, we read from right to left." Hersh, *The Samson Option*, 230.

7. Sadat's fear of the Israeli nuclear arsenal was a large part of what motivated his historic peacemaking journey to Jerusalem in November 1977. Farr, *The Third Temple's Holy of Holies*, 13, 14. Seymour Hersh reports that in a secret meeting with Israel's Prime Minister Menachem Begin "shortly after arriving" in Jerusalem, Sadat sought a "pledge not to use nuclear weapons against Egypt" as part of the peace treaty he was proposing. Begin did not acknowledge having nuclear weapons. Hersh, *The Samson Option*, 269.

8. McGeorge Bundy, *Danger and Survival: Choices about the Bomb in the First Fifty Years*. New York: Random House, 1988, 230.

9. On the U.S. side alone, more than ninety thousand nuclear weapons were produced over fifty years. Sherwin and Bird, *American Prometheus*, 423.

10. Kissinger, together with the nuclear theorist Herman Kahn and the physicist Edward Teller, is widely regarded as the figure behind the title character of Stanley Kubrick's 1964 film *Dr. Strangelove, or How I Learned to Stop Worrying and Love the Bomb*.

11. Israel developed the bomb in cooperation with France, which pursued the partnership as a counter to Nasser's Egypt, which was supporting the anti-French rebellion in Algeria. When the French successfully tested their first nuclear device in 1960, that "made two nuclear powers, not one — such was the depth of the collaboration" between France and Israel. Farr, *The Third Temple's Holy of Holies*, 6.

12. Kissinger, *Years of Upheaval*, 581.

13. Kissinger, *Years of Upheaval*, 581, 582, 589. In his own memoir, Nixon dodges the question of his absence from the Dobrynin crisis. "When Haig [then Nixon's chief of staff] informed me about this message, I said that he and Kissinger should have a meeting at the White House to formulate plans for a firm reaction to what amounted to a scarcely veiled threat of unilateral Soviet intervention. Words were not making our point — we needed action, even the shock of a military alert." *RN*, 938.

14. Nolan, *Guardians of the Arsenal*, 122.

15. www.onejerusalem.com/2009/01/06/golda-meir-on-children-and-war. This story of Meir's successful blackmailing of Kissinger, ironically, lends credence to the claim that Israel *had* to acquire a nuclear arsenal. With no way to force the American resupply, Israel might well have lost the war.

16. Grossman, *Writing in the Dark*, 23.

17. Grossman, *Writing in the Dark*, 44.

18. Farr, *The Third Temple's Holy of Holies*, 18, 19.

19. During the 2009 Gaza war, Hamas-fired Qassam rockets fell within about twenty miles of Dimona, where a plutonium production reactor had been operating since the 1960s. It is believed to have created enough material for up to two hundred nuclear weapons, which have been manufactured in an adjacent underground facility. Dimona is protected with sophisticated air and missile defenses, and is mostly a hardened target. Yet the very presence of the nuclear facility in the war zone defines the danger. While it is not inconceivable that even such primitive weapons as Hamas musters could damage the above-ground dome of the Dimona reactor and cause a widely fatal radiation leak, the larger point is that when Israel engages in high-stakes military operations against its enemies, it is a grand illusion to think that Israel's own nuclear reservation won't eventually be targeted, with a massive escalation of psychological and political tensions. Israel would surely justify its nuclear readiness now as a deterrent against Iran, whose leaders have sworn to exterminate the Jewish state, and perhaps Syria, which apparently has been engaged in a secret nuclear program of its own. Yet Israel's possession of the bomb adds to the pressures that drive Tehran's nuclear ambition. Will Israel's security continue to be enhanced by a nuclear arsenal that, more than deterring, gives enemies both motive and excuse to pursue their own? Convincing Tehran to limit its nuclear appetite requires every nuclear power, beginning with the United States, to recommit itself to nuclear abolition. What applies to one nation applies to all. That means Israel, too. In addition to supplying Israel's deterrent, Dimona creates radioactive pressure toward the proliferation of nuclear weapons throughout the region. Experts warn that such a "cascade," once flowing, would run from Iran to Saudi Arabia to Egypt to Turkey and perhaps to others. How would this make Israel safer?

20. See, for example, this 2010 statement by Egypt's ambassador to the United Nations: http://www.globalsecuritynewswire.org/gsn/nw201003114924.php.

21. *The Fate of the Earth* is the title of Jonathan Schell's pivotal 1982 book on the nuclear danger.

22. For a radio sound check, he counted backward from ten, concluding ". . . three, two, one — boom! There goes Moscow."

23. Neoconservative Catholics included Michael Novak, George Weigel, and Richard John Neuhaus. When the right-wing pundit Robert Novak and right-wing politician Newt Gingrich converted to Catholicism in the early 2000s, it seemed a perfect fit. See Clermont, *The Neo-Catholics*, 2010.

24. Dugger, "Does Ronald Reagan Expect Armageddon?"

25. In the Soviet Union, the key voice was Andrei Sakharov, who, as the father of the Soviet H-bomb, was a kind of Soviet Oppenheimer. Sakharov's dissent meshed with grassroots movements like Solidarity in Poland and the Democracy Forum in Czechoslovakia. In western Europe, a mass movement against the deployment of medium-range U.S. nuclear missiles (notably the Pershing) defined the 1980s. In America a nationwide nuclear freeze movement was supported by Hollywood films like *The Day After* and *The China Syndrome*. The celebrity scientist Carl Sagan was a leading voice.

26. "A great star fell from heaven, blazing like a torch, and it fell on a third of

the rivers and on fountains of water. The name of the star is Wormwood. A third of the waters became wormwood, and many men died of the water because it was made bitter." Revelation 8:10–11. Reagan's biographer Lou Cannon comments, "When Reagan learned that 'Chernobyl' is the Ukrainian for 'wormwood' he was certain that the disaster at Reactor Number 4 was indeed a portent of Armageddon." Cannon notes that in later relating this ominous fact, Reagan said that "'Chernobyl' was Ukrainian for 'Wedgwood.'" Cannon, *President Reagan*, 757.

27. That same shallow self-confidence was what enabled Reagan to do an abrupt about-face when a very different Soviet leader, Mikhail Gorbachev, came to power. Responding to Gorbachev's invitation, and to pressure from the American electorate, Reagan replaced his nuclear apocalypticism with a commitment to nuclear abolition. When asked, during his friendly visit to Red Square in 1988, about his earlier condemnation of the Soviet Union as "evil," he shrugged amiably, pointed at Gorbachev, and said, "It was evil, until he — until this one man made all the difference." Morris, *Dutch*, 647.

28. Esther 3:1–6.

29. Stern, *Terror in the Name of God*, 92. Stern's book showed me the connection between Goldstein and Amir.

30. In 2006, one-third of Israelis sampled told pollsters that they would support a pardon for Yigal Amir. Among self-identified "religious" Jews, the figure supporting pardon was 64 percent. http://www.ynetnews.com/articles/0,7340,L-3320266,00.html.

31. Omar Bakri Muhammad, a militant Lebanese Islamic activist, in an interview with the *Sunday Express* of London, said about Paul McCartney's planned trip to Israel, "If he values his life, Mr. McCartney must not come to Israel. He will not be safe there. The sacrifice operatives will be waiting for him." *New York Times*, September 17, 2008. McCartney went anyway and performed in Tel Aviv.

32. Around two dozen distinct terrorist groups, from Chechnya to the Middle East to Sri Lanka, use suicide as a weapon. Between 1985 and 2006, more than two hundred suicide bombers were women, about one in six. At first, the groups using women in this role were secular, although they assumed classic religious attitudes toward sacrifice and martyrdom. The first Palestinian woman to commit an act of suicide bombing did so in 2002, after which the Al Aqsa Martyrs Brigade set up a women's suicide-bombing unit, one of whose members was Ayat al-Akhras. Female suicide bombers may think they are rejecting the traditional role of gender subservience, but they "are actually operating under them. These include a well-scripted set of rules in which women sacrifice themselves . . . In a sense, martyrdom is the ultimate and twisted fulfillment of these ideals. So the spectacle of female suicide bombers doesn't challenge the patriarchy as much as provide evidence of its power. The message female suicide bombers send is that they are more valuable to their societies dead than they ever could have been alive." Mia Bloom, "Female Suicide Bombers," *Daedalus*, Winter 2007, 102.

33. For a description of Ayat al-Akhras's action, see Jason Keyser, "Female Suicide

Bomber Kills Two at Jerusalem Supermarket," *Independent,* March 30, 2002.
For a description of Palestinian men performing a marital dance the day after
a female blew herself up, killing six Israelis, see "The Bomber Next Door," *60
Minutes,* May 28, 2003. After these incidents, the number of female suicide
bombers increased, especially in Iraq. "Wearing billowy, black head-to-toe
garments, the female bombers have been able to conceal powerful explosives
and slip into crowded areas too heavily guarded for a male suicide bomber to
ease through undetected. While men often undergo physical searches, Islamic
rules do not allow male security officers to pat down women." Richard A. Op-
pel Jr., "8 Die in Iraq Suicide Bombing, Apparently by Woman," *New York
Times,* July 25, 2008. In general, female suicide bombers share with males the
same motivations, which a researcher with the Chicago Project on Suicide
Terrorism characterized as "a deep loyalty to their community combined with
a variety of personal grievances against enemy forces." The motivations may
or may not be explicitly religious, but the act draws on religious motifs of
sacrifice and martyrdom. Lindsey O'Rourke, "The Woman Behind the Bomb,"
International Herald Tribune, August 4, 2008.

34. Robin Wright, "Since 2001, a Dramatic Increase in Suicide Bombings,"
    http://www.washingtonpost.com/wp-dyn/content/article/2008/04/17
    /AR2008041703595.html.

35. Aslan, *No god but God,* 190.

36. Aslan, *No god but God,* 244.

37. Aslan, *No god but God,* 246–48.

38. For a discussion of how religion motivates many, but not all, suicide terrorists,
    see Pape, *Dying to Win,* 2005. Pape's recent book *Cutting the Fuse* explains that
    while foreign occupation is the "principal trigger" for suicide terror, "religious
    difference between the foreign occupier and the occupied is a key enabling
    factor" (86).

39. The president used the phrase during a press conference on the White House
    lawn on September 16, 2001. See, for example, *Christian Science Monitor,* Sep-
    tember 19, 2001.

40. I was one such liberal. See my book *Crusade: Chronicles of an Unjust War.* New
    York: Metropolitan Books, 2004. In my criticism of Bush, I highlighted his re-
    ligiosity as if it were exceptional. Only in writing this book did I see how Bush's
    responses were consistent with deep currents in American life and politics.

41. At the National Cathedral two days after the attack, he pledged to "rid the
    world of evil." In 2004, two shapers of the "Bush Doctrine," David Frum and
    Richard Perle, published a book titled *An End to Evil.*

42. Appearing in the same lens marked with the crosshairs that allowed soldiers
    to fix on targets were small engraved letters in sequence with the sight's serial
    number. For example, "2Cor 4:6," which reads "For God, who commanded
    the light to shine out of darkness, hath shined in our hearts, to give the light
    of knowledge of the glory of God in the face of Jesus Christ." The Trijicon
    Company had a $660 million contract to provide 800,000 gun sights to the
    army. Joseph Rhee, "U.S. Military Weapons Inscribed With Secret 'Jesus'

Bible Codes," January 18, 2010, http://abcnews.go.com/Blotter/us-military
-weapons-inscribed-secret-jesus-bible-code/story.html. After the New Testament citations on the gun sights became public in 2010, the manufacturer
stopped the practice.

43. George W. Bush, "Address to a Joint Session of Congress and the American
People," September 20, 2001, www.whitehouse.gov/news/releases/2001/09
/20010920-8.html.

44. This is reflected especially in the Obama defense budget, which allocated $5
trillion for the period 2010–2017, a 5 percent increase, in constant dollars,
over the Bush defense budget from 2002 to 2009. The Iraq and Afghanistan
wars, continued by Obama, were by far the most expensive in U.S. history. By
comparison, the Korean War cost $393,000 per person per year; Vietnam cost
$256,000 per person per year. As of 2010, Iraq and Afghanistan cost $792,000
per person per year. Project on Defense Alternatives, http://www.comw.org
/pda/fulltext/1001pdabr20exsum.pdf.

10. Conclusion: Good Religion

1. "The hollow shell of the 'secular democratic state' of the PLO had to be infused
with a 'religious soul.' As a consequence, the conflict became Islamicized, Palestinian grievances were reformulated as a historic clash of religions." Hamas,
established in 1988 as the agent of this, began its suicide bombing campaign in
1994. Hamas is an acronym for the Islamic Resistance Movement. Wistrich, *A
Lethal Obsession*, 733, 731.

2. Julius, *Trials of the Diaspora*, 583.

3. The danger, from the Jewish side, is caught by Gershom Scholem, who "feared
that Zionism's political fevers would awaken more primordial fevers . . . long
dormant but easily activated agents of messianism and apocalyptic thinking."
This summary is Sidra DeKoven Ezrahi's. She adds, "How can we stay close
to the sacred center, yet keep our distance?" Avishai, *The Hebrew Republic*,
111. On the Muslim fringe, meanwhile, traditional and limited antagonisms
with Christianity and Judaism "have been transformed into an apocalyptic
myth about the Jewish and Western threat to Islam as a whole. Drawing on the
Koran, hadith, and Muslim eschatology, Jews are described as adherents of the
great deceiver, the Dajjal — a kind of Muslim parallel to the Anti-Christ legend
. . . The bottom line is very clear: The End of Days will not come until all the
Jews have been killed." Wistrich, *A Lethal Obsession*, 744.

4. I acknowledge that in writing about fundamentalism, I write from outside it.
In the same way, in what follows, I write from outside Islam and Judaism, and
so my perceptions are necessarily limited.

5. Isaiah 55:8.

6. O'Malley, *Four Cultures of the West*, 6, 7.

7. Palestinian partisans succeeded in having Zionism denounced as racism at the
2001 United Nations Conference in Durban, South Africa, but even a Pales-

tinian like Edward Said had foreseen the wrong in such "sweeping rhetorical denunciation." Said, *The Question of Palestine*, 111.

8. Fromm, *The Heart of Man: Its Genius for Good and Evil.*

9. Isaiah 42:6. David Hartman is my special teacher on this tension between particularity and universality. See especially "Revelation and Creation: The Particular and the Universal in Judaism," *A Heart of Many Rooms*, 153–68.

10. A glib criticism of "Jewish exclusivism" has been a mark of Christian denigration of the Jewish religion, rooted in a reading of St. Paul. Yet Christianity's emphasis on the necessity of Jesus Christ for salvation, beginning with Paul, is more exclusive than anything in Judaism.

11. I owe this understanding to Sidra DeKoven Ezrahi.

12. Elon, *Jerusalem*, 17.

13. Elon, *Jerusalem*, 14.

14. Psalm 137.

15. Recall that 1 and 2 Maccabees are not in the canon of Judaism.

16. The Hellenizing Seleucids usually respected the religious diversity of their subjects, but in 167 BCE, probably because of pressures from rivals in Egypt, they imposed a new uniformity on the cults, forbidding Jewish observances. "The Maccabees are best understood as moderate fanatics. They were not in total revolt against Greek culture . . . they were fighting heroically for their traditions and the survival of their faith." They successfully retook Jerusalem in 164 and restored the Temple, a victory celebrated at Hanukkah. David Brooks, "Hanukkah Story Reflects Tragedy of Violent Political Strife," *New York Times*, December 13, 2009.

17. Burg, *The Holocaust Is Over*, 37.

18. Luke 13:1, 13:33. Recall that the Gospel of Luke was written years after the events it records, around 80 CE, in the thick of the Roman war against the Jews and after the Romans had leveled the Temple and slaughtered tens of thousands in Jerusalem. Luke's Gospel is more like a novel than a history, and uses the violence of Jerusalem as the pivot of the story. That is why, unlike the other Gospels, it has Jesus coming to the city only once, as an act of deliberate provocation — as an act of self-killing, if not suicide.

19. Matthew 16:22–23.

20. Matthew 16:22–23.

21. Kripal, *Esalen: America and the Religion of No Religion.*

22. "God is greater than religion, faith is greater than dogma." Heschel, *The Insecurity of Freedom*, 119.

23. St. Augustine, Sermon 52.16.

24. Paul Ricoeur wrote of surrendering "the immediacy of belief. But if we can no longer live the great symbolisms of the sacred in accordance with the original belief, we can, we modern men, aim at a second naiveté in and through criticism." *The Rule of Metaphor*, 318. See also Tracy, *On Naming the Present*, 138.

25. The Ten Commandments (Exodus 20:3, Deuteronomy 5:7) include the prohibition against false gods, but as we saw, there was an evolution from monolatry, the commitment to worship the Lord and not the other gods, to monotheism, the conviction that "the Lord is God in heaven above and on earth below:

there is none else" (Deuteronomy 4:39). Or, "I am the first and I am the last. Beside me there is no God" (Isaiah 44:6). As we saw, critical to this evolution was the insight of the captive Hebrews in Babylon, the breakthrough both to the idea that God is One in the sense of being the only one, and One in the sense of being the creative principle of cosmic unity.

26. Pelican, *Jesus Through the Centuries*, 106. The best expression of salvation as this change in God's mind is given by John Calvin: "God was at enmity with men until they were brought back into grace by the death of Jesus Christ." *Institutes of the Christian Religion* 2.16.2.

27. Bonhoeffer, *Letters and Papers from Prison*, 163.

28. Bonhoeffer, *Letters and Papers from Prison*, 219.

29. Such rejection of God in the name of justice defined the atheism of Marx, Camus, and Sartre, but their notions of justice, even first defined as they were by people responding to God, did not extend to women.

30. Niebuhr, *The Irony of American History*, 89.

Bibliography

Aamodt, Terrie D. *Righteous Armies, Holy Cause: Apocalyptic Imagery in the Civil War*. Macon, GA: Mercer University Press, 2002.

Aaron, Daniel. *America in Crisis*. New York: Knopf, 1952.

Allison, Graham. "Nuclear Disorder: Surveying Atomic Threats," *Foreign Affairs* 89, no. 1, January–February 2010.

Arendt, Hannah. *Eichmann in Jerusalem: A Report on the Banality of Evil*. New York: Penguin Classics, 1994.

Armstrong, Karen. *A History of God: The 4,000-Year Quest of Judaism, Christianity, and Islam*. New York: Ballantine Books, 1994.

———. *Jerusalem: One City, Three Faiths*. New York: Ballantine Books, 1996.

———. *Islam: A Short History*. New York: Modern Library, 2000.

———. *The Battle for God: A History of Fundamentalism*. New York: Ballantine Books, 2001.

———. *The Great Transformation: The Beginning of Our Religious Traditions*. New York: Knopf, 2006.

———. "The Holiness of Jerusalem: Asset or Burden?" *Journal of Palestine Studies* 27, no. 3, Spring 1998.

Asali, K. J., ed. *Jerusalem in History*. New York: Olive Branch Press, 2000.

Aslan, Reza. *No god but God: The Origins, Evolution, and Future of Islam*. New York: Random House, 2005.

———. *How to Win a Cosmic War: God, Globalization, and the End of the War on Terror*. New York: Random House, 2009.

———. "Islam's Long War Within," *Harvard Divinity Bulletin*, Autumn 2005.

Assmann, Jan. *Moses the Egyptian: The Memory of Egypt in Western Monotheism*. Cambridge: Harvard University Press, 1997.

Avishai, Bernard. *The Tragedy of Zionism: Revolution and Democracy in the Land of Israel*. New York: Farrar, Straus and Giroux, 1985.

———. *A New Israel: Democracy in Crisis, 1973–1988*. New York: Ticknor & Fields, 1990.

———. *The Hebrew Republic*. Orlando, FL: Harcourt, 2008.

Bailie, Gil. *Violence Unveiled: Humanity at the Crossroads.* New York: Crossroad, 1995.

Baltzell, E. Digby. *Puritan Boston and Quaker Pennsylvania.* New York: Free Press, 1979.

Barber, Noel. *Lords of the Golden Horn: From Suleiman the Magnificent to Kemal Atatürk.* London: Pan Books, 1976.

Barr, David. "Toward an Ethical Reading of the Apocalypse." Society of Biblical Literature 1997 Seminar Paper. Atlanta: Scholars Press, 1997.

Barth, Karl. *Church Dogmatics.* Edinburgh, Scotland: T. and T. Clark, 1957.

Bartlett, Anthony W. *Cross Purposes: The Violent Grammar of Christian Atonement.* Hamburg, PA: Trinity Press International, 2001.

Barton, George A. "The Jerusalem of David and Solomon," *Biblical World* 22, no. 1, July 1903, pp. 2, 8–21. http://links.jstor.org/sici?sici=0190-3578%28190307%2922%3A1%3C2%3ATJODAS%3E2.0.CO%3B2-W.

Bea, Cardinal Augustus. *The Church and the Jewish People.* Trans. Philip Loretz. New York: Harper & Row, 1966.

Bell, David. *The First Total War: Napoleon's Europe and the Birth of Warfare as We Know It.* Boston: Houghton Mifflin, 2007.

Bellah, Robert N. *The Broken Covenant: American Civil Religion in Time of Trial.* Chicago: University of Chicago Press, 1992.

Bellinger, Charles K. *The Genealogy of Violence: Reflections on Creation, Freedom, and Evil.* Oxford: Oxford University Press, 2001.

Ben-Ami, Shlomo. *Scars of War, Wounds of Peace: The Israeli-Arab Tragedy.* New York: Oxford University Press, 2006.

Benvenisti, Meron. "The Inevitable Bi-national Regime," *Challenge,* no. 99, September–October 2006.

Berger, Marshall J., and Thomas A. Idinopulos. *Jerusalem's Holy Places and the Peace Process.* Washington, DC: Washington Institute for Near East Policy, 1998.

Bloom, Harold. *The American Religion.* New York: Simon & Schuster, 1992.

Bonhoeffer, Dietrich. *Letters and Papers from Prison.* Trans. Reginald Fuller. New York: Macmillan, 1953.

Brock, Rita Nakashima, and Rebecca Ann Parker. *Saving Paradise: How Christianity Traded Love of This World for Crucifixion and Empire.* Boston: Beacon Press, 2008.

Brodie, Bernard. *The Absolute Weapon: Atomic Power and World Order.* New York: Harcourt, Brace, 1946.

Bronowski, Jacob. *Ascent of Man.* Boston: Little, Brown, 1974.

Brown, Joanne Carlson, and Carole R. Bohn, eds. *Christianity, Patriarchy, and Abuse: A Feminist Critique.* Cleveland: Pilgrim Press, 1989.

Brown, Raymond E. *An Introduction to the New Testament.* New York: Doubleday, 1996.

Buber, Martin. *Good and Evil.* Upper Saddle River, NJ: Prentice Hall, 1997.

Bundy, McGeorge. *Danger and Survival: Choices about the Bomb in the First Fifty Years.* New York: Random House, 1988.

Burg, Avraham. *The Holocaust Is Over, We Must Rise from Its Ashes*. New York: Palgrave Macmillan, 2008.

Butler, Jon. *Awash in a Sea of Faith: Christianizing the American People*. Cambridge: Harvard University Press, 1990.

Cannon, Lou. *President Reagan: The Role of a Lifetime*. New York: Simon & Schuster, 1991.

Carroll, James. *Constantine's Sword: The Church and the Jews*. Boston: Houghton Mifflin, 2001.

———. *House of War: The Pentagon and the Disastrous Rise of American Power*. Boston: Houghton Mifflin, 2006.

———. "Shoah in the News: Patterns and Meanings of News Coverage of the Holocaust." Joan Shorenstein Center on the Press, Politics, and Public Policy. Boston: Kennedy School of Government, Harvard University, 1997.

Carter, Jeffrey, ed. *Understanding Religious Sacrifice*. New York: Continuum, 2003.

Cavanaugh, William T. *The Myth of Religious Violence*. New York: Oxford University Press, 2009.

Cesarani, David. *Becoming Eichmann: Rethinking the Life, Crimes, and Trial of a "Desk Murderer."* Cambridge: Da Capo Press, 2007.

Chace, James. "After Hiroshima: Sharing the Atom Bomb," *Foreign Affairs*, January/February 1996.

Chehab, Zaki. *Inside Hamas: The Untold Story of the Militant Islamic Movement*. New York: Nation Books, 2007.

Chilton, Bruce. *The Temple of Jesus: His Sacrificial Program Within a Cultural History of Sacrifice*. University Park, PA: Pennsylvania State University Press, 1992.

———. *Abraham's Curse: The Roots of Violence in Judaism, Christianity, and Islam*. New York: Doubleday, 2008.

Clarke, John Henrik, ed. *William Styron's Nat Turner: Ten Black Writers Respond*. Boston: Beacon Press, 1968.

Clermont, Betty. *The Neo-Catholics: Implementing Christian Nationalism in America*. Atlanta: Clarity Press, 2010.

Cohen, Avner. *The Worst-Kept Secret: Israel's Bargain with the Bomb*. New York: Columbia University Press, 2010.

Cole, Peter. *Things On Which I've Stumbled*. New York: New Directions, 2008.

Conrad, Joseph. *Heart of Darkness*. Minneapolis: Filiquarian Publishing, 2006.

Conway, Jill Ker. *When Memory Speaks: Reflections on Autobiography*. New York: Knopf, 1998.

Corrasco, David. *City of Sacrifice: The Aztec Empire and the Role of Violence in Civilization*. Boston: Beacon Press, 1999.

Cragg, Kenneth, ed. *Readings in the Qur'an*. London: HarperCollins Religious, 1988.

Cronon, William. *Nature's Metropolis: Chicago and the Great West*. New York: W. W. Norton, 1991.

Crosly, Alfred W. *The Columbian Exchange: Biological and Cultural Consequences of 1492*. Westport, CT: Praeger (30th anniv. ed.), 2003.

Crossan, John Dominic. *The Historical Jesus: The Life of a Mediterranean Jewish Peasant*. San Francisco: HarperSanFrancisco, 1991.

————. *The Birth of Christianity*. San Francisco: HarperSanFrancisco, 1998.

————. *God and Empire: Jesus Against Rome, Then and Now*. San Francisco: HarperSanFrancisco, 2007.

————, and Jonathan L. Reed. *Excavating Jesus: Beneath the Stones, Behind the Texts*. San Francisco: HarperSanFrancisco, 2001.

Culotta, M. C. "The Temple, the Synagogue, and Hebrew Precedent," *Journal of the History of Ideas* 31, no. 2, April–June 1970, pp. 273–76. http://links.jstor.org/sici?

Dadosky, John D. *The Structure of Religious Knowing: Encountering the Sacred in Eliade and Lonergan*. Albany, NY: State University of New York Press, 2004.

Daniell, David. *The Bible in English: Its History and Influence*. New Haven: Yale University Press, 2003.

Delaney, Carol. "Columbus's Ultimate Goal: Jerusalem," *Comparative Studies in Society and History* 48, no. 22, 2006.

Dodwell, Henry. *The Founder of Modern Egypt: A Study of Muhammad Ali*. Cambridge, UK: Cambridge University Press, 1967.

Donald, David. *Lincoln Reconsidered*. New York: Random House, 1961.

Dunn, James G. D. *Unity and Diversity in the New Testament*. Valley Forge, PA: Trinity Press International, 1993.

Dunne, John S. *A Search for God in Time and Memory*. New York: Macmillan, 1967.

Durkheim, Emile. *Elementary Forms of Religious Life*. Trans. Carol Cosman. New York: Oxford University Press, 2001.

Eagleton, Terry. *Holy Terror*. New York: Oxford University Press, 2005.

Eco, Umberto. *Foucault's Pendulum*. New York: Harcourt Brace Jovanovich, 1988.

Ehrman, Bart D. *God's Problem*. New York: HarperCollins, 2008.

Eidelberg, Shlomo. *The Jews and the Crusaders: The Hebrew Chronicles of the First and Second Crusades*. Madison: University of Wisconsin Press, 1977.

Eisler, Diane. *The Chalice and the Blade: Our History, Our Future*. San Francisco: Harper & Row, 1987.

Eksteins, Modris. *Rites of Spring: The Great War and the Birth of the Modern Age*. Boston: Houghton Mifflin, 1989.

Eliade, Mircea. *Patterns in Comparative Religion*. Trans. Rosemary Sheed. Cleveland: World Publishing, 1963.

————. *A History of Religious Ideas*. Vol. 2: *From Guatama Buddha to the Triumph of Christianity*. Chicago: University of Chicago Press, 1982.

————. *The Sacred and the Profane: The Nature of Religion*. Trans. Willard R. Trask. San Diego: Harcourt Brace Jovanovich, 1987.

————. "The Quest for the 'Origins' of Religion," *History of Religions* 4, no. 1, Summer 1964, pp. 154–69. http://links.jstor.org/sici?sici=0018-2710%28196422%294%3A1%3C154%3ATQFT%22O%3E2.0.CO%3B2-J.

Elon, Amos. *Jerusalem: City of Mirrors*. Boston: Little, Brown, 1989.

Emmett, Chad F. "The Capital Cities of Jerusalem," *Geographical Review* 86, April 1996.

Esposito, John L. *Islam: The Straight Path*. New York: Oxford University Press, 1991.

Ezrahi, Sidra DeKoven. *Booking Passage: Exile and Homecoming in the Modern Jewish Imagination*. Berkeley: University of California Press, 2000.

———. "'To What Shall I Compare Thee?': Jerusalem as Ground Zero of the Hebrew Imagination," *Publications of the Modern Language Association* 122, no. 1, January 2007, 220–34.

Farr, Warner D. *The Third Temple's Holy of Holies: Israel's Nuclear Weapons.* Counterproliferation Papers, Future of Warfare Series No. 2, Maxwell Air Force Base, Alabama, 1999.

Faust, Drew Gilpin. *The Republic of Suffering: Death and the American Civil War.* New York: Knopf, 2008.

Feldman, Noah. *Divided by God.* New York: Farrar, Straus and Giroux, 2005.

Filson, Floyd V. "Temple, Synagogue, and Church," *Biblical Archaeologist* 7, no. 4, December 1944, pp. 77–88. http://links.jstor.org/sici?sici=0006-0895%28194412%297%3A4%3C77%3ATSAC%3E2.0.CO%3B2-T.

Fisk, Robert. *The Great War for Civilization: The Conquest of the Middle East.* New York: Vintage, 2007.

Flannery, Edward H. *The Anguish of the Jews: Twenty-three Centuries of Antisemitism.* New York: Paulist Press, 1985.

Francorum, Gesta. *Deeds of the Franks and Other Pilgrims to Jerusalem.* London: Thomas Nelson, 1962.

Fredriksen, Paula. *Jesus of Nazareth, King of the Jews.* New York: Knopf, 1999.

———. *Augustine and the Jews: A Christian Defense of Jews and Judaism.* New York: Doubleday, 2008.

Freeland, Richard M. *The Truman Doctrine and the Origins of McCarthyism.* New York: New York University Press, 1985.

Fromm, Erich. *The Heart of Man: Its Genius for Good, Its Genius for Evil.* New York: Harper & Row, 1964.

Fussell, Paul. *The Great War and Modern Memory.* New York: Oxford University Press, 1975.

Gaustad, Edwin S. *Roger Williams: Lives and Legacies.* New York: Oxford University Press, 2005.

Gellman, Rabbi Ezra, ed. *Essays on the Thought and Philosophy of Rabbi Kook.* Rutherford, NJ: Fairleigh Dickinson University Press, 1991.

Gilbert, Martin. *The Atlas of Jewish History.* New York: William Morrow, 1985.

Girard, René. *Violence and the Sacred.* Trans. Patrick Gregory. Baltimore: Johns Hopkins University Press, 1977.

———. *Things Hidden Since the Foundation of the World.* Trans. Michael Metteer and Stephen Bann. Stanford, CA: Stanford University Press, 1987.

———. *The Girard Reader.* Ed. James G. Williams. New York: Crossroad, 1996.

Goen, C. C. *Broken Churches, Broken Nation.* Macon, GA: Mercer University Press, 1985.

Gopin, Marc. *Holy War, Holy Peace: How Religion Can Bring Peace to the Middle East.* New York: Oxford University Press, 2002.

Gordis, Lisa M. *Opening Scripture: Bible Reading and Interpretive Authority in Puritan New England.* Chicago: University of Chicago Press, 2003.

Gordon, Bruce. *Calvin.* New Haven: Yale University Press, 2009.

Gowers, Andrew, and Tony Walker. *Behind the Myth: Yasser Arafat and the Palestinian Revolution.* New York: Olive Branch Press, 1992.

Grabar, Oleg. *The Shape of the Holy*. Princeton, NJ: Princeton University Press, 1996.

———— and Benjamin Z. Kedar, eds. *Where Heaven and Earth Meet: Jerusalem's Sacred Esplanade*. Austin: University of Texas Press, 2010.

Grainger, John. *The Battle for Palestine — 1917*. Rochester, NY: Boydell Press, 2006.

Greenberg, Kenneth S., ed. *Nat Turner: A Slave Rebellion in History and Memory*. New York: Oxford University Press, 2003.

Grose, Peter. *Israel in the Mind of America*. New York: Knopf, 1983.

Grossman, David. *Writing in the Dark: Essays on Literature and Politics*. Trans. Jessica Cohen. New York: Farrar, Straus and Giroux, 2010.

Hamdani, Abbas. "Columbus and the Recovery of Jerusalem," *Journal of the American Oriental Society* 99, no. 1, January–March 1979.

Harpur, James. *Revelations: The Medieval World*. New York: Henry Holt, 1995.

Hartman, David. *A Living Covenant: The Innovative Spirit in Traditional Judaism*. Woodstock, VT: Jewish Lights Publishing, 1997.

———. *A Heart of Many Rooms: Celebrating the Many Voices Within Judaism*. Woodstock, VT: Jewish Lights Publishing, 1999.

Hatch, Nathan O. *The Sacred Cause of Liberty*. New Haven: Yale University Press, 1977.

Heim, S. Mark. *Saved from Sacrifice: A Theology of the Cross*. Grand Rapids, MI: Eerdmans, 2006.

———. "Christ's Death to End Sacrifice." Religion Online, http://www.religion-online.org/showarticle.asp?title=2141%20.

———. "Why Does Jesus' Death Matter?" Religion Online, http://www.religion-online.org/showarticle.asp?title=2138%20.

Hersh, Seymour M. *The Samson Option: Israel, America, and the Bomb*. New York: Random House, 1991.

Heschel, Abraham Joshua. *The Sabbath: Its Meaning for Modern Man*. New York: Farrar, Straus and Young, 1951.

———. *The Insecurity of Freedom*. New York: Farrar, Straus and Giroux, 1966.

———. *Moral Grandeur and Spiritual Advocacy*. Ed. Susannah Heschel. New York: Noonday, 1997.

Hill, John Wesley. *Abraham Lincoln, Man of God*. New York: G. P. Putnam's Sons, 1920.

Hillenbrand, Carole. *The Crusades: Islamic Perspectives*. New York: Routledge, 2000.

Hitchens, Christopher. *God Is Not Great: How Religion Poisons Everything*. New York: Hachette, 2007.

Hofstadter, Richard. *The Paranoid Style in American Politics and Other Essays*. Chicago: University of Chicago Press, 1965.

Holm, Jean, and John Bowker, eds. *Sacred Place*. London: Pinter Publishers, 1994.

Hubert, Henri, and Marcel Mauss. *Sacrifice: Its Nature and Function*. Trans. W. D. Halls. Chicago: University of Chicago Press, 1964.

Idinopulos, Thomas A. *Jerusalem*. Chicago: Ivan R. Dee, 1991.

Ingle, H. Larry. *First Among Friends: George Fox and the Creation of Quakerism*. New York: Oxford University Press, 1996.

Jacoby, Susan. *Freethinkers: A History of American Secularism*. New York: Metropolitan Books, 2004.

Jeremias, Joachim. *Jerusalem in the Time of Jesus*. Philadelphia: Fortress Press, 1978.

Join-Lambert, Michel. *Jerusalem*. Trans. Charlotte Haldane. New York: Frederick Ungar, 1966.

Judt, Tony. *Postwar: A History of Europe Since 1945*. New York: Penguin, 2005.

Juergensmeyer, Mark. *Terror in the Mind of God: The Global Rise of Religious Violence*. Berkeley: University of California Press, 2000.

Julius, Anthony. *Trials of the Diaspora*. Oxford: Oxford University Press, 2010.

Keegan, John. *The First World War*. New York: Vintage, 2000.

Keenan, Dennis King. *The Question of Sacrifice*. Bloomington: Indiana University Press, 2005.

Kennan, George. "The Sources of Soviet Conduct," *Foreign Affairs*, July 1947.

Kenny, Anthony J. *Catholics, Jews, and the State of Israel*. Mahwah, NJ: Paulist Press, 1993.

Keyser, Jason. "Female Suicide Bomber Kills Two at Jerusalem Supermarket," *Independent*, March 30, 2002.

Khalidi, Rashid. *The Iron Cage: The Story of the Palestinian Struggle for Statehood*. Boston: Beacon Press, 2006.

———. *Sowing Crisis: The Cold War and American Dominance in the Middle East*. Boston: Beacon Press, 2009.

Kiser, John W. *Commander of the Faithful: The Life and Times of Emir Abd el-Kader*. Rhinebeck, NY: Monkfish Book Publishing, 2008.

Kissinger, Henry. *Years of Upheaval*. Boston: Little, Brown, 1982.

Klawans, Jonathan. *Purity, Sacrifice, and the Temple: Symbolism and Supersessionism in the Study of Ancient Judaism*. New York: Oxford University Press, 2006.

Kripal, Jeffrey J. *Esalen: America and the Religion of No Religion*. Chicago: University of Chicago Press, 2007.

Kugel, James. *How to Read the Bible: A Guide to Scripture, Then and Now*. New York: Free Press, 2007.

Küng, Hans. *Judaism: Between Yesterday and Tomorrow*. New York: Crossroad, 1992.

———. *Christianity: Essence, History, and Future*. New York: Continuum, 1995.

———. *Islam: Past, Present, and Future*. Oxford: Oneworld, 2007.

Landes, David. *The Wealth and Poverty of Nations: Why Some Are So Rich and Some So Poor*. New York: W. W. Norton, 1998.

LaPlante, Eve. *American Jezebel: The Uncommon Life of Anne Hutchinson, the Woman Who Defied the Puritans*. New York: HarperCollins, 2004.

Leakey, Richard. *Origins: What New Discoveries Reveal about the Emergence of Our Species and Its Possible Future*. New York: Anchor Doubleday, 1993.

LeBeau, Bryan F. "Christopher Columbus and the Matter of Religion," *Center for the Study of Religion and Society Newsletter* 4, no. 1. http://www.sodahead. com/united-states/christopher-columbus-and-the-matter-of-religion/blog-80803.

Lefebure, Leo D. *Revelation, the Religions, and Violence.* Maryknoll, NY: Orbis Books, 2000.

Levenson, Jon D. *The Death and Resurrection of the Beloved Son: The Transformation of Child Sacrifice in Judaism and Christianity.* New Haven: Yale University Press, 1993.

———. "The Temple and the World," *Journal of Religion,* July 1984.

Lewis, David Levering. *God's Crucible: Islam and the Making of Europe, 570–1215.* New York: Norton, 2008.

Lindqvist, Sven. *"Exterminate All the Brutes."* New York: New Press, 1996.

Lorenz, Konrad. *On Aggression.* San Diego: Harcourt Brace, 1963.

Macquarrie, John. *Principles of Christian Theology.* London: SCM Press, 2003.

Madigan, Kevin J., and Jon D. Levenson. *Resurrection: The Power of God for Christians and Jews.* New Haven: Yale University Press, 2008.

Maier, Pauline. *American Scripture: Making the Declaration of Independence.* New York: Vintage, 1998.

Makiya, Kanan. *The Rock: A Tale of Seventh-Century Jerusalem.* New York: Vintage, 2001.

Mandel, Paul. "The Loss of Center: Changing Attitudes Towards the Temple in Aggadic Literature," *Harvard Theological Review* 99, no. 1, January 2006. http://0-find.galegroup.com.library.law.suffolk.edu:80/itx/start.do?prodID=AONE.

Marius, Richard. *Martin Luther: The Christian Between God and Death.* Cambridge: Belknap Press, 1999.

Marty, Martin E. *Pilgrims in Their Own Land: 500 Years of Religion in America.* Boston: Little, Brown, 1984.

Mastnak, Tomaž. *Crusading Peace: Christendom, the Muslim World, and Western Political Order.* Berkeley: University of California Press, 2001.

Mattar, Philip. *The Mufti of Jerusalem: Al-Hajj Amin al-Husayni and the Palestinian National Movement.* New York: Columbia University Press, 1988.

McDougall, Walter A. *Promised Land, Crusader State: The American Encounter with the World Since 1776.* Boston: Houghton Mifflin, 1997.

Meacham, Jon. *American Gospel: God, the Founding Fathers, and the Making of a Nation.* New York: Random House, 2007.

Mearsheimer, John J., and Stephen M. Walt. *The Israel Lobby and U.S. Foreign Policy.* New York: Farrar, Straus and Giroux, 2007.

Meir, Golda. *My Life.* New York: G. P. Putnam's Sons, 1975.

Menocal, Maria Rosa. *The Ornament of the World: How Muslims, Jews, and Christians Created a Culture of Tolerance in Medieval Spain.* New York: Little, Brown, 2002.

Milbank, John. *Theology and Social Theory.* Malden, MA: Blackwell Publishing, 2006.

Miles, Jack. "Judaist Israel, Islamist Palestine," *Harvard Divinity Bulletin,* Autumn 2005.

Miller, Perry. *The American Puritans: Their Prose and Poetry.* Garden City, NY: Doubleday, 1956.

————. *Nature's Nation*. Cambridge: Belknap Press, 1967.

Millis, Walter, ed. *The Forrestal Diaries*. New York: Viking, 1951.

Mishal, Shaul, and Avraham Sela. *The Palestinian Hamas: Vision, Violence, and Coexistence*. New York: Columbia University Press, 2000.

Morison, Samuel Eliot. *Admiral of the Ocean Sea*. Boston: Little, Brown, 1991.

Morris, Benny. *1948: The First Arab-Israeli War*. New Haven: Yale University Press, 2008.

Morris, Edmund. *Dutch: A Memoir of Ronald Reagan*. New York: Modern Library, 1999.

Morse, Chuck. *The Nazi Connection to Islamic Terrorism: Adolf Hitler and Haj Amin al-Husseini*. New York: iUniverse, 2003.

Nasr, Seyyed Hossein. *The Heart of Islam: Enduring Values for Humanity*. San Francisco: HarperSanFrancisco, 2002.

Nicholson, Helen J. *Love, War, and the Grail: Templars, Hospitallers, and Teutonic Knights in Medieval Epic and Romance, 1150–1500*. Leiden, Netherlands: Brill, 2001.

Niebuhr, Reinhold. *The Irony of American History*. Chicago: University of Chicago Press, 2008.

Nixon, Richard. *RN: The Memoirs of Richard Nixon*. New York: Grosset and Dunlap, 1978.

Nolan, Janne E. *Guardians of the Arsenal: The Politics of Nuclear Strategy*. New York: Basic Books, 1989.

Nusseibeh, Sari, with Anthony David. *Once Upon a Country: A Palestinian Life*. New York: Farrar, Straus and Giroux, 2007.

Oates, Stephen B. *With Malice Toward None: The Life of Abraham Lincoln*. New York: Harper & Row, 1977.

Ochs, Peter, ed. *The Return to Scripture in Judaism and Christianity*. New York: Paulist Press, 1993.

O'Malley, John. *Four Cultures of the West*. Cambridge: Belknap Press, 2004.

Oren, Michael B. *Power, Faith, and Fantasy: America in the Middle East, 1776 to the Present*. New York: W. W. Norton, 2007.

Oz, Amos. *In the Land of Israel*. San Diego: Harcourt Brace Jovanovich, 1983.

Pagels, Elaine. *The Origin of Satan: How Christians Demonized Jews, Pagans, and Heretics*. New York: Vintage, 1996.

Pape, Robert A. *Dying to Win: The Strategic Logic of Suicide Terrorism*. New York: Random House, 2005.

————, and James K. Feldman. *Cutting the Fuse: The Explosion of Global Suicide Terrorism and How to Stop It*. Chicago: University of Chicago Press, 2010.

Pappe, Ilan. *The Ethnic Cleansing of Palestine*. Oxford: Oneworld, 2006.

Paton, Lewis Bayles. "Jerusalem in Bible Times: VI. Jerusalem in the Earliest Times," *Biblical World* 29, no. 6, June 1907, pp. 402, 409–19. http://www.jstor.org/sici?sici=0190-3578%28190706%2929%3A6%3C402%3AJIBTVJ%3E2.0.CO%3B2-S.

Pelican, Jaroslav. *Jesus Through the Centuries: His Place in the History of Culture*. New Haven: Yale University Press, 1985.

Perry, Mark. *Four Stars: The Inside Story of the Forty-Year Battle Between the Joint Chiefs of Staff and America's Civilian Leaders*. Boston: Houghton Mifflin, 1989.

Peters, F. E. *Jerusalem and Mecca: The Typology of the Holy City in the Near East*. New York: New York University Press, 1986.

Phillips, Jonathan, ed. *The First Crusade: Origins and Impact*. Manchester, UK: Manchester University Press, 1997.

Pinsky, Robert. *The Life of David*. New York: Schocken, 2005.

Purcell, Hugh. *Lloyd George*. London: Haus Publishing, 2006.

Rad, Gerhard von. *The Message of the Prophets*. New York: Harper & Row, 1962.

Rauf, Imam Feisal Abdul. *What's Right with Islam: A New Vision for Muslims and the West*. San Francisco: HarperSanFrancisco, 2004.

Read, Piers Paul. *The Templars*. New York: St. Martin's Press, 1999.

Rennie, Bryan S. *Reconstructing Eliade: Making Sense of Religion*. Albany: State University of New York Press, 1996.

Rhodes, Richard. *The Making of the Atomic Bomb*. New York: Simon & Schuster, 1993.

Ricoeur, Paul. *The Rule of Metaphor: Multidisciplinary Studies of the Creation of Meaning in Language*. Trans. Robert Czerny, K. McLaughlin, and J. Costello. Toronto: University of Toronto Press, 1977.

Robinson, James M. *A New Quest of the Historical Jesus*. London: Allenson, 1959.

Rossing, Barbara R. *The Rapture Exposed: The Message of Hope in the Book of Revelation*. New York: Basic Books, 2004.

Roth, Philip. *Indignation*. Boston: Houghton Mifflin, 2008.

Said, Edward W. *Orientalism*. New York: Pantheon, 1979.

———. *The Question of Palestine*. New York: Vintage, 1992.

Sanders, E. P. *Jesus and Judaism*. Philadelphia: Fortress Press, 1985.

———. *Judaism: Practice and Belief, 63 BCE–66 CE*. Philadelphia: Trinity Press International, 1992.

Santillana, Giorgio de. *The Crime of Galileo*. Chicago: University of Chicago Press, 1976.

Saperstein, Marc. *Moments of Crisis in Jewish-Christian Relations*. Philadelphia: Trinity Press International, 1989.

Schaffer, Ronald. *Wings of Judgment: American Bombing in World War II*. New York: Oxford University Press, 1985.

Schlesinger, Arthur, Jr. *The Cycles of American History*. Boston: Mariner Books, 1999.

Schneer, Jonathan. *The Balfour Declaration: The Origins of the Arab-Israeli Conflict*. New York: Random House, 2010.

Schultz, Eric B., and Michael J. Tougias. *King Philip's War: The History and Legacy of America's Forgotten Conflict*. Woodstock, VT: Countryman Press, 1999.

Schwager, Raymond, S.J. *Must There Be Scapegoats?: Violence and Redemption in the Bible*. Trans. Maria L. Assad. New York: Crossroad, 2000.

Schwartz, Regina M. *The Curse of Cain: The Violent Legacy of Monotheism*. Chicago: University of Chicago Press, 1997.

Scruton, Roger. *Spinoza*. Oxford: Oxford University Press, 1990.

Scully, Vincent Joseph. *The Earth, the Temple, and the Gods: Greek Sacred Architecture*. New Haven: Yale University Press, 1979.

Segev, Tom. *1949: The First Israelis*. New York: Free Press, 1998.

————. *The Seventh Million: The Israelis and the Holocaust*. New York: Henry Holt, 2000.

Sherwin, Martin J., and Kai Bird. *American Prometheus: The Triumph and Tragedy of J. Robert Oppenheimer*. New York: Knopf, 2005.

Shulevitz, Judith. *The Sabbath World: Glimpses of a Different Order of Time*. New York: Random House, 2010.

Silberman, Neil Asher. *Heavenly Powers: Unraveling the Secret History of the Kabbalah*. New York: Grosset/Putnam, 1998.

Silberstein, Laurence J., and Robert L. Cohn, eds. *The Other in Jewish Thought and History: Constructions of Jewish Culture and Identity*. New York: New York University Press, 1994.

Smith, Julie Ann. "My Lord's Native Land (1): Mapping the Christian Holy Land," *Church History* 76, no. 1, March 2007. http://o-find.galegroup.com.library. law.suffolk.edu:80/itx/start.do?prodID=AONE.

Soderland, Jean R., ed. *William Penn and the Founding of Pennsylvania: A Documentary History*. Philadelphia: University of Pennsylvania Press, 1983.

Stark, Rodney. *One True God: Historical Consequences of Monotheism*. Princeton, NJ: Princeton University Press, 2001.

————. *For the Glory of God: How Monotheism Led to Reformations, Science, Witch-Hunts, and the End of Slavery*. Princeton, NJ: Princeton University Press, 2003.

Steiner, George. "Our Homeland, the Text," *Salmagundi*, no. 66, Winter–Spring 1985.

Stephanson, Anders. *Manifest Destiny*. New York: Hill and Wang, 1995.

Stern, Jessica. *Terror in the Name of God: Why Religious Militants Kill*. New York: HarperCollins, 2003.

Stout, Harry S. *Upon the Altar of the Nation: A Moral History of the Civil War*. New York: Viking, 2006.

Studstill, Randall. "Eliade, Phenomenology, and the Sacred," *Religious Studies* 36, 2000, pp. 177–94.

Sumner, Charles. *The Works of Charles Sumner*, vol. 7. Boston: Lee & Shepard, 1873.

Susser, Asher. *The Rise of Hamas in Palestine and the Crisis of Secularism in the Arab World*. Waltham, MA: Crown Center for Middle East Studies, Brandeis University, 2010.

Swartley, Willard M., ed. *Violence Renounced: René Girard, Biblical Studies, and Peacemaking*. Studies in Peace and Scripture, vol. 4. Philadelphia: Pandora Press U.S., 2000.

Thurman, Judith. "First Impressions: What Does the World's Oldest Art Say About Us?" *The New Yorker*, June 23, 2008.

Tillich, Paul. *Dynamics of Faith*. New York: HarperCollins, 1957.

Tracy, David. *On Naming the Present: Reflections on God, Hermeneutics, and Church*. Maryknoll, NY: Orbis Books, 1994.

Tuveson, Ernest Lee. *Redeemer Nation: The Idea of America's Millennial Role.* Chicago: University of Chicago Press, 1968.

Wainstock, Dennis. *The Decision to Drop the Bomb.* Westport, CT: Praeger, 1996.

Walker, Peter. "The Land Called Holy: Palestine in Christian History and Thought," *Journal of Theological Studies* 45, no. 1, April 1994. http://0-find.galegroup. com.library.law.suffolk.edu:80/itx/start.do?prodID=AONE.

Weisburd, David. *Jewish Settler Violence: Deviance as Social Reaction.* University Park, PA: Pennsylvania State University Press, 1989.

Weschler, Lawrence. "Mayhem and Monotheism: The Good Book's Dark Side," *The New Yorker,* November 24, 1997, pp. 131–33.

Wessels, Antoine. *A Modern Arabic Biography of Muhammad: A Critical Study of Muhammad Husayn.* Leiden, Netherlands: Brill, 1972.

Whitehead, Alfred North. *Science and the Modern World.* New York: Free Press, 1997.

Whitfield, Stephen J. *The Culture of the Cold War.* Baltimore: Johns Hopkins University Press, 1991.

Whitman, Walt. *Essays in November: Prose Works.* Philadelphia: David McKay, 1892.

Widmer, Ted. *Ark of the Liberties: America and the World.* New York: Hill and Wang, 2008.

Wilken, Robert L. "Early Christian Chiliasm, Jewish Messianism, and the Idea of the Holy Land," *Harvard Theological Review* 79, no. 1/3.

Williams, James G. *The Bible, Violence, and the Sacred: Liberation from the Myth of Sanctioned Violence.* New York: HarperCollins, 1991.

Wilson, Charles Reagan. *Baptized in Blood: The Religion of the Lost Cause.* Athens: University of Georgia Press, 1980.

Wilson, E. O. *The Creation: An Appeal to Save Life on Earth.* New York: W. W. Norton, 2006.

Wistrich, Robert S. *A Lethal Obsession: Anti-Semitism from Antiquity to the Global Jihad.* New York: Random House, 2010.

Wood, James. "God in the Quad," *The New Yorker,* August 31, 2009.

Wylie, David. *The Abandonment of the Jews.* New York: Pantheon, 1984.

Wynn, Mark. "God, Pilgrimage, and Acknowledgement of Place," *Religious Studies* 43, 2007, pp. 145–63.

Yergin, Daniel. *Shattered Peace: The Origins of the Cold War and the National Security State.* Boston: Houghton Mifflin, 1978.

Young, Jeremy. *The Violence of God and the War on Terror.* New York: Seabury Books, 2008.

Zemer, Rabbi Dr. Moshe. *Evolving Halakhah: A Progressive Approach to Traditional Jewish Law.* Woodstock, VT: Jewish Lights Publishing, 1999.

Acknowledgments

James Parks Morton, as the longtime dean of the Cathedral of St. John the Divine and then as the founder of the Interfaith Center of New York, has been a prophet of interfaith reconciliation. David Hartman, the founder of the Shalom Hartman Institute in Jerusalem, is a living example of urgently needed religious magnanimity. The late Krister Stendahl, bishop of Stockholm and dean of the Harvard Divinity School, did more than anyone to open the Christian imagination to its contemporary ecumenical renewal. That these three men have been not just shapers of my thought but treasured friends is a wonder to me. I gratefully dedicate this book to them.

I did this work as a scholar-in-residence at Suffolk University in Boston, and acknowledge the sustenance I drew from generous Suffolk colleagues and students. Dean Kenneth Greenberg has been a pillar of support, even to reading the entire book in manuscript, offering the benefit of his sharp historian's eye. Professors Fred Marchant and Nir Eisikovits also read the manuscript and gave me astute advice. I am especially indebted to them for their readings and their friendship. Other Suffolk colleagues with whom I discussed this work include Professors Gregory Fried and Bryan Trabold and my fellow scholar-in-residence Robert Brustein. Suffolk students who gave me invaluable research help include Charles Ryan, Bora Hajnaj, Erin Bagan, Sam Nelson, Hillary Creedon, and Alysha MacDonald. Heartfelt thanks to you all.

The first time I publicly presented this book's material was at the Trinity Institute at Trinity Church, Wall Street. James Cole, Susannah Heschel, and Tariq Ramadan were my partners in the conversation, ably steered by Reverend Mark Richardson and Robert Scott. I acknowledge my debt to those distinguished colleagues and the Trinity Institute community.

I worked on this book as the Richman Visiting Professor at Brandeis University, where I had the support of President Yehuda Reinharz, Provost Marty Krauss, Chaplain Walter Cuenin, and my gifted teaching assistant, Timothy McCarty. It has been my privilege to be on the advisory board of the Brandeis International Center for Ethics, Justice, and Public Life, which focuses on issues closely related to my subject here. Its director, Daniel Terris, has been a particular inspiration and help, especially in the critical reading he gave of an early draft of this book. Thanks to all at Brandeis.

My association with the Center for the Study of Jewish-Christian-Muslim Relations at Merrimack College has been a boon for my work. In addition to numerous multifaith encounters, in which I have learned from and befriended Jewish, Christian, and Muslim dialogue partners, I have had the singular support of Director Padraic O'Hare, whose early reading of this book was invaluable. Not to mention his friendship. Thanks also to Joseph Kelley, Rabbi Robert Goldstein, and Joseph V. Montville, founder of the Abrahamic Family Reunion.

At the Shalom Hartman Institute in Jerusalem, I have been a privileged participant in the annual gathering of Jewish, Christian, and Muslim religious leaders for more than a decade. Thanks to conference organizers Menachem Fisch, David Neuhaus S.J., Muhammad Hourani, Paul Ballanfat, Kimberley Patton, Brenda Yagod, Peter A. Pettit, and Karla Suomala. I give special acknowledgment to Director Donniel Hartman. Jerusalem residents Rabbi Ron Kronish and Donald Moore S.J. have kept me apprised of developments with regular e-mail bulletins. Paulist Fathers Michael McGarry and Thomas Stransky have been my Jerusalem hosts and mentors across the years, and I acknowledge an old debt to them.

My ablest guides to Jerusalem have been my dear friends Bernard Avishai, who was a first reader of this work, and Sidra DeKoven Ezrahi, whose Jerusalem scholarship is matched by her welcoming spirit. Board chair of the Jerusalem YMCA Dorothy Harman facilitated a rare visit to the Al Aqsa Mosque Museum, where I was warmly received by Director Khader Salameh. I gratefully salute both Ms. Harman and Dr. Salameh. The distinguished Muslim scholar Reza Aslan gave me a careful reading and encouragement. I was privileged to retrace Abraham's first steps with the Abraham Path Initiative, led by Joshua Weiss under the sponsorship of the Global Negotiation Initiative at Harvard University.

Among the venues where I tested my thinking for this work were Boston College, with Father Thomas Kane C.S.P.; the Wellfleet Seminar, under Robert Jay Lifton's leadership; the American Academy of Arts and Sciences, ably led by Leslie Berlowitz; Wellesley College; the University of California at Santa Barbara; Loyola University, Chicago; Emmanuel College, under President Sister Janet Eisner S.N.D.; Claremont Graduate University; the Engelsberg Seminar in Sweden; the Kaufman Interfaith Institute, with Sylvia and Richard Kaufman; All Saints Episcopal Church in Pasadena, with my good friend Reverend Ed Bacon; the Urban-Suburban Group at the National Cathedral in Washington, hosted by the Very Reverends Samuel Candler and Samuel Lloyd; and Temple Kehillath Israel, led by Rabbi William Hamilton.

This work benefited enormously from conversations with Daniel Gibson, Brita Stendahl, Larry Kessler, Ali Asani, Askold Melnyczuk, and Martin Malin. I thank my fellow members of the Dean's Council at Harvard Divinity School, and Dean William Graham; my fellow trustees of the Boston Public Library, with board chair Jeffrey Rudman and library president Amy Ryan; and the Humanities Center at Harvard University, including, especially, Director Homi Baba and Mary Halpenny-Killip. For a time, I was a member of the Boston Study Group, and I acknowledge all that I learned about the Middle East from its members: Herbert C. Kelmann, Lenore G. Martin, Henry Steiner, Harvey Cox, Stephen M. Walt, Alan Berger, Augustus Richard Norton, Stephen Van Evera, and Everett Mendelsohn. I owe a special debt to the librarians of Suffolk and Harvard universities and of the Boston Public Library.

I drew on the work I was doing on this book for columns I published in the *Boston Globe,* where my editors are Peter Canellos, Dante Ramos, Marjorie Pritchard, and Don Macgillis. Thank you to the *Globe* and its readers.

I am deeply grateful to Houghton Mifflin Harcourt. Deanne Urmy, my editor there, drew on her own deep wisdom and knowledge to help me sharpen my argument. Her enthusiastic appreciation from start to finish was my most valued asset, and I gratefully acknowledge the stamp she has put on this book. Larry Cooper has been my manuscript editor for more than fifteen years — and it seems almost that many books. His work on this one has been indispensable. I salute Bruce Nichols, Andrea Schulz, Lori Glazer, Carla Gray, Taryn Roeder, Meagan Stacey, Nicole Angeloro, and all of the good people of Houghton Mifflin Harcourt who have brought this work to the world.

My agent and friend Donald Cutler is my partner in all the work I do. Unable to repay my debt to him, I say, again, a simple word of thanks. And finally, to those who sustain my work and life, I end with a fresh word of the old love — to Lizzy Carroll and James Jenkins, Patrick Carroll, and the pulse of my heart, Alexandra Marshall.

Index